Grammar and Writing 5

Student Edition

Second Edition

Christie Curtis

Mary Hake

Houghton Mifflin Harcourt Publishers, Inc.

Grammar and Writing 5

Second Edition

Student Edition

This edition is based on the work titled *Grammar and Writing 5* © 2006 by Mary E. Hake and Christie Curtis and originally published by Hake Publishing.

Printed in the U.S.A.

ISBN 978-0-544-04423-4

1 2 3 4 5 6 7 8 9 10   0928   22 21 20 19 18 17 16 15 14 13

4500425519   A B C D E F G

Contents

	Introduction	1
Lesson **1**	The Sentence: Two Parts	3
Lesson **2**	Four Types of Sentences	7
Lesson **3**	Simple Subjects • Simple Predicates	11
Lesson **4**	Reversed Subject and Predicate • Split Predicate	15
Lesson **5**	Complete Sentence or Sentence Fragment?	19
Lesson **6**	Correcting a Sentence Fragment	24
Lesson **7**	Action Verbs	28
Lesson **8**	Capitalizing Proper Nouns	31
Lesson **9**	Present Tense of Verbs	35
Lesson **10**	Past Tense of Regular Verbs	39
Lesson **11**	Concrete, Abstract, and Collective Nouns	44
Lesson **12**	Helping Verbs	49
Lesson **13**	Singular, Plural, Compound, and Possessive Nouns	53
Lesson **14**	Future Tense	58
Lesson **15**	Capitalization: Sentence, Pronoun *I*, and Poetry	63
Lesson **16**	Irregular Plural Nouns, Part 1	68
Lesson **17**	Irregular Plural Nouns, Part 2	73

Lesson **18**	Irregular Verbs, Part 1: *Be*, *Have*, and *Do*	79
Lesson **19**	Four Principal Parts of Verbs	85
Lesson **20**	Simple Prepositions, Part 1	90
Lesson **21**	Simple Prepositions, Part 2	96
Lesson **22**	Irregular Plural Nouns, Part 3	101
Lesson **23**	Complete Sentence or Run-on Sentence?	105
Lesson **24**	Correcting a Run-on Sentence	110
Lesson **25**	Capitalization: Titles	114
Lesson **26**	Capitalization: Outlines and Quotations	119
Lesson **27**	Dictionary Information About a Word, Part 1	124
Lesson **28**	Spelling Rules: Silent Letters *k*, *g*, *w*, *t*, *d*, and *c*	129
Lesson **29**	Spelling Rules: Silent Letters *p*, *b*, *l*, *u*, *h*, *n*, and *gh*	134
Lesson **30**	Dictionary Information About a Word, Part 2	139
Lesson **31**	Linking Verbs	144
Lesson **32**	Diagramming Simple Subjects and Simple Predicates	150
Lesson **33**	Spelling Rules: Suffixes, Part 1	155
Lesson **34**	Spelling Rules: Suffixes, Part 2	162
Lesson **35**	Spelling Rules: *ie* or *ei*	167
Lesson **36**	Phrases and Clauses	171
Lesson **37**	Diagramming a Direct Object	176
Lesson **38**	Capitalization: People Titles, Family Words, and School Subjects	181
Lesson **39**	Descriptive Adjectives	186

Lesson **40**	The Limiting Adjective • Diagramming Adjectives	191
Lesson **41**	Capitalization: Areas, Religions, and Greetings	197
Lesson **42**	Proper Adjectives	202
Lesson **43**	No Capital Letter	207
Lesson **44**	Object of the Preposition • The Prepositional Phrase	212
Lesson **45**	The Prepositional Phrase as an Adjective • Diagramming	218
Lesson **46**	Indirect Objects	224
Lesson **47**	The Period, Part 1	230
Lesson **48**	Coordinating Conjunctions	235
Lesson **49**	Diagramming Compound Subjects and Predicates	240
Lesson **50**	The Period, Part 2: Abbreviations and Decimals	246
Lesson **51**	The Predicate Nominative	252
Lesson **52**	Noun Case, Part 1: Nominative and Possessive	258
Lesson **53**	Noun Case, Part 2: Objective	263
Lesson **54**	The Predicate Adjective	269
Lesson **55**	Comparison Adjectives	275
Lesson **56**	Irregular Comparison Adjectives	283
Lesson **57**	The Comma, Part 1: Dates, Addresses, and Series	289
Lesson **58**	Appositives	295
Lesson **59**	The Comma, Part 2: Direct Address and Academic Degrees	300
Lesson **60**	The Comma, Part 3: Appositives	305

Lesson 61	Overused Adjectives • Unnecessary Articles	310
Lesson 62	Pronouns and Antecedents	315
Lesson 63	The Comma, Part 4: Greetings and Closings; Last Name First	322
Lesson 64	Personal Pronouns	327
Lesson 65	Irregular Verbs, Part 2	334
Lesson 66	Nominative Pronoun Case	340
Lesson 67	The Comma, Part 5: Introductory and Interrupting Elements; Afterthoughts	346
Lesson 68	The Comma, Part 6: Clarity	352
Lesson 69	Objective Pronoun Case	356
Lesson 70	Personal Pronoun Case Forms	363
Lesson 71	Diagramming Pronouns	369
Lesson 72	Possessive Pronouns and Possessive Adjectives	374
Lesson 73	Dependent and Independent Clauses • Subordinating Conjunctions	380
Lesson 74	The Comma, Part 7: Descriptive Adjectives and Dependent Clauses	386
Lesson 75	Compound Sentences • Coordinating Conjunctions	391
Lesson 76	The Comma, Part 8: Compound Sentences and Direct Quotations	398
Lesson 77	Relative Pronouns	403
Lesson 78	Pronoun Usage	411
Lesson 79	Interrogative Pronouns	417

Lesson 80	Quotation Marks, Part 1	425
Lesson 81	Quotation Marks, Part 2	430
Lesson 82	Demonstrative Pronouns	435
Lesson 83	Indefinite Pronouns	440
Lesson 84	Italics or Underline	447
Lesson 85	Irregular Verbs, Part 3	453
Lesson 86	Irregular Verbs, Part 4	458
Lesson 87	Irregular Verbs, Part 5	463
Lesson 88	The Exclamation Mark • The Question Mark	469
Lesson 89	Subject-Verb Agreement, Part 1	474
Lesson 90	Subject-Verb Agreement, Part 2	480
Lesson 91	Subject-Verb Agreement, Part 3	487
Lesson 92	Subject-Verb Agreement, Part 4	493
Lesson 93	Negatives • Double Negatives	498
Lesson 94	The Hyphen: Compound Nouns and Numbers	505
Lesson 95	Adverbs That Tell "How"	511
Lesson 96	Using the Adverb *Well*	517
Lesson 97	The Hyphen: Compound Adjectives	522
Lesson 98	Adverbs That Tell "Where"	529
Lesson 99	Word Division	534
Lesson 100	Adverbs That Tell "When"	539
Lesson 101	Adverbs That Tell "How Much"	544
Lesson 102	Comparison Adverbs	550

Lesson **103**	The Semicolon	556
Lesson **104**	Adverb Usage	561
Lesson **105**	The Colon	567
Lesson **106**	The Prepositional Phrase as an Adverb • Diagramming	573
Lesson **107**	Preposition or Adverb? • Preposition Usage	579
Lesson **108**	The Apostrophe: Possessives	585
Lesson **109**	The Apostrophe: Contractions; Omitting Digits and Letters	591
Lesson **110**	The Complex Sentence • The Compound-Complex Sentence	596
Lesson **111**	Active or Passive Voice	601
Lesson **112**	Interjections	606
	Appendix • Dictations	611
	Appendix • Journal Topics	619
	Index	625

Introduction

Welcome to a language arts program created for easy reading and instruction. Behind this program is a team of dedicated teachers who care about your success and want to present incremental teaching material in a simple format.

This program consists of a series of **daily lessons**, **review sets**, and **tests** that are carefully sequenced to develop a variety of skills and concepts. We include lessons on capitalization, punctuation, parts of speech, sentence structure, spelling rules, correct word usage, and dictionary skills with a focus on improving our writing.

To increase your understanding, you will learn to diagram sentences. Diagramming a sentence, like doing a puzzle, exercises your brain and helps you to see the structure of the sentence and the function of its parts. Knowing how to diagram an English sentence will make your future study of foreign languages much easier. It will also help you with correct word usage and punctuation as you write.

Because of the incremental nature of this program, **it is essential that the lessons be taught in order, that all review sets are completed, and that no lessons are skipped.**

In addition to the daily lessons, the program includes a series of **writing lessons**. These are designed to guide you through the process of composing a complete essay. Also included are weekly **dictations** for practice in spelling and punctuation. You will also be asked to keep a journal; the program contains suggested **journal topics**.

No matter your goals, mastery of the English language is one of the most valuable tools you can possess. It is our hope that this program provides you with a strong foundation not only for future language arts studies but also for a lifetime of satisfying and successful writing.

Best wishes!

LESSON 1

The Sentence: Two Parts

> **Dictation or Journal Entry**
> **Vocabulary:**
> *Essential* means "necessary." Green vegetables are an *essential* part of our diet.
> *Nonessential* means "not necessary." Cupcakes are a *nonessential* part of Freddy's diet.

A **sentence** is a group of words that expresses a complete thought.

The word groups below do *not* express a complete thought.

> Connecticut.
>
> Became a state in 1788.
>
> Fifty states.
>
> Make the United States.

While we often hear such groups of words in conversation, they are not sentences. They do not express a complete thought. However, we can combine the word groups above to make the following complete sentences:

> Connecticut became a state in 1788.
>
> Fifty states make the United States.

Two Parts of a Sentence

A sentence has **two parts,** (1) the subject and (2) the predicate. Both parts are necessary to make a complete sentence.

Subject Part

The **subject** of a sentence tells whom or what the sentence is about. Subjects are underlined below.

> <u>Connecticut</u> became a state in 1788.
>
> <u>Fifty states</u> make the United States.

Predicate Part

The **predicate** of a sentence tells what the subject does, is, or is like. Predicates are underlined below.

> Connecticut <u>became a state in 1788</u>.
>
> Fifty states <u>make the United States</u>.

Example 1 (a) Write the subject of this sentence:

> My sister visited New Hampshire last summer.

(b) Write the predicate of this sentence:

The United States bought Alaska from Russia.

Solution (a) We write, **"My sister,"** for it is the subject of the sentence; it tells *who* visited New Hampshire.

(b) We write, **"bought Alaska from Russia,"** for it is the predicate of the sentence; it tells what the United States *did*.

Example 2 Rewrite the sentences below. Then draw a vertical line between the subject and the predicate of each sentence.

My large, colorful map shows all fifty states.

The President lives at the White House.

Two sneaky pirates hid their treasure in a cave.

Solution We rewrite the sentences and draw vertical lines between the subjects and predicates:

My large, colorful map | shows all fifty states.

The President | lives at the White House.

Two sneaky pirates | hid their treasure in a cave.

Practice For a and b, write the subject of the sentence.

a. The United States admitted Alabama into Statehood in 1819.

b. The city of Montgomery became the state capital.

For c and d, write the predicate of the sentence.

c. The area of Alabama measures 52,423 square miles.

d. Land comprises 50,750 square miles.

Rewrite sentences e and f, drawing a vertical line between the subject and the predicate of each sentence.

e. Water covers 1673 square miles in Alabama.

f. Tyrell and Marisol live in Alabama.

For g and h, replace the blank with *essential* or *nonessential*.

   g. Adequate rainfall is _____ for farming.

   h. Learning to ride a unicycle is a(n) _____ part of one's education.

✓Review Set 1   Choose the correct word to complete sentences 1–8.

1. Water and sunshine are (essential, nonessential) for growing pine trees.

2. (*Essential, Nonessential*) means "not necessary."

3. Both the subject and the predicate are (essential, nonessential) parts of a complete sentence.

4. A complete sentence has (twelve, two) main parts.

5. The (subject, predicate) of the sentence tells whom or what the sentence is about.

6. The (subject, predicate) of the sentence tells what the subject does, is, or is like.

7. A (subject, sentence) is a word group that expresses a complete thought.

8. The two essential parts of a sentence are the subject and the (pirate, predicate).

Write the subject of sentences 9–12.

9. Farmers cultivate cotton and peanuts in Alabama.

10. Poultry and eggs provide income for Alabamians.

11. Lumber and wood products supplement the economy.

12. Alabama's flag has a crimson Saint Andrew's cross on a white background.

Write the predicate of sentences 13–16.

13. Alabama's flag resembles a Confederate Battle Flag.

14. The state bird of Alabama is the yellowhammer.

15. The yellowhammer belongs to the woodpecker family.

16. Florida, Georgia, Mississippi, and Tennessee border Alabama.

Rewrite sentences 17–25, drawing a vertical line between the subject and the predicate of each sentence.

17. Booker T. Washington founded a school in Tuskegee, Alabama.

18. Boll weevils destroyed a cotton crop!

19. George Washington Carver experimented with peanuts and other crops.

20. Julian made a peanut butter pie.

21. Sweet potato pie is my favorite.

22. Tyrone's chickens laid two dozen eggs!

23. His rooster crows too early.

24. Miss Snoot complains.

25. She wakes in a bad mood.

Four Types of Sentences

Dictation or Journal Entry
Vocabulary:
A *synonym* is a word that has the same or nearly the same meaning as another word. "Big" is a *synonym* of "large."

An *antonym* is word that means the opposite of another word. "Small" is an *antonym* of "large."

A group of words that expresses a complete thought is called a sentence. A capital letter begins each sentence. There are **four types of sentences.**

Declarative

A **declarative sentence** makes a statement and ends with a period.

> We were whistling "Dixie" while we worked.
>
> I located the Appalachian Mountains on the map.
>
> Cotton grows in the Black Belt of Alabama.

Interrogative

An **interrogative sentence** asks a question and ends with a question mark.

> Do you whistle while you work?
>
> Can you locate the Appalachians on the map?
>
> Where does cotton grow?

Imperative

An **imperative sentence** expresses a command or a request and ends with a period.

> Whistle while you work.
>
> Locate the Appalachian Mountains on the map.
>
> Plant some cotton.

Exclamatory

An **exclamatory sentence** shows excitement or strong feeling and ends with an exclamation point.

> Hooray!
>
> I found it!
>
> What a beautiful cotton sweater!

Example For a–d, write whether the sentence is declarative, interrogative, imperative, or exclamatory.

(a) Where is Alaska?

(b) *Fast* and *quick* are synonyms.

(c) Learn about the state of Alaska.

(d) It's snowing!

Solution (a) This is an **interrogative** sentence because it asks a question and ends with a question mark.

(b) This sentence makes a statement and ends with a period. It is **declarative.**

(c) This sentence commands you to do something, and it ends with a period. Therefore, it is **imperative.**

(d) This sentence ends with an exclamation point and shows strong feeling. We recognize the **exclamatory** sentence.

✓**Practice** For a–d, write whether the sentence is declarative, interrogative, imperative, or exclamatory.

a. What is the capital of Alaska?

b. I know!

c. Juneau is the capital of Alaska.

d. Find Alaska on the map.

For e and f, replace each blank with *synonyms* or *antonyms*.

e. *Bucket* and *pail* are _____.

f. *Failure* and *success* are _____.

✓**Review Set 2** Choose the correct word to complete sentences 1–12.

*Numbers in parentheses indicate the number of the lesson in which the concept was introduced.

1. (*Essential*, *Nonessential*) means "necessary."
*(1)

2. *Old* is a(n) (synonym, antonym) of *young*.
(2)

Grammar and Writing 5

Student Edition
Lesson 2

3. A(n) (declarative, interrogative) sentence makes a
(2) statement.

4. A(n) (declarative, interrogative) sentence asks a question.
(2)

5. An (interrogative, imperative) sentence expresses a
(2) command or request.

6. A(n) (declarative, exclamatory) sentence shows strong
(2) feeling.

7. Declarative and imperative sentences end with a (period,
(2) question mark).

8. The (subject, predicate) of a sentence tells whom or what
(1) the sentence is about.

9. The (subject, predicate) of the sentence tells what the
(1) subject does, is, or is like.

10. A sentence begins with a (lowercase, capital) letter.
(2)

11. An interrogative sentence ends with a (period, question
(2) mark).

12. An exclamatory sentence ends with a(n) (question mark,
(2) exclamation point).

For 13–17, write whether the sentence is declarative,
interrogative, exclamatory, or imperative.

13. Alaska became a state in 1959.
(2)

14. Wow, it's the biggest state!
(2)

15. Who is Jack London?
(2)

16. The bull moose stood seven feet tall and weighed over a
(2) thousand pounds.

17. Sketch a moose.
(2)

Write the subject of sentences 18–22.

18. The willow ptarmigan is the Alaskan state bird.
(1)

19. Seafood provides income for Alaska.
(1)

20. Moose and brown bears stroll through Alaskan cities.
(1)

21. The economy depends heavily on tourism.
(1)

22. Petroleum and natural gas undergird the economy as
(1) well.

Write the predicate of sentences 23–26.

23. Alaska adopted a state flag in 1959.
(1)

24. The blue background represents the sky, the sea, the
(1) lakes, and the wildflowers.

25. The Big Dipper contains seven stars.
(1)

26. No roads connect Juneau to the rest of the world.
(1)

27. Unscramble these words to make a declarative sentence:
(2)
  salmon   the   upstream   swam

28. Unscramble these words to make an interrogative
(2) sentence:

  is   where   Mount McKinley

Rewrite sentences 29 and 30, drawing a vertical line between the subject and the predicate.

29. Alaska's motto is "North to the Future."
(1)

30. People rushed to the goldfields.
(1)

LESSON 3

Simple Subjects • Simple Predicates

Dictation or Journal Entry

Vocabulary:

Abundant means "more than enough" or "plentiful." We can make many apple pies, for we have an *abundant* supply of apples.

Scarce means "insufficient for a need" or "not enough." Because of disease and pests, fruit was *scarce* in the orchard.

We have learned that a sentence has two main parts: (1) the subject and (2) the predicate. The subject is the part that tells whom or what the sentence is about. The predicate is the part that tells something about the subject. The sentences below have been divided into their two main parts—subjects and predicates.

COMPLETE SUBJECT	COMPLETE PREDICATE
A generous person	shares with others.
Daniel Boone..............	explored Kentucky.
A shaggy donkey	brays at midnight.
History	is fascinating.

The complete (whole) subject or predicate may be a single word or many words. However, a subject or predicate of many words always has an essential part that we call the *simple subject* or *simple predicate.*

Simple Subject The main word or words in a sentence that tell *who* or *what* is doing or being something is called the **simple subject.** In the sentence below, *Yoli* is the simple subject, because it tells *who* plays the trumpet.

> Brown-eyed *Yoli* | plays the trumpet.

In the sentences below, we have italicized the simple subjects.

> A generous *person* | shares with others.

> *Daniel Boone* | explored Kentucky.

> A shaggy *donkey* | brays at midnight.

> *History* | is fascinating.

Example 1 Write the simple subject from this sentence:

A good tennis player practices every day.

Solution Who or what practices every day? A good tennis player does, so **player** is the simple subject. (The word "tennis" tells what kind of player.)

Simple Predicate The **simple predicate** is the verb. A verb expresses action or being. In the sentence below, "described" is the simple predicate, because it tells what Mrs. Cameron did.

Mrs. Cameron <u>described</u> the Grand Canyon.

We have underlined the simple predicates of the sentences below.

ACTION: A generous *person* <u>shares</u> with others.

ACTION: *Daniel Boone* <u>explored</u> Kentucky.

ACTION: A shaggy *donkey* <u>brays</u> at midnight.

BEING: *History* <u>is</u> fascinating.

Notice that sometimes the simple predicate contains more than one word as in these sentences:

The *thief* <u>has returned</u> the tarts.

Dad <u>will be singing</u> with the choir.

You <u>should have done</u> your homework.

Example 2 Write the simple predicate of the sentence below.

A good tennis player practices every day.

Solution We examine the sentence and discover that the player "practices." Therefore, **practices** is the simple predicate.

✓**Practice** For a–c, write the simple subject of each sentence.
  a. Alabama's caves contain ancient human bones.

  b. Five states border Arizona.

  c. A long-legged roadrunner speeds across New Mexico's desert.

For d–f, write the simple predicate of each sentence.
  d. Navajo ranchers raise sheep in Arizona.

e. Arizona's flag displays the sun's rays.

f. The Colorado River formed the Grand Canyon.

For g and h, replace each blank with *abundant* or *scarce*.

g. During the winters, tourists are _____ in Alaska, for the temperatures are too cold for most people.

h. Oil and fish are _____ in Alaska.

✓**Review Set 3**   Choose the correct word to complete sentences 1–10.

*Numbers in parentheses indicate number of the lesson in which the concept was introduced.

1. The main word in a sentence that tells whom or what the
*(3) sentence is about is called the simple (subject, predicate).

2. The simple (subject, predicate) of a sentence tells whom
(3) or what the sentence is about.

3. The simple (subject, predicate) is the verb.
(3)

4. A (verb, subject) expresses action or being.
(3)

5. A complete sentence has two parts—a (subject, verb) and
(1) a predicate.

6. (*Essential, Nonessential*) means "not necessary."
(1)

7. *Abundant* means "(scarce, plentiful)."
(3)

8. *Abundant* and *plentiful* are (synonyms, antonyms).
(2, 3)

9. *Scarce* and *abundant* are (synonyms, antonyms).
(2, 3)

10. (Synonyms, Antonyms) are opposites.
(2)

Write the <u>simple subject</u> of sentences 11–14.

11. Mount McKinley is the tallest mountain in North
(3) America.

12. The United States purchased Alaska from Russia.
(3)

13. Mount Katmai erupted in 1912.
(3)

14. A blue-ice glacier inches down the mountain.
(3)

Write the simple predicate of sentences 15–18.

15. Most Alaskans live in houses, not igloos.
(3)

16. Russia lies two and one-half miles from Alaska.
(3)

17. Forget-me-nots are blooming on the hillsides.
(3)

18. A wolf has been following my dog sled.
(3)

19. Unscramble these words to make a declarative sentence:
(2) discovered   prospectors   gold

20. Unscramble these words to make an interrogative
(2) sentence:

famous   is   why   Wyatt Earp

21. Unscramble these words to make an exclamatory
(2) sentence:

snake   out   the   for   look

22. Unscramble these words to make an imperative sentence:
(2) step   watch   you   where

For sentences 23–26, write whether the sentence is declarative, interrogative, imperative, or exclamatory.

23. Describe Wyatt Earp.
(2)

24. Was he a lawman?
(2)

25. Wyatt Earp, his brothers, and Doc Holliday tamed Dodge
(2) City, Wichita, and Tombstone.

26. That's an amazing story!
(2)

Rewrite sentences 27–30, drawing a vertical line between the subject and the predicate of each sentence.

27. The river eroded the soil.
(1)

28. Many tourists have walked through this ghost town.
(1)

29. Coyotes are howling at the moon.
(1)

30. Spanish explorers were searching for "Cities of Gold."
(1)

LESSON 4

Reversed Subject and Predicate
• Split Predicate

> **Dictation or Journal Entry**
>
> **Vocabulary:**
>
> *Optimism* is the belief that things are not hopeless, that they will turn out for the best. Even in the worst of times, Jenny's *optimism* makes her expect a better future.
>
> *Pessimism* is the belief that things are bad and that they are going to get worse. Gloomy Glumford is full of *pessimism*; he sees the worst in everything and doesn't expect improvement.

Reversed Subject and Predicate

In most sentences, the subject of the sentence comes first, and the predicate follows.

(subject)   (predicate)

The *parade* | will start at two p.m.

However, sometimes the order of the subject and predicate is reversed so that the predicate comes before the subject as in the sentences below.

(predicate)   (subject)

Here comes the *parade*.

Under the gate crawled my neighbor's *cat*.

Example 1

Write the simple subject and the simple predicate of this sentence:

Deep in the cave lies a dusty chest.

Solution

We remember that sometimes the predicate comes before the subject. The simple subject of this sentence is **chest.** What does the chest do? It "lies." The simple predicate is **lies.** Do not be confused by the word "cave." It is not the subject. "Deep in the cave" tells where the chest lies.

Split Predicate

In interrogative sentences, we usually find parts of the predicate split by the subject as in this sentence:

Did *you* answer the question?

In the sentence above, the simple subject is *you*, and the simple predicate is did answer.

Example 2

Write the simple predicate of this sentence:

Has Lucky found the treasure?

Solution   The subject *Lucky* <u>has found</u>. Therefore, the simple predicate is <u>**has found**</u>.

✓**Practice**   For a and b, replace the blank with *optimism* or *pessimism*.

    a. Some people might experience _____ during a disastrous fire or flood.

    b. Molly's _____ made her hopeful.

Write the simple subject of sentences c and d.

    c. There are many ladybugs in Delaware.

    d. Deep in a hole lives a hungry gopher.

Write the simple predicate of sentences e and f.

    e. Have the ducks migrated south?

    f. Did you hear that tall tale?

More Practice   See "More Practice Lesson 4" in Student Workbook.

✓**Review Set 4**   Choose the correct word to complete sentences 1–10.

*Numbers in parentheses indicate number of the lesson in which the concept was introduced.

    1. The main word in a sentence that tells what the subject does, is, or is like is called the simple (subject, predicate).
    (3)

    2. The simple (subject, predicate) of a sentence tells whom or what the sentence is about.
    (3)

    3. The simple predicate is the (subject, verb).
    (3)

    4. A verb expresses (action, pessimism) or being.
    (3)

    5. A complete (verb, sentence) has two parts—a subject and a predicate.
    (1)

    6. Food and water are (essential, nonessential) for survival.
    (1)

    7. (*Abundant, Scarce*) means "not enough."
    (3)

    8. *Pessimism* and *optimism* are (synonyms, antonyms).
    (2, 4)

    9. *Plentiful* and *abundant* are (synonyms, antonyms).
    (2, 3)

10. (Synonyms, Antonyms) are words that mean the same or almost the same.
(2)

For 11–16, write the simple subject of each sentence.

11. Many Arkansans enjoy folk music.
(3, 4)

12. On the fence sat a mockingbird.
(3, 4)

13. Over there are some apple blossoms.
(3, 4)

14. Was William J. Clinton born in Arkansas?
(3, 4)

15. In Arkansas, agriculture thrives.
(3, 4)

16. Above my head flew three wild turkeys.
(3, 4)

For 17–22, write the simple predicate of each sentence.

17. Do watermelons grow in Arkansas?
(3, 4)

18. I wandered along a scenic trail in the Ozarks.
(3, 4)

19. Did you catch a catfish?
(3, 4)

20. Pivot Rock balances on a small base.
(3, 4)

21. When will the bus arrive in Little Rock?
(3, 4)

22. Up the river chugged a steamboat.
(3, 4)

For sentences 23–26, write whether the sentence is declarative, interrogative, imperative, or exclamatory.

23. Enter at your own risk.
(2)

24. Have you seen the Arkansas River?
(2)

25. Arkansas entered the Union in 1836.
(2)

26. Look, the egg is hatching!
(2)

27. Unscramble these words to make an interrogative sentence:
(2)

fly   can   turkeys

Rewrite sentences 28–30, drawing a vertical line between the subject and the predicate of each sentence.

28. My uncle found a diamond in Arkansas.
(1)

29. Laborers are harvesting cotton and rice.
(1)

30. The Mississippi River divides Arkansas and Mississippi.
(1)

LESSON 5

Complete Sentence or Sentence Fragment?

Dictation or Journal Entry

Vocabulary:

Homophones are words that sound the same but differ in spelling and meaning. *There* and *their* are *homophones*.

There means "at or in that place." Please put the box up *there* on the shelf.

Their is the possessive form of *they*: *their* vacation, *their* house, *their* idea. They parked *their* car in the lot.

Complete Sentences

A **complete sentence** expresses a complete thought. It has both a subject and a predicate. The following are **complete sentences**.

California is the Golden State.

What is the capital of California?

Please find Sacramento on the map.

Notice that the sentence above, "Please find Sacramento on the map," does not appear to have a subject. It is an imperative sentence, a command. The subject *you* is understood.

(You) please find Sacramento on the map.

Fragments

A piece of a sentence is called a **fragment.** When a sentence fragment fails to tell us who or what is doing the action, it is missing the subject. The following sentence fragments are missing subjects.

Mops the floor. (who?)

Is slipping on the soapy floor. (who or what?)

If we identify the subject (who or what is doing the action), and we do not know what it is doing, the expression is missing a verb. The sentence fragments below are missing verbs.

The tallest trees on Earth. (do what? are what?)

The tourist in the funny hat. (does what?)

If the subject or verb is missing, we identify the expression as a **fragment.** Other errors that result in fragments are leaving out punctuation marks or using the *to* form and *ing* form of the verb.

	COMPLETE SENTENCES
FRAGMENTS	
The surfer riding a wave.	The surfer rides a wave.
	The surfer riding a wave saw a dolphin.
Carla to play goalie.	Coach asked Carla to play goalie.
	Carla wanted to play goalie.

Example Tell whether each of the following is a complete sentence or a sentence fragment.

   (a) Mr. McFuddle snores.

   (b) A tall redwood tree growing near the coast.

   (c) Two quail chicks left their nest.

   (d) To cross the Golden Gate Bridge.

Solution (a) **Complete sentence.**

   (b) This expression is missing part of the verb, so it is a **sentence fragment.** [Corrected: A tall redwood tree is growing near the coast. (or) I saw a tall redwood tree growing near the coast.]

   (c) **Complete sentence.**

   (d) This expression uses the *to* form of the verb, and it lacks a subject. It is not a complete thought. It is a **sentence fragment.** [Corrected: I want to cross the Golden Gate Bridge. (or) Shall we cross the Golden Gate Bridge?]

✓ **Practice** For a–d, write whether each word group is a sentence fragment or complete sentence.

   a. The California quail eats seeds and insects.

   b. Perching in a tree to avoid danger.

   c. To measure the height of a giant sequoia.

   d. Sequoias are the tallest trees on Earth.

For e–g, replace each blank with the correct vocabulary word from this lesson.

e. _____ is a giant sequoia!

f. Quails build _____ nests on the ground.

g. *Won* and *one* are _____.

More Practice Write whether each word group is a complete sentence or a sentence fragment.

1. Inside the dusty chest with rusty hinges.

2. Cleo dreams about treasure.

3. I have a map.

4. A cold, dark cavern with a musty smell.

5. To see through the darkness.

6. A friend holding a lantern.

Review Set 5 Choose the correct word to complete sentences 1–10.

*Numbers in parentheses indicate number of the lesson in which the concept was introduced.

1. A complete sentence has both a subject and a (fragment, predicate).
(3)

2. A piece of a sentence is called a sentence (fragment, homophone).
(5)

3. The simple (subject, predicate) is the verb.
(3)

4. If a sentence fragment fails to tell who or what is doing the action, it is missing the (subject, predicate).
(5)

5. If a sentence fails to tell what the subject is or is doing, it is missing a (subject, predicate).
(5)

6. *Two* and *too* are (synonyms, antonyms, homophones).
(5)

7. Please place the keys (there, their) on the table.
(5)

8. Full of (optimism, pessimism), Dr. Dimview thinks that life will go from bad to worse, that things are hopeless.
(4)

9. We have more than enough tomatoes; they are (abundant, scarce).
(3)

10. *Happy* and *joyful* are (homophones, antonyms,
(2)   synonyms).

For 11–18, write whether the word group is a complete
sentence or a sentence fragment.

11. Cassidy smiled.
(5)

12. Waves pounding the rocks.
(5)

13. Seals dive and splash.
(5)

14. To see the biggest telescope.
(5)

15. Drilling for oil.
(5)

16. A city with many vehicles.
(5)

17. Golden poppies blanket the hills.
(5)

18. People seek their fortunes.
(5)

Write the simple subject of sentences 19–21.

19. Does California have gold?
(3, 4)

20. Along came the forty-niners.
(3, 4)

21. Have you climbed Mount Whitney?
(3, 4)

Write the simple predicate of sentences 22–24.

22. Does California have gold?
(3, 4)

23. Along came the forty-niners.
(3, 4)

24. Have you climbed Mount Whitney?
(3, 4)

For sentences 25–28, write whether the sentence is
declarative, interrogative, imperative, or exclamatory.

25. The surf is up!
(2)

26. Death Valley lies 282 feet below sea level.
(2)

27. Visit the Palomar Observatory.
(2)

28. Have you seen Lake Tahoe?
(2)

29. Unscramble these words to make an interrogative sentence:
(2)   toast   burned   the   who

30. Rewrite the following sentence, drawing a vertical line
(1)   between the subject and the predicate:

California has the tallest and oldest trees in the world.

Correcting a Sentence Fragment

Dictation or Journal Entry
Vocabulary:
Its is the possessive (owning) form of *it*: *its* place, *its* paws, *its* engine. The bird returned to *its* nest.
It's is the shortened form of "it is." I think *it's* time for lunch.

We have learned that a complete sentence expresses a complete thought and that it has both a subject and a predicate. On the other hand, a **sentence fragment** is a piece of a sentence, missing a subject or predicate or proper punctuation marks.

Correcting Fragments   We can correct sentence fragments by adding subjects, verbs, and punctuation marks.

Example 1   Correct this sentence fragment: Hissed at me.

Solution   There is more than one right answer. We add a subject to tell who or what hissed.

My *kitten* <u>hissed</u> at me.

A *snake* <u>hissed</u> at me.

Example 2   Correct this sentence fragment: The suspension bridge.

Solution   There are different ways to correct this sentence fragment. We can add an action verb telling "what the suspension bridge does."

The suspension *bridge* <u>sways</u> in the wind.

We can also add a being verb to tell "what the suspension bridge is."

The suspension *bridge* <u>is</u> very high.

✓**Practice**   For a–d, rewrite and correct each sentence fragment, making a complete sentence. There is more than one correct answer.

a. Found a big silver nugget.

b. An enormous dinosaur.

c. My best friend.

d. Was sharpening its claws.

For e and f, replace each blank with *its* or *it's*.

    e. (Its, It's) a sunny day!

    f. The cat wiggled (its, it's) whiskers.

✓ **More Practice** For 1–5, correct each sentence fragment, making a complete sentence. There is more than one correct answer.

    1. A mean-looking bearded pirate.

    2. A box of gold coins.

    3. To find the coins.

    4. Searched the cave.

    5. Makes its home in the cave.

✓ **Review Set 6** Choose the correct word to complete sentences 1–10.

    1. The athletes wore (there, their) uniforms to the award
    (5) ceremony.

    2. Even though life is hard, James's (optimism, pessimism)
    (4) causes him to see a bright future.

    3. We do not have enough cucumbers to make a jar of
    (3) pickles. Our garden cucumbers are (abundant, scarce) this year.

    4. *Happy* and *sad* are (synonyms, antonyms, homophones).
    (2)

    5. (Essential, Nonessential) parts are necessary.
    (1)

    6. I think (its, it's) going to rain.
    (6)

    7. An (exclamatory, interrogative) sentence ends with a
    (2) question mark.

    8. The simple (subject, predicate) of a sentence is the verb.
    (3)

    9. A verb expresses (optimism, action, pessimism) or being.
    (3)

    10. An (exclamatory, interrogative) sentence ends with an
    (2) exclamation point.

For 11–14, write whether the word group is a complete sentence or a sentence fragment.

11. Skiing on the slopes of Vail, Colorado.
(5)

12. *Flea* and *flee* are homophones.
(5)

13. The 1858 gold rush.
(5)

14. Denver is the capital of Colorado.
(5)

For 15–18, rewrite and correct each sentence fragment, making a complete sentence. There is more than one correct answer.

15. To hike to Pike's Peak.
(6)

16. My favorite place in the whole world.
(6)

17. Grazing in the meadow.
(6)

18. Two bald eagles.
(6)

Write the simple subject of sentences 19–21.

19. Powdery snow fell in Colorado today.
(3, 4)

20. At the top of that tree sits a falcon.
(3, 4)

21. Did the miners find silver?
(3, 4)

Write the simple predicate of sentences 22–24.

22. Powdery snow fell in Colorado today.
(3, 4)

23. At the top of that tree sits a falcon.
(3, 4)

24. Did the miners find silver?
(3, 4)

For sentences 25–28, write whether the sentence is declarative, interrogative, imperative, or exclamatory.

25. The window is broken.
(2)

26. Who broke the window?
(2)

27. Tell me the truth.
(2)

28. I'm so sorry!
(2)

29. Unscramble these words to make a declarative sentence:
(2)

irrigate   ranchers   fields   their

30. Rewrite the following sentence, drawing a vertical line
(1) between the subject and the predicate:

Bighorn sheep dot Colorado's slopes.

Action Verbs

> **Dictation or Journal Entry**
>
> **Vocabulary:**
> To *conceal* is to put or keep out of sight; hide. We shall *conceal* our house key where no one will find it.
>
> To *disclose* is to make known; uncover. Will you *disclose* the secret recipe so that others can enjoy it?

Action Verbs A sentence is made up of a subject and a verb. The verb tells what the subject is or does. An **action verb** describes what the subject does or did. *Served* is an action verb in the sentence below. It tells what Connecticut did.

Connecticut <u>served</u> America's first hamburger.

Sometimes a sentence has more than one action verb. In the sentence below, *ticks* and *chimes* are two action verbs telling what the old clock does.

The old clock <u>ticks</u> loudly and <u>chimes</u> every hour.

Example Identify each action verb in these sentences.

(a) We shall build new towns but preserve scenic areas.

(b) Connecticut's inventors revolutionized industry.

(c) Eli Whitney's ideas started mass production.

Solution (a) The action verbs **build** and **preserve** tell what "we" shall do.

(b) The action verb **revolutionized** tells what "inventors" did.

(c) The action verb **started** tells what "ideas" did.

✓ Practice Write each action verb in sentences a–c.

a. Connecticut's colonial laws influenced the Constitution of the United States.

b. Birdwatchers spotted and admired the robins, Connecticut's state birds.

c. The Mohicans named Connecticut after its long tidal river.

For d and e, replace each blank with *conceal* or *disclose*.

    d. Elle and Al tried to _____ their bag of wildbird seed so that the squirrels could not find it.

    e. If they _____ the hiding place, the squirrels might eat all the wildbird seed.

Review Set 7 Choose the correct word to complete sentences 1–5.

    1. If you (conceal, disclose) the hiding place, it will no

(7) longer be a secret.

    2. A bear left (its, it's) tracks in the mud.

(6)

    3. *There* and (*here, their, where*) are homophones.

(5)

    4. (Optimism, Pessimism) is the belief that things will only

(4) get worse.

    5. *Plentiful* is a synonym of (*abundant, scarce*).

(2, 3)

Write each action verb in sentences 6–10.

    6. Amelia visited Connecticut, the Constitution State.

(7)

    7. Connecticut's factories manufacture color TVs.

(7)

    8. The original thirteen states included Connecticut.

(7)

    9. The red hen clucked at me and scratched the ground.

(7)

    10. Out at sea, a whale breached and blew.

(7)

For 11–14, write whether the word group is a complete sentence or a sentence fragment.

    11. The magnificent state of New York.

(5)

    12. Welcomes people from all over the world.

(5)

    13. Glaciers carved lakes in upstate New York.

(5)

    14. Massachusetts lies north of Connecticut.

(5)

For 15–18, rewrite and correct each sentence fragment, making a complete sentence. There is more than one correct answer.

15. A noisy helicopter.
(6)

16. To see the Statue of Liberty.
(6)

17. A delicious snack food.
(6)

18. Photographing Niagara Falls.
(6)

Write the simple subject of sentences 19–21.

19. Dairy products contribute to Connecticut's economy.
(3, 4)

20. Are the roses blooming in New York?
(3, 4)

21. Inside the trap is an enormous lobster.
(3, 4)

Write the simple predicate of sentences 22–24.

22. Dairy products contribute to Connecticut's economy.
(3, 4)

23. Are the roses blooming in New York?
(3, 4)

24. Inside the trap is an enormous lobster.
(3, 4)

For sentences 25–28, write whether the sentence is declarative, interrogative, imperative, or exclamatory.

25. Wow, lobster is expensive!
(2)

26. Did you trap that lobster?
(2)

27. Lobsters have exoskeletons and large pinchers.
(2)

28. Stay away from the pinchers.
(2)

29. Unscramble these words to make an exclamatory sentence:
(2) lobster   the   me   pinched

30. Rewrite the following sentence, drawing a vertical line
(1) between the subject and the predicate:

Lobster flourishes off the coast of Connecticut.

Capitalizing Proper Nouns

Dictation or Journal Entry:

Vocabulary:

The Greek root *geo-*, as in *geography* and *geology*, means "Earth."

Geography is the study of Earth's natural surface, including its climate and the plant, animal, and human life in different areas. In my *geography* class, I studied how the major rivers, lakes, and mountain ranges of North America have affected human activity.

Geology is the science that deals with Earth's structure, composition, and history, including the natural changes that have taken place on Earth's surface. In our *geology* class, we discussed how volcanic activity, erosion, and earthquakes have shaped landforms; we also learned to identify various rocks and minerals.

Proper Nouns A noun is a name word—a person, place, or thing. A noun may be common or proper. A *common noun* does not name a specific person, place, or thing. A **proper noun** does name a specific person, place, or thing and requires a capital letter.

Common noun—cat; **Proper noun—Spookie**

We capitalize every proper noun.

COMMON NOUN	PROPER NOUN
country	United States
lake	Lake Erie
day	Friday
month	August
girl	Laura Ingalls
book	*Homer Price*

Common Nouns Within Proper Nouns When a common noun such as "lake," "river," "mountain," "street," or "school" is a part of a proper noun, we capitalize it as in the examples below.

COMMON NOUN	PROPER NOUN
street	Lora Street
school	Dana Junior High School
ocean	Atlantic Ocean
family	Ware Family
river	Delaware River

Small Words Within Proper Nouns When the following small words are parts of a proper noun, we do not capitalize them unless they are the initial or final word:

a, an, and, at, but, by, for, from,

if, in, into, of, on, the, to, with

Notice the examples below.

The Little House on the Prairie
Proctor and Gamble Company
Gulf of Maine
House of Commons
Ivan the Terrible

Example Capitalize letters in these sentences as needed.

(a) The main character is tom sawyer.

(b) Have you read *lord of the rings?*

(c) The dixon family helped to build hoover dam.

(d) Many americans are immigrants.

Solution (a) We capitalize **Tom Sawyer** because it is a specific person.

(b) **Lord** and **Rings** are capitalized because they are words of a book title. We do not capitalize the small words *of* and *the.*

(c) **Dixon Family** is a specific family and needs capital letters. Also, **Hoover Dam** is a specific dam.

(d) **Americans** is capitalized because it is a group of people from a specific country.

Practice Rewrite sentences a–e, capitalizing each proper noun.

a. The dutch formed a whaling colony in 1631.

b. They named the colony lewes.

c. Let's read the book *hans brinker or the silver skates.*

d. The capital city of delaware is dover.

e. In 1609, henry hudson sailed into delaware bay.

For f–h, replace each blank with the correct vocabulary word from this lesson.

f. The Greek root _____ means "Earth."

g. Both geology and _____ study parts of Earth's surface.

h. _____ is the science of Earth's composition—its rocks and minerals, for example.

Review Set 8   Choose the correct word to complete sentences 1–5.

1. The Greek root *geo-* means "(Earth, study, science)."
(8)

2. Pirates tried to (conceal, disclose) the treasure where no one would find it.
(7)

3. Don't tell; (its, it's) a secret.
(6)

4. The poodles wagged (there, their) tails when they saw me.
(5)

5. *Plentiful* is an antonym of (*abundant, scarce*).
(2, 3)

Write and capitalize each proper noun in sentences 6–8.

6. Can we fish in noxingtown pond?
(8)

7. lynne reid banks wrote *the indian in the cupboard*.
(8)

8. Long ago, french immigrants established companies in delaware.
(8)

Write each action verb in sentences 9 and 10.

9. Leroy tiptoes into the kitchen and makes a sandwich.
(7)

10. Have mice nibbled this cheese?
(7)

For 11–14, write whether the word group is a complete sentence or a sentence fragment.

11. Building the first log cabins.
(5)

12. European workers took factory jobs.
(5)

13. To start the car and rev the engine.
(5)

14. Winds blew.
(5)

For 15–18, rewrite and correct each sentence fragment, making a complete sentence. There is more than one correct answer.

15. Migrating ducks and geese.
(6)

16. The peach blossoms.
(6)

17. To play the trombone.
(6)

18. A blue hen from Delaware.
(6)

Write the simple subject of sentences 19–21.

19. The first log cabins were built (in Delaware.)
(3, 4)

20. Up the stream swam a salamander.
(3, 4)

21. Are the geese resting at the swamp?
(3, 4)

Write the simple predicate of sentences 22–24.

22. The first log cabins were built in Delaware.
(3, 4)

23. Up the stream swam a salamander.
(3, 4)

24. Are the geese resting at the swamp?
(3, 4)

For sentences 25–28, write whether the sentence is declarative, interrogative, imperative, or exclamatory.

25. Memorize the fifty states and their capitals.
(2)

26. Mills in Wilmington made flour, paper, and cloth.
(2)

27. Where do the geese go in winter?
(2)

28. Horseshoe crabs can go a whole year without food!
(2)

29. Unscramble these words to make an interrogative sentence:
(2)   oranges   grow   do   Delaware   in

30. Rewrite the following sentence, drawing a vertical line
(1)   between the subject and the predicate:

Delaware was the first state in the union.

LESSON 9

Present Tense of Verbs

Dictation or Journal Entry

Vocabulary:

An _archipelago_ is a group or chain of many islands. The West Indies form an _archipelago_ over two thousand miles long in the Caribbean Sea.

An _estuary_ is the wide mouth of a river where the current meets the sea and is affected by the tides. Many water birds inhabit that marshy _estuary_ near the Caribbean Sea.

Tense means "time." Verbs tell us not only what action is occurring but also when it is occurring. The form of a verb, or the verb tense, changes in order to show when the action takes place. Three simple verb tenses are present, past, and future. In this lesson, we will talk about the present tense.

Present Tense

The **present tense** refers to action that is happening now. We add an _s_ when the subject is singular, except when the pronoun is _I_ or _you_.

PLURAL SUBJECTS AND PRONOUNS _I_ AND _YOU_	SINGULAR SUBJECTS
Chickens <u>cluck</u>.	The chicken <u>clucks</u>.
Ducks <u>quack</u>.	A duck <u>quacks</u>.
I <u>leap</u>.	She <u>leaps</u>.
We <u>sleep</u>.	He <u>sleeps</u>.
They <u>laugh</u>.	Moe <u>laughs</u>.
You <u>sing</u>.	Tina <u>sings</u>.
Phil and Jenny <u>talk</u>.	Grandma <u>talks</u>.

When a verb ends in _s, x, z, ch,_ or _sh,_ we add _es_ when the subject is singular.

PLURAL SUBJECTS AND PRONOUNS _I_ AND _YOU_	SINGULAR SUBJECTS
We <u>rush</u>.	Athena <u>rushes</u>.
Insects <u>buzz</u>.	An insect <u>buzzes</u>.
Horses <u>munch</u>.	The horse <u>munches</u>.
Kittens <u>hiss</u>.	A kitten <u>hisses</u>.
Cooks <u>mix</u> ingredients.	Ted <u>mixes</u> ingredients.

When a verb ends in a consonant and a _y,_ we change the _y_ to _i_ and add _es_ for the singular form.

I <u>dry</u> the dishes.
They <u>empty</u> the trash.

He <u>dries</u> the dishes.
Lillian <u>empties</u> the trash.

Example   Replace each blank with the singular present tense form of the verb.

(a) You <u>reply</u>. He _____.

(b) Birds <u>fly</u>. A robin _____.

(c) Babies <u>cry</u>. A baby _____.

(d) Sodas <u>fizz</u>. One soda _____.

(e) They <u>guess</u>. She _____.

Solution   (a) **replies** (Since the verb ends in *y*, we change the *y* to *i* and add *es*.)

(b) **flies** (Since the verb ends in *y*, we change the *y* to *i* and add *es*.)

(c) **cries** (Since the verb ends in *y*, we change the *y* to *i* and add *es*.)

(d) **fizzes** (The verb ends in *z*, so we add *es*.)

(e) **guesses** (The verb ends in *s*, so we add *es*.)

✓ **Practice**   For a and b, replace each blank with the correct vocabulary word from this lesson.

a. The islands of the West Indies form a chain, or _____.

b. The mouth of a river might form an _____.

For c–f, replace each blank with the singular present tense form of the underlined verb.

c. Dan and Quan <u>wash</u>. Dad _____.

d. Kim and Chris <u>wish</u>. Juan _____.

e. People <u>reply</u>. One woman _____.

f. They <u>try</u>. She _____.

Review Set 9 Choose the correct word to complete sentences 1–5.

1. An estuary is the wide mouth of a (platypus, river, hippopotamus).
   (9)

2. We might learn the names of mountains and rivers in a (biography, photography, geography) class.
   (8)

3. If you *disclose* something, you (hide, uncover) it.
   (7)

4. If (its, it's) raining, we'll wear our boots.
   (6)

5. (There, Their) is the possessive form of *they*.
   (5)

6. Write and capitalize each proper noun from the following sentence:
   (8)

   On friday a shuttle will launch from the kennedy space center.

For 7 and 8, replace the blank with the singular present tense form of the underlined verb.

7. Many frogs <u>catch</u> flies. One frog _____ flies.
   (9)

8. Some peacocks <u>fly</u>. One peacock _____.
   (9)

Write each action verb in sentences 9 and 10.

9. Tourists flock to Florida in the winter.
   (7)

10. A twelve-foot long alligator opens its mouth and snaps at a frog.
    (7)

For 11–14, write whether the word group is a complete sentence or a sentence fragment.

11. One famous person in Florida.
    (5)

12. To hunt for seashells along the sandy shore.
    (5)

13. Did Juan Ponce de León find the Fountain of Youth?
    (5)

14. Cape Canaveral, a major tourist attraction.
    (5)

For 15–18, rewrite and correct each sentence fragment, making a complete sentence. There is more than one correct answer.

15. A crocodile in the Everglades.
(6)

16. Picking bushels of juicy oranges.
(6)

17. To vacation in the Sunshine State.
(6)

18. An aggressive, grayish-brown mockingbird.
(6)

Write the simple subject of sentences 19–21.

19. Juan Ponce de León claimed Florida for Spain.
(3, 4)

20. Do panthers live in the Everglades?
(3, 4)

21. Out of the swamp crawled an enormous crocodile.
(3, 4)

Write the simple predicate of sentences 22–24.

22. Ponce de León claimed Florida for Spain.
(3, 4)

23. Do panthers live in the Everglades?
(3, 4)

24. Out of the swamp crawled an enormous crocodile.
(3, 4)

For sentences 25–28, write whether the sentence is declarative, interrogative, imperative, or exclamatory.

25. Please do not tease the alligators.
(2)

26. Wow, their jaws are strong!
(2)

27. Where are the Florida Keys?
(2)

28. Lemons, oranges, and grapefruits come from Florida.
(2)

29. Unscramble these words to make an imperative sentence:
(2)
water   plenty   drink   of

30. Rewrite the following sentence, drawing a vertical line
(1)   between the subject and the predicate:

My friend from Michigan enjoys Florida's warm winters.

Past Tense of Regular Verbs

We remember that *tense* means "time," that verbs tell us not only what action is occurring but also when it is occurring. The form of a verb, or the verb tense, changes in order to show when the action takes place. Three simple verb tenses are present, past, and future. In this lesson, we will talk about past tense of regular verbs. There are many irregular verb forms that we will learn later.

Past Tense   The **past tense** shows action that has already occurred. To form the past tense of regular verbs, we add *ed*.

talk—talked

bark—barked

When a one-syllable verb ends in a single consonant, we double the consonant and add *ed*.

chip—chipped

tap—tapped

When a verb ends in *e*, we drop the *e* and add *ed*.

rake—raked

live—lived

When the verb ends in *y*, we change the *y* to *i* and add *ed*.

try—tried

supply—supplied

Example 1   Write the past tense form of each verb.

(a) slap   (b) care   (c) cry

(d) pat   (e) worry   (f) move

Solution   (a) **slapped** (Since this is a short verb ending in a consonant, we double the consonant and add *ed*.)

(b) **cared** (The verb ends in *e*, so we drop the *e* and add *ed*.)

(c) **cried** (The verb ends in *y*, so we change the *y* to *i* and add *ed*.)

(d) **patted** (Since this is a short verb ending in a consonant, we double the consonant and add *ed*.)

(e) **worried** (The verb ends in *y*, so we change the *y* to *i* and add *ed*.)

(f) **moved** (The verb ends in *e*, so we drop the *e* and add *ed*.)

Errors to Avoid Do not use the present tense form for the past tense.

NO: Yesterday, Ben <u>calls</u> me twice.
YES: Yesterday, Ben <u>called</u> me twice.

NO: Last night, we <u>work</u> late.
YES: Last night, we <u>worked</u> late.

NO: A week ago, Mia <u>studies</u> the map.
YES: A week ago, Mia <u>studied</u> the map.

Do not shift from past to present in the same phrase.

NO: She <u>looked</u> everywhere but <u>discovers</u> nothing.
YES: She <u>looked</u> everywhere but <u>discovered</u> nothing.

NO: The sparrow <u>chirped</u> and <u>flaps</u> its wings.
YES: The sparrow <u>chirped</u> and <u>flapped</u> its wings.

Example 2 Choose the correct form of the verb to complete each sentence.

(a) Daniel washed the dishes and (mops, mopped) the floor.

(b) A while ago, I (slip, slipped) on the icy walkway.

Solution (a) Daniel washed the dishes and **mopped** the floor.

(b) A while ago, I **slipped** on the icy walkway.

✓**Practice** For a and b, replace each blank with *flora* or *fauna*.

a. The _____ of a region is its animals.

b. The _____ of a region is its plants.

For c–j, write the past tense form of each verb.

c. clap   **d.** bury   **e.** drop   **f.** race

g. dry   **h.** hike   **i.** dip   **j.** step

For k and l, choose the correct verb form.

k. Yesterday, an alligator (escapes, escaped) from the zoo.

l. It crawled down Main Street and (swallows, swallowed) a flower pot.

Review Set 10

Choose the correct word to complete sentences 1–5.

1. A (tree, bird, bush) is an example of *fauna*.
(10)

2. An island might be a part of an (estuary, archipelago).
(9)

3. We might learn to identify rock and minerals in a (biology, geology, theology) class.
(8)

4. If you *conceal* something, you (hide, uncover) it.
(7)

5. A spider spun (its, it's) web inside the lampshade.
(6)

6. Write and capitalize each proper noun from the following sentence:
(8)

In florida's capital city, tallahassee, you can stroll through the beautiful maclay gardens.

For 7 and 8, replace the blank with the singular present tense form of the underlined verb.

7. Some alligators <u>hiss</u>. An alligator _____.
(9)

8. Two cooks <u>fry</u> yams. One cook _____ yams.
(9)

Write each action verb in sentences 9 and 10.

9. Golfers putt, chip, and drive golf balls.
(7)

10. Casey squeezed six oranges and drank the juice.
(7)

For 11–14, write whether the word group is a complete sentence or a sentence fragment.

11. In the birders' paradise along the coast.
(5)

12. River otters and bears in untamed bogs and marshes.
(5)

13. Peanuts grow on the roots of the plant.
(5)

14. Colonists grew peanuts in Georgia.
(5)

For 15–18, rewrite and correct each sentence fragment, making a complete sentence. There is more than one correct answer.

15. Bumper-to-bumper traffic on the highway.
(6)

16. Growing large, delicious peaches.
(6)

17. The friendliest animal of all.
(6)

18. To become President of the United States.
(6)

Write the simple subject of sentences 19–21.

19. Does the gin separate the seeds from the cotton?
(3, 4)

20. Into the bog dove the otter.
(3, 4)

21. Here comes the parade!
(3, 4)

Write the simple predicate of sentences 22–24.

22. Does the gin separate the seeds from the cotton?
(3, 4)

23. Into the bog dove the otter.
(3, 4)

24. Here comes the parade!
(3, 4)

For sentences 25 and 26, choose the correct verb form.

25. My cousin called me and (chats, chatted) for an hour.
(10)

26. Yesterday, we (pick, picked) a bushel of peaches.
(10)

27. For a–d, write the past tense form of the verb.
(10) (a) clip   (b) try   (c) chat   (d) deny

28. Write whether the following sentence is declarative,
(2) interrogative, imperative, or exclamatory:

Georgia is the Empire State of the South.

29. Unscramble these words to make a declarative sentence:
(2)

came   Jimmy Carter   Georgia   from

30. Rewrite the following sentence, drawing a vertical line between the subject and the predicate:
(1)

Mills in Georgia make paper from trees.

LESSON 11

Concrete, Abstract, and Collective Nouns

> **Dictation or Journal Entry**
>
> **Vocabulary:**
> A *peninsula* is a body of land almost entirely surrounded by water, usually connected with the mainland by an isthmus. Florida is mainly a large *peninsula* extending between the Atlantic Ocean and the Gulf of Mexico.
>
> An *isthmus* is a narrow strip of land bordered by water and connecting two larger bodies of land. The *Isthmus* of Panama connects North America with South America.

We know that a noun is a person, place, or thing. We group nouns into these classes: common, proper, concrete, abstract, and collective.

We have learned the difference between common and proper nouns. In this lesson, we will learn the difference between concrete and abstract nouns. We will also learn to recognize collective nouns.

Concrete Nouns
A **concrete noun** names a person, place, or thing. It may be either common or proper.

CONCRETE COMMON	CONCRETE PROPER
car	Ford
doctor	Dr. Cho
city	Savannah

Abstract Nouns
An **abstract noun** names something that cannot be seen or touched. It names something that you can only think about. An abstract noun can be common or proper as well.

ABSTRACT COMMON NOUNS	ABSTRACT PROPER NOUNS
religion	Judaism
holiday	Thanksgiving Day
nationality	Irish
language	Mandarin
day	Monday

Example 1 Tell whether each noun is concrete or abstract.

      (a) Islam   (b) hope

      (c) Persian Gulf   (d) truth

      (e) book   (f) optimism

Solution (a) **abstract** (Islam is a religion.)

      (b) **abstract** (We can only *think* about hope.)

      (c) **concrete**   (d) **abstract**

      (e) **concrete**   (f) **abstract**

Collective Nouns A **collective noun** names a collection of persons, places, animals, or things. We list a few examples below.

      PERSONS: team, crew, class, army, family, chorus

      ANIMALS: flock, herd, school (fish), litter

      PLACES: Africa, Asia, Europe, Latin America

      THINGS: batch, bunch, assortment, collection, multitude

Example 2 Write the collective noun from each sentence.

      (a) A yoke of oxen lumbered up the steep path.

      (b) The Apache tribe demonstrated native dances.

      (c) The United States helped tsunami victims.

      (d) Yasmin bakes a batch of banana muffins every Saturday.

Solution (a) **yoke**   (b) **tribe**

      (c) **United States**   (d) **batch**

Practice For a and b, replace each blank with *peninsula* or *isthmus*.

      a. A(n) _____ is a narrow strip of land connecting two larger bodies of land.

      b. The state of Florida is mainly a(n) _____.

      For c–f, tell whether each noun is abstract or concrete.

      c. whale   **d.** peace

e. Buddhism   **f.** cotton gin

For g and h, write the collective noun that you find in each sentence.

g. We peeled, boiled, and mashed a bushel of potatoes for our feast.

h. The colony at Plymouth celebrated the first Thanksgiving.

More Practice

For 1–12, tell whether each noun is abstract or concrete.

1. optimism
2. carrot
3. peninsula
4. joy
5. tiger
6. pessimism
7. courage
8. cheese
9. peach
10. nose
11. shoe
12. hope

Write each collective noun that you find in sentences 13–15.

13. Mirta's class admired her butterfly collection.

14. A school of fish swam among a fleet of ships.

15. A swarm of flies lands on an assortment of sandwiches at the picnic.

✓ Review Set 11

Choose the correct word to complete sentences 1–5.

1. A (cat, mouse, weed) is an example of *flora*.
(10)

2. Fresh water might mix with salty seawater in a(n) (estuary, synonym, homophone).
(9)

3. The Greek prefix *geo-* means "(life, God, Earth)."
(8)

4. *Conceal* and *disclose* are (synonyms, antonyms, homophones).
(2, 7)

5. We'll have a picnic if (its, it's) not too cold.
(6)

6. Write and capitalize each proper noun from the following sentence:
(8)

In the gulf of mexico, hurricane rita gathered force.

For 7 and 8, replace the blank with the singular present tense form of the underlined verb.

7. Some princesses <u>kiss</u> frogs. One princess _____
(9) a frog.

8. Two ducks <u>fly</u> south. One duck _____ south.
(9)

Write each action verb in sentences 9 and 10.

9. Stone Mountain depicts Robert E. Lee, Jefferson Davis,
(7) and Stonewall jackson.

10. Martin Luther King lived and worked in Atlanta.
(7)

For 11–14, write whether the word group is a complete sentence or a sentence fragment.

11. Known as America's greatest botanical garden.
(5)

12. Okefenokee Swamp is a national wildlife refuge.
(5)

13. To settle along the Chattahoochee River.
(5)

14. Did that granite come from a Georgia rock quarry?
(5)

For 15 and 16, rewrite and correct each sentence fragment, making a complete sentence. There is more than one correct answer.

15. An aggressive alligator in the Okefenokee swamp.
(6)

16. To protect endangered animals.
(6)

17. For a–d, write whether the noun is concrete or abstract.
(11) (a) estuary   (b) faith   (c) archipelago   (d) fear

18. Write each collective noun that you find in this sentence:
(11) A gaggle of geese gobbled up all the bread crumbs.

Write the simple subject of sentences 19–21.

19. Daniel Boone led settlers through the Cumberland Gap to
(3, 4) Kentucky.

20. Did that stallion race in the Kentucky Derby?
(3, 4)

21. Around the bend goes Secretariat!
(3, 4)

Write the simple predicate of sentences 22–24.

22. Daniel Boone led settlers through the Cumberland Gap to
(3, 4) Kentucky.

23. Did that stallion race in the Kentucky Derby?
(3, 4)

24. Around the bend goes Secretariat!
(3, 4)

For sentences 25 and 26, choose the correct verb form.

25. Long ago, settlers (name, named) Georgia after George II
(10) of England.

26. Hollis picked fresh peaches and (bakes, baked) them in a
(10) pie.

27. For a–d, write the past tense form of the verb.
(10) (a) chop   (b) fry   (c) pit   (d) reply

28. Write whether the following sentence is declarative,
(2) interrogative, imperative, or exclamatory:

Secretariat crossed the finish line!

29. Unscramble these words to make an exclamatory sentence:
(2) cave   that   deep   is

30. Rewrite the following sentence, drawing a vertical line
(1) between the subject and the predicate:

Georgia's nickname, the Empire State of the South, refers
to its size and wealth.

Helping Verbs

Dictation or Journal Entry

Vocabulary:

A *strait* is a narrow waterway or channel connecting two larger bodies of water. The *Strait* of Magellan separates the Tierra del Fuego archipelago from the mainland of South America.

A *lagoon* is a pond or shallow body of seawater partly or completely enclosed by land or by a coral reef. Conchs often live in shallow waters, such as at the bottom of a *lagoon*.

Helping Verbs We know that every predicate contains a verb. Sometimes, the verb is more than one word in the sentence. The main verb may have one or more **helping verbs.** The main verb shows the action; the helping verbs do not show action, but they help to form the verb tense.

You <u>might have read</u> many good books.

In the sentence above, "read" is the main verb, and "might" and "have" are helping verbs. "Might have read" is called a verb phrase.

Memorize these common helping verbs:

is, am, are, was, were, be, being, been,

has, have, had, may, might, must,

can, could, do, does, did,

shall, will, should, would

Example In the following sentences, write the entire verb phrase and circle each helping verb.

(a) Erin should have been watching Kilauea, the world's most active volcano.

(b) She might have seen an eruption.

(c) Instead, she has been shopping for Hawaiian clothing.

(d) Unlike Erin, Coleman will have witnessed several volcanic eruptions before sundown.

Solution (a) **should have been** watching (*Should, have,* and *been* are helping verbs for the main verb "watching.")

(b) **might have** seen

(c) has been shopping

(d) will have witnessed

✓ Practice   **a.** Study the helping verbs listed in this lesson. Memorize them one line at a time. Practice saying them *in order* (perhaps to your teacher or a friend). Then write as many as you can from memory.

For sentences b–e, write the entire verb phrase and circle each helping verb.

b. Dale must have been harvesting sugarcane today.

c. He should have called me.

d. I could have helped him.

e. Tomorrow I shall volunteer my services.

For f and g, replace each blank with *strait* or *lagoon*.

f. A _____ is a narrow waterway connecting two larger bodies of water.

g. A _____ is like a pond.

More Practice   See "More Practice Lesson 12" in Student Workbook.

✓ Review Set 12   Choose the correct word to complete sentences 1–7.

1. Florida is mainly a large (archipelago, estuary, peninsula).
(11)

2. Walnut trees are an example of (flora, fauna).
(10)

3. An archipelago is a group or chain of many (pearls, islands, lakes).
(9)

4. The Greek prefix (*geo-, bio-, theo-*) means "Earth."
(8)

5. To (conceal, disclose) is to make known; uncover.
(7)

6. Last night, I trembled when a gorilla (taps, tapped) on my door.
(10)

7. At seven p.m., I closed the book and (turn, turned) off the
(10) computer.

8. Write and capitalize each proper noun from the following
(8) sentence: My friend rosalba wants to attend the
university of hawaii at manoa.

For 9 and 10, replace the blank with the singular present
tense form of the underlined verb.

9. All the students <u>try</u> hard. One student _____ hard.
(9)

10. Four cars <u>miss</u> the turn. A car _____ the turn.
(9)

Write each action verb in sentences 11 and 12.

11. Polynesians paddled canoes from one island to another.
(7)

12. Hawaii exports sugar and imports cars.
(7)

13. From memory, write the common helping verbs listed in
(12) this lesson.

For sentences 14 and 15, write the entire verb phrase, circling
each helping verb.

14. Next month Kai will be surfing at Waikiki Beach.
(12)

15. You should have seen Mauna Loa's eruption!
(12)

For 16–19, write whether the word group is a complete
sentence or a sentence fragment.

16. Walking through lush Kauai rain forests.
(5)

17. Waves crash against the beach.
(5)

18. Megan wears a red hibiscus in her hair.
(5)

19. To slice a fresh pineapple and eat it.
(5)

20. Rewrite and correct the following sentence fragment,
(6) making a complete sentence: My favorite summertime
activities.

21. For a–d, write whether the noun is concrete or abstract.
(11)
(a) lagoon   (b) idea   (c) happiness   (d) strait

STOP

22. Write each collective noun that you find in this sentence:
(11) A pod of whales amused the rowing team.

Write the simple subject of sentences 23 and 24.

23. The world's biggest dormant volcano is Haleakala.
(3, 4)

24. Away flew the Hawaiian goose.
(3, 4)

Write the simple predicate of sentences 25 and 26.

25. The world's biggest dormant volcano is Haleakala.
(3, 4)

26. Away flew the Hawaiian goose.
(3, 4)

27. For a–d, write the past tense form of the verb.
(10) (a) jog   (b) rely   (c) mop   (d) dry

28. Write whether the following sentence is declarative,
(2) interrogative, imperative, or exclamatory: The volcano is
erupting!

29. Unscramble these words to make a declarative sentence:
(2)
alphabet   Hawaiian   the   twelve   letters   has

30. Rewrite the following sentence, drawing a vertical line
(1) between the subject and the predicate:

My cousin on Maui has planted a macadamia nut tree.

Singular, Plural, Compound, and Possessive Nouns

Singular or Plural

Nouns are either singular or plural. A **singular noun** names only one person, place, or thing. A **plural noun** names more than one person, place, or thing.

SINGULAR NOUNS	PLURAL NOUNS
orchid	orchids
perch	perches
cliff	cliffs
mango	mangoes

Example 1 Tell whether each noun is singular or plural.

(a) fox   (b) wishes   (c) clips

(d) mole   (e) stories   (f) monkey

Solution (a) **singular**   (b) **plural**   (c) **plural**

(d) **singular**   (e) **plural**   (f) **singular**

Compound

A noun made up of two or more words is a **compound noun.** Sometimes we write a compound noun as one word:

baseball, freeway, keyboard

Often we write compound nouns as two words:

elementary school, post office, swimming pool

Other compound nouns are hyphenated:

brother-in-law, hand-me-down, take-off

There is no pattern for determining whether to spell a compound noun as one word, two separate words, or one hyphenated word. We must use the dictionary.

Example 2 Write the compound nouns from this list:

encyclopedia	eyelash
show-off	dictionary

Solution The compound nouns from the list above are **eyelash** and **show-off.**

Possessive A **possessive noun** tells "who" or "what" owns something. Possessive nouns can be either singular or plural. The possessive form of nouns has an apostrophe and an *s* added to them:

an *elephant's* trunk	the *volcano's* ashes
anybody's guess	the *cat's* name
somebody's shoe	a *fish's* fin
nobody's business	a *bull's* horns

Usually only an apostrophe is added to plural nouns when they end with the letter *s*:

two *elephants'* trunks	some *boys'* bicycles
the *horses'* saddles	the *nurses'* opinions
the *Wigginses'* chicken	several *ranchers'* cattle

Example 3 Write the possessive noun from each sentence.

(a) Have you made a card for Mother's Day?

(b) Please give me your parents' names.

(c) Isabel's bicycle has a flat tire.

(d) My friend's optimism encourages me.

Solution (a) **Mother's** (b) **parents'** (c) **Isabel's** (d) **friend's**

Practice For a–d, write whether each noun is singular or plural.

a. cherries   **b.** rectangle

c. Venus   **d.** sons

e. Write each compound noun from this list:

son-in-law	check mark
doorknob	Mississippi

For f and g, write the possessive noun from each sentence.

    f. Do you know Idaho's nickname?

    g. Have you seen the gem collectors' garnets?

For h and i, replace each blank with *tributary* or *delta*.

    h. We might find a _____, or triangular area of land, at the mouth of a river.

    i. A river or stream that flows into a larger river or stream is called a _____.

More Practice See "Corny Chronicle #1" in Student Workbook. Have fun!

Review Set 13 Choose the correct word to complete sentences 1–8.

    1. A strait is a narrow waterway connecting two larger
    (12) bodies of (dinosaurs, water, ice).

    2. A peninsula is a body of land almost entirely surrounded
    (11) by (water, mountains, clouds).

    3. Horses are an example of (flora, fauna).
    (10)

    4. An (archipelago, estuary) is the wide mouth of a river
    (9) where the current meets the sea.

    5. (Essential, Nonessential) supplies are not necessary.
    (1)

    6. After building a snowman, Norma removed her gloves
    (10) and (rubs, rubbed) her cold fingers.

    7. At six a.m., I picked up a leash and (walk, walked) the
    (10) dog.

    8. *Tributaries* is a (singular, plural) noun.
    (13)

    9. Write and capitalize each proper noun from the following
    (8) sentence: A young shoshone guide, sacagawea, led lewis and clark across the bitterroot range.

For 10 and 11, replace the blank with the singular present tense form of the underlined verb.

10. Two shoppers <u>hurry</u>. One shopper _____.
(9)

11. Some groomers <u>brush</u> horses. A groomer _____
(9) horses.

12. Write each action verb in the following sentence: My dog
(7) Vixen leaps fences, digs holes, and chases cats.

13. From memory, write the common helping verbs listed in
(12) Lesson 12.

For sentences 14 and 15, write the entire verb phrase, circling each helping verb.

14. The world's first ski lift was built in 1935.
(12)

15. In Sun Valley, Idaho, Lisha might ride the oldest ski lift
(12) in the world.

For 16 and 17, write whether the word group is a complete sentence or a sentence fragment.

16. National forests cover more than a third of Idaho.
(5)

17. Planting and harvesting potatoes in the Snake River
(5) Valley.

18. Write each compound noun from this list:
(13)
warm-up   trailblazer

caterpillar   pathfinder

19. Write the possessive noun from this sentence: Idaho's
(13) sawmills process pine, spruce, and fir trees.

20. Rewrite and correct the following sentence fragment,
(6) making a complete sentence: To pick bing cherries near
Boise, Idaho.

21. For a–d, write whether the noun is concrete or abstract.
(11) (a) baboon   (b) harmony   (c) mercy   (d) dentist

22. Write each collective noun that you find in this sentence:
(11) This crop of potatoes came from Idaho Falls.

Write the simple subject of sentences 23 and 24.

23. There are sparkling, snow-topped mountains in Idaho.
(3, 4)

24. Has Ms. Galindo been skiing all day?
(3, 4)

Write the simple predicate of sentences 25 and 26.

25. There are sparkling, snow-topped mountains in Idaho.
(3, 4)

26. Has Ms. Galindo been skiing all day?
(3, 4)

27. For a–d, write the past tense form of the verb.
(10) (a) slip   (b) hurry   (c) scrub   (d) reply

28. Write whether the following sentence is declarative,
(2) interrogative, imperative, or exclamatory: Why do
beavers build dams?

29. Unscramble these words to make an imperative sentence:
(2) vegetables   eat   your   green

30. Rewrite the following sentence, drawing a vertical line
(1) between the subject and the predicate:

A band of mountain men have been telling tall tales.

Future Tense

> **Dictation or Journal Entry**
>
> **Vocabulary:**
>
> A *hemisphere* is one half of Earth, as divided by the equator or by the Greenwich meridian. The equator divides Earth into the Northern and Southern *hemispheres*; the Greenwich meridian divides it into the Eastern and Western *hemispheres.*
>
> A *meridian* is an imaginary circle on Earth's surface passing through the North and South poles. A *meridian* is also known as a line of longitude, a measure of the distance in degrees east or west of Greenwich, England.

The **future tense** refers to action that has not yet occurred. The future tense is usually formed with the helping verbs *shall* or *will*. With the pronouns *I* and *we*, the use of *shall* is preferable in formal writing.

He *will* play.	We *shall* play.
They *will* talk.	I *shall* talk.
You *will* help.	We *shall* help.
Jasmin *will* come.	She and I *shall* come.
Sam *will* leave.	We *shall* leave.
Kevin and Juan *will* sing.	I *shall* sing.

Example 1 Complete the future tense verb form by replacing each blank with *will* or *shall*, as you would do in formal writing.

(a) Anthony _____ play the tuba in the next parade.

(b) Shalene and I _____ march with the band.

(c) It _____ snow tomorrow.

(d) I _____ build a snow fort.

Solution (a) Anthony **will** play the tuba in the next parade.

(b) Shalene and I **shall** march with the band.

(c) It **will** snow tomorrow.

(d) I **shall** build a snow fort.

Errors to Avoid Do not use the present for the future tense.

NO: Tomorrow I <u>rake</u> the leaves.
YES: Tomorrow I <u>shall rake</u> the leaves.

NO: We race next Thursday.
YES: We shall race next Thursday.

NO: Next week she plays her cello.
YES: Next week she will play her cello.

Example 2 Identify the following underlined verbs as present, past or future tense.

(a) Utah borders Idaho.

(b) Grandma will bake pies for Thanksgiving.

(c) Ben laughed.

Solution (a) **present**   (b) **future**   (c) **past**

Example 3 Write the correct form of the verb.

(a) The orchestra (future of *perform*) tonight.

(b) Babies often (present of *fill*) their mouths too full.

(c) A miner (past of *search*) for gold.

(d) My dog (present of *bury*) his bones.

Solution (a) The orchestra **will perform** tonight.

(b) Babies often **fill** their mouths too full.

(c) A miner **searched** for gold.

(d) My dog **buries** his bones.

✓Practice For sentences a–d, tell whether the underlined verb is present, past, or future tense.

a. Many people enjoy the outdoors.

b. The students will plan a trip.

c. Shall I call you later?

d. Clarence asked for a ride.

For e–g, write the correct form of the verb.

e. Moses (past of *telephone*) Egypt.

f. Tassoula (future of *prove*) her case.

g. The parrot (present of *talk*) loudly.

For h–k, replace each blank with *will* or *shall*, as you would do in formal writing, in order to complete the future tense form of the verb.

h. That little fir tree _____ grow tall.

i. We _____ eat healthful foods.

j. They _____ agree with us.

k. I _____ fly to Idaho next summer.

For l and m, replace each blank with *hemisphere* or *meridian*.

l. We use imaginary _____ lines on Earth to measure distance in degrees east or west.

m. Since the United States is north of the equator, we say that it is in the Northern _____.

✓ **Review Set 14**

Choose the correct word to complete sentences 1–8.

1. The Tennessee River is a major (delta, tributary, isthmus)
(13) of the Ohio River.

2. A (strait, lagoon) might be completely enclosed by land
(12) or by a coral reef.

3. An isthmus is a narrow strip of (land, water, paper).
(11)

4. (Flora, Fauna) refers to animals of a particular
(10) region.

5. Geology is the science that deals with (Earth's,
(8) mankind's, Saturn's) structure, composition, and history.

6. Clyde picked up his suitcase and (carries, carried) it to
(10) the car.

7. We (will, shall) pass through the Strait of Magellan next
(14) week.

8. *Isthmus* is a (singular, plural) noun.
(13)

9. Write and capitalize each proper noun from the following
(8) sentence: florida is mainly a large peninsula extending
between the atlantic ocean and the gulf of mexico.

For 10 and 11, replace the blank with the singular present
tense form of the underlined verb.

10. Some students <u>worry</u>. One student _____.
(9)

11. Meg and Jon <u>rush</u> home. Uncle Ben _____ home.
(9)

12. Write each action verb in the following sentence: As Beth
(7) shuffles into the kitchen, mice dart here and there.

13. From memory, write the common helping verbs listed in
(12) Lesson 12.

14. In the following sentence, write the entire verb phrase,
(12) circling each helping verb: By 1838, John Deere had
perfected his steel plow.

15. In the following sentence, write whether the underlined
(10) verb phrase is present, past, or future tense: George Ferris
<u>invented</u> the first Ferris wheel.

For 16 and 17, write whether the word group is a complete
sentence or a sentence fragment.

16. On land as flat as a pancake.
(5)

17. Most of Illinois is flat.
(5)

18. Write each compound noun from this list:
(13)
abundance   place mat

archipelago   cookbook

19. Write the possessive noun from this sentence: Abraham
(13) Lincoln wanted to move the state's capital to Springfield.

20. Rewrite and correct the following sentence fragment,
(6) making it a complete sentence: Eating more fresh fruits
and vegetables.

21. For a–d, write whether the noun is concrete or abstract.
(11)
(a) estuary   (b) courage   (c) isthmus   (d) patience

22. Write each collective noun that you find in this sentence:
(11) Has the road crew finished their work yet?

23. Write the simple subject of the following sentence: Does
(3, 4) that amazing hero work in Metropolis, Illinois?

24. For the following sentence, write the correct form of the
(14) verb: We (future of *pull*) weeds tomorrow.

Write the simple predicate of sentences 25 and 26.

25. We can buy farm machinery from a company in Illinois.
(3, 4)

26. May I borrow your tractor?
(3, 4)

27. For a–d, write the past tense form of the verb.
(10) (a) dip   (b) marry   (c) rub   (d) bury

28. Write whether the following sentence is declarative,
(2) interrogative, imperative, or exclamatory: The Willis
Tower (formerly known as Sears Tower) is a skyscraper in
Chicago, Illinois.

29. Unscramble these words to make an interrogative sentence:
(2) we ˙the field shall plow

30. Rewrite the following sentence, drawing a vertical line
(1) between the subject and the predicate:

The Great Chicago Fire destroyed much of the city in
1871.

Capitalization: Sentence, Pronoun *I*, and Poetry

Dictation or Journal Entry

Vocabulary:

Latitude is a distance north or south of the equator. The imaginary *latitude* lines form circles around Earth running east and west, parallel to the equator.

Longitude is a distance on Earth's surface, measured in degrees east and west of Greenwich, England. The imaginary lines of *longitude* pass through the North and South poles.

Look at the latitude and longitude lines on a globe. What country lies at latitude 30° north and longitude 105° east?

There are many reasons why words require capitalization. Since proper nouns name a specific person, place, or thing, they need to be capitalized. We also remember that a common noun linked with a proper noun requires a capital letter. Therefore, the word "ocean" is capitalized in "Pacific Ocean."

However, little words such as *a*, *of*, *the*, *an*, and *in* are not capitalized when they are part of a proper noun (as in the Strait of Magellan, the Gulf of Mexico, and John the Baptist).

Now we will learn more about capitalization.

First Word of Every sentence   The **first word of every sentence** requires a capital letter.

> Cardinals build bowl-like nests in bushes.
>
> They eat seeds, insects, snails, and maple sap.
>
> Male cardinals have bright red feathers and a black face.

The Pronoun *I*   The **pronoun *I*** is always capitalized, no matter where it is placed in the sentence.

> I shall learn which words to capitalize.
>
> Do I use a capital letter there?
>
> Rules, I am told, help students with their writing.

First Word in a Line of Poetry   The **first words of each line in most poetry** are usually capitalized.* For example, Joseph Rodman Drake (1795–1820) begins "The American Flag" with:

> When Freedom from her mountain height
>
> Unfurled her standard to the air...

Jack Appleton Everard's poem "The Quiet Courage" reads:

With gentle patience that no man might boast
She does her daily task, year after year,
Meeting her worries as they come, she waits—
In her brave smile there is no sign of fear.

* However, for effect, some poets purposely do not capitalize first words of their lines of poetry.

Example   Add capital letters wherever needed.

(a) May i read you a poem?

(b) look at that covered bridge!

(c) An anonymous poet capitalizes the first word of each line of the poem "Twelfth Song of the Thunder:"

the voice that beautifies the land!
the voice above,
the voice of the thunder
within the dark cloud....

Solution   (a) We capitalize the pronoun *I* in this sentence.

(b) Since the first word in every sentence must be capitalized, we write, "**L**ook at that covered bridge!"

(c) We write,
The voice that beautifies the land!
The voice above,
The voice of the thunder
Within the dark cloud....

Practice   Write each word that should be capitalized in a–c.

a. in march of last year, i moved to indianapolis, indiana.

b. Henry Wadsworth Longfellow capitalized the first word of each line in his poem, "Paul Revere's Ride," which begins like this:
listen my children and you shall hear
of the midnight ride of paul revere
on the eighteenth of april in seventy-five
hardly a man is now alive
who remembers that famous day and year.

c. the ohio river forms the southern border of indiana.

For d and e, replace each blank with *latitude* or *longitude*.

✓ **d.** The distance east or west of Greenwich, England is called

_____.

✓ **e.** The distance north or south of the equator is called

_____.

More Practice   See "More Practice Lesson 15" in Student Workbook.

✓**Review Set 15**   Choose the correct word(s) to complete sentences 1–8.

1. A (hemisphere, lagoon, meridian) is also known as a line
(14) of longitude, a measure of the distance in degrees east or
west of Greenwich, England.

2. A tributary may be a (mountain, stream, desert).
(13)

3. A lagoon is a (strait, pond, isthmus).
(12)

4. A(n) (isthmus, geography, lagoon) is a narrow strip of
(11) land.

5. *Down* is a(n) (antonym, synonym) of *up*.
(2)

6. Stephanie and Bill pulled weeds and (work, worked) in
(5, 10) (there, their) garden all day.

7. I (will, shall) conceal the trophy over (there, their) behind
(5, 14) the podium.

8. *Homophones* is a (singular, plural) noun.
(13)

9. Rewrite the following sentence, adding capital letters as
(8, 15) needed: the isthmus of panama connects north america
with south america.

For 10 and 11, replace the blank with the singular present
tense form of the underlined verb.

10. Carpenters <u>carry</u> lumber. A carpenter _____ lumber.
(9)

11. Two cadets <u>polish</u> their shoes. A cadet _____ his
(9) shoes.

12. Write each action verb in the following sentence: The
(7) ship sailed east across the Pacific Ocean all day Tuesday
and crossed the International Date Line the next morning.

13. From the following list, write the word that is *not* a
(12) helping verb: is, am, are, was, where, be, being, been.

14. In the following sentence, write the entire verb phrase,
(12) circling each helping verb: My cousin has been playing
professional baseball for twelve years.

15. In the following sentence, write whether the underlined
(14) verb phrase is present, past, or future tense: Race car fans
<u>will flock</u> to Indianapolis for the Indy 500.

For 16 and 17, write whether the word group is a complete
sentence or a sentence fragment.

16. A famous international car race on Memorial Day
(5) weekend.

17. Cars race for five hundred miles.
(5)

18. Write each compound noun from this list:
(13)

playground   mechanic

peninsula   footprint

19. Write each possessive noun from this sentence:
(13) Longfellow's poem talks about Paul Revere's ride to the
Old North church.

20. Rewrite and correct the following sentence fragment,
(6) making a complete sentence: To ride a galloping horse.

21. For a–d, write whether the noun is concrete or abstract.
(11)
(a) synonym   (b) raccoon   (c) island   (d) grace

22. Write the collective noun in this sentence: A drove of
(11) pigs wallows in the mud.

23. Write the simple subject of the following sentence: Some
(3, 4) residents in Gary, Indiana, work at the nation's largest
steel mills.

24. For the following sentence, write the correct form of the
(14) verb: We (future of *bake*) bread tomorrow.

25. Write the simple predicate of the following sentence:
(3, 4) Some residents in Gary, Indiana, work at the nation's
largest steel mills.

26. Rewrite the following lines of poetry, adding capital
(15) letters as needed:

birds of a feather flock together,
and so will pigs and swine;
rats and mice will have their choice,
and so will i have mine.

27. For a–d, write the past tense form of the verb.
(10) (a) hug   (b) skip   (c) hop   (d) bully

28. Write whether the following sentence is declarative,
(2) interrogative, imperative, or exclamatory: Tell me about
your future plans.

29. Unscramble these words to make a declarative sentence:
(2)

cabin   log   Abe Lincoln's   in   is   Indiana

30. Rewrite the following sentence, drawing a vertical line
(1) between the subject and the predicate:

John Chapman planted apple trees from Pennsylvania to
Illinois.

Irregular Plural Nouns, Part 1

Dictation or Journal Entry:

Vocabulary:
An *arroyo* is the bed of a stream, or a gully. An *arroyo* is also a small river or stream. Lizards and horned toads now live in the dry, sandy *arroyo* carved out by running water.

An *atoll* is a circular coral reef rising above and surrounding a lagoon. Soil built up on the *atoll*, and plants began to grow, eventually creating an island.

Plural Nouns

We never form a plural with an apostrophe. In most cases, we make a singular noun plural by adding an *s*.

SINGULAR	PLURAL
dog	dogs, NOT dog's
bone	bones
pen	pens
paper	papers

Irregular Forms

Some nouns have irregular plural forms. We must learn these. We add *es* to a singular noun ending in the following letters: *s, sh, ch, x, z.*

SINGULAR	PLURAL
James	Jameses
loss	losses
bush	bushes
bench	benches
fox	foxes
Gómez	Gómezes
buzz	buzzes

We add an *s* when a singular noun ends with *ay, ey, oy,* or *uy.*

SINGULAR	PLURAL
way	ways
key	keys
boy	boys
guy	guys

We change *y* to *i* and add *es* when a singular noun ends in a consonant plus *y.*

SINGULAR	PLURAL
spy	spies
baby	babies
party	parties
tributary	tributaries

Example For a–p, write the plural form of each singular noun.

    (a) strait   (b) torch   (c) box   (d) bay

    (e) guess   (f) lagoon   (g) supply   (h) wish

    (i) alley   (j) toy   (k) waltz   (l) isthmus

    (m) guy   (n) sky   (o) address   (p) López

Solution (a) **straits** (regular)   (b) **torches** (ends in *ch*)

    (c) **boxes** (ends in *x*)   (d) **bays** (ends in *ay*)

    (e) **guesses** (ends in *ss*)   (f) **lagoons** (regular)

    (g) **supplies** (ends in consonant plus *y*)

    (h) **wishes** (ends in *sh*)   (i) **alleys** (ends in *ey*)

    (j) **toys** (ends in *oy*)   (k) **waltzes** (ends in *z*)

    (l) **isthmuses** (ends in *s*)   (m) **guys** (ends in *uy*)

    (n) **skies** (ends in consonant plus *y*)

    (o) **addresses** (ends in *ss*)   (p) **Lópezes** (ends in *z*)

✓**Practice** For a and b, replace each blank with *arroyo* or *atoll*.

    a. An _____ is a ring of coral in the sea.

    b. An _____ is a small river or river bed.

For c–p, write the plural form of each singular noun.

    c. moss   **d.** lake   **e.** donkey   **f.** brush

    g. Burgess   **h.** boundary   **i.** delta   **j.** wrench

    k. day   **l.** tax   **m.** turkey   **n.** toy

    o. berry   **p.** puppy

Choose the correct word(s) to complete sentences 1–8.

1. Longitude measures distance east or west while (isthmus,
(15) strait, latitude) measures distance north or south.

2. A (delta, estuary, meridian) is an imaginary circle on
(14) Earth's surface, passing through the North and South
poles.

3. A delta is often shaped like a(n) (circle, triangle,
(13) elephant).

4. A (strait, lagoon, peninsula) is a pond.
(12)

5. (Optimism, Pessimism) is the belief that things will get
(4) better.

6. The Curtises raked leaves and (trim, trimmed) trees in
(5, 10) (there, their) yard this morning.

7. Jan and I (will, shall) be (there, their) soon.
(5, 14)

8. We (never, sometimes, always) form a plural with an
(16) apostrophe.

9. Rewrite the following sentence, adding capital letters as
(8, 15) needed: yes, i think julia lives near the mississippi river,
in memphis, tennessee.

For 10 and 11, replace the blank with the singular present
tense form of the underlined verb.

10. Two cooks <u>fry</u> potatoes. One cook _____ potatoes.
(9)

11. Some workers <u>wax</u> cars. A worker _____ cars.
(9)

12. Write each action verb in the following sentence: A
(7) pessimist believes the bad and expects the worst.

13. From the following list, write the word that is *not* a
(12) helping verb: has, have, had, may, might, munch, can,
could.

14. In the following sentence, write the entire verb phrase,
(12) circling each helping verb: Abe Lincoln was born in
Kentucky on February 12, 1809.

15. In the following sentence, write whether the underlined
(14) verb phrase is present, past, or future tense: Bev and Leon
<u>will attend</u> the Kentucky Derby in May.

For 16 and 17, write whether the word group is a complete
sentence or a sentence fragment.

16. The Kentucky Derby race lasts about two minutes.
(5)

17. An abundance of fragrant purple flowers with yellow
(5) centers.

18. Write each compound noun from this list:
(13)
    president   refrigerator

    toothbrush   mailbox

19. Write the possessive noun from this sentence: Who
(13) captured Daniel Boone's daughter?

20. Rewrite and correct the following sentence fragment,
(6) making a complete sentence: A strong, thoroughbred
racehorse.

21. For a–d, write whether the noun is concrete or abstract.
(11) (a) antonym   (b) mercy   (c) ocean   (d) frog

22. Write each collective noun that you find in this sentence:
(11) The cast presented scenes from *Little House on the
Prairie.*

23. Write the simple subject of the following sentence: Daniel
(3, 4) Boone's daughter shows her courage and cleverness.

24. For the following sentence, write the correct form of the
(14) verb: I (future of *answer*) your questions on Wednesday.

25. Write the simple predicate of the following sentence: Did
(3, 4) Daniel Boone's daughter survive the capture?

26. Rewrite the following lines of poetry, adding capital
(15) letters as needed:

    mary had a little lamb.
    its fleece was white as snow.
    and everywhere that mary went
    the lamb was sure to go.

27. Write the past tense form of the verb *try*.
(10)

28. Write whether the following sentence is declarative,
(2) interrogative, imperative, or exclamatory: Have you seen
Kentucky's bluegrass?

29. For a–d, write the plural of each noun.
(16)
(a) key   (b) baby   (c) lunch   (d) cherry

30. Rewrite the following sentence, drawing a vertical line
(1) between the subject and the predicate:

Colorful American goldfinches peck at thistle seeds.

Irregular Plural Nouns, Part 2

We continue our study of plural nouns.

Irregular Forms Some singular nouns change completely in their plural forms.

SINGULAR	PLURAL
woman	women
man	men
person	people
tooth	teeth
foot	feet

Other nouns are the same in their singular and plural forms.

SINGULAR	PLURAL
moose	moose
deer	deer
cod	cod

Dictionary When we are uncertain, we use a dictionary to check plural forms. If the plural form of the noun is regular (only add *s* to the singular noun), then the dictionary will not list it. Sometimes the dictionary will list two plural forms for a noun. The first one listed is the preferred one. (Example: cactus *n.*, *pl.* cacti, cactuses)

Example 1 Write the plural form of each of the following singular nouns. Use a dictionary if you are in doubt.

(a) mouse   (b) ox   (c) child   (d) sheep

Solution (a) **mice** (irregular form)   (b) **oxen** (irregular form)

(c) **children** (irregular form)

(d) We check the dictionary and find that the plural of sheep is **sheep.**

Nouns Ending in *f, ff, fe* For most nouns ending in *f, ff,* and *fe,* we add *s* to form the plural.

SINGULAR	PLURAL
cuff	cuffs
gulf	gulfs
safe	safes

However, for some nouns ending in *f* and *fe,* we change the *f* to *v* and add *es.*

SINGULAR	PLURAL
life	lives
calf	calves
wolf	wolves

Nouns Ending in *o* We usually add *s* to form the plurals of nouns ending in *o,* especially if they are musical terms.

SINGULAR	PLURAL
archipelago	archipelagos
auto	autos
solo	solos
piano	pianos
alto	altos
soprano	sopranos
banjo	banjos

However, the following are important exceptions:

SINGULAR	PLURAL
echo	echoes
hero	heroes
veto	vetoes
tomato	tomatoes
potato	potatoes
torpedo	torpedoes
mosquito	mosquitoes

(There are more!)

Since there are many more exceptions, we must check the dictionary to be sure of the correct spelling.

Example 2 Write the plural form of each of the following singular nouns. Use a dictionary if you are in doubt.

(a) puff   (b) piano   (c) hero   (d) half

Solution (a) **puffs** (word ending in *ff*)

(b) **pianos** (musical term ending in *o*)

(c) We notice that the word *hero* is in the list of exceptions to words ending in *o*. We check the dictionary and find that the plural of *hero* is **heroes.**

(d) We check the dictionary and find that the plural of *half* is **halves.**

✓**Practice** For a–i, write the plural form of each singular noun. Use the dictionary if you are in doubt.

a. cliff   **b.** tomato   **c.** chief

d. knife   **e.** salmon   **f.** tooth

g. goose   **h.** cello   **i.** zoo

For j and k, replace each blank with *Tropic of Cancer* or *Tropic of Capricorn.*

j. The _____ runs through Australia.

k. The _____ runs through Mexico.

More Practice Write the plural of each noun.

1. cross   2. bunch   3. boy   4. lunch

5. bush   6. boss   7. cherry   8. bay

9. sheep   10. man   11. lady   12. woman

13. person   14. mouse   15. goose   16. cliff

17. leaf   18. loaf   19. alto   20. potato

✓**Review Set 17** Choose the correct word(s) to complete sentences 1–8.

1. An atoll is a circular coral reef surrounding a
   (16) (hemisphere, estuary, lagoon).

2. Latitude measures distance north or south while (flora,
(15) longitude, fauna) measures distance east or west.

3. The Greenwich meridian divides Earth into Eastern
(14) and Western (isthmuses, estuaries, hemispheres).

4. A (strait, delta, homophone) is often shaped like a
(13) triangle.

5. Inside my desk, everything has (it's, its) place.
(6)

6. Elle and her grandmother chatted about the hot weather
(5, 10) and (sip, siped, sipped) (there, their) iced tea.

7. (Its, It's) raining!
(6)

8. We never form a (plural, possessive) noun with an
(16) apostrophe.

9. Rewrite the following sentence, adding capital letters as
(8, 15) needed: every sunday, juan jogs down myrtle street in
monrovia, california.

For 10 and 11, replace the blank with the singular present
tense form of the underlined verb.

10. Two women <u>reply</u>. One woman _____.
(9)

11. Children <u>wish</u>. A child _____.
(9)

12. Write each action verb in the following sentence: An
(7) optimist believes the good and expects the best.

13. From the following list, write the word that is *not* a
(12) helping verb: can, could, do, does, dip, shall, will,
should, would.

14. In the following sentence, write the entire verb phrase,
(12) circling each helping verb: Have you tasted jambalaya?

15. In the following sentence, write whether the underlined
(10) verb phrase is present, past, or future tense: Troy <u>waded</u>
through the bayou.

For 16 and 17, write whether the word group is a complete sentence or a sentence fragment.

16. Louisiana is also called the "Pelican State."
(5)

17. Special names for bits of stuff.
(5)

18. Write each compound noun from this list:
(13)
scarcity   railroad
celebration   spaceship

19. Write the possessive noun from this sentence: The
(13) pelican's pouch can hold nearly three gallons of fish and water.

20. Rewrite and correct the following sentence fragment,
(6) making a complete sentence: A brown pelican with its long gray bill.

stop →

21. For a–d, write whether the noun is concrete or abstract.
(11) (a) idea   (b) desert   (c) truth   (d) wolf

22. Write each collective noun that you find in this sentence:
(11) The colony grew its own fruits and vegetables.

23. Write the simple subject of the following sentence: *Mardi*
(3, 4) *Gras* means "fat Tuesday."

24. For the following sentence, write the correct form of the
(14) verb: We (future of *paint*) the house this spring.

25. Write the simple predicate of the following sentence:
(3, 4) May I taste the jambalaya and crawfish?

26. Rewrite the following lines of poetry, adding capital
(15) letters as needed:

twinkle, twinkle, little star.
how i wonder what you are,
up above the world so high,
like a diamond in the sky.

27. Write the past tense form of the verb *clap*.
(10)

28. Write whether the following sentence is declarative,
(2) interrogative, imperative, or exclamatory: Louis
Armstrong played the trumpet.

29. For a–d, write the plural of each noun.
(16, 17) (a) piano   (b) bench   (c) life   (d) child

30. Rewrite the following sentence, drawing a vertical line
(1) between the subject and the predicate:

The people of Louisiana listen to Cajun music.

Irregular Verbs, Part 1: *Be*, *Have*, and *Do*

Three of the most frequently used verbs in the English language are *be*, *have*, and *do*. The tenses of these verbs are irregular; they do not fit the pattern of the regular verbs. Therefore, we must memorize them.

Points of View Verb forms often change according to three points of view:

(1) First person, the speaker—*I* or *we*

(2) Second person, the person or thing spoken to—*you*

(3) Third person, the person or thing spoken of—*he, she, it, they,* and singular or plural nouns

Below are charts showing the verb forms of *be*, *have*, and *do*.

Be

	PRESENT		PAST	
	SINGULAR	PLURAL	SINGULAR	PLURAL
1ST PERSON	I am	we are	I was	we were
2ND PERSON	you are	you are	you were	you were
3RD PERSON	he is	they are	he was	they were

Have

	PRESENT		PAST	
	SINGULAR	PLURAL	SINGULAR	PLURAL
1ST PERSON	I have	we have	I had	we had
2ND PERSON	you have	you have	you had	you had
3RD PERSON	he has	they have	he had	they had

Do

	PRESENT		PAST	
	SINGULAR	PLURAL	SINGULAR	PLURAL
1ST PERSON	I do	we do	I did	we did
2ND PERSON	you do	you do	you did	you did
3RD PERSON	he does	they do	he did	they did

Example Complete each sentence with the correct form of the verb.
   (a) She (present of *have*) red hair.

   (b) You (present of *be*) so helpful!

   (c) I (past of *be*) on time.

   (d) We (past of *do*) our homework last night.

   (e) He (present of *do*) chores each day.

   (f) They (past of *have*) an abundance of ripe tomatoes.

Solution (a) She **has** red hair.

   (b) You **are** so helpful!

   (c) I **was** on time.

   (d) We **did** our homework last night.

   (e) He **does** chores each day.

   (f) They **had** an abundance of ripe tomatoes.

✓**Practice** Write the correct verb form to complete sentences a–f.
   a. Jazz, classical, and rock (present of *be*) types of music.

   b. Raynor (present of *have*) a healthful lifestyle.

   c. He (present of *do*) exercises to strengthen his muscles.

   d. Sarah (past of *have*) spinach and eggs for dinner.

   e. We (past of *be*) washing the car.

   f. I (past of *do*) my chores.

For g and h, replace each blank with *Torrid Zone* or *timberline.*
   g. It is cold above the _____.

   h. The _____ is a warm, tropical region.

1. For a–d, choose the correct present tense form of the verb *be*.
   (a) I (am, are, is)   (b) You (am, are, is)
   (c) He (am, are, is)   (d) They (am, are, is)

2. For a–d, choose the correct present tense form of the verb *have*.
   (a) I (have, has)   (b) You (have, has)
   (c) She (have, has)   (d) We (have, has)

3. For a–d, choose the correct present tense form of the verb *do*.
   (a) I (do, does)   (b) You (do, does)
   (c) It (do, does)   (d) They (do, does)

4. For a–d, choose the correct past tense form of the verb *be*.
   (a) I (was, were)   (b) You (was, were)
   (c) He (was, were)   (d) They (was, were)

For 5–16, choose the correct verb form for each sentence.

5. John (do, does) his daily chores.

6. He (have, has) brown hair.

7. Mr. Luz (were, was) my teacher last year.

8. (Are, Is) you an optimist?

9. They (was, were) pessimistic.

10. Alba and Beth (is, are) friends.

11. (Was, Were) you there?

12. (Was, Were) your sister with you?

13. Isabel (have, has) a snapping turtle.

14. (Do, Does) Isabel like turtles?

15. I (are, is, am) studying geography.

16. John (do, did) five loads of wash today.

Review Set 18 ✓ Choose the correct word(s) to complete sentences 1–8.

1. The Tropic of Cancer and the Tropic of Capricorn are
   (17) imaginary lines running parallel to the (meridian, equator, oceans).

2. An atoll is a (horned toad, coral reef).
(16)

3. (Latitude, Longitude) is a distance east or west of Greenwich, England.
(15)

4. The equator divides Earth into the Northern and Southern (peninsulas, archipelagos, hemispheres).
(14)

5. An (archipelago, isthmus) is a narrow strip of land bordered by water and connecting two larger bodies of land.
(11)

6. Elle and her grandmother (was, were) still sipping their iced tea when a salesperson (call, called).
(10, 12)

7. (Its, It's) snowing up (their, there) on the mountain.
(5, 6)

8. Ted and Pat (am, is, are) wearing (their, there) coats.
(5, 18)

9. Rewrite the following sentence, adding capital letters as needed: this february, i would like to sail to catalina island.
(8, 15)

For 10 and 11, replace the blank with the singular present tense form of the underlined verb.

10. Some men <u>dry</u> dishes. One man _____ dishes.
(9)

11. Children <u>wash</u> dishes. A child _____ dishes.
(9)

12. Write each action verb in the following sentence: Henry feeds the poor and visits the sick.
(7)

13. From the following list, write the word that is *not* a helping verb: do, does, did, shall, bill, should, would.
(12)

14. In the following sentence, write the entire verb phrase, circling each helping verb: Amit might have painted that lighthouse.
(12)

15. In the following sentence, write whether the underlined verb phrase is present, past, or future tense: The Pine Tree State <u>has</u> beautiful evergreen forests.
(9)

For 16 and 17, write whether the word group is a complete sentence or a sentence fragment.

16. Forests cover nearly ninety percent of Maine's land.
(5)

17. Produces wood for ice-cream sticks, paper, canoes, and
(5) toothpicks.

√ **18.** Write each compound noun from this list:
(13)

meridian   earthworm

baseball   discovery

19. Write the possessive noun from this sentence: One of
(13) Maine's inventions is earmuffs.

√ **20.** Rewrite and correct the following sentence fragment,
(6) making a complete sentence: An active little chickadee with a black cap.

21. For a–d, write whether the noun is concrete or abstract.
(11)
(a) joy   (b) ladybug   (c) honor   (d) whale

22. Write each collective noun that you find in this sentence:
(11) A herd of cattle rests among the oak trees.

23. Write the simple subject of the following sentence: Along
(3, 4) came Leif Erickson, an Icelandic explorer.

24. For the following sentence, write the correct form of the
(18) verb: We (past of *be*) happy about our success.

25. Write the simple predicate of the following sentence: Was
(3, 4) that ship built in Maine?

26. Rewrite the following lines of poetry, adding capital
(15) letters as needed:

a diller, a dollar, a ten o'clock scholar!
what makes you come so soon?
you used to come at ten o'clock;
now you come at noon.

27. Write the past tense form of the verb *drop*.
(10)

28. Write whether the following sentence is declarative,
(2) interrogative, imperative, or exclamatory: Watch out for
the lobster's claw!

29. For a–d, write the plural of each noun.
(16, 17) (a) sheep   (b) church   (c) thief   (d) potato

30. Rewrite the following sentence, drawing a vertical line
(1) between the subject and the predicate:

Maine has a jagged coastline with rocky cliffs.

LESSON 19

Four Principal Parts of Verbs

Four Principal Parts

Every verb has **four** basic forms, or **principal parts.** In order to form all the tenses of each verb, we need to learn these principal parts: the present tense, the present participle, the past, and the past participle.

(1) Present Tense

The first principal part is the singular verb in its **present tense** form, which is used to express *present time*, something that is *true at all times*, and *future time*:

talk   earn   wish   move

(2) Present Participle

The second principal part, used to form the progressive tenses (continuing action), is preceded by a form of the *be* helping verb. The **present participle** is formed by adding *ing* to the singular verb:

(is) talking   (are) earning   (is) wishing   (are) moving

(3) Past Tense

The third principal part of a verb, used to express *past time*, is the **past tense,** which we form by adding *ed* to most verbs.

talked   earned   wished   moved

(4) Past Participle

The fourth principal part of a verb, used to form the *perfect* tenses, is the **past participle.** It is preceded by a form of the *have* helping verb. With regular verbs, the past and the past participle are the same.

PAST	PAST PARTICIPLE
talked	(have) talked
earned	(has) earned
wished	(have) wished
moved	(has) moved

Example Complete the chart by writing the second, third, and fourth "principal parts" (present participle, past tense, and past participle) of each verb.

Verb	Present Participle	Past Tense	Past Participle
help	(is) helping	helped	(has) helped
(a) cook	_____	_____	_____
(b) clean	_____	_____	_____
(c) farm	_____	_____	_____
(d) pitch	_____	_____	_____
(e) ask	_____	_____	_____

Solution

Verb	Present Participle	Past Tense	Past Participle
(a) cook	**(is) cooking**	**cooked**	**(has) cooked**
(b) clean	**(is) cleaning**	**cleaned**	**(has) cleaned**
(c) farm	**(is) farming**	**farmed**	**(has) farmed**
(d) pitch	**(is) pitching**	**pitched**	**(has) pitched**
(e) ask	**(is) asking**	**asked**	**(has) asked**

Practice For a–e, complete the chart by writing the second, third, and fourth "principal parts" (present participle, past tense, and past participle) of each verb.

Verb	Present Participle	Past Tense	Past Participle
a. act	_____	_____	_____
b. want	_____	_____	_____
c. walk	_____	_____	_____
d. view	_____	_____	_____
e. work	_____	_____	_____

For f and g, replace each blank with the correct vocabulary word.

f. You would wear a jacket in the _____, for it is cold there.

g. You might see lions and zebras in an African _____.

Review Set 19

Choose the correct word(s) to complete sentences 1–9.

1. Large trees do not grow above the (base line, timberline, starting line).
(18)

2. The Tropic of Cancer and the Tropic of Capricorn mark the northern and southern borders of the (arctic, tropic, antarctic) region of Earth.
(17)

3. A(n) (atoll, arroyo, tributary) is a coral reef surrounding a lagoon.
(16)

4. (Latitude, Longitude) is a distance north or south of the equator.
(15)

5. A strait is a narrow passage of (atmosphere, water, land).
(12)

6. Eliza (do, does) yard work each week.
(18)

7. (Its, It's) fun for Eliza to work out (their, there) in the yard.
(5, 6)

8. James (have, has) brown eyes.
(18)

9. The (present, past) participle of the verb *mix* is *(is) mixing*.
(18)

10. Rewrite the following sentence, adding capital letters as needed: is salem, oregon, in the willamette valley?
(8, 15)

11. Replace the blank below with the singular present tense form of the underlined verb.
(9)

People <u>apply</u> for jobs. A person _____ for a job.

12. Write each action verb in the following sentence: Molly mows the lawn and sweeps the driveway.
(7)

13. From the following list, write the word that is *not* a helping verb: is, am, far, was, were, be, being, been.
(12)

14. In the following sentence, write the entire verb phrase,
(12) circling each helping verb: Does the state of Maryland
have an estuary?

15. In the following sentence, write whether the underlined
(9) verb phrase is present, past, or future tense: Some people
in Maryland <u>catch</u> fish, blue crabs, and oysters.

For 16 and 17, write whether the word group is a complete
sentence or a sentence fragment.

16. In Baltimore Harbor during the War of 1812.
(5)

17. Francis Scott Key wrote "The Star Spangled Banner."
(5)

18. Write each compound noun from this list:
(13)
encyclopedia   moonlight

sunflower   dictionary

19. Write the possessive noun from this sentence:
(13)
Chesapeake Bay is our country's largest estuary.

20. Rewrite and correct the following sentence fragment,
(6) making a complete sentence: To sail across the Atlantic
Ocean.

21. For a–d, write whether the noun is concrete or abstract.
(11)
(a) anteater   (b) happiness   (c) sadness   (d) elbow

22. Write each collective noun that you find in this sentence:
(11) My family has moved to Baltimore, Maryland.

23. Write the simple subject of the following sentence: Has
(3, 4) Clarissa been jousting?

24. For the following sentence, write the correct form of the
(18) verb: My dog (present of *have*) fleas.

25. Write the simple predicate of the following sentence: Has
(3, 4) Clarissa been jousting in the tournament?

26. Rewrite the following lines of poetry, adding capital
(15) letters as needed:

i scream,
you scream,
we all scream
for ice cream!

27. For the verb *mix*, write the (a) present participle, (b) past
(19) tense, and (c) past participle.

28. Write whether the following sentence is declarative,
(2) interrogative, imperative, or exclamatory: George
Washington selected the site of the national capital,
Washington, D.C.

29. For a–d, write the plural of each noun.
(16, 17) (a) berry   (b) monkey   (c) half   (d) tomato

30. Rewrite the following sentence, drawing a vertical line
(1) between the subject and the predicate:

A long bridge stretches across the Chesapeake Bay.

Simple Prepositions, Part 1

Dictation or Journal Entry

Vocabulary:

A *mesa*, from the Spanish word meaning "table," is a flat-topped hill or mountain with steep sides. We can see many *mesas* in the southwestern plains of the United States.

A *chasm* is a deep, wide crack in Earth's surface; a gorge. Did an earthquake cause that huge *chasm*?

Prepositions

Prepositions are words belonging to the part of speech that shows the relationship between a noun or pronoun and another word. Notice how a preposition (italicized) shows the space relationship between a bug and the straw:

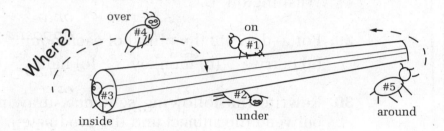

Bug #1 is *on* the straw. Bug #2 is *under* the straw. Bug #3 is *inside* the straw. Bug #4 is jumping *over* the straw. Bug #5 is walking *around* the straw.

Prepositions also show time relationships:

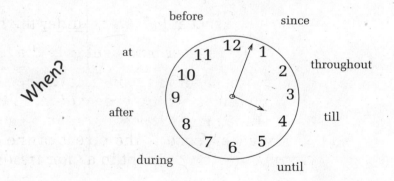

Noah giggled *before* lunch, *at* lunch, *during* lunch, *throughout* lunch, *after* lunch, and *until* midnight. He's been giggling *since* yesterday!

Besides showing space and time relationships, prepositions also show abstract (thought or idea) relationships. The prepositions listed below show abstract relationships.

concerning	except	like	regarding
considering	excepting	of	save
despite	for	opposite	unto

Simple Prepositions

Some prepositions are single words while others are gr[oups] of words such as *across from, along with, apart fro[m], means of,* etc. In this lesson we will learn to recognize s[ingle] word prepositions, **simple prepositions,** which we [list] alphabetically here. To help you memorize these, we list them in four columns.

1	2	3	4
aboard	beside	inside	since
about	besides	into	through
above	between	like	throughout
across	beyond	near	till
after	but	of	to
against	by	off	toward
along	concerning	on	under
alongside	considering	onto	underneath
amid	despite	opposite	until
among	down	out	unto
around	during	outside	up
at	except	over	upon
before	excepting	past	via
behind	for	regarding	with
below	from	round	within
beneath	in	save	without

Simple prepositions are underlined in the sentences below. Notice how they show the relationship between "went" and "fence."

The soccer ball went <u>under</u> the fence.

The soccer ball went <u>over</u> the fence.

A person, place, or thing always follows a preposition. We call this word the **object of the preposition.** In the first sentence, we see that *fence* is the object of the preposition *under*. In the second sentence, *fence* is the object of the preposition *over*. We will practice this concept in a later lesson.

Example   Underline each preposition in sentences a–c.

(a) Pilgrims aboard the Mayflower arrived at Plymouth Rock in 1620.

(b) Settlers in Massachusetts and throughout New England understood the importance of education.

(c) Barrett came from Martha's Vineyard with vivid descriptions of its beauty.

Solution (a) Pilgrims **aboard** the Mayflower arrived **at** Plymouth Rock **in** 1620.

(b) Settlers **in** Massachusetts and **throughout** New England understood the importance **of** education.

(c) Barrett came **from** Martha's Vineyard **with** vivid descriptions **of** its beauty.

Practice **a.** Memorize the first column of prepositions: Study the column for a moment, then cover it, and say the prepositions to yourself or to a friend. Repeat this until you can say all the prepositions in the first column.

b. Now follow the instructions for Practice "a" in order to memorize the second column of prepositions, and say them to yourself or to a friend.

c. Have a "preposition contest" with yourself or with a friend to see how many prepositions you can write in one minute.

For d–f, list all the prepositions that you find in each sentence.

d. At the café, I ordered Boston cream pie for dessert.

e. Quan and Cruz traveled from Cambridge to Boston.

f. Martha's Vineyard Island lies near Nantucket Island, off the coast of Massachusetts.

For g and h, replace each blank with the correct vocabulary word from this lesson.

g. The dark and deep _____, or crack, in the mountain made a safe hiding place for raccoons.

h. The southwestern portion of the United States has flat-topped hills called _____.

More Practice For 1 and 2, replace each blank with the missing preposition from your alphabetical list of simple prepositions in this lesson (columns 1 and 2).

1. aboard, about, _____, across, _____, against, along, alongside, amid, among, _____, at, _____, behind, _____, beneath

2. beside, besides, _____, beyond, _____, by, concerning, considering, despite, _____, during, except, _____, for, _____, in

Write each preposition that you find in sentences 3–8.

3. Looking for adventure, my dog Rex leaps over our gate and runs through the streets.

4. He sniffs along the ground and barks at cats and squirrels.

5. Sometimes he goes to the park and chases ducks around the lake.

6. Opposite the park is his favorite restaurant.

7. During lunch, someone might share a sandwich with him.

8. Rex wants a sandwich without mayonnaise on it.

Review Set 20

Choose the correct word(s) to complete sentences 1–9.

1. Savanna is a (tropical, frozen, arctic) region.
(19)

2. (Plants, Animals, Trees) generally do not grow above the
(18) timberline.

3. The Torrid Zone, or tropics, lies between the Tropic of
(18) Cancer and the Tropic of (Leo, Capricorn, Taurus).

4. A(n) (peninsula, arroyo, atoll) is a circular coral reef.
(16)

5. To (conceal, disclose) is to make known; uncover.
(7)

6. I (am, is, are) older than he.
(18)

7. A rabbit left (its, it's) footprints (their, there) in the
(5, 6) snow.

8. Lillian (do, does) crossword puzzles every day.
(18)

9. The (present, past) participle of the verb *mix* is *(has)*
(18) *mixed.*

10. Rewrite the following sentence, adding capital letters as needed: at the store, i bought washington apples, idaho potatoes, and wisconsin cheese.
(8, 15)

11. Replace the blank below with the singular present tense form of the underlined verb.
(9)

Sam and Joe <u>mix</u> paint. Amy _____ paint.

12. Write each action verb in the following sentence: Ms. Lum gathers eggs from the hen house, milks the cows, and then drives her tractor to town for groceries.
(7)

13. From the following list, write the word that is *not* a helping verb: has, have, mad, may, might, must, can.
(12)

14. In the following sentence, write the entire verb phrase, circling each helping verb: Out in the flooded fields, Margaret has been harvesting cranberries today.
(12)

15. In the following sentence, write whether the underlined verb phrase is present, past, or future tense: Henry Ford and Ransom E. Olds <u>invented</u> the first gasoline-powered cars in 1896.
(10)

16. Write whether the following word group is a complete sentence or a sentence fragment: Four of the five Great Lakes.
(5)

17. Write each preposition that you find in the following sentence: The state of Michigan is divided into two parts.
(20)

18. Replace each blank below with a preposition from the alphabetical list (column 1) provided in this lesson.
(20)

aboard, about, above, _____, _____, against, along, _____, amid, _____, around, at, before, behind, _____, beneath

19. Write the compound, possessive noun from the following sentence: Unfortunately, the eyewitness's account did not help us to solve the mystery.
(13)

20. Rewrite and correct the following sentence fragment, making a complete sentence: Wearing a warm, woolen sweater on a cold, winter morning.
(6)

21. For a–d, write whether the noun is concrete or abstract.
(11) (a) butterfly   (b) patience   (c) stop sign   (d) democracy

22. Write each collective noun that you find in this sentence:
(11) A shipment of automobiles is leaving Detroit, Michigan.

23. Write the simple subject of the following sentence: Did
(3, 4) the Kelloggs make the first corn flakes?

24. For the following sentence, write the correct form of the
(18) verb: My dog (past tense of *have*) fleas.

25. Write the simple predicate of the following sentence: Did
(3, 4) the Kelloggs make the first corn flakes?

26. Rewrite the following lines of poetry, adding capital
(15) letters as needed:

the bee is not afraid of me,
i know the butterfly;
the pretty people in the woods
receive me cordially.

27. For the verb *answer*, write the (a) present participle, (b)
(19) past tense, and (c) past participle.

28. Write whether the following sentence is declarative,
(2) interrogative, imperative, or exclamatory: Michigan's
Upper Peninsula extends east from Wisconsin.

29. For a–d, write the plural of each noun.
(16, 17) (a) fox   (b) discovery   (c) butterfly   (d) ostrich

30. Rewrite the following sentence, drawing a vertical line
(1) between the subject and the predicate:

Both tart and sweet cherries grow in Michigan.

Simple Prepositions, Part 2

In this lesson, we continue to practice memorizing prepositions and identifying them in a sentence.

We will focus on memorizing the third and fourth columns of simple prepositions:

3	4
inside	*since*
into	*through*
like	*throughout*
near	*till*
of	*to*
off	*toward*
on	*under*
onto	*underneath*
opposite	*until*
out	*unto*
outside	*up*
over	*upon*
past	*via*
regarding	*with*
round	*within*
save	*without*

Practice **a.** Memorize preposition column #3. Study the column for a moment, then cover it, and say the prepositions to yourself or to a friend. Repeat this until you can say all the prepositions in the third column.

b. Now, follow the Practice "a" instructions in order to memorize column #4 so that you can say this list of prepositions to yourself or to a friend.

c. Have a "preposition contest" with yourself or with a friend to see how many prepositions you can write in one minute.

Write each preposition that you find in sentences d–f.

d. During the Civil War, Jefferson Davis served as president of the Confederate States.

e. Underneath an avocado tree sits Kurt with his two sisters, Molly and Melody.

f. Since six o'clock in the evening, the three children have been guarding the avocados from hungry, nocturnal animals.

For g and h, replace each blank with *plateau* or *fissure.*

g. A slight earthquake caused a long, narrow _____ in the rock.

h. Amparo lives on a high, flat _____ in Arizona.

More Practice For 1 and 2, replace each blank with the missing preposition from your alphabetical list of simple prepositions in this lesson (columns 3 and 4).

1. inside, into, like, _____, of, _____, on, onto, opposite, _____, outside, over, _____, regarding, _____, save

2. since, through, _____, till, _____, toward, under, _____, until, _____, up, upon, via, _____, within, without

For 3–22, write whether each word is a noun, verb, or preposition. Write "N" for noun, "V" for verb, or "P" for preposition.

3. said   **4.** muffin   **5.** upon   **6.** went

7. with   **8.** bird   **9.** ran   **10.** until

11. bush   **12.** into   **13.** eat   **14.** car

15. from   **16.** sing   **17.** like   **18.** under

19. jacket   **20.** during   **21.** sky   **22.** hoped

Review Set 21 Choose the correct word(s) to complete sentences 1–9.

1. A mesa is a mountain or hill that resembles a (20) (motorcycle, volcano, table).

2. The savanna is a tropical, treeless, grassy (mountain, hill, plain).
(19)

3. Trees generally do not grow above the (Torrid Zone, timberline, equator).
(18)

4. The Tropic of (Orion, Gemini, Cancer) and the Tropic of Capricorn are imaginary lines on Earth's surface, marking the borders of the tropics, or Torrid Zone.
(17)

5. *For* and *four* are (synonyms, antonyms, homophones).
(5)

6. Amelia (have, has) darker hair than I.
(18)

7. (Its, It's) too hot to wax the car out (their, there) in the sun today.
(5, 6)

8. Juan (do, does) his chores before school.
(18)

9. The (present, past) participle of the verb *pour* is *(has) poured*.
(18)

10. Rewrite the following sentence, adding capital letters as needed: in july, i shall visit the smithsonian institution in washington, d.c.
(8, 15)

11. Replace the blank below with the singular present tense form of the underlined verb.
(9)

They <u>copy</u> the dictation. Kurt _____ the dictation.

12. Write each action verb in the following sentence: Ms. Lum repairs a flat tire on her tractor, fills its tank with gasoline, and then sings happy songs all the way home.
(7)

13. From the following list, write the word that is *not* a helping verb: may, might, rust, can, could, do, does, did.
(12)

14. In the following sentence, write the entire verb phrase, circling each helping verb: Farmers can cultivate healthy crops in the soil next to the Mississippi River.
(12)

15. In the following sentence, write whether the underlined verb phrase is present, past, or future tense: Restaurants <u>buy</u> shrimp from Biloxi, Mississippi.
(9)

16. Write whether the following word group is a complete sentence or a sentence fragment: The fragrant blossoms of magnolia trees in Mississippi.
(5)

17. Write each preposition that you find in the following sentence: On a steamboat with two smokestacks, we cruised up and down the Mississippi River.
(20, 21)

18. Replace each blank below with a preposition from the alphabetical list (column 3) provided in this lesson.
(20, 21)

inside, _____, like, near, of, _____, on, onto, opposite, _____, _____, over, past, regarding, _____, save

19. Write the compound, possessive noun from the following sentence: The factbook's information was outdated; therefore, I did not use it for my research paper.
(13)

20. Rewrite and correct the following sentence fragment, making a complete sentence: A Mississippi steamboat with two smokestacks and a paddle wheel.
(6)

21. For a–d, write whether the noun is concrete or abstract.
(11)
(a) beetle   (b) entomology   (c) endurance   (d) snail

22. Write each collective noun that you find in this sentence: A mockingbird swoops over a flock of pigeons.
(11)

23. Write the simple subject of the following sentence: Did Jefferson Davis grow up in Mississippi?
(3, 4)

24. For the following sentence, write the correct form of the verb: The dogs (past tense of *be*) scratching.
(18)

25. Write the simple predicate of the following sentence: Did Jefferson Davis grow up in Mississippi?
(3, 4)

26. Rewrite the following lines of poetry, adding capital letters as needed:
(15)

if all the world were paper,
and all the sea were ink,
if all the trees
were bread and cheese,
what should we have to drink?

27. For the verb *laugh*, write the (a) present participle, (b)
(19) past tense, and (c) past participle.

28. Write whether the following sentence is declarative,
(2) interrogative, imperative, or exclamatory: Ouch, a red ant
stung me!

29. For a–d, write the plural of each noun.
(16, 17) (a) inch   (b) photocopy   (c) blue jay   (d) wolf

30. Rewrite the following sentence, drawing a vertical line
(1) between the subject and the predicate:

Grover and Annie Mae raise catfish in their pond.

Irregular Plural Nouns, Part 3

> **Dictation or Journal Entry**
> **Vocabulary:**
> The Latin word *placare*, meaning "to soothe or calm," appears in the English words *placate, placid, and implacable.*
>
> To *placate* is to calm the hostility of; to appease. The salesperson tried to *placate* the angry customer.
>
> *Placid* means "calm or peaceful; undisturbed." The *placid* water on the lake had no ripples. Gentle Miss Sylvia has a *placid* temperament.
>
> *Implacable* means "not able to be placated or appeased." Defending her cub, the furious mother bear became *implacable.*

We continue our study of irregular plural nouns. In this lesson, we shall learn the plural forms of compound nouns and nouns ending in *ful.*

Compound Nouns We make the main element plural in a compound noun.

SINGULAR	PLURAL
brother-in-law	*brothers*-in-law
commander in chief	*commanders* in chief
officer of the law	*officers* of the law
justice of the peace	*justices* of the peace
king of Spain	*kings* of Spain
matron of honor	*matrons* of honor
groomsman	grooms*men*
bridesmaid	brides*maids*

Nouns Ending in *ful* We form the plurals of nouns ending in *ful* by adding an *s* at the end of the word.

SINGULAR	PLURAL
handful	handfuls
spoonful	spoonfuls

Example Write the plural form of each of the following singular nouns. Use a dictionary if you are in doubt.

(a) cupful   (b) sister of the bride   (c) son-in-law

Solution (a) **cupfuls** (word ending in *ful*)

(b) **sisters of the bride** (compound noun)

(c) **sons-in-law** (compound noun)

✓ Practice For a–d, write the plural form of the singular noun.

    a. mother-in-law   **b.** chief of staff

    c. mouthful   **d.** pailful

For e–h, replace the blank with the correct vocabulary word from this lesson.

    e. When the wind stopped blowing, the water on the lake became _____.

    f. The Latin word _____ means "to soothe or calm."

    g. It's no use trying to _____ a mad hornet.

    h. A mad hornet is _____.

✓ Review Set 22 Choose the correct word(s) to complete sentences 1–9.

    1. A fissure is a (mountain, mammal, crack).
    (21)

    2. A chasm is a gorge, or (mystery, lump, crack) in
    (20) Earth's surface.

    3. A layer of soil remains frozen in the (savanna, tundra,
    (19) tropic) region.

    4. The Torrid Zone is near Earth's (equator, poles).
    (18)

    5. To (conceal, disclose) is to put or keep out of sight; hide.
    (7)

    6. Dan and Ben (is, am, are) brothers.
    (18)

    7. Ben and Dan watched (their, there) dog bury (its, it's)
    (5, 6) bone in Ms. Lum's garden.

    8. Juanita (do, does) her homework at the library.
    (18)

    9. The (present, past) participle of the verb *disturb* is *(is)*
    (19) *disturbing*.

    10. Rewrite the following sentence, adding capital letters as
    (8, 15) needed: in our solar system, mercury and venus are the only planets without moons.

11. Replace the blank below with the singular present tense
(9) form of the underlined verb.

Bank tellers <u>cash</u> checks. A teller _____ checks.

12. Write each action verb in the following sentence: Did Ms.
(7) Lum water the garden and feed the cow before she left?

13. From the following list, write the word that is *not* a
(12) helping verb: do, does, did, shall, will, should, wood.

14. In the following sentence, write the entire verb phrase,
(12) circling each helping verb: Through Missouri, Clarisse
may follow the same route as the old Pony Express.

15. In the following sentence, write whether the underlined
(10) verb phrase is present, past, or future tense: Mark Twain
<u>lived</u> in Hannibal, Missouri, from age seven to eighteen.

16. Write whether the following word group is a complete
(5) sentence or a sentence fragment: In 1904, the St. Louis
World's Fair introduced ice-cream cones.

17. Write each preposition that you find in the following
(20, 21) sentence: About the time of Judd's birthday, he received
twenty-five dollars from his aunt.

18. From the following list, write the word that is *not* a
(20, 21) preposition: aboard, about, above, across, asked, against,
along, alongside, amid, among, around, at, before, behind.

19. Write the compound, possessive noun from the following
(13) sentence: The artist made the storybook's illustrations too
scary for young children.

20. Rewrite and correct the following sentence fragment,
(6) making a complete sentence:

Tapping their feet to country music.

21. For a–d, write whether the noun is concrete or abstract.
(11)
(a) Mars   (b) astronomy   (c) honesty   (d) planet

22. Write each collective noun that you find in this sentence:
(11) A pack of wolves moves across the plain.

23. Write the simple subject of the following sentence: From the Appalachian highlands to the Ozark Plateau came a fiddler with her delightful folk music.
(3, 4)

24. For the following sentence, write the correct form of the verb: Ms. Lum (present of *have*) six sheep.
(18)

25. Write the simple predicate of the following sentence: From the Appalachian highlands to the Ozark Plateau came a fiddler with her delightful folk music.
(3, 4)

26. Rewrite the following lines of poetry, adding capital letters as needed:
(15)

red sky at night,
sailor's delight;
red sky at morning,
sailor's warning.

27. For the verb *sail*, write the (a) present participle, (b) past tense, and (c) past participle.
(19)

28. Write whether the following sentence is declarative, interrogative, imperative, or exclamatory:
(2)

Missouri touches eight other states.

29. For a–d, write the plural of each noun.
(17, 22)
(a) calf   (b) attorney at law   (c) spoonful   (d) sheep

30. Rewrite the following sentence, drawing a vertical line between the subject and the predicate:
(1)

A white-haired fiddler in a plaid shirt fiddled faster and faster.

Complete Sentence or
Run-on Sentence?

Dictation or Journal Entry

Vocabulary:

The Latin word *loqui,* meaning "to talk," appears in the English words *ventriloquist* and *elocution.*

A *ventriloquist* is one who speaks without moving the lips. The *ventriloquist* pretended to carry on a conversation with a puppet.

Elocution is the art of public speaking, including pronunciation, tone, and gestures. Ms. Smiley gave an excellent speech; her *elocution* was flawless.

Run-on Sentences   A sentence is complete only if it expresses a complete thought. Two complete thoughts written or spoken as one sentence without proper punctuation or connecting words is called a **run-on sentence,** as shown below.

> Hepzy went to Montana she saw fifty glaciers. (Run-on)

Sometimes we put a comma where there should be a period.

> Hepzy went to Montana, she saw fifty glaciers. (Run-on)

Other times, we join sentences with *and*'s, *and-so*'s, or *but*'s. If we omit the joining words or punctuation between sentences, we have a run-on sentence.

RUN-ON SENTENCE:
Some people have no pets other people have one or two some people have many.

COMPLETE SENTENCE:
Some people have no pets, and other people have one or two, but some people have many.

Example   Tell whether each of the following is a complete sentence or a run-on sentence.

(a) Montana has big mountains it has prairies too.

(b) Miners find gold, silver, and precious gems in Montana.

(c) Summers are warm winters are cold.

(d) High in the cedar tree, the meadowlark is singing.

Solution (a) This expression is two complete thoughts without punctuation. Therefore it is a **run-on sentence.** (Corrected: Montana has big mountains. It has prairies too.)

(b) **Complete sentence**

(c) This is two complete thoughts without connecting words or punctuation, so it is a **run-on sentence.** (Corrected: Summers are warm, but winters are cold.)

(d) **Complete sentence**

✓Practice For a–d, write whether each word group is a complete sentence or a run-on sentence.

a. Helena is the capital of Montana it is near the Missouri River.

b. Captain William Clark explored Montana in 1803.

c. General George Custer fought Native Americans at Little Bighorn.

d. Custer lost the battle it was Custer's Last Stand.

For e–g, replace each blank with the correct word from the vocabulary section of this lesson.

e. The Latin word *loqui* means "to _____."

f. If you speak well in public, you might be praised for your _____.

g. A _____ speaks without moving his or her lips.

More Practice Write whether each word group is a complete sentence or a run-on sentence.

1. I can't open the chest its hinges are rusty.

2. Can you open it?

3. I have a tool let's use it.

4. Look at this treasure!

5. It's too dark I can't see.

6. Please bring a lantern.

Choose the correct word(s) to complete sentences 1–9.

1. *Implacable* means "not able to be (concealed, disclosed,
(22) calmed)."

2. A small fissure might eventually become a (mesa, tundra,
(21) chasm).

3. A (mesa, savanna, chasm) is a deep, wide crack in
(20) Earth's surface.

4. The tundra is a (hot, warm, cold) region.
(19)

5. Geography is the study of (sun's, moon's, Earth's)
(8) natural surface.

6. Trees (was, were) more scarce as we approached the
(18) timberline.

7. Zebras like the African savannas, but (its, it's) too hot
(5, 6) (their, there) for me.

8. (Do, Does) a layer of soil remain frozen in the tundra?
(18)

9. *(Has) concealed* is the (present, past) participle of the
(19) verb *conceal.*

10. Rewrite the following sentence, adding capital letters as
(8, 15) needed: one of montana's richest gold deposits is in
virginia city.

11. Replace the blank below with the singular present tense
(9) form of the underlined verb.

   Cooks <u>mash</u> potatoes. Alex _____ potatoes.

12. Write each action verb in the following sentence: Melody
(7) made a birthday card, signed it, and mailed it.

For sentences 13 and 14, write the entire verb phrase, circling
each helping verb.

13. Bison have been thriving out there on the range.
(12)

14. Can grasshoppers survive on a glacier?
(12)

15. In the following sentence, write whether the underlined verb phrase is present, past, or future tense:
(14)

My family <u>will appreciate</u> the peace and quiet of Montana.

16. Write whether the following word group is a complete sentence, a sentence fragment, or a run-on sentence:
(23)

Only six people per square mile in this part of the country.

17. Write each preposition that you find in the following sentence:
(20, 21)

In Montana, a city named Butte rhymes with "cute."

18. From the following list, write the word that is *not* a preposition: beside, besides, between, beyond, but, buy, concerning, considering, despite, down, during, except.
(20, 21)

19. Write the compound, possessive noun from the following sentence:
(13)

The gentleman's optimism and good humor cheered everyone.

20. Rewrite and correct the following sentence fragment, making a complete sentence:
(6)

To canoe down the river through Montana's wild lands.

21. For a–d, write whether the noun is concrete or abstract.
(11)
(a) atoll   (b) astronomer   (c) courage   (d) geology

22. Write each collective noun that you find in this sentence:
(11)

With my binoculars, I spotted a herd of cattle in the distance.

23. Write the simple subject of the following sentence:
(3, 4)
Have the mountain climbers reached the summit yet?

24. For the following sentence, write the correct form of the verb:
(18)

Ms. Lum (present of *do*) her chores early each morning.

25. Write the simple predicate of the following sentence:
(3, 4) Have the mountain climbers reached the summit yet?

26. Rewrite the following lines of poetry (song lyrics), adding
(15) capital letters as needed:

i've been working on the railroad
all the livelong day
i've been working on the railroad
just to pass the time away

27. For the verb *disclose*, write the (a) present participle, (b)
(19) past tense, and (c) past participle.

28. Write whether the following sentence is declarative,
(2) interrogative, imperative, or exclamatory:

Where did you find that precious sapphire?

29. For a–d, write the plural of each noun.
(17, 22) (a) shelf (b) justice of the peace (c) cupful (d) deer

30. Rewrite the following sentence, drawing a vertical line
(1) between the subject and the predicate:

Two huge bison with thick brown coats were minding
their own business.

Correcting a Run-on Sentence

Dictation or Journal Entry

Vocabulary:
The Latin root _val-_, meaning "strength," appears in the English words _valor_ and _valiant_.

Valor is outstanding courage, or great bravery, especially in battle. The soldiers who fought for our freedom will always be remembered for their _valor_.

Valiant is an adjective meaning "brave or courageous." The _valiant_ warriors refused to retreat.

We have learned that two or more complete thoughts written or spoken as one sentence without proper punctuation or connecting words is called a **run-on sentence.**

Correcting Run-ons   We correct run-on sentences by adding punctuation or connecting words, and by removing unnecessary words.

Example   Correct this run-on sentence:

Hepzy has a red hen she feeds it corn.

Solution   We see that the run-on sentence above has two subjects and two predicates, or two complete thoughts.

subject | predicate   subject | predicate
Hepzy | has a red hen   she | feeds it corn

We may add a period and capital letter to make two complete sentences.

Hepzy has a red hen. She feeds it corn.

Or we may add a comma and a connecting word to make a complete compound sentence. We shall learn more about compound sentences in a later lesson.

Hepzy has a red hen, and she feeds it corn.

✓**Practice**   For a–d, rewrite and correct each run-on sentence. There is more than one correct answer.

a. My friends in Nebraska grow corn they also raise pigs.

b. Some ranchers felt lonely they had cornhusking parties with neighbors.

c. Corn grows well in Nebraska some of it is fed to livestock.

d. On the prairie, wood was scarce people built homes of sod.

For e–g, replace each blank with the correct word from the vocabulary section of this lesson.

e. The Latin root *val-* means "_____."

f. The word _____ is an abstract noun meaning "great bravery."

g. The word _____ is an adjective meaning "brave or courageous."

More Practice For 1–5, correct each run-on sentence. There is more than one correct answer.

1. It's too dark I can't see.

2. I have a map let's find the cave.

3. Please come with me I need your help.

4. Bats live here they sleep during the day.

5. Bats wake they startle me!

Review Set 24 Choose the correct word(s) to complete sentences 1–9.

1. Elocution is the art of public (transportation, defense, speaking).
(23)

2. (*Implacable, Optimistic, Pessimistic*) means "not able to be calmed or appeased."
(22)

3. A (plateau, fissure, savanna) is a long, narrow opening or crack.
(21)

4. A (mesa, tundra, chasm) is a flat-topped hill or mountain with steep sides.
(20)

5. A(n) (lagoon, atoll, arroyo) is a gully, or the bed of a stream.
(16)

6. Conchs and shrimp (is, are) abundant in the lagoon.
(18)

7. Mr. and Mrs. Blue noticed that (there, their) car had lost (its, it's) antenna.
(5, 6)

8. (Has, Have) the ships passed through the Strait of Magellan yet?
(18)

9. *(Is) placating* is the (present, past) participle of the verb *placate*.
(19)

10. Rewrite the following sentence, adding capital letters as needed: nebraska's capital, lincoln, is named after president abraham lincoln.
(8, 15)

11. Replace the blank below with the singular present tense form of the underlined verb.
(9)

My eyeglasses <u>magnify</u> small objects. A microscope _____ small objects.

12. Write each action verb in the following sentence: A peacock struts into the garden, pecks among the flowers, and calls for its mate.
(7)

For sentences 13 and 14, write the entire verb phrase, circling each helping verb.

13. Shall we follow the Oregon Trail?
(12)

14. Cowboys have been roping steer for decades.
(12)

15. In the following sentence, write whether the underlined verb phrase is present, past, or future tense: Cattle <u>stampede</u> across the plain.
(9)

16. Write whether the following word group is a complete sentence, a sentence fragment, or a run-on sentence:
(23)

You are a good corn husker you should join the contest.

17. Write each preposition that you find in the following sentence: In Nebraska, archaeologists have found fossils of prehistoric elephants with long tusks.
(20, 21)

18. From the following list, write the word that is *not* a preposition: inside, into, lake, near, of, off, on, onto, opposite, out, outside, over, past, regarding, round.
(20, 21)

19. Write the proper, possessive noun from the following sentence: Unfortunately, Mr. Blue's pessimism proved contagious, discouraging everyone in the group.
(13)

20. Rewrite and correct the run-on sentence below. There
⁽²⁴⁾ is more than one correct answer.

This is Arbor Day we shall plant trees.

21. For a–d, write whether the noun is concrete or abstract.
⁽¹¹⁾ (a) valor   (b) elocution   (c) estuary   (d) isthmus

22. Write each collective noun that you find in this sentence:
⁽¹¹⁾ The committee has decided to plant river birch trees.

23. Write the simple subject of the following sentence: There
^(3, 4) were mammoths in Nebraska!

24. For the following sentence, write the correct form of the
⁽¹⁸⁾ verb: We (future of *be*) friends forever.

25. Write the simple predicate of the following sentence:
^(3, 4) There were mammoths in Nebraska!

26. Rewrite the following lines of poetry (song lyrics), adding
⁽¹⁵⁾ capital letters as needed:

o beautiful for spacious skies,
for amber waves of grain,
for purple mountain majesties
above the fruited plain!

27. For the verb *conceal*, write the (a) present participle, (b)
⁽¹⁹⁾ past tense, and (c) past participle.

28. Write whether the following sentence is declarative,
⁽²⁾ interrogative, imperative, or exclamatory: Please do not
disturb the cranes beside the Platte River.

29. For a–d, write the plural of each noun.
^(17, 22) (a) estuary   (b) sister-in-law   (c) fistful   (d) country

30. Rewrite the following sentence, drawing a vertical line
⁽¹⁾ between the subject and the predicate:

Cattle, corn, pigs, and oil provide economic stability for
Nebraska.

Capitalization: Titles

Dictation or Journal Entry

Vocabulary:

The Latin word *ignis* means "fire."

To *ignite* is to burn or set on fire. In order to cook our dinner, we must *ignite* the gas in this stove.

Igneous rocks are those formed by the solidification of the molten material within the earth. Granite and obsidian are *igneous rocks*, formed as molten material cools and solidifies.

We have learned to capitalize proper nouns, common nouns when they are a part of proper nouns, the pronoun *I*, the first word of every sentence, and the first word in every line of most poetry. We have also learned that little words like *of*, *and*, and *an* are not capitalized when part of a proper noun.

Titles   Titles require special capitalization. In titles, we capitalize the following:

1. The first and last words of a title

2. All verbs (action or being words)

3. All other words in the title except certain short words

4. A preposition with five or more letters (such as *outside, underneath, between,* etc.)

Notice the examples below.

Heidi

The Outsiders

"The Emperor's New Clothes"

Unless located first or last in the title, words like *a, an, and, the, but, or, for, nor,* and prepositions with four letters or fewer do not need a capital letter.

Where the Red Fern Grows

"The Tortoise and the Hare"

Sound of Music

The Door in the Wall

Example   Provide capital letters as needed in the following titles.
(a) *old yeller*

(b) *the courage of sarah noble*

(c) "the giant shoes"

(d) "down in the valley"

Solution   (a) **Old Yeller.** We capitalize the first and last words in a book title.

(b) ***The Courage of Sarah Noble*** is also a book. The little word *of* is not capitalized. The first and last words as well as the important words require a capital letter.

(c) "**The Giant Shoes**" is a story title. We capitalize the first and last words and all important words.

(d) "**Down in the Valley**" is a song title. We do not capitalize the little words *in* and *the* because they are not first or last words in the title.

✓**Practice**   Rewrite titles a–d, adding capital letters as needed.

  a. *winnie the pooh*

  b. *the call of the wild*

  c. *the house at pooh corner*

  d. "home on the range"

For e–g, replace each blank with the correct vocabulary word from this lesson.

  e. We might find _____ where a volcano exploded in the past.

  f. The Latin word _____ means "fire."

  g. To light the candle, I shall _____ a match.

More Practice   See "More Practice Lesson 25" in Student Workbook.

Review Set 25   Choose the correct word to complete sentences 1–9.

  1. A(n) (implacable, valiant, placid) person is brave or courageous.
  (24)

  2. A(n) (optimist, pessimist, ventriloquist) talks without moving his or her lips.
  (23)

  3. The Latin word *placare* means "to (calm, disturb, shout)."
  (22)

4. A plateau is relatively (hilly, flat, deep).
(21)

5. (Savanna, Tundra, Arroyo) is a vast, flat, frozen plain in
(19) the North.

6. The two essential parts of a sentence are the subject and
(1) the (predator, predictor, predicate).

7. (There, Their) is a horse with (it's, its) saddle on
(5, 6) backwards!

8. Alida (do, does) sit-ups and push-ups to strengthen her
(18) muscles.

9. *(Has) ignited* is the (present, past) participle of the verb
(19) *ignite.*

10. Rewrite the following sentence, adding capital letters as
(8, 15) needed: one of the world's biggest dams is hoover dam in
nevada.

11. Replace the blank below with the singular present tense
(9) form of the underlined verb.
Geese <u>fly</u> south. A goose _____ south.

12. Write each action verb in the following sentence:
(7)
A cowboy fell off a bull, tumbled onto the ground, and
rolled under the fence to safety.

13. In the following sentence, write the entire verb phrase,
(12) circling each helping verb:

Has the cowboy broken any bones?

14. Write the following book title, using correct
(25) capitalization: *the cat in the hat*

15. In the following sentence, write whether the underlined
(14) verb phrase is present, past, or future tense: I <u>shall mail</u>
you a postcard from Lake Tahoe.

16. Write whether the following word group is a complete
(23) sentence, a sentence fragment, or a run-on sentence:

Hoover Dam spans the Colorado River and forms Lake
Mead.

17. Write each preposition that you find in the following sentence: In the Mojave Desert, a rattlesnake slithers around a cactus and under a rock.
(20, 21)

18. From the following list, write the word that is *not* a preposition: save, since, through, throughout, till, tool, toward, under.
(20, 21)

19. Write the proper, possessive noun from the following sentence: Nevada's deserts have seven different types of rattlesnakes.
(13)

20. Rewrite and correct the run-on sentence below. There is more than one correct answer.
(24)

Prospectors went to Virginia City there they found silver and gold.

21. For a–d, write whether the noun is concrete or abstract.
(11)

(a) cowboy   (b) ghost town   (c) adventure   (d) success

22. Write each collective noun that you find in this sentence: The mule team carried heavy packs over the rugged mountain pass.
(11)

23. Write the simple subject of the following sentence: Have you visited Carson City, Nevada's capital?
(3, 4)

24. For the following sentence, write the correct form of the verb: We (past of *be*) friends in our youth.
(18)

25. Write the simple predicate of the following sentence: Have you visited Carson City, Nevada's capital?
(3, 4)

26. Rewrite the following lines of Robert Frost's poem, adding capital letters as needed:
(15)

i left you in the morning,
and in the morning glow
you walked a way beside me
to make me sad to go.

27. For the verb *ignite*, write the (a) present participle, (b) past tense, and (c) past participle.
(19)

28. Write whether the following sentence is declarative,
(2) interrogative, imperative, or exclamatory: Over here! It's
a silver nugget!

29. For a–d, write the plural of each noun.
(17, 22) (a) sky   (b) lord of England   (c) tubful   (d) prefix

30. Rewrite the following sentence, drawing a vertical line
(1) between the subject and the predicate:

The state of Nevada mines silver, copper, and turquoise.

Capitalization: Outlines and Quotations

Dictation or Journal Entry
Vocabulary:
The Greek word *metamorphosis* means "transformation."

Metamorphosis is the process by which certain animals undergo changes as they develop. By *metamorphosis* a tadpole becomes a frog.

Metamorphic rocks are those that have been changed from their original form by great heat and pressure. Marble and slate are *metamorphic rocks*.

We have learned to capitalize proper nouns, common nouns when they are a part of proper nouns, the pronoun *I*, the first word of every sentence, and the first word in every line of most poetry. We have learned that little words like *of*, *and*, and *an* are not capitalized when part of a proper noun and that titles require special capitalization.

In this lesson we shall learn the correct capitalization of outlines and quotations.

Outlines   We learn to organize written material by outlining. **Outlines** require capital letters for the Roman numerals and for the letters of the first major topics. We also capitalize the first letter of the first word in each line of an outline.

> I. Things to see in Alabama
>   A. Rivers and streams
>   B. Mountains
>   C. Museums
>
> II. Things to see in Georgia
>   A. Wildlife
>   B. Plantations
>   C. Monuments and historical sites

Quotations   We capitalize the first word of a dialogue **quotation,** as shown below.

> The teacher asked, "Is Perlina asleep in class?"
>
> Perlina's friend said, "Wake up, Perlina!"
>
> Perlina replied, "Please, don't bother me."

Example   Provide capital letters as needed.
(a) i. kinds of maps

        a. political maps
        b. physical maps
        c. climate maps

   (b) Mrs. Curtis explains, "you can see the state boundaries
       on a political map."

Solution (a) We remember that outlines require capital letters for their
           Roman numerals, major topics, and first words.

     I. **K**inds of maps
        A. **P**olitical maps
        B. **P**hysical maps
        C. **C**limate maps

   (b) We use a capital *y* in "**Y**ou can see the state boundaries
       on a political map."

✓Practice Rewrite a–c, using correct capitalization.
       a. i. types of trees
               a. deciduous trees
               b. evergreen trees

       b. andrew angles said, "your grandmother and i came from
           scotland."

       c. then he explained, "it was difficult leaving our families."

   For d–f, replace each blank with the correct vocabulary word
   from this lesson.
       d. The Greek word meaning "transformation" is _____.

       e. Great heat and pressure transform material into
           _____ such as slate and marble.

       f. By _____ a caterpillar becomes a butterfly.

More Practice See "More Practice Lesson 26" in Student Workbook.

✓Review Set 26 Choose the correct word to complete sentences 1–9.
       1. Igneous (lumber, rocks, trees) form as molten material
       (25) cools and solidifies.

       2. A valiant person is (cowardly, nice, brave).
       (24)

       3. (Optimism, Elocution, Persecution) is the art of public
       (23) speaking.

4. *Placid* means "(angry, disturbed, peaceful)."
(22)

5. The Torrid Zone is (warm, cold, freezing).
(18)

6. The word *danger* is a(n) (abstract, concrete) noun.
(11)

7. Daniel and Susan think (its, it's) too cold in (there, their)
(5, 6) state.

8. Alida (have, has) strong muscles because she exercises
(18) daily.

9. *(Is) exercising* is the (present, past) participle of the verb
(19) *exercise.*

10. Rewrite the following sentence, adding capital letters as
(8, 15) needed: joseph said, "the honeybee is new jersey's state
bug."

11. Replace the blank below with the singular present tense
(9) form of the underlined verb.

Snakes <u>hiss</u>. A snake _____.

12. Write the action verb in the following sentence:
(7)

Lilah drives across the George Washington Bridge from
New Jersey to New York City.

13. In the following sentence, write the entire verb phrase,
(12) circling each helping verb:

That restaurant should have offered eggplant parmesan
on its menu.

14. Write the following song title, using correct
(25) capitalization: "i've been working on the railroad"

15. In the following sentence, write whether the underlined
(10) verb phrase is present, past, or future tense: John Henry
<u>worked</u> hard on the railroad.

16. Write whether the following word group is a complete
(23) sentence, a sentence fragment, or a run-on sentence:

Living in Alabama, the Heart of Dixie, the land of cotton.

17. Write each preposition that you find in the following sentence:
(20, 21)

During the night, I couldn't see the rocks alongside the road without my flashlight.

18. From the following list, write the word that is *not* a preposition: underneath, until, unto, up, upon, understand, via, with, within, without.
(20, 21)

19. Write the proper, possessive noun from the following sentence:
(13)

In the 1920s, boll weevils destroyed Alabama's cotton harvest.

20. Rewrite and correct the run-on sentence below. There is more than one correct answer.
(24)

New Jersey has beautiful beaches people like to come to the shore.

21. Rewrite the following sentence fragment, making a complete sentence:
(6)

To swim in the ocean with jellyfish, sharks, and eels.

22. Write each compound noun that you find in this sentence:
(13)

We can use that lighthouse for a landmark.

23. Write the simple subject of the following sentence:
(3, 4)

Far to the east of California lies New Jersey.

24. For the following sentence, write the correct form of the verb: We (present of *be*) friends now.
(18)

25. Write the simple predicate of the following sentence:
(3, 4)

Far to the east of California lies New Jersey.

26. Rewrite the following outline, adding capital letters as
(26) needed:

    i. the globe
      a. continents
      b. oceans
    ii. locating places
      a. hemispheres
      b. latitude and longitude

27. For the verb *play*, write the (a) present participle, (b) past
(19) tense, and (c) past participle.

28. Write whether the following sentence is declarative,
(2) interrogative, imperative, or exclamatory: Is Perlina
awake now?

29. For a–d, write the plural of each noun.
(17, 22) (a) lady   (b) brother-in-law   (c) shovelful   (d) man

30. Rewrite the following sentence, drawing a vertical line
(1) between the subject and the predicate:

The state of New Jersey protects plants and animals in the
Pine Barrens.

Dictionary Information
About a Word, Part 1

> **Dictation or Journal Entry**
>
> **Vocabulary:**
>
> _Sediment_ is matter that settles to the bottom of a liquid. On the bottom of the pan of water, I noticed some sparkling gold _sediment_!
>
> _Sedimentary rocks_ are those formed in layers from materials deposited by water, wind, or ice. Limestone and sandstone are _sedimentary rocks_.

Definitions A dictionary's main function is to provide word meanings. Since a single word may have many meanings, we carefully read all its definitions.

Parts of Speech Usually, an italicized abbreviation indicates the part of speech of the word being defined. A dictionary's front or back matter explains its abbreviations, like the ones below.

_n._	noun	_v._	verb
adj.	adjective	_adv._	adverb
pron.	pronoun	_prep._	preposition
conj.	conjunction	_interj._	interjection
_v.t._	transitive verb	_v.i._	intransitive verb

Spelling The boldfaced word that begins a dictionary entry gives the accepted spelling. If there are two or more accepted spellings, these are given as well. The dictionary also provides the spelling of irregular plurals, principal parts of verbs, comparative or superlative forms of adjectives, and other grammatical changes in word forms.

Syllable Division The boldfaced dictionary entry shows syllable division by a dot or by a space.

con·ceal   con ceal

Pronunciation Using a fixed symbol for each of the common English sounds, the pronunciation guide respells the entry word with accent marks to show which syllables are spoken with more stress than the others. A heavier mark indicates the heaviest accent, or stress on the syllable; a lighter mark indicates a lighter accent.

Penn·syl·va·nia   pen´ səl vān´ yə

Example   Use a dictionary to complete the following.

(a) Write two different definitions for the word *witness*.

(b) Write the part of speech indicated by the dictionary for the word *indolence*.

(c) Write two accepted spellings for the plural of *cactus*.

(d) Rewrite the word *optimistic* showing its syllable division.

(e) Rewrite the word *ornate* showing its pronunciation, including accent marks.

Solution   (a) Answers will vary. **1. one who has seen or heard something. 2. to see or hear something.**

(b) **noun**   (c) **cactuses, cacti**

(d) **op·ti·mis·tic**   (e) **ôr nāt´**

Practice   Use a dictionary to answer a–e.

a. Write two different meanings for the word *battle*.

b. The word *gentility* is what part of speech?

c. Write two accepted spellings for the plural of *brother*.

d. Rewrite the word *perpendicular* showing its syllable division.

e. Rewrite the word *disclose* showing its pronunciation.

For f and g, replace each blank with the correct vocabulary word from this lesson.

✓ f. _____ settles to the bottom of a liquid.

✓ g. _____ form in layers from materials deposited by water, wind, or ice.

✓ **Review Set 27**   Choose the correct word to complete sentences 1–9.

1. (Candy, Salt, Metamorphic) rocks have been changed
(26) from their original form by great heat and pressure.

2. Igneous rocks form when (cotton, polyester, molten)
$^{(25)}$ material cools and solidifies.

3. (Valor, Flora, Fauna) is outstanding courage, or great
$^{(24)}$ bravery, especially in battle.

4. A ventriloquist (chews, talks, smiles) without moving his
$^{(23)}$ or her lips.

5. (*Placid, Fissure, Plateau*) means "calm or peaceful;
$^{(22)}$ undisturbed."

6. The word *mesa* is a(n) (abstract, concrete) noun.
$^{(11)}$

7. Oops, a lizard left (it's, its) tail over (their, there).
$^{(5, 6)}$

8. The washing machine (do, does) its job.
$^{(18)}$

9. *(Has) washed* is the (present, past) participle of the verb
$^{(19)}$ *wash.*

10. Rewrite the following sentence, adding capital letters as
$^{(26)}$ needed: besly said, "next tuesday i shall take the train to
santa fe, new mexico."

11. Replace the blank below with the singular present tense
$^{(9)}$ form of the underlined verb.

Sodas <u>fizz</u>. A soda _____.

12. Write each action verb in the following sentence:
$^{(7)}$
Perlina yawns and rubs her eyes.

13. In the following sentence, write the entire verb phrase,
$^{(12)}$ circling each helping verb:

Riley's ancestors might have built an adobe pueblo in
New Mexico.

14. Write the following story title, using correct
$^{(25)}$ capitalization: "the hunting of the great bear"

15. In the following sentence, write whether the underlined
$^{(14)}$ verb phrase is present, past, or future tense: That
roadrunner <u>will exceed</u> the speed limit!

16. Write whether the following word group is a complete
(23) sentence, a sentence fragment, or a run-on sentence:

New Mexico grows chili peppers they are very hot.

17. Write each preposition that you find in the following
(20, 21) sentence:

In 1947, a spaceship with aliens supposedly crashed at
Alamogordo, New Mexico.

18. Use a dictionary: (a) The word *atoll* is what part of
(27) speech? (b) Write its pronunciation.

19. Write the possessive noun from the following sentence:
(13)
Do roadrunners' legs get tired?

20. Rewrite and correct the run-on sentence below. There is
(24) more than one correct answer.

Ilbea ate a chili pepper tears came to her eyes.

21. Rewrite the following sentence fragment, making a
(6) complete sentence:

An unidentified flying object in the night sky.

22. Write the collective noun that you find in this sentence:
(11)
Sadly, the entire citrus grove is infested with white flies.

23. Write the simple subject of the following sentence:
(3, 4)
Through the Land of Enchantment runs the roadrunner.

24. For the following sentence, write the correct form of the
(18) verb: The roadrunner (present of *have*) strong legs.

25. Write the simple predicate of the following sentence:
(3, 4)
Through the Land of Enchantment runs the roadrunner.

26. Rewrite the following outline, adding capital letters as
(26) needed:

i. products of new mexico
   a. agricultural products
   b. industrial products

27. For the verb *cry*, write the (a) present participle, (b) past
(19) tense, and (c) past participle.

28. Write whether the following sentence is declarative,
(2) interrogative, imperative, or exclamatory: One of the
world's great wonders is Carlsbad Caverns.

29. For a–d, write the plural of each noun.
(17, 22)   (a) echo   (b) editor in chief   (c) knife   (d) city

30. Rewrite the following sentence, drawing a vertical line
(1) between the subject and the predicate:

Migrants from the East headed west by wagon train.

Spelling Rules: Silent Letters
k, g, w, t, d, and *c*

> **Dictation or Journal Entry**
>
> **Vocabulary:**
>
> A *caldera* is a large depression resulting from the explosion or collapse of the center of a volcano. The volcano's *caldera* looks like a huge basin.
>
> *Magma* is the molten rock that lies beneath Earth's surface. Lava and igneous rocks are formed as the hot *magma* cools.

Why Are Some Letters Silent?

The English language contains many words that are spelled differently than they are pronounced. There are several reasons for this.

As the language changed and grew through the centuries, the way people pronounced a word often changed, yet the way the word was spelled remained the same.

Some early scholars insisted on applying Latin rules of spelling to English words. (Since English borrowed the Latin alphabet, this idea was logical.)

More words were borrowed from other languages, and their foreign spellings were kept.

In the midst of this, the printing press appeared. It helped to "freeze" the spelling of all these words, no matter how irregular. Most English words are spelled today just as they were in the 1500s. As a result, there are many words that contain letters we no longer (or never did) pronounce.

The Letter *k*

A silent *k* at the beginning of a word is always followed by an *n*.

know   **k**nock   **k**neel   **k**nife

The Letter *g*

A silent *g* may also be followed by an *n* at the beginning or the end of a word.

gnat   **g**naw   fei**g**n   rei**g**n   campai**g**n

The Letter *w*

A silent *w* can come before the letter *r*.

wrinkle   **w**ritten   **w**rench   **w**reath

Sometimes the silent *w* comes before the letter *h*.

whole   **w**ho   **w**hose

Other silent *w*'s appear in the words *answer, sword,* and *two*.

The Letter _t_ A silent _t_ can follow the letter _s_.

> cas*t*le   rus*t*le   lis*t*en   has*t*en

A silent _t_ can also come before the letters _ch_.

> Sco*t*ch   ma*t*ch   ske*t*ch   pi*t*ch

Not all words that end with the "ch" sound have a silent _t_ (_much, rich, attach, such, sandwich_, etc.). When in doubt, check the dictionary.

Other silent _t_'s appear in words borrowed from the French, such as _ballet_, _depot_, _debut_, _gourmet_, and _mortgage_.

The Letter _d_ The letters _ge_ usually follow a silent _d_.

> fu*d*ge   e*d*ge   bri*d*ge   do*d*ge   ba*d*ge

We also find silent _d_'s in these words:

> a*d*jective   a*d*just   We*d*nesday   han*d*some

The Letter _c_ A silent _c_ can follow the letter _s_.

> s*c*issors   s*c*ene   s*c*ience   s*c*ent

Example Rewrite these words and circle each silent letter.

    (a) kneel   (b) answer   (c) wrong

    (d) badger   (e) gnarl   (f) itch

Solution (a) (k)neel   (b) ans(w)er   (c) (w)rong

    (d) ba(d)ger   (e) (g)narl   (f) i(t)ch

Practice Rewrite words a–h, circling each silent letter.

    a. wrestle   **b.** whose   **c.** gnome   **d.** listen

    e. knot   **f.** knees   **g.** scenery   **h.** whistle

For i and j, replace each blank with the correct vocabulary word from this lesson.

    i. Igneous rocks are solidified _____.

    j. From a helicopter we could see inside the _____ of the volcano.

Review Set 28 Choose the correct word to complete sentences 1–9.

    1. Sedimentary rocks form in (volcanoes, layers, lumps)
    (27) from sediment deposited by water, wind, or ice.

2. Metamorphic rocks have been (destroyed, disclosed,
(26) changed) from their original form by great heat and
pressure.

3. To ignite is to (disclose, burn, freeze).
(25)

4. Valor is outstanding (beauty, grace, courage).
(24)

5. Good study habits are necessary, or (essential,
(1) nonessential), for success in school.

6. The word *ladies* is a (plural, possessive) noun.
(11)

7. (It's, Its) not fatal if lizards lose (their, there) tails.
(5, 6)

8. Sheung and Amy (is, was, were) singing a duet.
(18)

9. *(Is) snoring* is the (present, past) participle of the verb
(19) *snore.*

10. Rewrite the following sentence, adding capital letters as
(26) needed: rosa said, "my family and i saw two plays in new
york city."

11. Replace the blank below with the singular present tense
(9) form of the underlined verb.

Ting and Mae <u>fish</u>. Tyler _____.

12. Write each action verb in the following sentence:
(7)
Maxwell thinks before he speaks.

13. In the following sentence, write the entire verb phrase,
(12) circling each helping verb:

Great Grandpa Petersen must have entered the United
States through Ellis Island.

14. Write the following story title, using correct
(25) capitalization: "ali baba and the forty thieves"

15. In the following sentence, write whether the underlined
(10) verb is present, past, or future tense: New York <u>offered</u>
several new plays on Broadway last year.

16. Write whether the following word group is a complete
(23) sentence, a sentence fragment, or a run-on sentence:

Seeing the Statue of Liberty on Ellis Island in the harbor.

17. Write each preposition that you find in the following
(20, 21) sentence:

Despite strong winds, the small plane flew north along
the Hudson River, over the Appalachian Mountains,
around Adirondack Park, and into Syracuse.

18. Use a dictionary: (a) The word *exalt* is what part of
(27) speech? (b) Write its pronunciation.

19. Rewrite the following words, circling each silent letter:
(28)
(a) knead   (b) sign   (c) watch

20. Rewrite and correct the run-on sentence below. There is
(24) more than one correct answer.

The Niagara River has magnificent waterfalls have you
seen them?

21. Rewrite the following sentence fragment, making a
(6) complete sentence:

To take the elevator to the eighty-sixth floor of the Empire
State Building.

22. Write the compound noun that you find in this sentence:
(13)
New York has been the gateway to the United States.

23. Write the simple subject of the following sentence:
(3, 4)
Did glaciers create the Finger Lakes?

24. For the following sentence, write the correct form of the
(18) verb: Icicles (past of *be*) forming above the windows.

25. Write the simple predicate of the following sentence:
(3, 4)
Did glaciers create the Finger Lakes?

26. Rewrite the following lines of poetry, adding capital
(15) letters as needed:

an apple a day
keeps the doctor away.

27. For the verb *dry*, write the (a) present participle, (b) past
(19) tense, and (c) past participle.

28. Write whether the following sentence is declarative,
(2) interrogative, imperative, or exclamatory: New York has
more than 18,000 dairy farms!

29. For a–d, write the plural of each noun.
(17, 22) (a) logo   (b) bookshelf   (c) pailful   (d) county

30. Rewrite the following sentence, drawing a vertical line
(1) between the subject and the predicate:

The Erie Canal links the Atlantic and the Great Lakes.

Spelling Rules: Silent Letters
p, *b*, *l*, *u*, *h*, *n*, and *gh*

Dictation or Journal Entry

Vocabulary:

A *meteor* is a body from space that has entered Earth's atmosphere, where it burns brightly as it falls. A *meteor* is also known as a "falling star."

A *meteorite* is a meteor that has fallen to Earth. Some *meteorites* have created large craters in Earth's surface.

The Letter *p*   The Greek language is a source of many words that contain a silent *p*. The silent *p* usually occurs before the letters *n*, *s*, and *t*.

      pneumonia   **p**salm   **p**sychology   **p**terodactyl

Other words with a silent *p* include *receipt, cupboard,* and *corps.*

The Letter *b*   Many words contain the letter *m* followed by a silent *b*.

      plum**b**   com**b**   succum**b**   clim**b**   lam**b**

Other silent *b*'s are found in the words *debt, doubt,* and *subtle.*

The Letter *l*   Many words that contain a silent *l* follow a similar pattern: an *l* followed by a consonant that makes the *l* difficult to pronounce.

      chalk   talk   walk   yolk   folk

      palm   calm   would   could   should

      calf (calves)   half (halves)

Other silent *l*'s are found in the words *colonel* and *salmon.*

The Letter *u*   A silent *u* usually follows the letter *g*. It reminds us to pronounce the *g* with a "hard" sound (*g*) rather than a "soft" sound (*j*), at either the beginning or the end of the word.

      g**u**ardian   g**u**ess   g**u**ide   plag**u**e   vag**u**e

The Letter *h*   A silent *h* usually follows *c*, *r*, or *g,* as in these words:

      sc**h**eme   ac**h**e   r**h**ombus

      ag**h**ast   g**h**ost   r**h**eumatism

An initial *h* can also be silent, as in the words ***h**onor,* ***h**our,* and ***h**eir.*

The Letters gh The letter combination *gh* is always silent when it comes before the letter *t*.

light   daughter   freight   bought

bright   taught   straight   thought

A *gh* at the end of a word can be silent as well:

weigh   thorough   though   sigh

sleigh   dough   bough   high

The Letter n Sometimes the letter *m* is followed by a silent *n*, as in these words:

column   condemn   hymn   solemn

Example Rewrite these words, circling each silent letter.

(a) dough   (b) should   (c) walk   (d) crumb

(e) ache   (f) limb   (g) through   (h) hymn

(i) would   (j) subtle   (k) psalm   (l) guard

Solution (a) **dough**   (b) **should**   (c) **walk**   (d) **crumb**

(e) **ache**   (f) **limb**   (g) **through**   (h) **hymn**

(i) **would**   (j) **subtle**   (k) **psalm**   (l) **guard**

Practice Rewrite words a–l, circling each silent letter.

a. guess   **b.** although   **c.** chorus   **d.** rhyme

e. could   **f.** calf   **g.** sight   **h.** corps

i. pneumonia   **j.** debt   **k .** tomb   **l.** yolk

For m and n, replace each blank with the correct vocabulary word from this lesson.

m. I saw a falling star, or _____ in the night sky.

n. Was that large crater caused by a _____?

Review Set 29 Choose the correct word to complete sentences 1–9.

1. Magma is molten (wood, rock, cheese) that lies beneath
(28) Earth's surface.

2. Sedimentary (rocks, people, animals) form in layers from
(27) materials deposited by water, wind, or ice.

3. By (evaporation, metamorphosis, photosynthesis) a silk
(26) worm becomes a moth.

4. To (placate, conceal, ignite) is to burn or set on fire.
(25)

5. A(n) (synonym, antonym) is a word that has the same or
(2) nearly the same meaning as another word.

6. The word *meteor* is a(n) (abstract, concrete) noun.
(11)

7. (Their, There) is ample evidence that Earth rotates on
(5, 6) (it's, its) axis.

8. Tony (do, does, did) two crossword puzzles yesterday.
(10, 18)

9. *(Has) done* is the (present, past) participle of the verb
(19) *do.*

10. Rewrite the following sentence, adding capital letters as
(26) needed: the ship's captain said, "while out at sea, i
spotted cape hatteras lighthouse, warning me of
hazardous waters ahead."

11. Replace the blank below with the singular present tense
(9) form of the underlined verb.

People <u>apply</u> for jobs. Someone _____ for a job.

12. Write each action verb in the following sentence:
(7)
A powerful beacon warns us of danger and lights our way
to safety.

13. In the following sentence, write the entire verb phrase,
(12) circling each helping verb:

Without the lighthouse, our ship might have crashed on
Diamond Shoals.

14. Write the following poem title, using correct
(25) capitalization: "the arrow and the song"

15. In the following sentence, write whether the underlined
(14) verb is present, past, or future tense: We <u>shall proceed</u> to shore cautiously.

16. Write whether the following word group is a complete
(23) sentence, a sentence fragment, or a run-on sentence:

North Carolina lies in the southeastern part of the United States.

17. Write each preposition that you find in the following
(20, 21) sentence:

After the storm, the ship sailed through Long Bay, around Cape Fear, and into Onslow Bay for supplies.

18. Use a dictionary: (a) The word *placid* is what part of
(27) speech? (b) Write its pronunciation.

19. Rewrite the following words, circling each silent letter:
(28, 29)
(a) know   (b) light   (c) limb

20. Rewrite and correct the run-on sentence below. There is
(24) more than one correct answer.

Orville and Wilbur Wright successfully flew for the first time in 1903 they departed from Kitty Hawk, North Carolina.

21. Rewrite the sentence fragment below, making a complete
(6) sentence. There is more than one correct answer.

The notorious pirate Blackbeard.

22. Write the collective noun that you find in this sentence:
(11)
A shipment of new tables arrived today.

23. Write the simple subject of the following sentence:
(3, 4)
Was this furniture crafted in North Carolina?

24. For the following sentence, write the correct form of the
(18) verb: That dreadful pirate (present of *have*) a black beard, not a red one.

25. Write the simple predicate of the following sentence:
(3, 4) Was this furniture crafted in North Carolina?

26. Rewrite the following outline, adding capital letters as needed:

    i. florida's wetlands
      a. the world's largest swamp
      b. endangered species

27. For the verb *do*, write the (a) present participle, (b) past tense, and (c) past participle.

28. Write whether the following sentence is declarative, interrogative, imperative, or exclamatory: Watch the horizon for the lighthouse.

29. For a–d, write the plural of each noun.
    (a) trout   (b) child of the King   (c) axis   (d) industry

30. Rewrite the following sentence, drawing a vertical line between the subject and the predicate:
Many ships have sunk off the coast of North Carolina.

Dictionary Information About a Word, Part 2

> **Dictation or Journal Entry**
> **Vocabulary:**
>
> *Vertebrate* means "having a backbone or spinal column." Fish, amphibians, reptiles, birds, and mammals are *vertebrate* animals.
>
> *Invertebrate* means "having no backbone; not vertebrate." Starfish, spiders, insects, and worms are *invertebrate* creatures.

We have learned that dictionaries provide the following information about a word: definitions, parts of speech, spelling, syllable division, and pronunciation. In this lesson we shall see that dictionaries also provide etymologies, field labels, synonyms, and antonyms.

Etymologies

Etymologies are word histories showing the word's original language and meaning. Usually, the dictionary's front matter explains abbreviations used to indicate the languages from which words come. The symbol < or the abbreviation *fr.* may mean "from." See examples below.

DICTIONARY ABBREVIATION	MEANING
< F	from French
< Heb-Aram	from Hebrew-Aramaic
fr. OE	from Old English
< Gr	from Classical Greek
< Heb	from Hebrew
fr. L	from Latin

Field Labels

Some dictionary words are not part of our general vocabulary but have to do with a special subject, area, or usage. These words may have **field labels** such as the ones below.

SUBJECT LABELS

Med. (medicine)	*Chem.* (chemistry)
Zool. (zoology)	*Music*
Baseball	*Comput.* (Computer Science)

AREA LABELS

Netherl. (Netherlandic)	*Scotland*
Northwest U.S.	*NGmc* (North Germanic)

USAGE LABELS

Dialect	Slang	Rare
Informal	Old-fashioned	Literary
Archaic	Obsolete	Vulgar

Synonyms and Antonyms At the end of an entry, a dictionary may list **synonyms** (SYN, words of similar meaning) and/or **antonyms** (ANT, words of opposite meaning).

Example Use a dictionary to complete the following.

(a) The word *resuscitate* comes from what language?

(b) Write the field label given to the word *pianissimo*.

(c) Write a synonym of the word *prudent*.

Solution (a) **Latin**   (b) *Music*   (c) **careful**

Practice Use a dictionary to answer a–c.

a. Write the origin of the word *fricative*.

b. Write the field label given to the word *stapes*.

c. Write an antonym of the word *forbid*.

For d and e, replace each blank with the correct vocabulary word from this lesson.

✓ d. The tiger has a backbone; it is a(n) _____ animal.

✓ e. The starfish does not have a backbone; it is a(n) _____ sea creature.

Review Set 30 Choose the correct word to complete sentences 1–8.

1. A large (meteorite, homophone, arroyo) might create a
(29) crater in Earth's surface.

2. Lava and igneous rocks form as (sediment, magma,
(28) tundra) cools.

3. (Valor, Elocution, Sediment) is matter that settles to the
(27) bottom of a liquid.

4. Metamorphosis is the process by which animals (eat, sleep, change).
(26)

5. We do not have many redheads in our family; redheads are (abundant, scarce, meteors).
(3)

6. The word *dog's* is a (plural, possessive) noun.
(13)

7. A(n) (meteorite, caldera, etymology) shows a word's original language and meaning.
(30)

8. Synonyms are words of (similar, opposite) meaning.
(30)

9. Write the past tense form of the verb *skip*.
(10)

10. Rewrite the following sentence, adding capital letters as needed: lilah asked, "have you ever experienced a north dakota blizzard?"
(26)

11. Replace the blank below with the singular present tense form of the underlined verb.
(9)

People <u>qualify</u> for jobs. Someone _____ for a job.

12. Write each action verb in the following sentence:
(7)

The cold wind stings my eyes, bites my nose, and whistles in my ears.

13. In the following sentence, write the entire verb phrase, circling each helping verb:
(12)

Trouble can teach us patience.

14. Write the following book title, using correct capitalization: *why the chicken crossed the road*
(25)

15. In the following sentence, write whether the underlined verb is present, past, or future tense: A swarm of grasshoppers <u>invaded</u> the wheat field before harvest time.
(10)

16. Write whether the following word group is a complete sentence, a sentence fragment, or a run-on sentence:
(23)

The North Dakota farmer endured a drought and a dust storm then came the grasshopper invasion.

17. Write each preposition that you find in the following
(20, 21) sentence:

At the library on Tuesday, I looked through the
encyclopedia for a picture of a North Dakota field with
sunflowers in bloom.

18. Use a dictionary: (a) The word *plateau* is what part of
(27, 30) speech? (b) Write its pronunciation. (c) Write its
etymology.

19. Rewrite the following words, circling each silent letter:
(28, 29)
(a) bridge   (b) hour   (c) talk

20. Rewrite and correct the run-on sentence below. There is
(24) more than one correct answer.

Little ground squirrels flick their tails then they dive back
into their burrows on the prairie.

21. Rewrite the sentence fragment below, making a complete
(6) sentence. There is more than one correct answer.

Growing sunflowers over ten feet tall.

22. Write the compound noun that you find in this sentence:
(13) Migrating waterfowl made temporary homes on our
pond.

23. Write the simple subject of the following sentence:
(3, 4) After the dust storm came the insects.

24. For the following sentence, write the correct form of the
(14) verb:

We (future of *harvest*) the durum wheat in September.

25. Write the simple predicate of the following sentence:
(3, 4) After the dust storm came the insects.

26. For the verb *try*, write the (a) present participle, (b) past
(19) tense, and (c) past participle.

27. Write whether the following sentence is declarative,
(2) interrogative, imperative, or exclamatory: Do I want to
ride a hundred miles in a covered wagon?

28. Rewrite the rhyme, adding capital letters as needed.
(15)

twelve pairs hanging high,
twelve knights riding by,
each knight took a pear,
and yet left a dozen there.

29. For a–d, write the plural of each noun.
(17, 22)

(a) wife   (b) spoonful   (c) key   (d) country

30. Rewrite the following sentence, drawing a vertical line
(1) between the subject and the predicate:

All the giant golden sunflowers turn their faces to the sunshine.

Linking Verbs

> **Dictation or Journal Entry**
> **Vocabulary:**
> An *asset* is something valuable or useful; an advantage. Knowing the rules of grammar is a great *asset* for a writer or a speaker.
>
> A *liability* is something that works to one's disadvantage; a handicap. Not knowing the rules of grammar was a *liability* in writing papers for science, history, and English classes.

Linking Verbs A **linking verb** "links" the subject of a sentence to the rest of the predicate. It does not show action, and it is not "helping" an action verb. Its purpose is to connect a name or description to the subject.

Woody <u>was</u> a folksinger.

In the sentence above, *was* links "Woody" with "folksinger." The word *folksinger* names Woody's occupation.

Woody <u>was</u> successful.

In the sentence above, *was* links "Woody" with "successful." The word *successful* describes Woody.

Watch Out! We must carefully examine our sentences. Some verbs can be used as either linking or action verbs, as shown in the two sentences below.

Dan <u>looks</u> happy today. (*Looks* is a linking verb. It links "Dan" with "happy.")

Dan <u>looks</u> at the mistletoe. (*Looks* is an action verb, not a linking verb. Dan is doing something.)

Common Linking Verbs Common linking verbs include all of the "to be" verbs:

is, am, are, was, were, be, being, been

The following are also common linking verbs. Memorize these:

look, feel, taste, smell, sound

seem, appear, grow, become

remain, stay

Identifying Linking Verbs To tell whether a verb is a linking verb, we replace it with a form of the verb "to be"—*is, am, are, was, were, be, being, been*, as in the example below.

Yin feels optimistic.

We replace *feels* with *is*.

Yin *is* optimistic.

Since the sentence still makes sense, we know that *feels* is a linking verb in this sentence. Now let us examine the word *feels* in the sentence below.

Yin *feels* the warmth of the sun.

We replace *feels* with *is*.

Yin *is* the warmth of the sun.

The sentence no longer makes sense, so we know that *feels* is not a linking verb in this sentence.

Example Identify and write the linking verb, if any, in each sentence.

(a) Woody Guthrie was a famous songwriter.

(b) Homesteaders seemed eager for land.

(c) Oklahoma became home for Sooners.

(d) A winter journey proved tragic.

(e) Luis looks at the Trail of Tears.

Solution (a) The linking verb *was* links "Woody Guthrie" to "songwriter."

(b) The verb *seemed* links "homesteaders" to "eager."

(c) The verb *became* links "Oklahoma" to "home."

(d) The verb *proved* links "journey" to "tragic."

(e) We replace the verb *looks* with *is*: Luis *is* the Trail of Tears. The sentence no longer makes sense, so we know that the word *looks* is not a linking verb in this sentence. There are **no linking verbs** in this sentence.

Practice a. Study the linking verbs (including the "to be" verbs) listed in this lesson. Memorize them line by line. Then say them to your teacher or to a friend.

b. Have a "linking verb contest" with yourself or with a partner: Write as many as you can from memory in one minute.

Write the linking verbs, if any, from sentences c–j.

c. Oklahoma City became the capital of Oklahoma.

c-l

d. Chisholm Trail was popular for cattle drives.

e. The tornado appears close!

f. Tulsa remains famous for oil.

g. Mistletoe seems abundant here.

h. That music sounds sad.

i. I smell a cattle ranch.

j. The cattle ranch smells pungent.

For k and l, replace each blank with the correct vocabulary word from this lesson.

k. Poor eating habits are a(n) _____ for one's health.

l. Good eating habits are a(n) _____ for one's health.

More Practice   Write each linking verb from sentences 1–10.

1. That smiley student seems optimistic.

2. Taco Treat remains the best restaurant in the area.

3. Mr. Phan stayed strong in the race.

4. The twins felt energetic after swimming in the lake.

5. Andrew appeared surprised when his little sister tasted the dog food.

6. Dog food tastes rather bland.

7. In the waiting room, I grew restless.

8. Cat food smells fishy.

9. Difficult concepts become simple with practice.

10. The person on the phone sounded friendly.

For 11–16, tell whether each verb is action or linking.

11. She <u>tastes</u> the soup.   **12.** The soup <u>tastes</u> salty.

13. He <u>sounds</u> the alarm.   **14.** It <u>sounds</u> urgent.

15. Gus <u>smells</u> the fire.   **16.** The air <u>smells</u> smoky.

✓ **Review Set 31** Choose the correct word to complete sentences 1–8.

1. Spiders, insects, and worms are (vertebrate, invertebrate)
(30) animals, for they have no backbone.

2. A meteorite is a (chasm, mesa, meteor) that has fallen to
(29) Earth.

3. (Flora, Fauna, Magma) is molten rock beneath Earth's
(28) surface.

4. Sediment is matter that settles to the bottom of a (page,
(27) liquid, basket).

5. *Optimism* and (*synonym, pessimism, metamorphosis*)
(4) are antonyms.

6. The word *safety* is a(n) (concrete, abstract) noun.
(11)

7. A linking (noun, verb) links the subject of a sentence to
(31) the rest of the predicate.

8. Antonyms are words of (similar, opposite) meaning.
(30)

9. Write the past tense form of the verb *hop.*
(10)

10. Rewrite the following sentence, adding capital letters as
(26) needed:

mr. chen said, "the famous ballerina maria tallchief was a
native american from fairfax, Oklahoma."

11. Replace the blank below with the singular present tense
(9) form of the underlined verb.

People <u>cash</u> checks. Someone _____ a check.

12. Write each action verb in the following sentence:
(7)

Miss Fortune counted her assets and considered her liabilities.

13. In the following sentence, write the entire verb phrase,
(12) circling each helping verb:

Miss Fortune might have counted more liabilities than assets.

14. Write the following song title, using correct
(25) capitalization: "america the beautiful"

15. Write the linking verb in the following sentence:
(31)

The oil grew more valuable.

16. Write whether the following word group is a complete
(23) sentence, a sentence fragment, or a run-on sentence:

Oklahoma is shaped like a pan.

17. Write each preposition that you find in the following
(20, 21) sentence:

Thousands of Native Americans died during their relocation to Oklahoma.

18. Use a dictionary: (a) The word *livid* is what part of
(27, 30) speech? (b) Write its pronunciation. (c) Write its etymology.

19. Rewrite the following words, circling each silent letter:
(28, 29)
(a) whose   (b) sigh   (c) folk

20. Rewrite and correct the run-on sentence below. There is
(24) more than one correct answer.

Pam lives in Oklahoma City her husband works in the oil fields.

21. Rewrite the sentence fragment below, making a complete
(6) sentence. There is more than one correct answer.

To escape the tornado.

22. Write the collective noun that you find in this sentence:
(11)

Mr. Cua presented a spray of red roses to Anna.

23. Write the simple subject of the following sentence:
(3, 4)

The Sooners claimed their land early.

24. For the following sentence, write the correct form of the
(18) verb:

Byron (present of *fry*) bananas for lunch.

25. Write the simple predicate of the following sentence:
(3, 4)

The Sooners claimed their land early.

26. For the verb *worry*, write the (a) present participle, (b)
(19) past tense, and (c) past participle.

27. Write whether the following sentence is declarative,
(2) interrogative, imperative, or exclamatory:

Here comes a twister!

28. Rewrite the outline below, adding capital letters as
(26) needed.

    i. resources of oklahoma
      a. oil
      b. cattle
      c. wheat

29. For a–d, write the plural of each noun.
(17, 22)

    (a) sheep   (b) sister-in-law   (c) donkey   (d) liability

30. Rewrite the following sentence, drawing a vertical line
(1) between the subject and the predicate:

Oklahoma's twisters must have surprised the settlers.

Diagramming Simple Subjects and Simple Predicates

> **Dictation or Journal Entry**
>
> **Vocabulary:**
>
> The Greek root _pan_ means "all."
>
> A _panacea_ is a remedy for all diseases or evils; a cure-all. More money is not a _panacea_ for our social problems.
>
> _Pan American_ means "including or relating to all the countries or people of North, Central, and South America." A _Pan American_ peace-keeping organization meets in Washington, D.C.

We have learned to find the simple subject and simple predicate of a sentence. Now we will learn how to **diagram** our sentence according to this pattern:

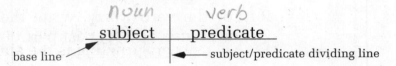

The subject and predicate sit on a horizontal "base line" and are separated by a vertical line that passes through the base line. Below is a **simple subject and simple predicate diagram** of this sentence.

Egbert tripped on his shoelace.

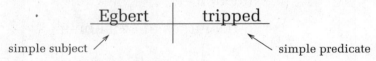

As you can see above, we place the simple subject on the left and the simple predicate on the right. We separate the two with a vertical line.

Example 1 Diagram the simple subject and predicate of the following sentence:

The sun shines in Egbert's eyes.

Solution The "who or what" (subject) of the sentence is "sun." The action words connected with sun (predicate) is "shines."

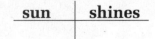

Example 2 Diagram the simple subject and predicate of the following sentence:

Egbert is a good student.

Solution We refer to the list of helping verbs and linking verbs in the previous lessons. "Is" is a linking verb in this sentence. We ask ourselves, "Who or what *is*?" The answer is the subject, Egbert.

Egbert	is

Example 3 Diagram the simple subject and predicate of this sentence:

Egbert's stomach has been growling.

Solution We recall our list of helping verbs and see that the verb phrase has been growling is the simple predicate telling what *stomach* (subject) has been doing.

stomach	has been growling

✓Practice Diagram the simple subject and the simple predicate of sentences a–d.

a. Big trees cover nearly half of Oregon.

b. Oregon's hazelnuts taste delicious.

c. Spotted owls hoot through the night.

d. Do you fish for salmon?

For e–g, replace each blank with the correct vocabulary word from this lesson.

e. The _____ group included people from North, Central, and South America.

f. _____ is a Greek root meaning "all."

g. Immunizations help to prevent disease, but they are not a _____.

Review Set 32 Choose the correct word to complete sentences 1–8.

1. *Liability* and *asset* are (synonyms, antonyms).
(31)

2. A(n) (vertebrate, invertebrate, valiant) creature has no backbone.
(30)

3. A (meteor, magma, caldera) is also known as a "falling star."
(29)

4. A caldera is a large (river, ocean, depression) or basin in a volcano.
(28)

5. (*There*, *Their*) means "at or in that place."
(5)

6. The word *coaches* is a (plural, possessive) noun.
(13)

7. In a sentence diagram, the subject goes on the (left, right).
(32)

8. In a sentence diagram, the predicate goes on the (left, right).
(32)

9. Write the past tense form of the verb *mop.*
(10)

10. Rewrite the following sentence, adding capital letters as needed:
(26)

    jamaica king said, "the people of oregon care about their environment."

11. Replace the blank below with the singular present tense form of the underlined verb.
(9)

    Cooks <u>mash</u> potatoes. Herbert _____ potatoes.

12. Write each action verb in the following sentence:
(7)

    Strong winds blast the shore and create huge waves.

13. In the following sentence, write the entire verb phrase, circling each helping verb:
(12)

    Loggers have been banned from owl territory.

14. Write the following story title, using correct capitalization: "chased by the trail"
(25)

15. Write the linking verb in the following sentence:
(31) The rare spotted owl feels comfortable in Oregon's thick, dark woods.

16. Write whether the following word group is a complete
(23) sentence, a sentence fragment, or a run-on sentence:

Having the nickname "Beaver State."

17. Write each preposition that you find in the following
(20, 21) sentence:

Since 1990 the state has banned logging within two thousand acres of a spotted owl's nest.

18. Use a dictionary: (a) The word *serene* is what part of
(27, 30) speech? (b) Write its pronunciation. (c) Write its etymology.

19. Rewrite the following words, circling each silent letter:
(28, 29)
   (a) who   (b) high   (c) guard

20. Rewrite and correct the run-on sentence below. There is
(24) more than one correct answer.

Oregon's Columbia River has a strong current it powers plants that provide electricity.

21. From memory, write the linking verbs listed in Lesson
(31) 31.

22. Write the compound noun that you find in this sentence:
(13)
A lonely lighthouse stands on the rocky coast.

23. For the following sentence, write the correct form of the
(10) verb:

We (past of *fry*) bananas for lunch.

24. For the verb *carry*, write the (a) present participle, (b)
(19) past tense, and (c) past participle.

25. Write whether the following sentence is declarative,
(2) interrogative, imperative, or exclamatory:

Do not disturb the spotted owls.

26. Rewrite the following lines of poetry, adding capital letters as needed:

(15)

elizabeth, elspeth, betsy, and bess,
they all went together to see a bird's nest;

27. For a–d, write the plural of each noun.

(17, 22)

(a) box   (b) mugful   (c) Tuesday   (d) ability

Diagram the simple subject and simple predicate of sentences 28–30.

28. There go the pirates!

(32)

29. The hoodlum with a patch over his eye looks scary.

(32)

30. Has that pirate boarded the ship?

(32)

Spelling Rules: Suffixes, Part 1

Dictation or Journal Entry
Vocabulary:
Dispensable means "unessential or unimportant." I shall eliminate *dispensable* items from my backpack so that it won't be so heavy.

Indispensable means "absolutely necessary or essential." Proper nutrition is *indispensable* for good health.

As we will learn later, we use the suffixes *-er* and *-est* to form comparison adjectives and adverbs. In this lesson, we will examine some rules for adding suffixes. As always, we check the dictionary if we are not sure how a word is spelled.

Words Ending in *y*   A final *y* usually changes to *i* when suffixes (except for the suffix *-ing*) are added:

deny + able = deniable

modify + er = modifier

fry + ed = fried

pity + ful = pitiful

bury + s = buries

worry + some = worrisome

ready + ly = readily

dry + est = driest

glory + ous = glorious

happy + ness = happiness

funny + er = funnier

bounty + ful = bountiful

but: denying, modifying, frying, pitying, burying, worrying, readying, drying, glorying

When preceded by a vowel, the final *y* does not change to *i* when a suffix is added.

toy + ing = toying

play + ed = played

enjoy + able = enjoyable

gray + est = grayest

Exceptions   Important exceptions include the following:

$$lay + ed = laid$$
$$pay + ed = paid$$
$$say + ed = said$$
$$day + ly = daily$$

Example 1   Add suffixes to these words ending in *y*.

(a) replay + ed = _____

(b) crazy + er = _____

(c) messy + ness = _____

(d) plenty + ful = _____

(e) happy + ly = _____

Solution   (a) replay + ed = **replayed** (The *y* is preceded by a vowel, so it does not change to an *i*.)

(b) crazy + er = **crazier** (The final *y* usually changes to *i* when suffixes are added.)

(c) messy + ness = **messiness**

(d) plenty + ful = **plentiful**

(e) happy + ly = **happily**

Words Ending in a Silent *e*   We usually drop the silent *e* before adding a suffix beginning with a vowel (including the suffix -*y*).

$$fame + ous = famous$$
$$wire + y = wiry$$
$$wave + y = wavy$$
$$come + ing = coming$$
$$separate + tion = separation$$
$$live + able = livable$$
$$blue + ish = bluish$$
$$sense + ible = sensible$$

However, we keep the final *e* when we add a suffix beginning with a consonant.

$$encourage + ment = encouragement$$
$$like + ness = likeness$$
$$tire + less = tireless$$
$$rare + ly = rarely$$
$$shame + ful = shameful$$

Exceptions Exceptions to the rules above include the following words:

$$judge + ment = judgment$$
$$argue + ment = argument$$
$$wise + dom = wisdom$$
$$gentle + ly = gently$$
$$true + ly = truly$$

Also, when adding *-ous* or *-able* to a word ending in *ge* or *ce*, we keep the final *e* to indicate the soft sound of the *c* (as in *celery*) or *g* (as in *giant*).

$$manage + able = manageable$$
$$trace + able = traceable$$
$$change + able = changeable$$
$$outrage + ous = outrageous$$
$$courage + ous = courageous$$

Example 2 Add suffixes to these words ending in a silent *e*.

(a) conceive + able = _____

(b) please + ing = _____

(c) cease + ing = _____

(d) safe + ly = _____

(e) brave + ly = _____

(f) manage + able = _____

(g) gentle + ly = _____

Solution (a) conceive + able = **conceivable** (We usually drop the silent *e* when the suffix begins with a vowel.)

(b) please + ing = **pleasing**

(c) cease + ing = **ceasing**

(d) safe + ly = **safely** (We usually keep the final *e* when the suffix begins with a consonant.)

(e) brave + ly = **bravely**

(f) manage + able = **manageable** (We keep the silent *e* after the *g* to retain the soft *g* sound.)

(g) gentle + ly = **gently** (This is an exception to the rule.)

√ **Practice** Add suffixes to words a–k.

a. beauty + ful = _____

b. gloomy + ness = _____

c. merry + est = _____

d. cheery + ly = _____

e. plate + ful = _____

f. bite + ing = _____

g. live + ly = _____

h. drive + er = _____

i. knowledge + able = _____

j. rate + ing = _____

k. clue + less = _____

For l and m, replace each blank with the correct vocabulary word from this lesson.

l. Fresh water is _____ for survival.

m. We can do without _____ items.

Review Set 33

Choose the correct word to complete sentences 1–6.

1. The Greek root (*pan, geo-, dia-*) means "all."
(32)

2. A liability is a(n) (advantage, disadvantage, vertebrate).
(31)

3. Vertebrate animals have a (mother-in-law, backbone, disease).
(30)

4. One might see a meteor in the (ocean, sky, kitchen).
(29)

5. (Its, It's) snowing!
(6)

6. The word *panacea* is a(n) (concrete, abstract) noun.
(11)

7. Add suffixes to the following words ending in *y*:
(33) (a) rely + able   (b) play + ing

8. Add suffixes to the following words ending in a silent *e*:
(33) (a) love + ing   (b) care + ful

9. Write the past tense form of the verb *deny*.
(10)

10. Rewrite the following sentence, adding capital letters as needed:
(26)

miss fortune said, "i lost my purse in pennsylvania."

11. Replace the blank below with the singular present tense form of the underlined verb.
(9)

Kids <u>brush</u> their teeth. Lori _____ her teeth.

12. Write each action verb in the following sentence:
(7)

The keystone sits in the center of an arch and binds the other stones together.

13. In the following sentence, write the entire verb phrase, circling each helping verb:
(12)

Miss Fortune must have misplaced her purse.

14. Write the following title to Shakespeare's play, using correct capitalization: "the merchant of venice"
(25)

15. Write the linking verb in the following sentence:
(31)

Pittsburg remains famous for its steel.

16. Write whether the following word group is a complete sentence, a sentence fragment, or a run-on sentence:
(23)

William Penn believed in religious freedom he treated Native Americans with respect.

17. Write each preposition that you find in the following sentence:
(20, 21)

Without the keystone, the other stones of the arch will not hold together.

18. Use a dictionary: (a) The word *bouquet* is what part of speech? (b) Write its pronunciation. (c) Write its etymology.
(27, 30)

19. Rewrite the following words, circling each silent letter:
(28, 29)
(a) walk   (b) design   (c) knot

20. Rewrite and correct the run-on sentence below. There is more than one correct answer.
(24)

On February 2, Punxsutawney Phil saw his shadow he predicts six more weeks of winter.

21. From memory, write the linking verbs listed in Lesson 31.
(31)

22. Write the collective noun that you find in this sentence:
(11)
William Penn founded his colony in 1682.

23. For the following sentence, write the correct form of the verb:
(10)

Elle (past of *grin*) at me.

24. For the verb *marry*, write the (a) present participle, (b) past tense, and (c) past participle.
(19)

25. Write whether the following sentence is declarative, interrogative, imperative, or exclamatory:
(2)

Why do we call Pennsylvania the Keystone State?

26. Rewrite the following outline, adding capital letters as needed:
(26)

    i. pennsylvania's agriculture
      a. dairy products
      b. fresh vegetables
      c. eggs

27. For a–d, write the plural of each noun.
(17, 22)
    (a) fax   (b) man   (c) piccolo   (d) duty

Diagram the simple subject and simple predicate of sentences 28–30.

28. Here come my friends!
(32)

29. That soccer player in the red jersey seems happy.
(32)

30. Did her team win the game?
(32)

Spelling Rules: Suffixes, Part 2

> **Dictation or Journal Entry**
> **Vocabulary:**
> The Latin word *clamare* means "to shout or cry out."
>
> A *clamor* is a loud outcry, or an uproar. From far away we could hear the hungry monkeys making a *clamor* for food.
>
> A *proclamation* is a public announcement. Everyone heard the king's *proclamation* regarding the new laws.

Doubling Final Consonants

When a one-syllable word ends with a single consonant preceded by a single vowel, we double the final consonant before adding a suffix that begins with a vowel.

$$drop + ed = dropped$$
$$sin + er = sinner$$
$$trip + ing = tripping$$
$$big + est = biggest$$
$$run + y = runny$$

Exceptions include the words *bus* (bused), *sew* (sewing), *bow* (bowed), and *tax* (taxing).

When a word of two or more syllables ends with a single consonant preceded by a single vowel, we double the final consonant if the word is accented (stressed) on the last syllable.

$$forget + ing = forgetting$$
$$repel + ed = repelled$$
$$submit + ed = submitted$$

Do Not Double

We **do not** double the final consonant of any of the words described above (words ending with a single consonant preceded by a single vowel) when adding a suffix that begins with a consonant.

$$sad + ly = sadly$$
$$spot + less = spotless$$
$$mad + ness = madness$$

We **do not** double the final consonant if it is preceded by two vowels or another consonant:

$$rain + ed = rained$$
$$warm + ly = warmly$$
$$broad + est = broadest$$

$$\text{dish} + \text{ful} = \text{dishful}$$

Example Add suffixes to these words.

(a) chop + ing = _____

(b) commit + ed = _____

(c) bad + ly = _____

(d) pain + less = _____

(e) luck + y = _____

Solution (a) chop + ing = **chopping** (We double the final consonant when we add a suffix beginning with a vowel.)

(b) commit + ed = **committed** (When a two-syllable word is accented on the final syllable, we double the final consonant if it is preceded by a single vowel.)

(c) bad + ly = **badly** (When the suffix begins with a consonant, we do not double the final consonant before adding the suffix.)

(d) pain + less = **painless** (A final consonant preceded by two vowels is not doubled.)

(e) luck + y = **lucky** (A final consonant preceded by another consonant is not doubled.)

Practice Add suffixes to words a–e.

a. tap + ed = _____

b. stop + ing = _____

c. glad + ly = _____

d. benefit + ed = _____

e. flat + ness = _____

For f–h, replace each blank with the correct vocabulary word from this lesson.

f. The governor will issue a _____ explaining his new public policies.

g. Angry protestors created a _____ in the streets.

h. _____ is a Latin word meaning "to shout or cry out."

√ **Review Set 34** Choose the correct word to complete sentences 1–6.

1. *Indispensable* and *essential* are (synonyms, antonyms, (33) peninsulas).

2. (North, South, Pan) American refers to all countries of (32) North, Central, and South America.

3. A(n) (asset, liability, tributary) works to one's (31) disadvantage.

4. *Invertebrate* means "having no (teeth, backbone, eyes)." (30)

5. An (archipelago, estuary, isthmus) is a group or chain of (9) many islands.

6. The word *porcupine's* is a (plural, possessive) noun. (13)

7. Add suffixes to the following words: (33) (a) glory + ous   (b) scare + y

8. Add suffixes to the following words: (34) (a) win + ing   (b) glad + ly

9. Write the past tense form of the verb *clap*. (10)

10. Rewrite the following sentence, adding capital letters as (26) needed:

"no," said miss fortune, "i did not leave my purse at a bus station in philadelphia."

11. Replace the blank below with the singular present tense (9) form of the underlined verb.

Kids <u>rush</u> to school. Nicholas _____ to school.

12. Write each action verb in the following sentence: (7)

Roger Williams left Massachusetts and started the colony of Providence for religious freedom.

13. In the following sentence, write the entire verb phrase, (12) circling each helping verb:

Nelda has been fishing off the coast of Rhode Island.

14. Write the following book title, using correct
(25) capitalization: *gone with the wind*

15. Write the linking verb in the following sentence:
(31)
Rhode Island looks very small on a United States map.

16. Write whether the following word group is a complete
(23) sentence, a sentence fragment, or a run-on sentence:

Rhode Island, the smallest state in area.

17. Write each preposition that you find in the following
(20, 21) sentence:

Near the southern border of Rhode Island lies the
Narragansett Indian Reservation.

18. Use a dictionary: (a) The word *enclave* is what part of
(27, 30) speech? (b) Write its pronunciation. (c) Write its
etymology.

19. Rewrite the following words, circling each silent letter:
(28, 29)
    (a) wrote   (b) edge   (c) hymn

20. Rewrite and correct the sentence fragment below, making
(6) a complete sentence. There is more than one correct
answer.

The state of Rhode Island, the smallest in area.

21. From memory, write the linking verbs listed in
(31) Lesson 31.

22. Write the compound noun that you find in this sentence:
(13)
Tugboats pulled the barge through the busy harbor.

23. For the following sentence, write the correct form of the
(9) verb:

Elle (present of *grin*) at everyone.

24. For the verb *hurry*, write the (a) present participle, (b)
(19) past tense, and (c) past participle.

Stop

25. Write whether the following sentence is declarative,
(2) interrogative, imperative, or exclamatory:

Providence is the capital of Rhode Island.

26. Rewrite the following lines of poetry, adding capital
(15) letters as needed:

a wise old owl sat in an oak;
the more he heard, the less he spoke;
the less he spoke, the more he heard;
why aren't we all like that wise old bird?

27. For a–d, write the plural of each noun.
(17, 22) (a) tax   (b) woman   (c) letter of reference   (d) duty

Diagram the simple subject and simple predicate of sentences
28–30.

28. Over the moon leaps the cow.
(32)

29. The cow high in the sky appears frantic.
(32)

30. Will the cow return safely to Earth?
(32)

Spelling Rules: *ie* or *ei*

Dictation or Journal Entry
Vocabulary:

Kin is a noun meaning "one's whole family; one's relatives." Most of his *kin* live in Central America.

Akin means "related by blood, or of the same family." Your uncle and my brother-in-law are *akin*, for they have the same grandmother. The mouse is *akin* to the rat. *Akin* also means "similar." Honesty and integrity are *akin*.

To determine whether to use *ie* or *ei* to make the long *e* sound in a word, we recall this rhyme:

Use *i* before *e*
Except after *c*
Or when sounded like *ay*
As in *neighbor* and *weigh*.

USE *i* BEFORE *e*:

believe   yield   shield   brief   view

chief   priest   niece   relieve   achieve

EXCEPT AFTER *c*:

ceiling   receive   conceit

deceive   conceive   perceive

OR WHEN SOUNDED LIKE *ay*:

neighbor   weigh   freight   reign

Exceptions   The following words are exceptions to the rule. We must memorize them.

either   neither   leisure   seize

ancient   height   forfeit   weird

Example   Write the words that are spelled correctly.

(a) yeild, yield   (b) beleive, believe

(c) cieling, ceiling   (d) receipt, reciept

(e) nieghbor, neighbor   (f) wiegh, weigh

Solution   (a) **yield** (Use *i* before *e*.)   (b) **believe**

(c) **ceiling** (Except after *c*.)   (d) **receipt**

(e) **neighbor** (Or when sounded as *ay*.)

(f) **weigh**

✓**Practice**   For a–f, write the words that are spelled correctly.

    a. achieve, acheive   **b.** peice, piece

    c. recieve, receive   **d.** conciet, conceit

    e. freight, frieght   **f.** fiegn, feign

For g and h, replace each blank with the correct vocabulary word from this lesson.

    g. One's relatives are one's _____.

    h. _____ means "similar, or of the same family."

✓**Review Set 35**   Choose the correct word to complete sentences 1–6.

    1. The mayor might issue a (panacea, caldera, proclamation)
    (34) to keep people informed.

    2. A(n) (invertebrate, dispensable, indispensable) item is
    (33) essential.

    3. The Greek root *pan* means "(fire, all, table)."
    (32)

    4. A(n) (asset, vertebrate, liability) is something valuable or
    (31) useful; an advantage.

    5. (Flora, Fauna, Latitude) refers to plants in a particular
    (10) region.

    6. The word *porcupine* is a(n) (abstract, concrete) noun.
    (11)

    7. Add suffixes to the following words:
    (33) (a) fly + er   (b) come + ing

    8. Add suffixes to the following words:
    (34) (a) shop + ed   (b) warm + est

    9. For a and b, write the word that is spelled correctly.
    (35) (a) beleive, believe   (b) receive, recieve

10. Rewrite the following sentence, adding capital letters as
(26) needed:

miss fortune asked, "have you seen my purse?"

11. Replace the blank below with the singular present tense
(9) form of the underlined verb.

People <u>express</u> joy. Abdul _____ joy.

12. Write each action verb in the following sentence:
(7)
The Rhode Island Red hen clucked and laid an egg.

13. In the following sentence, write the entire verb phrase,
(12) circling each helping verb:

People in Charleston, South Carolina, have been weaving
sweetgrass baskets for over three hundred years.

14. Write the following story title, using correct
(25) capitalization: "king arthur and the round table"

15. Write the linking verb in the following sentence:
(31)
The cotton gin proved helpful to farmers.

16. Write whether the following word group is a complete
(23) sentence, a sentence fragment, or a run-on sentence:

South Carolina's shape is like a piece of pie.

17. Write each preposition that you find in the following
(20, 21) sentence:

After the Civil War, South Carolina's economy suffered
through hard times.

18. Use a dictionary: (a) The word *dictate* is what part of
(27, 30) speech? (b) Write its pronunciation. (c) Write its
etymology.

19. Rewrite the following words, circling each silent letter:
(28, 29)
(a) comb   (b) glisten   (c) psalm

20. Rewrite and correct the run-on sentence below. There is
(24) more than one correct answer.

South Carolina is the Palmetto State its capital is
Columbia.

21. From the following list, write the word that is *not* a
(31) linking verb: is, am, far, was, were, be, being, been.

22. Write the collective noun that you find in this sentence:
(11)

A flock of Carolina wrens just flew into that palmetto tree.

23. For the following sentence, write the correct form of the
(14) verb:

Elle (future of *smile*) at the camera.

24. For the verb *move*, write the (a) present participle, (b)
(19) past tense, and (c) past participle.

25. Write whether the following sentence is declarative,
(2) interrogative, imperative, or exclamatory:

The Civil War began at Fort Sumter in Charleston Harbor.

26. Rewrite the following poem, adding capital letters as
(15) needed:

use *i* before *e*
except after *c*
or when sounded like *ay*
as in *neighbor* and *weigh*.

27. For a–d, write the plural of each noun.
(17, 22)
(a) inch (b) deer (c) son-in-law (d) dairy

Diagram the simple subject and simple predicate of sentences 28–30.

28. First comes the silly cow.
(32)

29. The little dog's laugh sounds hysterical.
(32)

30. Does the dish really run away with the spoon?
(32)

Phrases and Clauses

> **Dictation or Journal Entry**
> **Vocabulary:**
> *Avarice* is greed for wealth. *Avarice* caused the unkind queen to raise taxes.
>
> *Avaricious* means "greedy." The *avaricious* queen wants more gold and more precious jewels.

Phrases

[handwritten: Not both]

A **phrase** is a group of words used as a single word in a sentence. A phrase may contain nouns and verbs, but it does not have both a subject and a predicate. Below are some phrases.

> aboard the ship
> in addition to the gift
> may have docked
> during the night
> might have asked

Clauses

[handwritten: subject & predicate]

A **clause** is a group of words with a subject and a predicate. In the clauses below, we have italicized the simple subjects and underlined the simple predicates.

> before the *game* began
> as *you* may know
> but *they* claim innocence
> for the *baseball* flies into left field
> (*you*) Look up!

Example 1 Tell whether each group of words is a phrase or a clause.

(a) when Nashville became famous

(b) inside the mansion

(c) along the ridge of the Smoky Mountains

(d) before you called

(e) Watch out!

Solution (a) This group of words is a **clause.** It has both a subject (Nashville) and a predicate (became).

(b) This group of words is a **phrase.** It does not have a subject or predicate.

(c) This is a **phrase**. It has no subject or predicate.

(d) This is a **clause**. Its subject is *you*; its predicate is <u>called</u>.

(e) This is a **clause**. We remember that the subject, *you*, of an imperative sentence is understood. (*You*) <u>Watch</u> out!

Every complete sentence has at least one clause. Some sentences have more than one clause. We have italicized the simple subjects and underlined the simple predicates in each clause of the sentence below. Notice that it contains three clauses (three subject and predicate combinations).

Before *I* <u>went</u> to Nashville, but after *I* <u>wrote</u> the song, *I* <u>bought</u> the guitar.

Below, we have diagrammed the simple subjects and simple predicates of each clause from the sentence above.

Before I went to Nashville,	I	went

but after I wrote the song,	I	wrote

I bought the guitar.	I	bought

Example 2   Diagram the simple subjects and simple predicates of the clauses in this sentence:

The star sang popular rock-and-roll songs until his untimely death ended his career.

Solution   We examine the sentence and find that there are two clauses:

1. The *star* <u>sang</u> popular rock-and-roll songs
2. until his untimely *death* <u>ended</u> his career

We diagram the first clause: | **star** | **sang** |
|---|---|

We diagram the second clause: | **death** | **ended** |
|---|---|

✓ **Practice**   For a–d, tell whether the group of words is a phrase or a clause.

   a. since she went to Nashville

   b. regarding country and western music

c. then you can come home

d. after studying Tennessee

Diagram each simple subject and simple predicate in clauses e–g.

e. before the concert began

f. but they sang off key

g. for David Crockett remains King of the Wild Frontier

For h and i, replace each blank with the correct vocabulary word from this lesson.

h. *Greedy* and _____ have the same meaning.

i. *Greed* and _____ are synonyms.

✓**Review Set 36** Choose the correct word to complete sentences 1–6.

1. *Kin* is a noun meaning "one's whole (enchilada, family, city)."
(35)

2. A proclamation is a public (telephone, announcement, beach).
(34)

3. (*Dispensable, Panacea, Indispensable*) means "unessential or unimportant."
(33)

4. A panacea is a remedy for (some, no, all) diseases or evils.
(32)

5. (There, Their) were four little sparrows in the nest.
(5)

6. The word *porcupines* is a (plural, possessive) noun.
(13)

7. Add suffixes to the following words:
(33)
(a) ready + ly   (b) play + er

8. Add suffixes to the following words:
(34)
(a) big + est   (b) wish + ful

9. For a and b, write the word that is spelled correctly.
(35)
(a) chief, cheif   (b) cieling, ceiling

10. Rewrite the following sentence, adding capital letters as needed:
(26)

the docent at graceland said, "here is mr. presley's study."

11. Replace the blank below with the singular present tense form of the underlined verb.
(9)

Men <u>press</u> buttons. A man _____ a button.

12. Write whether the following word group is a phrase or a clause: if you follow directions
(36)

13. In the following sentence, write the entire verb phrase, circling each helping verb:
(12)

Elvis's car collection might have impressed some fans.

14. Rewrite the following song title, using correct capitalization: "the hawaiian wedding song"
(25)

15. Write the linking verb in the following sentence:
(31)

Memphis, Tennessee, became the home of rock-and-roll music.

16. Write whether the following word group is a complete sentence, a sentence fragment, or a run-on sentence:
(23)

In Tennessee, Nashville is famous for country and western music Memphis is known for rock-and-roll.

17. Write each preposition that you find in the following sentence:
(20, 21)

Stp

The road winds around the mountain, under a bridge, and through a long tunnel.

18. Use a dictionary: (a) The word *digraph* is what part of speech? (b) Write its pronunciation. (c) Write its etymology.
(27, 30)

19. Rewrite the following words, circling each silent letter:
(28, 29)

(a) knee   (b) scent   (c) honor

20. Rewrite and correct the following sentence fragment, making a complete sentence.
(6)

to explore deep, dark caves

21. From the following list, write the word that is *not* a linking verb: look, feel, taste, smell, pound, seem, appear.
(31)

22. Write the compound noun that you find in this sentence:
(13)

We can wear sunglasses to protect our eyes.

23. For the following sentence, write the correct form of the verb:
(14)

I (future of *smile*) for the photographer.

24. For the verb *study*, write the (a) present participle, (b) past tense, and (c) past participle.
(19)

25. Write whether the following sentence is declarative, interrogative, imperative, or exclamatory:
(2)

Who is King of the Wild Frontier?

26. Rewrite the following outline, adding capital letters as needed:
(26)

    i. animal husbandry in tennessee
      a. poultry
      b. pigs
      c. horses

27. For a–d, write the plural of each noun.
(17, 22)

(a) ranch   (b) cattle   (c) church mouse   (d) diary

28. Diagram the simple subject and simple predicate of each clause in the following sentence: Van will sing if you will play the guitar.
(36)

Diagram the simple subject and simple predicate of sentences 29–30.

29. Away runs the dish.
(32)

30. Catch that runaway dish!
(32)

Diagramming a Direct Object

Finding the Direct Object

A **direct object** follows an *action verb* and tells who or what receives the action.

Texas's football team won a big game.

action verb   direct object

We can answer these three questions to find the direct object of a sentence:

1. What is the verb in the sentence?

2. Is it an *action verb*?

3. Who or what receives the action? (direct object)

We will follow the steps above to find the direct object of this sentence:

A gardener plants bluebonnets.

QUESTION 1: What is the verb?
ANSWER: The verb is "plants."

QUESTION 2: Is it an *action verb*?
ANSWER: Yes.

QUESTION 3: Who or what receives the action?
ANSWER: *Bluebonnets* are "planted."

Therefore, "bluebonnets" is the direct object.

Example 1 Follow the procedure above to find the direct object of this sentence:

An armadillo crosses the road.

Solution We answer the questions as follows:

QUESTION 1: What is the verb?
ANSWER: The verb is "crosses."

QUESTION 2: Is it an *action verb*?
ANSWER: Yes.

QUESTION 3: Who or what receives the action?
ANSWER: The *road* receives the "crossing."

Therefore, **road** is the direct object.

Example 2 Answer the three questions above to find the direct object of this sentence:

Austin is the capital of Texas.

Solution We answer the questions as follows:

QUESTION 1: What is the verb?
ANSWER: The verb is "is."

QUESTION 2: Is it an *action verb*?
ANSWER: No. "Is" is a linking verb.

Therefore, this sentence has **no direct object.**

Diagramming the Direct Object Below is a diagram of the simple subject, simple predicate, and direct object of this sentence.

A gardener planted bluebonnets.

gardener	planted	bluebonnets.
(subject)	(verb)	(direct object)

Notice that a vertical line after the action verb indicates a direct object.

Example 3 Diagram the simple subject, simple predicate, and direct object of this sentence:

An armadillo crosses the road.

armadillo	crosses	road
(subject)	(verb)	(direct object)

Practice For a–d, write the direct object, if there is one, in each sentence.

a. Many Texans eat chili.

b. Cattle and oil are famous symbols of Texas.

                   twirls
c. A rancher ~~is twirling~~ a lasso.

Diagram the simple subject, simple predicate, and direct object of sentences d and e.

✓ **d.** Many Texans eat chili.

              twirls

✓ **e.** A rancher ~~is twirling~~ a lasso.

For f and g, replace each blank with the correct vocabulary word from this lesson.

✓ **f.** The avaricious queen's many possessions became an _____, for she did not have room to store them.

✓ **g.** The old, squeaky bicycle might _____ the cyclist in her race.

Review Set 37

Choose the correct word to complete sentences 1–6.

1. (Panacea, Asset, Avarice) is greed.
(36)

2. Leopards and tigers are (optimistic, pessimistic, akin), for both are cats.
(35)

3. The Latin word (*placare*, *ignis*, *clamare*) means "to shout or cry out."
(34)

4. *Dispensable* means "(essential, unessential, necessary)."
(33)

5. A(n) (estuary, peninsula, meridian) is a body of land almost entirely surrounded by water.
(11)

6. The word *avarice* is a(n) (abstract, concrete) noun.
(11)

7. Add suffixes to the following words:
(33)
    (a) modify + er   (b) sense + ible

8. Add suffixes to the following words:
(34)
    (a) fun + y   (b) mad + ness

9. For a and b, write the word that is spelled correctly.
(35)
    (a) brief, breif   (b) decieve, deceive

10. Rewrite the following sentence, adding capital letters as needed:
(26)

a newscaster reported, "oil production increased in texas this year."

11. Replace the blank below with the singular present tense form of the underlined verb.
(9)

Cows <u>munch</u> hay. A cow _____ hay.

12. Write whether the following word group is a phrase or a clause: for the seventy-seventh time today
(36)

13. In the following sentence, write the entire verb phrase, circling each helping verb:
(12)

Lucas could have lassoed the longhorn.

14. Write the following poem title, using correct capitalization: "the children's hour"
(25)

15. Write the linking verb in the following sentence:
(31)

Alba grew confident in grammar.

16. Write whether the following word group is a complete sentence, a sentence fragment, or a run-on sentence:
(23)

The Johnson Space Center is located in Texas.

17. Write each preposition that you find in the following sentence:
(20, 21)

Spread butter on sliced bread and sprinkle it with cheese.

18. Use a dictionary: (a) The word *couplet* is what part of speech? (b) Write its pronunciation. (c) Write its etymology.
(27,30)

19. Rewrite the following words, circling each silent letter:
(28, 29)
   (a) badge   (b) receipt   (c) thought

20. Rewrite and correct the run-on sentence below. There is more than one correct answer.
(24)

The frog leaped from the water it landed on my shoe.

21. From the following list, write the word that is *not* a linking verb: sound, seem, disappear, grow, remain, stay.
(31)

22. Write the collective noun that you find in this sentence:
(11)

A herd of longhorn cattle grazed near the Alamo.

23. For the following sentence, write the correct form of the
(10) verb:

Jenny (past of *rip*) open the package.

24. For the verb *rip*, write the (a) present participle, (b) past
(19) tense, and (c) past participle.

25. Write whether the following sentence is declarative,
(2) interrogative, imperative, or exclamatory:

Wow, this Texas cheese bread is delicious!

26. Rewrite the following lines of poetry, adding capital
(15) letters as needed:

grammar rules are fun to learn,
but an *A* is hard to earn.

27. For a–d, write the plural of each noun.
(17, 22)
(a) roach   (b) solo   (c) teaspoonful   (d) library

28. Diagram the simple subject and simple predicate of each
(36) clause in the following sentence: Throughout the day,
Van has been singing, and Jan has been playing the
guitar.

Diagram the simple subject, simple predicate, and direct
object of sentences 29–30.

29. Robert is reading a novel.
(32, 37)

30. Has Christie found her accordion yet?
(32, 37)

Capitalization: People Titles, Family Words, and School Subjects

Dictation or Journal Entry

Vocabulary:

To *exalt* is to praise or glorify. An arrogant king *exalts* himself.

To *humiliate* is to lower the pride or dignity of; to shame or embarrass. Discussing the king's former mistakes might *humiliate* him.

We continue to learn about capitalization. We have learned that proper nouns require capital letters and that common nouns are capitalized when they are a part of a proper noun. We also capitalize parts of an outline, the first word of a sentence, the first word of every line of poetry, the pronoun *I*, the first word in a direct quotation, and the important words in titles. Now we will add more capitalization rules.

Titles Used with Names of People

Titles used with names of people require a capital letter. Often, these are abbreviations. We capitalize initials because they stand for names of people.

Mr. and Mrs. Francisco Ramirez

Dr. Bryce Darden

General Ulysses S. Grant

Aunt Ila Mae

Sir Lancelot

Grandma Mihoko

Family Words

When **family words** such as *father, mother, grandmother,* or *grandfather* are used instead of a person's name, these words are capitalized. However, they are not capitalized when words such as *my, your, his, our,* or *their* are used before them.

Did you catch a fish, *Mom*?
I asked *my mom* if she had caught a fish.

He wanted *Grandpa* to come over.
He wanted *his grandpa* to come over.

School Subjects

When the name of a school subject comes from a proper noun, it is capitalized. Otherwise it is not.

English

German

Spanish

math

biology

language arts

Example Correct the following sentences by adding capital letters.

   (a) Can dr. dan d. laser fix my eyesight?

   (b) please help father clear the table.

   (c) my favorite classes are english, history, and french.

Solution (a) We capitalize **Dr.** because it is a title used with the name of a person. We capitalize **Dan D. L**aser because it is a proper noun, and the letter *D* is an initial.

   (b) We capitalize **P**lease because it is the first word of the sentence. **F**ather requires a capital because it is used instead of a person's name.

   (c) **M**y is the first word of the sentence. **E**nglish and **F**rench come from proper nouns, so we capitalize them.

✓**Practice** Add capital letters where they are needed.

   a. are you taking spanish this year?

   b. i think grandpa cuts his own hair.

   c. have you seen the orthodontist dr. u. b. straight?

   d. i should call my aunt and uncle.

   For e and f, replace each blank with the correct vocabulary word from this lesson.

   e. Wise people _____ truth and justice.

   f. Do not _____ your friends by pointing out their flaws.

More Practice See "More Practice Lesson 38" in Student Workbook.

✓**Review Set 38** Choose the correct word to complete sentences 1–6.

   1. To (conceal, disclose, encumber) is to burden or weigh
   (37) down.

   2. *Avaricious* and *greedy* are (synonyms, antonyms,
   (36) homophones).

   3. (*Vertebrate, Invertebrate, Akin*) means "similar or of the
   (35) same family."

4. A (panacea, clamor, meteor) is an outcry or uproar.
(34)

5. A (strait, peninsula, tundra) is a narrow waterway
(12) connecting two larger bodies of water.

6. The word *James's* is a (plural, possessive) noun.
(13)

7. Add suffixes to the following words:
(33)
(a) sunny + er (b) admire + ation

8. Add suffixes to the following words:
(34)
(a) begin + ing (b) sad + ness

9. For a and b, write the word that is spelled correctly.
(35)
(a) shield, sheild (b) perceive, percieve

10. Rewrite the following sentence, adding capital letters as
(26) needed:

ms. lim asked, "have you tried the texas cheese bread?"

11. Replace the blank below with the singular present tense
(9) form of the underlined verb.

Songs <u>pacify</u> babies. A song _____ a baby.

12. Write whether the following word group is a phrase or a
(36) clause: while the crickets were chirping

13. In the following sentence, write the entire verb phrase,
(12) circling each helping verb:

You should have seen that armadillo!

14. Write the following sentence, using correct
(38) capitalization: yes, mom is taking a spanish class from
professor reyna.

15. Write the linking verb in the following sentence:
(31)
On the map, Texas looks enormous.

16. Write whether the following word group is a complete
(23) sentence, a sentence fragment, or a run-on sentence:

A name meaning "allies or friends."

17. Write each preposition that you find in the following sentence:

Austin lies along the banks of the Colorado River.

18. Use a dictionary: (a) The word *didactic* is what part of speech? (b) Write its pronunciation. (c) Write its etymology.

19. Rewrite the following words, circling each silent letter:

(a) comb   (b) half   (c) reign

20. Rewrite and correct the sentence fragment below, making a complete sentence. There is more than one correct answer.

Fishing for marlin near Padre Island.

21. From the following list, write the word that is *not* a linking verb: is, am, are, was, where, be, being, been.

22. Write the compound noun that you find in this sentence:

During the storm, I searched for my raincoat.

23. For the following sentence, write the correct form of the verb:

Jalaliya (past of *snip*) the ribbon with a pair of scissors.

24. For the verb *snip*, write the (a) present participle, (b) past tense, and (c) past participle.

25. Write whether the following sentence is declarative, interrogative, imperative, or exclamatory:

Remember the Alamo.

26. Rewrite the following outline, adding capital letters as needed:

i. produce from texas
   a. bunches of carrots
   b. bags of peanuts

27. For a–c, write the plural of each noun.

(a) anniversary   (b) birthday   (c) queen of England

28. Diagram the simple subject and simple predicate of each
(36) clause in the following sentence: While Pac was
trimming the bushes, Jud was examining ants with a
magnifying glass.

Diagram the simple subject, simple predicate, and direct
object of sentences 29–30.

29. Has Tyler polished his shoes?
(32, 37)

30. Florinda might have left her trumpet under her chair.
(32, 37)

Descriptive Adjectives

Dictation or Journal Entry
Vocabulary:

Dogma, a noun, is a formally stated belief, religious or non-religious, that is viewed as authoritative. The Organization for the Fair Treatment of Catfish states its *dogma* and goals on its website.

Dogmatic, an adjective, does not refer to an automatic dog; rather, it refers to stating beliefs or opinions in an authoritative and often arrogant manner. The *dogmatic* lecturer did not allow for differences of opinion.

An adjective is a word that describes a person, place, or thing. There are many different kinds of adjectives. There are **limiting** adjectives such as *a*, *an*, and *the*; **demonstrative** adjectives such as *this*, *that*, *those*, and *these*; and **possessive** adjectives such as *his*, *her*, *their*, *our*, *its*, *your*, and *my*.

Descriptive Adjectives

In this lesson we will concentrate on **descriptive adjectives**, which describe a person, place, or thing. Sometimes they answer the question, "What kind?" Descriptive adjectives are italicized below.

noisy parrot

addition problem

tired, grumpy student

Often descriptive adjectives come before the person, place, or thing, as in the sentences below.

Curious kittens explore.

Pessimistic people expect *bad* news.

Sometimes descriptive adjectives come after the noun or pronoun, as in the example below.

Katya, *tall* and *elegant*, came from Russia.

Some descriptive adjectives end in suffixes like these:

–able	*comfortable, lovable, washable, believable*
–al	*unusual, natural, eventual, casual*
–ful	*joyful, hopeful, graceful, thankful*
–ible	*terrible, sensible, visible, possible*
–ive	*sensitive, secretive, creative, expensive*
–less	*tireless, fearless, useless, careless*
–ous	*enormous, poisonous, famous, curious*
–y	*funny, tasty, cheery, windy*

Example 1 Write each descriptive adjective in sentences a–c.

(a) Thankful people make pleasant companions.

(b) Tireless settlers built stable communities.

(c) The ride, long and bumpy, ended abruptly.

Solution (a) **Thankful** (describes "people"), **pleasant** (describes "companions")

(b) **Tireless** (describes "settlers"), **stable** (describes "communities")

(c) **long, bumpy** (describes "ride")

Improving Our Writing Descriptive adjectives help us to draw pictures using words. They make our writing more precise and more interesting. For example, clouds can be *high, low, scattered, billowy, puffy, wispy, animal-shaped, ominous, gloomy, dark, white, gray,* or *crimson.* Stars can be *gleaming, faint, distant, twinkling, bright,* or *dim.* When we write, we can use descriptive adjectives to create more detailed pictures.

Example 2 Replace each blank with a descriptive adjective to add more detail to the word "personality" in this sentence:

The boss has a _____, _____ personality.

Solution Our answers will vary. Here are some possibilities: ***gloomy, miserable, obnoxious, pessimistic, playful, happy, phony, deceitful, wicked, sarcastic, friendly, pleasant, joyful, optimistic,*** and ***confident.***

Practice Write each descriptive adjective in sentences a–c.

a. The car, old and rusty, will not start.

b. Healthful foods make delicious meals.

c. I like ripe, juicy peaches.

For d–f, write two descriptive adjectives to describe each noun.

d. puppy   **e.** voice   **f.** sweater

For g and h, replace each blank with the correct vocabulary word from this lesson.

g. Not many members questioned the _____ of the organization.

h. The _____ leader never allowed people to question the official rules of the organization.

More Practice See "Corny Chronicle #2" in Student Workbook. Have fun!

✓ **Review Set 39** Choose the correct word to complete sentences 1–6.

1. *Humiliate* and (*conceal*, *disclose*, *shame*) have almost the same meaning.
(38)

2. To encumber is to (help, burden, rescue).
(37)

3. A(n) (implacable, placid, avaricious) person always wants more; he or she is greedy.
(36)

4. *Akin* means "(different, unrelated, similar)."
(35)

5. (Its, It's) is the shortened form of "it is."
(6)

6. The word *dogma* is a(n) (abstract, concrete) noun.
(11)

7. Add suffixes to the following words:
(33)
   (a) pity + ful   (b) say + ed

8. Add suffixes to the following words:
(34)
   (a) drop + ing   (b) warm + er

9. For a and b, write the word that is spelled correctly.
(35)
   (a) veiw, view   (b) nieghbor, neighbor

10. Write each descriptive adjective from the following sentence:
(39)
   Have you seen the enormous, salty lake in Utah?

11. Replace the blank below with the singular present tense form of the underlined verb.
(9)
   People <u>reach</u> their goals. Ivy _____ her goals.

12. Write whether the following word group is a phrase or a
(36) clause: up the street from the gas station

13. In the following sentence, write the entire verb phrase,
(12) circling each helping verb:

Has Karis been floating on the river all day?

14. Rewrite the following book title, using correct
(25) capitalization: *the swiss family robinson*

15. Write the linking verb in the following sentence:
(31)

Provo, Utah, remains the steel center of the West.

16. Write whether the following word group is a complete
(23) sentence, a sentence fragment, or a run-on sentence:

Zion Narrows Canyon is deep and narrow you can see
stars from its bottom in the daytime.

17. Write each preposition that you find in the following
(20, 21) sentence:

On her raft, Karis drifted down the river until sunset.

18. Use a dictionary: (a) The word *digitate* is what part of
(27,30) speech? (b) Write its pronunciation. (c) Write its
etymology.

19. Rewrite the following words, circling each silent letter:
(28, 29)
(a) kneel   (b) two   (c) guard

20. Rewrite and correct the run-on sentence below. There is
(24) more than one correct answer.

In Utah's Great Salt Lake, floating is easy swimming
underwater is difficult.

21. From the following list, write the word that is *not* a
(31) linking verb: look, feel, paste, smell, sound, seem, appear.

22. Write the collective noun that you find in this sentence:
(11)

A cluster of grapes ripens on the vine.

23. For the following sentence, write the correct form of the verb:

(14)

Mr. Masood and I (future of *sing*) a duet at the festival.

24. For the verb *snap*, write the (a) present participle, (b) past tense, and (c) past participle.

(19)

25. Replace each blank with a descriptive adjective to add more detail to the word "backpack" in the sentence below. There are many possible answers.

(39)

The traveler carried a _____, _____ backpack.

26. Rewrite the following lines of poetry, adding capital letters as needed:

(15)

i have a hunch
it's time for lunch.

27. For a–c, write the plural of each noun.

(17, 22)

(a) dictionary   (b) avocado   (c) ruler of Spain

28. Diagram the simple subject and simple predicate of each clause in the following sentence:

(36)

The teacher asks a question, and Perlina scratches her head.

Diagram the simple subject, simple predicate, and direct object of sentences 29–30.

29. Perlina has been counting the freckles on her arm.

(32, 37)

30. Is Perlina rubbing her eyes now?

(32, 37)

The Limiting Adjective •
Diagramming Adjectives

> **Dictation or Journal Entry**
> **Vocabulary:**
> *Tangible* means "capable of being touched." Concrete nouns are generally *tangible* while abstract nouns are not.
>
> *Intangible* means "not capable of being perceived by the sense of touch." Faith and knowledge are *intangible*.

Limiting adjectives help to define, or "limit," a noun or pronoun. They tell "which one," "what kind," "how many," or "whose." There are six categories of limiting adjectives. They include articles, demonstrative adjectives, numbers, possessive adjectives (both pronouns and nouns), and indefinites.

Articles Articles are the most commonly used adjectives, and they are also the shortest—*a, an*, and ***the***.

a tree	*the* tree
a pen	*the* pen
an apple	*the* apple
an explorer	*the* explorer

We use *a* before words beginning with a consonant sound, and *an* before words beginning with a vowel sound. It is the sound and not the spelling that determines whether we use *a* or *an*:

an hour	*a* human being
an umbrella	*a* university
an R-rating	*a* rat
an X-ray	*a* xylophone

Demonstrative Adjectives WHICH ONE?

this town singular	*that* city S
these sticks plural	*those* stones P

Numbers HOW MANY?

three lemons	*four* marbles	*one* pig
twenty-six miles	*sixteen* years	*fifty* states

| **Possessive Adjectives** | Both pronouns and nouns commonly function as adjectives. They answer the question, WHOSE? |

Pronouns WHOSE?

| *her* pen | *its* place | *my* name |
| *our* country | *their* socks | *your* idea |

Nouns WHOSE?

| *Bob's* bicycle | *Omar's* hat | *Lily's* cat |
| *Meg's* book | *Rosa's* dream | *Pat's* shoe |

Indefinites HOW MANY?

| *some* wagons | *few* members | *many* ships |
| *several* hikers | *no* food | *any* syrup |

Example 1 Write each limiting adjective that you find in these sentences.

(a) I admire their company for helping the farmers.

(b) That company gives its leftovers to feed the pigs.

(c) Many pigs reject one flavor of ice cream.

(d) Molly's pig wants his ice cream in a cone.

Solution

(a) **their, the**   (b) **That, its, the**

(c) **Many, one**   (d) **Molly's, his, a**

Diagramming Adjectives We diagram adjectives by placing them on a slanted line beneath the noun or pronoun they describe, or "limit."

Molly's (possessive adjective) *cute* (descriptive adjective) piglet has eaten.

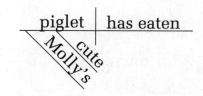

In this sentence, *Molly's* and *cute* tell "whose" and "what kind" of piglet, so we attach them to the word "piglet."

Example 2 Diagram this sentence:

Many hungry pigs eat the ice cream.

Solution We see that the adjectives *many* and *hungry* describe "pigs," and the adjective *the* describes "ice cream," so we diagram the sentence like this:

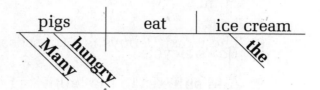

✓**Practice** For a and b, replace each blank with the correct vocabulary word from this lesson.

a. Sticks and stones are _____; they can be touched.

b. Forgiveness and joy are _____; they cannot be touched.

Write each limiting adjective that you find in sentences c–f.

c. Juan's teacher plays several instruments.

d. Some instruments add to the harmony.

e. This band has two drummers.

f. That drummer is my sister.

g. Diagram this sentence: Amir plays these golden bells.

More Practice See "More Practice Lesson 40" in Student Workbook.

Review Set 40 Choose the correct word to complete sentences 1–6.

1. A (dogmatic, timid, fearful) person speaks with authority
(39) and sometimes arrogance.

2. To humiliate is to shame or (exalt, praise, embarrass).
(38)

3. A heavy suitcase might (encumber, encourage, enable) a
(37) traveler.

4. Avarice is (generosity, patience, greed).
(36)

5. The Latin word (*clamare, placare*) means "to soothe or
(22) calm."

6. The word *Debbys* is a (possessive, plural) noun.
(13)

7. Add suffixes to the following words:
(33)
(a) crazy + ness   (b) pay + ed

8. Add suffixes to the following words:
(34)
(a) mop + ed   (b) rain + ing

9. For a and b, write the word that is spelled correctly.
(35)
(a) priest, preist   (b) reciept, receipt

10. Write each descriptive adjective from the following
(39) sentence:

Lush, colorful trees in Vermont attract appreciative
spectators.

11. Replace the blank below with the singular present tense
(9) form of the underlined verb.

People <u>rely</u> on you. Your teacher _____ on you.

12. Write whether the following word group is a phrase or a
(36) clause: before Maya crushes the cans

13. In the following sentence, write the entire verb phrase,
(12) circling each helping verb:

Should Luey have stuck his finger in the maple syrup?

14. Rewrite the following sentence, using correct
(38) capitalization: sergeant smug asked mom if she
passed her fourth grade english class.

15. Write the linking verb in the following sentence:
(31)
"The Green Mountain State" seems appropriate for
Vermont.

16. Write whether the following word group is a complete
(23) sentence, a sentence fragment, or a run-on sentence:

Forty gallons of maple tree sap will make one gallon of
Vermont syrup.

17. Write each preposition that you find in the following
(20, 21) sentence:

Luey waited underneath the maple tree near the cabin.

18. Use a dictionary: (a) The word *rapport* is what part of
(27,30) speech? (b) Write its pronunciation. (c) Write its
etymology.

19. Rewrite the following words, circling each silent letter:
(28, 29)
    (a) sign   (b) listen   (c) honesty

20. Rewrite and correct the following sentence fragment,
(6) making a complete sentence:

Pouring maple syrup on the pancakes.

21. From the following list, write the word that is *not* a
(31) linking verb: seem, appear, blow, become, remain, stay.

22. Write each limiting adjective from the following
(40) sentence:

This morning, Max's two poodles chewed several holes
in his backpack.

23. For the following sentence, write the correct form of the
(10) verb:

The thirsty collie (past of *empty*) her water dish.

24. For the verb *empty*, write the (a) present participle, (b)
(19) past tense, and (c) past participle.

25. Replace each blank with a descriptive adjective to add
(39) more detail to the word "traveler" in the sentence below.
There are many possible answers.

A _____, _____ traveler steps off the bus.

26. Rewrite the following sentence, adding capital letters as
(26)   needed: addicus said, "there is a copy of *the wizard of oz*
on ms. blue's bookshelf."

27. For a–c, write the plural of each noun.
(17, 22)
(a) Monday   (b) brush   (c) private investigator

28. Diagram the simple subject and simple predicate of each
(36)   clause in the following sentence:

While others are taking the test, Perlina is chewing the
eraser on her pencil.

Diagram each word of sentences 29–30.

✓ **29.** Mr. Hake can wiggle his ears.
(37, 40)

✓ **30.** Can you wiggle your ears?
(37, 40)

Capitalization: Areas, Religions, and Greetings

> **Dictation or Journal Entry**
>
> **Vocabulary:**
>
> *Cognizance,* a noun, is knowledge or perception. The boss has *cognizance* of her employee's past accomplishments.
>
> *Cognizant,* an adjective, means "having knowledge; aware." Are you *cognizant* of the benefits of good nutrition?

Proper capitalization becomes easier with practice. We remember to capitalize titles, family words when used as names, and the names of school subjects that come from proper nouns. Refer to an earlier capitalization lesson if you are in doubt. Now let's look at a few more capitalization rules.

Areas of the Country

We capitalize *North, South, East, West, Midwest, Northeast,* etc., when they refer to **certain areas of the country.**

Glaciers helped to shape the Northeast.

The Southwest usually has sunny weather.

The population of the Western states is growing.

Many immigrants have come from the Far East.

However, we do not capitalize these words when they indicate a direction. See the examples below.

Nan drives east to school and south to the library.

Vermont is west of New Hampshire.

The Mississippi River flows from north to south.

Religious References

We capitalize **religions and their members, works regarded as sacred,** and **references to a supreme being.**

Hatti is a Hindu.

Jews worship Jehovah.

The Catholics offered people a silent retreat.

Those passages are from the Koran.

Greeting and Closing of a Letter

We capitalize the first words in the **greeting and closing of a letter.** For example:

Dear Dvorjac,

My thoughtful aunt,

To whom it may concern:

Yours truly,

Warmly,

Gratefully,

Example Provide capital letters as needed.

(a) Pioneers moved to the west.

(b) The compass told us which way was north.

(c) There is a buddhist temple on that street.

(d) The girl wrote, "my dear cousin," and ended her letter with, "love, elle."

Solution (a) We capitalize **W**est, because it refers to a specific section of the United States.

(b) No correction is needed.

(c) We capitalize **B**uddhist because it is the name of a religion.

(d) We capitalize **M**y because it is the first word of a letter's greeting. However, because "cousin" is not the name of a specific person, and because it is preceded by the word "my," we do not capitalize it. **L**ove needs a capital because it is the first word of the closing. We capitalize **E**lle because it is a proper noun, or a specific person.

✓**Practice** Rewrite a–d with correct capitalization.

a. these passages are from the king james bible.

b. when i traveled in the east, i tasted lobster and crab.

c. look at the northwest corner of the map.

d. dear dad,

   i am having fun at camp.

      your son,

      alex

For e and f, replace each blank with the correct vocabulary word from this lesson.

e. False advertising will not fool a _____ buyer.

f. A buyer's _____ of the facts will prevent foolish purchases.

Review Set 41 Choose the correct word to complete sentences 1–6.

1. Something that is (tangible, intangible, dogmatic) cannot
(40) be perceived by the sense of touch.

2. A dogmatic speaker is (humble, authoritative, shy).
(39)

3. To exalt is to (humiliate, praise, criticize).
(38)

4. An (arroyo, encumbrance, atoll) is a hindrance or burden.
(37)

5. (*Chasm*, *Mesa*, *Savanna*) is a Spanish word meaning
(20) "table."

6. The word *octopus's* is a (possessive, plural) noun.
(13)

7. Add suffixes to the following words:
(33)
(a) lazy + ness   (b) day + ly

8. Add suffixes to the following words:
(34)
(a) commit + ed   (b) cloud + less

9. For a and b, write the word that is spelled correctly.
(35)
(a) niece, neice   (b) deceit, deciet

10. Write each descriptive adjective from the following
(39) sentence:

Fertile soil in Vermont produces tasty fruits.

11. Rewrite the following sentence, using correct
(41) capitalization.

nancy attends a lutheran church in the northeast.

12. Write whether the following word group is a phrase or a
(36) clause: with bats under the bridge

13. In the following sentence, write the entire verb phrase,
(12) circling each helping verb:

Has Jo been hiking in the forested mountains of Vermont?

14. Rewrite the following song title, using correct
(25) capitalization: "a bicycle built for two"

15. Write the linking verb in the following sentence:
(31)

Vermont's economy appears strong.

16. Write whether the following word group is a complete
(23) sentence, a sentence fragment, or a run-on sentence:

To make the best cheddar cheese in the nation.

17. Write each preposition that you find in the following
(20, 21) sentence:

In the quarry near the forest, I discovered marble beneath
some rubble.

18. Use a dictionary: (a) The word *dearth* is what part of
(27,30) speech? (b) Write its pronunciation. (c) Write its
etymology.

19. Rewrite the following words, circling each silent letter:
(28, 29)
(a) design   (b) lamb   (c) hourly

20. Rewrite and correct the run-on sentence below. There is
(24) more than one correct answer.

Crossing the Connecticut River is a covered bridge it is
one of the longest in the world.

21. Write whether the following sentence is declarative,
(2) interrogative, imperative, or exclamatory:

Concord Academy was the first school for training
teachers.

22. Write each limiting adjective from the following
(40) sentence:

Since Max's backpack had many holes in it, Max gave his
two poodles that backpack.

23. For the following sentence, write the correct form of the
(9) verb:

The thirsty collie (present of *empty*) her water dish.

24. For the verb *spy*, write the (a) present participle, (b) past
(19) tense, and (c) past participle.

25. Replace each blank with a descriptive adjective to add more detail to the word "hair" in the sentence below. There are many possible answers.
(39)

A teacher with _____, _____ hair nods and smiles.

26. Rewrite the following sentence, adding capital letters as needed:
(26)

mortimer asked, "how many copies of *robinson crusoe* does mr. garza have?"

27. For a–c, write the plural of each noun.
(17, 22)

(a) copy   (b) axis   (c) secret agent

28. Diagram the simple subject and simple predicate of each clause in the following sentence:
(36)

Perlina was solving a mystery while her classmates were sleeping.

Diagram each word of sentences 29–30.

29. Perlina is taking a difficult test.
(37, 40)

30. Will Perlina pass this test?
(37, 40)

LESSON 42

Proper Adjectives

Common Adjectives

An adjective can be common or proper. Common adjectives are formed from common nouns and are not capitalized.

COMMON NOUN	COMMON ADJECTIVE
peace	peaceful
gift	gifted
rain	rainy
joy	joyful

Proper Adjectives

Proper adjectives are formed from proper nouns and are always capitalized. Sometimes the word doesn't change at all, as in the examples below.

PROPER NOUN	PROPER ADJECTIVE
Labrador	Labrador (retriever)
Canada	Canada (geese)
Washington	Washington (apple)
Idaho	Idaho (potato)

Often the form of the proper adjective does change, as in the examples below.

PROPER NOUN	PROPER ADJECTIVE
Ireland	Irish (stew)
China	Chinese (food)
France	French (artist)
Spain	Spanish (dance)

Example 1

For sentences a–d, write each proper adjective followed by the noun it describes.

(a) I am proud to wave the American flag.

(b) Mexican food often includes rice and beans.

(c) My grandfather plays the French horn.

(d) Strawberries topped the Belgian waffle.

Solution (a) **American flag** (b) **Mexican food**

(c) **French horn** (d) **Belgian waffle**

Example 2 Diagram this sentence:

Mrs. Papazian served an Armenian roll.

Solution We place the proper adjective "Armenian" underneath the word it describes—"roll."

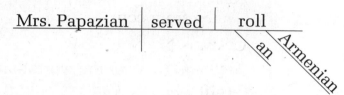

Practice For sentences a–d, write each proper adjective followed by the noun it describes.

a. Do you like Italian sausage with your pasta?

b. A Renaissance fair draws large crowds.

c. Listen to the Scottish bagpipes!

d. Peng demonstrated the Chinese martial arts.

e. Diagram this sentence: Bob wore a Hawaiian shirt.

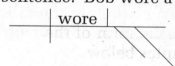

For f and g, replace each blank with the correct vocabulary word from this lesson.

f. _____ people save; they do not waste.

g. _____ people are wasteful.

Review Set Choose the correct word to complete sentences 1–6.
42
1. *Cognizant* and *ignorant* are (synonyms, antonyms, homophones).
(41)

2. (*Avaricious, Dogmatic, Tangible*) means "capable of being
(40) touched."

3. (Avarice, Tundra, Dogma) is a formally stated belief that
(39) is viewed as authoritative.

4. To (humiliate, exalt, encumber) is to praise or glorify.
(38)

5. The Latin word (*placare*, *unim*, *loqui*) means "to talk."
(23)

6. The word *volcano* is a(n) (abstract, concrete) noun.
(11)

7. Add suffixes to the following words:
(33)
(a) ready + ly   (b) come + ing

8. Add suffixes to the following words:
(34)
(a) win + ing   (b) rain + ed

9. For a and b, write the word that is spelled correctly.
(35)
(a) relieve, releive   (b) freight, frieght

10. Write each proper adjective from the following sentence:
(42)
Quan made a sandwich with French bread and Canadian bacon.

11. Rewrite the following letter, using correct capitalization.
(41)
dear quan,
        please don't eat all of the canadian bacon.
                    your brother,
                    sheung

12. Write whether the following word group is a phrase or a
(36) clause: since Quan ate the Canadian bacon

13. In the following sentence, write the entire verb phrase,
(12) circling each helping verb:

You might have heard of the magician Harry Houdini.

14. Rewrite the following sentence, using correct
(38) capitalization: next semester, dad will take mr. castro's spanish class.

15. Write the linking verb in the following sentence:
(31)
Houdini's escapes from handcuffs and boxes sound impossible.

16. Write whether the following word group is a complete
(23) sentence, a sentence fragment, or a run-on sentence:

Houdini escaped again it's amazing!

17. Write each preposition that you find in the following
(20, 21) sentence:

Throughout the night, he dreamed about stars beyond our
solar system.

18. Use a dictionary: (a) The word *distaff* is what part of
(27,30) speech? (b) Write its pronunciation. (c) Write its
etymology.

19. Rewrite the following words, circling each silent letter:
(28, 29)

(a) knot   (b) written   (c) climb

20. Rewrite and correct the following sentence fragment,
(6)   making a complete sentence:

To taste cheese from Wisconsin.

21. Write the word from this list that *cannot* be a linking
(31) verb: is, am, are, was, were, flea, being, been, look, feel.

22. Write each limiting adjective from the following
(40) sentence:

Elle rode her bicycle three times around the Harts'
farm that day.

23. For the following sentence, write the correct form of the
(14) verb:

I (future of *feed*) the horses next.

24. For the verb *wrap*, write the (a) present participle, (b) past
(19) tense, and (c) past participle.

25. Replace each blank with a descriptive adjective to add
(39) more detail to the word "jogger" in the sentence below.
There are many possible answers.

I waved to the _____, _____ jogger.

26. Rewrite the following rhyme, adding capital letters as
(15) needed:

it's raining, it's pouring,
the old man is snoring...

27. For a–c, write the plural of each noun.
(17, 22)

(a) branch   (b) calf   (c) son-in-law

28. Diagram the simple subject and simple predicate of each
(36) clause in the following sentence:

When the bell rang, Ms. Hoo stood and the class applauded.

Diagram each word of sentences 29–30.

29. My frugal brother has saved his old shoelaces.
(37, 40)

30. Have you saved your old shoelaces?
(37, 40)

No Capital Letter

Dictation or Journal Entry
Vocabulary:
Paternal means "of, relating to, or like a father." My *paternal* grandmother came from the Middle East.

Maternal means "of, relating to, or like a mother." The bear's *maternal* instincts caused her to protect and defend her cubs.

Most grammar books teach us when to capitalize words, but this lesson reminds us when **not** to capitalize words.

Common Nouns

Common nouns such as animals, plants, foods, objects, medical conditions, and pastimes are not capitalized. If a proper adjective (descriptive word) appears with the noun, we capitalize only the proper adjective, not the common noun. Below are some examples.

COMMON NOUN	COMMON NOUN WITH PROPER ADJECTIVE
cow	Holstein cow
elm tree	Italian cypress
trumpet	Steinway piano
flu	German measles
roller coaster	Ferris wheel
chess	Chinese checkers

Example 1 Add capital letters where needed.

(a) Bright orange california poppies cover the hillsides.

(b) Do you prefer lemonade or english tea?

(c) On rainy days, I play games such as checkers and chess.

(d) Do you play the french horn?

(e) Doctors recommend boosters for whooping cough and tetanus.

Solution (a) We capitalize *California,* a proper adjective. However, *poppies* is not capitalized because plants are common nouns.

(b) We capitalize *English,* a proper adjective. However, *lemonade* and *tea* are not capitalized because foods and beverages are common nouns.

(c) We do not add capital letters. Games and pastimes such as *checkers* and *chess* are common nouns.

(d) We capitalize *French,* a proper adjective. However, we do not capitalize *horn* because objects such as musical instruments are common nouns.

(e) We do not add capital letters. Most medical conditions are common nouns.

Seasons of the Year We do not capitalize **seasons of the year**: fall, winter, spring, and summer.

In the summer, we swim more often than we do in the winter.

Hyphenated Words We treat a **hyphenated word** as if it were a single word. If it is a proper noun or the first word of a sentence, we capitalize only the first word, not all the parts of the hyphenated word. See the examples below.

Twenty-one years is a long life for a dog!

Next, Attorney-at-law Nora Lin will ask questions.

Example 2 Add capital letters where needed in this sentence:

Last spring, sister-in-law Ann gave me the family's scottish shortbread recipe.

We capitalize *Scottish* because it is a proper adjective. We capitalize *Sister-in-law* because it is a family word used as part of a name. We do not capitalize *spring* because it is a season of the year. We do not capitalize *shortbread* because it is a food, a common noun.

✓ Practice For a and b, replace each blank with the correct vocabulary word from this lesson.

a. Your _____ relatives are those on your mother's side of the family.

b. Your _____ relatives are those on your father's side of the family.

For c–g, write and capitalize each word that needs a capital letter.

c. Jan's favorite sport is volleyball.

d. Stringed instruments include the violins, violas, cellos, and fiddles.

e. Did you find your fortune in the chinese cookie?

f. we harvest our vegetables in summer and fall.

g. twenty-four children played the game of hide-and-seek.

More Practice See "More Practice Lesson 43" in Student Workbook.

Review Set 43 Choose the correct word to complete sentences 1–6.

1. (*Avaricious, Dogmatic, Frugal*) means "avoiding waste;
(42) saving; economical."

2. (Avarice, Kin, Cognizance) is knowledge or perception.
(41)

3. *Intangible* means "not able to be perceived by the sense of
(40) (duty, responsibility, touch)."

4. Dogma is (water, belief, land).
(39)

5. The Latin word *loqui* means "to (calm, disturb, talk)."
(23)

6. The word *committee* is a (compound, collective) noun.
(11)

7. Add suffixes to the following words:
(33) (a) steady + ly   (b) peace + ful

8. Add suffixes to the following words:
(34) (a) sip + ing   (b) broad + est

9. For a and b, write the word that is spelled correctly.
(35) (a) weigh, wiegh   (b) acheive, achieve

10. Write each proper adjective from the following sentence:
(42) A Russian wolfhound buries his bone beneath the Australian willow tree.

11. Rewrite   the   following   sentence,   using   correct
(41, 43) capitalization.

my jewish friend lenny won the chess championship in the western division.

12. Write whether the following word group is a phrase or a
(36) clause: after a long, hard game of chess

13. In the following sentence, write the entire verb phrase,
(12) circling each helping verb:

May I sample that cheese?

14. Rewrite the following story title, using correct
(25) capitalization: "the race for the south pole"

15. Write the linking verb in the following sentence:
(31)

Wisconsin cheddar remains my favorite.

16. Write whether the following word group is a complete
(23) sentence, a sentence fragment, or a run-on sentence:

Wisconsin makes more cheese than any other state.

17. Write each preposition that you find in the following
(20, 21) sentence:

A border collie herds sheep alongside the river and
through a gate.

18. Use a dictionary: (a) The word *poultice* is what part of
(27,30) speech? (b) Write its pronunciation. (c) Write its
etymology.

19. Rewrite the following words, circling each silent letter:
(28, 29)
(a) pneumonia   (b) would   (c) pitch

20. Rewrite and correct the run-on sentence below. There is
(24) more than one correct answer.

Please bring some cheese I am baking bread.

21. Write whether the following sentence is declarative,
(2) interrogative, imperative, or exclamatory:

Bloomer, Wisconsin, is the rope-jumping capital of the
world.

22. Write each limiting adjective from the following
(40) sentence:

On my way out the door, I left those two books on Ms.
Hoo's desk.

23. For the following sentence, write the correct form of the
(9) verb:

Ms. Hoo (present of *hush*) her students.

24. For the verb *deny*, write the (a) present participle, (b) past
(19) tense, and (c) past participle.

25. Replace each blank with a descriptive adjective to add
(39) more detail to the word "vehicle" in the sentence below.
There are many possible answers.

Ms. Hoo drives a _____, _____ vehicle.

26. Rewrite the following sentence, adding capital letters as
(26) needed:

ms. hoo said, "my car was made in france, not
in japan."

27. For a–c, write the plural of each noun.
(17, 22)
(a) leaf   (b) bison   (c) mouthful

28. Diagram the simple subject and simple predicate of each
(36) clause in the following sentence:

Ms. Hoo drove her car, but I walked, and my friends rode
their bicycles.

Diagram each word of sentences 29–30.

29. My maternal ancestors built some rustic cabins.
(37, 40)

30. Did Dan's paternal ancestors build teepees?
(37, 40)

Object of the Preposition •
The Prepositional Phrase

py. 70

Object of the Preposition

We have learned to recognize common prepositions—connecting words that link a noun or pronoun to the rest of the sentence. In this lesson, we will identify the **object of the preposition,** which is the noun or pronoun that follows the preposition. Every preposition must have an object. Otherwise, it is not a preposition. We italicize prepositions and star their objects in the phrases below.

at the *corner	*down* the *stairs
on the *table	*through* the *tunnel
around the *lake	*like* a *bull
within a *year	*for* your *homework
across *town	*behind* *him
except *her	*with* *admiration
in the *library	*considering* the *snow

Prepositions may have compound objects:

Ivy hikes *through* *rain and *sleet.

Gus thinks *about* *villains and *heroes.

Example 1

Circle the object (or objects) of each preposition in these sentences.

(a) *Before* dark, I went *to* the store *for* milk and water.

(b) I walked *over* the bridge and *toward* the sunset.

Solution

(a) *Before* **dark,** I went *to* the **store** *for* **milk** and **water.**

(b) I walked *over* the **bridge** and *toward* the **sunset.**

Prepositional Phrase   A prepositional phrase begins with a preposition and contains a noun and its modifiers. We italicize prepositional phrases below.

> Josh's consistent effort raised his grade *in English.*
>
> Laura wrote Ariel *concerning their friendship.*
>
> Ms. Hoo stomped *into the noisy classroom.*
>
> Justin hit the baseball *beyond all the fielders.*

There can be more than one prepositional phrase in a sentence:

> Omar finds the answers *to his questions* (1) *in bizarre places* (2).
>
> A pony leaped *over the fence* (1) and trotted *through the town* (2).
>
> *After school* (1), let's jog *along the horse trail* (2) *around the park* (3).

Example 2   For each sentence, write each prepositional phrase, circling the objects of the prepositions.

(a) Rumors of Big Foot spread throughout Washington within a few weeks.

(b) Some places on the west side of the Cascade Mountains received 180 inches of rain.

(c) Lava from Mount St. Helens flowed down the slopes and onto flat land.

Solution   (a) **of (Big Foot)**   **throughout (Washington)** **within a few (weeks)**

(b) **on the west (side)**   **of the (Cascade Mountains)**   **of (rain)**

(c) **from (Mount St. Helens)**   **down the (slopes)** **onto flat (land)**

Practice   For sentences a–d, write each prepositional phrase, circling the object(s) of the preposition.

a. Fungus grows around us and causes sneezing in some of us.

b. Apples come to us from Washington by truck and train.

c. The east side of the Cascade Mountains is like a desert.

d. Beyond the shoreline, seals jump off rocks into the ocean.

For e and f, replace each blank with the correct vocabulary word from this lesson.

e. _____ people are wise and cautious.

f. _____ people are unwise.

More Practice Write each prepositional phrase, circling the object of each preposition in these sentences.

1. At sunrise, Ms. Hoo looks at her clock, thinks about her students, and gets into her car.

2. She drives past a house with daffodils in the yard.

3. Along the way she honks at a cow in the middle of the road.

4. The cow steps to the left, so Ms. Hoo passes it on the right.

5. Near the school, Ms. Hoo slows for pedestrians.

6. Without doubt, Ms. Hoo will arrive on time for class.

Review Set 44 Choose the correct word to complete sentences 1–6.

1. (Paternal, Maternal, Nocturnal) refers to a father.
   (43)

2. *Frugal* means "avoiding (waste, work, people)."
   (42)

3. Cognizance is (sediment, bravery, knowledge).
   (41)

4. *Tangible* means "able to be (heard, painted, eaten, touched)."
   (40)

5. The Latin root *val-* means "(calm, talk, strength)."
   (24)

6. The word *ladies* is a (plural, possessive) noun.
   (13)

7. Add suffixes to the following words:
(33) (a) bury + ed   (b) beauty + ful

8. Add suffixes to the following words:
(34) (a) top + ed   (b) refer + ed

9. For a and b, write the word that is spelled correctly.
(35) (a) reign, riegn   (b) yeild, yield

10. Write each proper adjective from the following sentence:
(42) Ivy snacks on Washington apples and American cheese.

11. Rewrite the following letter, using correct capitalization.
(41, 43) dear james,

      please join me for dinner on saturday. i shall serve boston baked beans.

                              love,
                              ima

12. Write whether the following word group is a phrase or a
(36) clause: while Ima was baking the beans

13. In the following sentence, write the entire verb phrase,
(12) circling each helping verb:

Next week, thousands of planes will be flying to Oshkosh, Wisconsin.

14. Rewrite the following sentence, using correct
(38) capitalization: i believe dr. rhombus was mother's geometry professor.

15. Write the linking verb in the following sentence:
(31) At the time, your idea seemed prudent.

16. Write whether the following word group is a complete
(23) sentence, a sentence fragment, or a run-on sentence:

I like malted milk it was invented in Racine, Wisconsin, in 1887.

17.
(44) From the following sentence, write each prepositional phrase, circling the object of each preposition:

With ease the gopher snake slithered through the door, down the stairs, and into the basement.

18.
(27,30) Use a dictionary: (a) The word *recede* is what part of speech? (b) Write its pronunciation. (c) Write its etymology.

19.
(28, 29) Rewrite the following words, circling each silent letter:

    (a) edge   (b) guest   (c) high

20.
(6) Rewrite and correct the following sentence fragment, making a complete sentence:

Washington, D.C., our nation's capital.

21.
(31) From the following list, write the word that could *not* be a linking verb: look, feel, taste, smell, sound, throughout.

22.
(40) Write each limiting adjective from the following sentence:

In a few minutes, Ms. Hoo will find Jasmin's crickets and my two books on her desk.

23.
(10) For the following sentence, write the correct form of the verb:

Ms. Hoo (past of *try*) not to laugh.

24.
(19) For the verb *stop*, write the (a) present participle, (b) past tense, and (c) past participle.

25.
(39) Replace each blank with a descriptive adjective to add more detail to the word "snake" in the sentence below. There are many possible answers.

Jasmin has a _____, _____ snake.

26.
(26) Rewrite the following outline, adding capital letters as needed:

    i. gopher snakes
      a. where they live
      b. what they eat

27. For a–c, write the plural of each noun.
(17, 22)

(a) waltz   (b) penny   (c) auto

28. Diagram the simple subject and simple predicate of each
(36) clause in the following sentence:

The trouble starts when Ann opens the cage and Rufus escapes.

Diagram each word of sentences 29–30.

29. My prudent cousin eats many green vegetables.
(37, 40)

30. Have you been eating your vegetables?
(37, 40)

The Prepositional Phrase as an Adjective • Diagramming

Dictation or Journal Entry

Vocabulary:

Malice, a noun, is desire to cause injury or pain to another; evil intent. Full of *malice,* the villain took pleasure in the hero's misfortune.

Malicious, an adjective, means "showing malice or resulting from malice." The *malicious* person seemed to enjoy other people's pain and suffering.

Adjective Phrases

We remember that a phrase is a group of words that functions as a single word. Prepositional phrases function as a single word, and some modify a noun or pronoun, so we call them **adjective phrases.** This type of prepositional phrase answers an adjective question— "Which one?" "What kind?" or "How many?" The adjective phrases are italicized in the following examples:

My friend *from Denmark* speaks Danish. (The adjective phrase *from Denmark* modifies the noun "friend," and tells "which one.")

Jake likes stories *about dinosaurs.* (The adjective phrase *about dinosaurs* modifies the noun "stories," and tells "what kind.")

I shall request seats *for seven.* (The adjective phrase *for seven* modifies the noun "seats," and tells "how many.")

Example 1 Write the adjective phrase and tell which noun or pronoun it modifies.

(a) The clock in the kitchen has stopped.

(b) Did you write a book for children?

(c) We have reservations for thirteen.

Solution (a) The phrase **in the kitchen** modifies **clock.** It tells "which one."

(b) The phrase **for children** modifies **book.** It tells "what kind."

(c) The phrase **for thirteen** modifies **reservations.** It tells "how many."

Diagramming Prepositional Phrases

To diagram a prepositional phrase, we place the preposition on a slanted line attached to the word that the phrase modifies. We place the object of the preposition on a horizontal line at the bottom of the slanted preposition line:

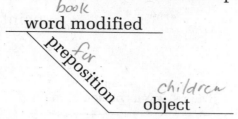

Let's diagram this sentence:

Amy has a backpack (with wheels.)

Amy | has | backpack
with wheels
preposition
object

Example 2 Diagram this sentence:

The outside (of my house) needs paint.

Solution The phrase **of my house** modifies the subject of the sentence, **outside**. We place the preposition **of** on a slanted line connected to **outside**. Then we place the object, **house**, on the horizontal line. The word **my** describes **house**, so we place it on a slanted line connected to the word it modifies.

The outside of my house needs paint.

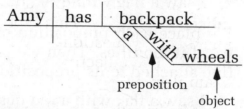

Sometimes a prepositional phrase immediately follows another one, as in the sentence below.

Some (of the paint) (around the windows) is peeling.

In the sentence above, the first prepositional phrase, **of the paint**, modifies the subject **some**. The second prepositional phrase, **around the windows**, modifies the noun **paint**. We show this by diagramming the sentence:

Some of the paint around the windows is peeling.

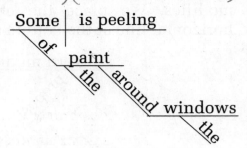

Example 3 Diagram this sentence:

I saw a flag with a red design on a yellow background.

Solution We place each preposition on a slanted line underneath the word it modifies. Then we place each object on a horizontal line attached to its preposition.

I saw a flag with a red design on a yellow background.

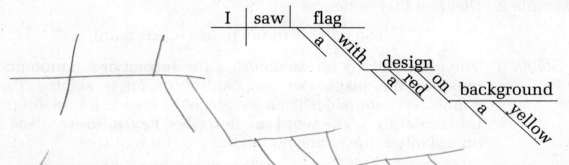

Practice For a–c, write which noun is described by each italicized prepositional phrase.

    a. Elle drew a picture *of a roadrunner.*

    b. The flag *of New Mexico* displays an ancient sun symbol.

    c. This symbolizes friendship *among different cultures.*

In sentences d and e, write the prepositional phrase. Then write the noun it describes.

    d. I have a surprise for you.

    e. The road through the forest is unpaved.

For f and g, replace each blank with the correct vocabulary word from this lesson.

f. Trying to start a fight, the villain made a _____ statement.

g. _____, a noun, is evil intent.

Diagram sentences h and i.

h. Wally likes stories about spies.

i. I used a recipe for muffins with nuts.

Review Set 45

Choose the correct word to complete sentences 1–6.

1. (*Extravagant, Prudent, Imprudent*) means "having or
(44) exercising good judgment."

2. (Paternal, Maternal, Nocturnal) refers to a mother.
(43)

3. A frugal person is (extravagant, wasteful, economical).
(42)

4. *Cognizance* and *knowledge* are (synonyms, antonyms,
(41) homophones).

5. The Latin word *ignis* means "(calm, fire, talk)."
(25)

6. The word *malice* is a(n) (abstract, concrete) noun.
(11)

7. Add suffixes to the following words:
(33) (a) fry + ed   (b) sleepy + ness

8. Add suffixes to the following words:
(34) (a) mat + ed   (b) prefer + ed

9. For a and b, write the word that is spelled correctly.
(35) (a) beleif, belief   (b) wieght, weight

10. Write the proper adjective from the following sentence:
(42) From far away, I could hear some Scottish bagpipes.

11. Rewrite the following sentence, using correct
(41, 43) capitalization: out in the wild west, a baptist preacher read from the holy bible.

12. Write whether the following word group is a phrase or a clause: with hot corn muffins and butter
(36)

13. In the following sentence, write the entire verb phrase, circling each helping verb:
(12)

Giancarlo should have brought his guitar.

14. Rewrite the following story title, using correct capitalization: "adrift on an ice pan"
(25)

15. Write the linking verb in the following sentence:
(31)

Those cherry blossoms smell so sweet!

16. Write whether the following word group is a complete sentence, a sentence fragment, or a run-on sentence:
(23)

The Library of Congress is the world's largest library.

17. From the following sentence, write each prepositional phrase, circling the object of each preposition:
(44)

For fun, I wrote a note to my friend, stuffed it into a bottle, and threw it into the sea.

18. Use a dictionary: (a) The word *rotund* is what part of speech? (b) Write its pronunciation. (c) Write its etymology.
(27,30)

19. Rewrite the following words, circling each silent letter:
(28, 29)

(a) wrist   (b) rhombus   (c) sigh

20. Rewrite and correct the run-on sentence below. There is more than one correct answer.
(24)

We toured the White House then we saw the Jefferson and Lincoln Memorials.

21. Write whether the following sentence is declarative, interrogative, imperative, or exclamatory:
(2)

Don't touch George Washington's false teeth.

22. Write each limiting adjective from the following sentence:
(40)

At her desk, Ms. Hoo is squashing Jasmin's crickets with my two books!

23. For the following sentence, write the correct form of the verb:

(9)

Jasmin's snake (present of *hiss*).

24. For the verb *multiply*, write the (a) present participle, (b) past tense, and (c) past participle.

(19)

✓**25.** Replace each blank with a descriptive adjective to add more detail to the word "muffins" in the sentence below. There are many possible answers.

(39)

Ms. Hoo bakes _____, _____ muffins.

✓**26.** Rewrite the following sentence, adding capital letters as needed: jasmin asks, "where are my jerusalem crickets?"

(26)

27. For a–c, write the plural of each noun.

(17, 22)

(a) public library   (b) apology   (c) Tuesday

28. Diagram the simple subject and simple predicate of each clause in the following sentence:

(36)

Ms. Hoo is shouting, and students are searching, for their pet has disappeared.

Diagram each word of sentences 29–30.

29. My prudent cousin eats a variety of healthful foods.

(40, 45)

30. A frantic search for Rufus has begun.

(40, 45)

Indirect Objects

Dictation or Journal Entry

Vocabulary:

Literate means "able to read and write." Most of the townspeople are *literate*; they can read the ballot and vote for a candidate.

Illiterate means "unable to read or write." Terry teaches *illiterate* people to read and write.

Indirect Objects

An action verb may have two kinds of objects: (1) A direct object receives the action directly. (2) An **indirect object** receives the action indirectly. It tells *to whom* or *for whom* the action was done.

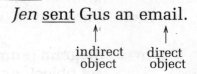

Jen <u>sent</u> Gus an email.

indirect   direct
object   object

In the sentences below, we have starred the direct objects and placed parentheses around the indirect objects, and the subject is in italics.

Duke <u>gave</u> (us) a *concert.

<u>Did</u> *you* <u>leave</u> (him) a *key?

Please <u>toss</u> (her) the *ball.

In order to have an indirect object, a sentence must have a direct object. The indirect object usually follows the verb and precedes the direct object. One test of an indirect object is that it can be expressed alternately by a prepositional phrase introduced by *to* or *for:*

Jen sent an email *to Gus.*

Duke gave a concert *for us.*

Did you leave a key *for him?*

Please toss the ball *to her.*

Indirect objects can be compound:

I <u>gave</u> (Jen) and (him) the *volleyball.

Example 1

Identify the indirect objects, if any, in each sentence.

(a) *Gus* <u>ordered</u> his friend a vanilla shake.

(b) Each year the *teacher* <u>gives</u> his class a lecture on insects.

(c) *Jen* <u>tossed</u> the volleyball.

(d) A caring young *man* <u>found</u> the stray cat a home.

Solution   (a) Gus ordered a vanilla shake *for* his friend. Therefore, **friend** is the indirect object.

(b) The teacher gives a lecture *to* his class. Therefore, **class** is the indirect object.

(c) This sentence has **no indirect object.**

(d) The man found a home *for* the cat. Therefore, **cat** is the indirect object.

Below is a diagram showing the simple subject, simple predicate, direct object, and indirect object of this sentence:

We <u>bought</u> (Ms. Hoo) *flowers.

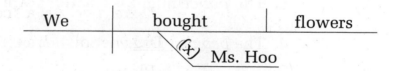

Notice that the indirect object (Ms. Hoo) is attached beneath the verb by a slanted line, as though it were a prepositional phrase with the preposition (x) understood, not stated.

Example 2   Diagram the simple subject, simple predicate, direct object, and indirect object of each sentence from Example 1.

Solution   (a) *Gus* <u>ordered</u> his friend a vanilla shake.

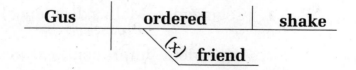

(b) Each year the *teacher* <u>gives</u> his class a lecture on insects.

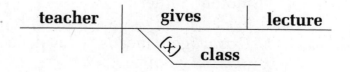

(c) *Jen* <u>tossed</u> the volleyball.

Jen	tossed	volleyball

(d) A caring young *man* <u>found</u> the stray cat a home.

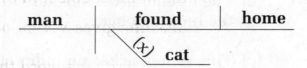

man	found	home

✓ **Practice**   For a and b, replace each blank with the correct vocabulary word from this lesson.

a. _____ people cannot read or write.

b. _____ people can read and write.

Write the indirect object, if any, in sentences c–f.

c. The *police* <u>might issue</u> him a warning.

d. The *beagle* <u>brings</u> her owner a tennis ball.

e. *Coaches* <u>give</u> their teams instructions.

f. One *student* <u>returns</u> to the library.

g. Diagram the <u>simple subject</u>, <u>simple predicate</u>, <u>direct object</u>, and <u>indirect object</u> of the sentence below.

Ms. Hoo read us a poem.

Review Set 46   Choose the correct word to complete sentences 1–6.

1. (Cognizance, Malice, Prudence) is evil intent.
(45)

2. A (prudent, imprudent, extravagant) person is wise and
(44) cautious.

3. *Paternal* means "of, relating to, or like a (porcupine,
(43) mother, father)."

4. *Extravagant* means "(frugal, economical, wasteful)."
(42)

5. The Latin word (*loqui, placare, ignis*) means "fire."
(25)

6. The word *doorknob* is a (compound, collective) noun.
(11)

7. Add suffixes to the following words:
(33, 34) (a) grip + ing   (b) creepy + est

8. Write the indirect object in the following sentence:
(46)

Mr. Yamashita gives Vivian painting lessons.

9. For a and b, write the word that is spelled correctly.
(35) (a) greif, grief   (b) sleigh, sliegh

10. Write the proper adjective from the following sentence:
(42)

The Jerusalem cricket is one of the ugliest bugs on the planet.

11. Rewrite the following letter, using correct capitalization:
(41, 43)

dear ms. hoo,

   i am sorry about rufus's disappearance. we shall continue the search.

                              respectfully,
                              ann

12. Write whether the following word group is a phrase or a
(36) clause: if Rufus needs food and water

13. In the following sentence, write the entire verb phrase,
(12) circling each helping verb:

Could the crickets have jumped into her purse?

14. Rewrite the following sentence, using correct
(38) capitalization: did deputy jesse learn to fix flat tires in dr. funk's latin class?

15. Write the linking verb in the following sentence:
(31)

Wyoming remains windy.

16. Write whether the following word group is a complete
(23) sentence, a sentence fragment, or a run-on sentence:

Wyoming was once part of the Wild West.

17. From the following sentence, write each prepositional phrase, circling the object of each preposition:

(44)

Is Rufus hiding under the seat of William's bicycle?

18. Use a dictionary: (a) The word *arid* is what part of speech? (b) Write its pronunciation. (c) Write its etymology.

(27,30)

19. Rewrite the following words, circling each silent letter:

(28, 29)

(a) doorknob   (b) science   (c) adjective

20. Rewrite and correct the following sentence fragment, making a complete sentence:

(6)

Hearing the song of a meadowlark.

21. From the following list, write the word that could *not* be a linking verb: seem, appear, grow, beware, remain, stay.

(31)

22. Write each limiting adjective from the following sentence:

(40)

For three hours, the students have been looking throughout their classroom for this pet.

23. For the following sentence, write the correct form of the verb:

(14)

Rufus (future of *find*) food and water.

24. For the verb *glorify*, write the (a) present participle, (b) past tense, and (c) past participle.

(19)

25. Replace each blank with a descriptive adjective to add more detail to the word "hat" in the sentence below. There are many possible answers.

(39)

Ms. Hoo wears a _____, _____ hat.

26. Rewrite the following lines of poetry, adding capital letters as needed:

(15)

a cat came fiddling out of a barn
with a pair of bagpipes under her arm.

27. For a–c, write the plural of each noun.

(17, 22)

(a) mother-in-law   (b) peach   (c) Wednesday

28. Diagram the simple subject and simple predicate of each
(36) clause in the following sentence:

Moses empties all the cupboards, and Rosa moves the
desks while other students squeal with alarm.

Diagram each word of sentences 29–30.

29. An illiterate goat ate six pages from the end of my novel.
(40, 45)

30. Quan handed me the remains of the novel.
(45, 46)

The Period, Part 1

Dictation or Journal Entry

Vocabulary:

Momentary means "lasting only a short time." When the mosquito bit me, the pain was *momentary*.

Momentous means "of great importance or consequence." The child's birth was a *momentous* event.

Punctuation marks help the reader to understand the meaning of what is written. **Periods** help the reader to know where a sentence begins and ends, but there are other uses for the period as well.

Declarative Sentence

A **declarative sentence** (statement) needs a period at the end.

Wyoming has the lowest population of any state.

Moose and bison graze on the plains.

Imperative Sentence

An **imperative sentence** (command) needs a period at the end.

Look at that herd of elk.

Watch where you are stepping.

Initials

We place periods after the **initials** in a person's name.

Delron J. Nation

J. K. Schade

A. Tori King

Outline

In an **outline**, letters and numbers require a period after them.

I. Resources in Wyoming
A. Oil
B. Uranium

Example

Add periods where they are needed in each expression.

(a) I. Agriculture in Wyoming
A. Crops
B. Farm animals

(b) Visit Yellowstone National Park.

(c) Glaciers carved the Teton peaks.

(d) William F. Cody is known as "Buffalo Bill."

Solution (a) We place periods after the numbers and letters in an **outline.**

    I. Agriculture in Wyoming
       A. Crops
       B. Farm animals

(b) We place a period at the end of an **imperative sentence.** Visit Yellowstone National Park.

(c) We place a period at the end of a **declarative sentence.** Glaciers carved the Teton peaks.

(d) We place periods after **initials** in a person's name. This is also a **declarative sentence.**
William F. Cody is known as "Buffalo Bill."

Practice Add periods as needed in a–d.

  a. I Rodeo competitions
      A Riding broncos
      B Roping steer

  b. J B Hoven wrote a novel called *The Bucking Bronco*

  c. Don't be ridiculous

  d. Eagles soar among the clouds

For e and f, replace each blank with the correct vocabulary word from this lesson.

  e. There was only a _____ calm during the storm, and then the rain began pounding the roof again.

  f. The coronation of the king was a _____ occasion.

More Practice See "More Practice Lesson 47" in Student Workbook.

Review Set 47 Choose the correct word to complete sentences 1–6.

  1. (*Malicious, Literate, Illiterate*) means "able to read and
  (46) write."

  2. (*Malicious, Cognizant, Prudent*) means "wanting to cause
  (45) injury or pain to another."

3. *Imprudent* means "(cautious, wise, unwise)."
(44)

4. *Maternal* means "of, relating to, or like a (mother, mouse, father)."
(43)

5. (*Val-*, *Loqui*, *Placare*) is a Latin root meaning "strength."
(24)

6. The word *collie's* is a (plural, possessive) noun.
(13)

7. Add suffixes to the following words:
(33, 34)
(a) dry + ing   (b) big + er

8. Write the indirect object in the following sentence:
(46)
Please read me the list of books by Laurence Yep.

9. For a and b, write the word that is spelled correctly.
(35)
(a) beleiving, believing   (b) deceiving, decieving

10. Write each proper adjective from the following sentence:
(42)
Does Rufus like Swiss cheese on Russian rye bread?

11. Rewrite the following sentence, using correct
(41, 43) capitalization:
black-collared lizards live in deserts of the southwest.

12. Write whether the following word group is a phrase or a
(36) clause: the omnivorous bearded dragon

13. In the following sentence, write the entire verb phrase,
(12) circling each helping verb:
Books can broaden our understanding of other cultures.

14. Rewrite the following song title, using correct
(25) capitalization: "on the sunny side of the street"

15. Write the linking verb in the following sentence:
(31)
The horseback riders grew weary.

16. Write whether the following word group is a complete
(23) sentence, a sentence fragment, or a run-on sentence:
Francie, an eighth grade African American girl.

17. From the following sentence, write each prepositional phrase, circling the object of each preposition:
(44)

Everyone at the school except the principal knows about this missing pet.

18. Use a dictionary: (a) The word *bailiff* is what part of speech? (b) Write its pronunciation. (c) Write its etymology.
(27,30)

19. Rewrite the following words, circling each silent letter:
(28, 29)
    (a) walking   (b) scent   (c) badge

20. Rewrite the following sentence, adding periods as needed:
(47)

I believe A J Gallo plays the violin

21. Write whether the following sentence is declarative, interrogative, imperative, or exclamatory:
(2)

Have you heard of Buffalo Bill?

22. Write each limiting adjective from the following sentence:
(40)

The principal raises his eyebrows when he enters Ms. Hoo's classroom, for many students have panicked.

23. For the following sentence, write the correct form of the verb:
(9)

Rufus (present of *catch*) crickets.

24. For the verb *simplify*, write the (a) present participle, (b) past tense, and (c) past participle.
(19)

25. Replace each blank with a descriptive adjective to add more detail to the word "story" in the sentence below. There are many possible answers.
(39)

Ms. Hoo tells a _____, _____ story.

26. Rewrite the following sentence, adding capital letters as needed:
(26, 43)

the principal says, "a bearded dragon belongs in central australia, not in a classroom."

27. For a–c, write the plural of each noun.
(17, 22)
    (a) fistful   (b) cherry   (c) tray

28. Diagram the simple subject and simple predicate of each
(36) clause in the following sentence:

The principal scowls, and Ms. Hoo snaps her fingers, so the students take their seats.

Diagram each word of sentences 29–30.

29. Jasmin's giggle broke the momentary silence.
(40, 45)

30. I made Quan two pieces of toast with jelly.
(45, 46)

Coordinating Conjunctions

Dictation or Journal Entry
Vocabulary:
Plausible means "apparently true; believable; likely." Roger's explanation is *plausible.* I believe it.

Implausible means "not believable; unlikely." The child's wild story seemed *implausible.* I didn't believe it.

Conjunctions are connecting words. They connect words, phrases, and clauses. There are three kinds of conjunctions: coordinating, correlative, and subordinating. In this lesson, we will learn to recognize coordinating conjunctions.

Coordinating Conjunctions

We use a **coordinating conjunction** to join parts of a sentence that are equal in form. Parts of sentences, such as words, phrases, and clauses, are called **elements**. A coordinating conjunction connects a word to a word, a phrase to a phrase, or a clause to a clause. When joined by a conjunction, they are called **compound elements**.

Here are the common coordinating conjunctions:

and   but   or   nor   for   yet   so

They may join a **word** to another **word**:

aunt *and* uncle	Rachel *or* Leah	better *or* worse
firm *yet* kind	walk *and* run	slowly *but* surely

They may join a **phrase** to another **phrase**:

singing loudly *or* humming softly

over the meadow *and* through the woods

They may connect a **clause** to another **clause**:

Anna rushes to the car, *for* she is late.

Quan searches for his python, *but* he can't find it.

Example Circle each coordinating conjunction that you find in these sentences.

(a) Andrew cut his hair and changed his shirt and pants, but he still looked like his twin brother.

(b) I shall ride my bicycle or walk, for I need the exercise.

(c) Ms. Hoo wants to go home and rest, yet she has too many papers to grade.

(d) Ariana brought the ball and bat, but she forgot her glove.

(e) It's not raining, so you may play soccer or baseball.

Solution   (a) Andrew cut his hair (and) changed his shirt (and) pants, (but) he still looked like his twin brother.

(b) I shall ride my bicycle (or) walk, (for) I need the exercise.

(c) Ms. Hoo wants to go home (and) rest, (yet) she has too many papers to grade.

(d) Ariana brought the ball (and) bat, (but) she forgot her glove.

(e) It's not raining, (so) we can play soccer (or) baseball.

✓ **Practice**   **a.** Replace each blank to complete the list of coordinating conjunctions.

_____, but, _____, nor, _____, yet, _____

b. Replace each blank to complete the list of coordinating conjunctions.

and, _____, or, _____, for, _____, so

c. Memorize the seven coordinating conjunctions, and say them to a friend or teacher.

Write each coordinating conjunction, if any, that you find in sentences d–g.

d. Harry washed and dried his white shirt, but it still has red and yellow food stains on it.

e. Harry didn't use detergent or bleach, nor did he use hot water.

f. Harry is disappointed, for the shirt was his favorite, yet now it is ruined.

g. Today is payday, so Harry will buy a new shirt.

For h and i, replace each blank with the correct vocabulary word from this lesson.

h. Roger's reason for coming late seemed _____, or believable.

i. Nelly didn't believe Roger's excuse; she thought it was _____.

Review Set 48 Choose the correct word to complete sentences 1–6.

1. (*Paternal, Maternal, Momentary*) means "lasting only a short time."
(47)

2. *Illiterate* means "unable to (speak, swim, read)."
(46)

3. Malice is desire to do (good, evil, better).
(45)

4. (Prudent, Imprudent, Extravagant) people usually make wise decisions.
(44)

5. The Latin root *val-* means "(talk, calm, strength)."
(24)

6. The word *valor* is a(n) (abstract, concrete) noun.
(11)

7. Add suffixes to the following words:
(33, 34) (a) lay + ed   (b) spin + ing

8. Write the indirect object in the following sentence:
(46)
Joseph gave Dolly some of his grapes.

9. For a and b, write the word that is spelled correctly.
(35) (a) breifcase, briefcase   (b) thier, their

10. Write each coordinating conjunction from the following sentence:
(48)
The cobra and the python are sleeping, but the king snake is wide awake.

11. Rewrite the following letter, using correct capitalization:
(41, 43) dear ann,

perhaps i shall retire and move to north dakota.
sincerely,
ms. hoo

12. Write whether the following word group is a phrase or a
(36) clause: as Perlina snoozed

13. In the following sentence, write the entire verb phrase,
(12) circling each helping verb:

Instead of Brady, Cole might be passing the football.

14. Rewrite the following sentence, using correct
(38) capitalization: i think officer ambush has issued more
speeding tickets than any other officer in the west.

15. Write the linking verb in the following sentence:
(31)
Quan's story about the python sounds plausible to me.

16. Write whether the following word group is a complete
(23) sentence, a sentence fragment, or a run-on sentence:

Erica wrote an essay, a poem, and a research report all in
one day.

17. From the following sentence, write each prepositional
(44) phrase, circling the object of each preposition:

Beside William's chair are bits of bread amid pieces of
torn paper.

18. Use a dictionary: (a) The word *bequest* is what part of
(27,30) speech? (b) Write its pronunciation. (c) Write its
etymology.

19. Rewrite the following words, circling each silent letter:
(28, 29)
(a) handsome   (b) chalk   (c) scene

20. Rewrite the following sentence, adding periods as needed:
(47)

Give my regards to Paul R Flores

21. Write the word from this list that is *not* a linking verb: is,
(31) am, are, was, were, be, being, been, hook, feel, taste, smell.

22. Write each proper or limiting adjective from the
(40, 42) following sentence:

This morning, Eva squeezed some Florida oranges for six
glasses of juice.

23. For the following sentence, write the correct form of the verb:
(10)

Sergio (past of *hum*) a ragtime tune.

24. For the verb *hum*, write the (a) present participle, (b) past
(19) tense, and (c) past participle.

25. Replace each blank with a descriptive adjective to add
(39) more detail to the word "personality" in the sentence. There are many possible answers.

Rufus has a(n) _____, _____ personality.

26. Rewrite the following outline, adding capital letters and
(26, 47) periods as needed:

    i thomas's hobbies
      a reading mysteries
      b riding bikes
      c playing the trumpet

27. For a–c, write the plural of each noun.
(17, 22)

    (a) child of the king   (b) hobby   (c) trout

28. Diagram the simple subject and simple predicate of each
(36) clause in the following sentence:

After Jasmin snorts, her face turns red, and everyone looks her way.

Diagram each word of sentences 29–30.

29. Does the principal fear long, slender reptiles?
(40, 45)

30. Ms. Hoo gives the principal a plausible explanation for
(45, 46) the crickets in her classroom.

LESSON 49

Diagramming Compound Subjects and Predicates

Compound Subjects
The predicate or verb of a sentence may have more than one subject, as in the sentence below.

Terence and *Chase* <u>raced</u>.

In this sentence, the verb "raced" has two subjects: "Terence" and "Chase." We call this a **compound subject**.

Compound Predicates
Likewise, a subject may have more than one predicate, as in the sentence below.

Rosa <u>ran</u> and <u>jumped</u>.

In this sentence, the subject "Rosa" has two predicates: "ran" and "jumped." We call this a **compound predicate**.

Diagramming
To diagram a compound subject or a compound predicate, we place each part of the compound on a separate, horizontal line. We write the conjunction on a vertical dotted line that joins the horizontal lines.

COMPOUND SUBJECT DIAGRAM:

Mr. Yee and *Mrs. Haw* <u>laughed</u>.

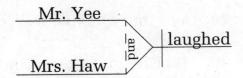

COMPOUND PREDICATE DIAGRAM:

Miss Hoop <u>shoots</u> and <u>scores</u>.

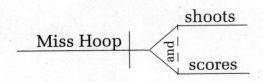

COMPOUND SUBJECT AND COMPOUND PREDICATE DIAGRAM:

Mirta and *Yoli* <u>shout</u> and <u>cheer</u>.

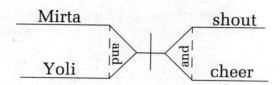

Example Diagram the subjects and predicates of each sentence.

(a) Jessica and Jocelyn chatted.

(b) A canary chirps and sings.

(c) Librarians, engineers, and teachers conceive and present new ideas.

Solution (a) This sentence contains a compound subject.

Jessica and *Jocelyn* <u>chatted</u>.

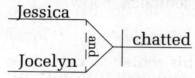

(b) This sentence has a compound predicate. The subject *canary* does two things. It <u>chirps</u> and <u>sings</u>.

A *canary* <u>chirps</u> and <u>sings</u>.

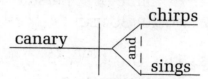

(c) This sentence has a compound subject (*Librarians, engineers, teachers*) and a compound predicate (<u>conceive</u>, <u>present</u>).

Librarians, engineers, and *teachers* <u>conceive</u> and <u>present</u> new ideas.

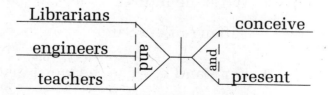

✓ Practice For a and b, replace each blank with the correct vocabulary word from this lesson.

    a. Though nervous, the pianist gave a _____ performance. Most of the audience enjoyed it.

    b. Cruelty to animals is _____.

Diagram the <u>simple subjects</u> and <u>simple predicates</u> of sentences c–e.

    c. Drummers and guitarists practice daily.

    d. The pianist bows and smiles at the audience.

    e. Sheep and cattle roam and graze in the valley.

More Practice See "More Practice Lesson 49" in Student Workbook.

Review Set 49 Choose the correct word to complete sentences 1–6.

    1. *Plausible* means "apparently (funny, true, false)."
    (48)

    2. (*Momentary, Momentous, Dispensable*) means of "great importance or consequence."
    (47)

    3. *Literate* means "able to (dance, read, sing) and write."
    (46)

    4. A malicious person wants to cause (laughter, harm, healing).
    (45)

    5. The Greek word (*ignis, metamorphosis, loqui*) means "transformation."
    (26)

    6. The word *family* is a (collective, compound) noun.
    (11)

    7. Add suffixes to the following words:
    (33, 34) (a) dry + est   (b) hop + ed

    8. Write the indirect object in the following sentence:
    (46)
    Tiffany offers Sarah a new pencil.

    9. For a and b, write the word that is spelled correctly.
    (35) (a) peice, piece   (b) biege, beige

10. Write the seven common coordinating conjunctions (48) listed in Lesson 48.

11. Rewrite the following sentence, using correct (41, 43) capitalization:

in october we enjoy fall colors in the northeast.

12. Write whether the following word group is a phrase or a (36) clause:

an intolerable amount of homework

13. In the following sentence, write the entire verb phrase, (12) circling each helping verb:

Elizabeth could have run the mile much faster.

14. Rewrite the following book title, using correct (25) capitalization: *the tales of uncle remus*

15. Write the linking verb in the following sentence: (31)

She felt miserable.

16. Write whether the following word group is a complete (23) sentence, a sentence fragment, or a run-on sentence:

Citrus fruits came from Southeast Asia now they grow in the United States.

17. From the following sentence, write each prepositional (44) phrase, circling the object of each preposition:

The dogs are sniffing throughout the classroom, around books, under desks, and behind cabinets.

18. Use a dictionary: (a) The word *scant* is what part of (27,30) speech? (b) Write its pronunciation. (c) Write its etymology.

19. Rewrite the following words, circling each silent letter: (28, 29)
(a) gnaw   (b) wrench   (c) solemn

20. Rewrite the following sentence, adding periods as needed: (47)

Jack B Nimble burned his toes

21. Write whether the following sentence is declarative, interrogative, imperative, or exclamatory: Did Ms. Hoo let the dogs out?

(2)

22. Write each proper or limiting adjective from the following sentence:

(40, 42)

Those Labrador retrievers are following the scent of several reptiles.

23. For the following sentence, write the correct form of the verb:

(9)

Sergio (present of *identify*) the subject of the sentence.

24. For the verb *identify*, write the (a) present participle, (b) past tense, and (c) past participle.

(19)

25. Replace each blank with a descriptive adjective to add more detail to the word "cage" in the sentence below. There are many possible answers.

(39)

Rufus has a(n) _____, _____ cage.

26. Rewrite the following sentence, adding capital letters as needed:

(26,)

the principal complains, "this chaos is intolerable."

27. For a–c, write the plural of each noun.

(17, 22)

(a) Labrador retriever   (b) foot   (c) capful

28. Diagram the simple subject and simple predicate of each clause in the following sentence:

(36)

Crickets hop here and there, and Ms. Hoo steps aside as a dog sniffs her feet.

Diagram each word of sentences 29–30.

29. Crickets and reptiles avoid dogs with cold, wet noses.

(45, 49)

30. The principal gives Ms. Hoo a stern lecture on the
(45, 46) importance of order in the classroom.

LESSON 50

The Period, Part 2: Abbreviations and Decimals

Abbreviations

Sometimes we shorten words by abbreviating them. **Abbreviations** often require periods. Because there are so many abbreviations, and because some abbreviations are used for more than one word, we check our dictionaries. Below are some common abbreviations that require periods. While it is important to become familiar with these abbreviations, we do not normally use abbreviations in formal writing. **When in doubt, spell it out.**

Time of Day

a.m. (Latin *ante meridiem*, "before noon")

p.m. (Latin *post meridiem*, "after noon")

Days of the Week

Sun. (Sunday)   Thurs. (Thursday)

Mon. (Monday)   Fri. (Friday)

Tues. (Tuesday)   Sat. (Saturday)

Wed. (Wednesday)

Months of the Year

Jan. (January)   July (no abbreviation)

Feb. (February)   Aug. (August)

Mar. (March)   Sept. (September)

Apr. (April)   Oct. (October)

May (no abbreviation) Nov. (November)

June (no abbreviation) Dec. (December)

Personal Titles

Mr. (Mister)   Miss (no abbreviation)

Mrs. (Mistress; a married woman)

Ms. (any woman, especially one whose marital status is unknown)

Jr. (Junior)   Sr. (Senior)

Dr. (Doctor)   Rev. (Reverend)

Prof. (Professor)   Pres. (President)

Gen. (General)	Capt. (Captain)
Sen. (Senator)	Rep. (Representative)

Proper Place Names We may abbreviate the following words when they appear in addresses as part of a proper place name (as in *Main Street*). They are not abbreviated when they are used as common nouns (as in *down the street*).

St. (Street)	Rd. (Road)
Dr. (Drive)	Blvd. (Boulevard)
Pl. (Place)	Ave. (Avenue)
Mt. (Mount, Mountain)	Bldg. (Building)

Compass Directions Compass directions may be abbreviated when they appear in addresses as part of a proper place name.

N. (North)	N.E. (Northeast)
S. (South)	N.W. (Northwest)
E. (East)	S.E. (Southeast)
W. (West)	S.W. (Southwest)

Others Here are a few other commonly-used abbreviations.

Inc. (Incorporated)	etc. (Latin *et cetera,* "and so forth")
Co. (Company)	est. (estimated)
Ltd. (Limited)	cont. (continued)
govt. (government)	anon. (anonymous)
dept. (department)	misc. (miscellaneous)

Decimal Point We use a period as a **decimal point** to show dollars and cents and to show the place value of numbers. Note: When we read a number, the "and" shows where the decimal point belongs.

$3.20 (three dollars and twenty cents)

6.5 (six and five tenths)

Example Add periods as needed in a–d.

(a) Mrs Cabrera lives at 117 N Pine St

(b) A bouquet of roses costs $999 (nine dollars and 99 cents).

(c) The notice reads "Homework due Wed Jan 21."

(d) I will see Dr Hetzel at ten am tomorrow.

Solution (a) **Mrs.** (Mistress), **N.** (North), and **St.** (Street), are abbreviations that require periods.

(b) **$9.99** requires a period as a decimal point to show nine dollars *and* ninety-nine cents.

(c) **Wed.** (Wednesday) and **Jan.** (January) are abbreviations that require periods.

(d) **Dr.** (doctor) and **a.m.** (*ante meridiem*, "before noon") are abbreviations that require periods.

Practice Add periods as needed in a–h. (Hint: When a sentence ends with an abbreviation that requires a period, that same period serves as the final punctuation!)

a. Mr and Mrs Hatti drove south on Baldwin Ave

b. School begins at 8 a m each weekday

c. Ms Lim winked at Ms Hoo

d. The Rev Freddy Rivas performed the marriage ceremony

e. Capt H R Montgomery commands the troops

f. "Gimme Toy Co" was the name on the box

g. Prof Werks wrote, "Hike to Mt Whitney in Aug"

h. We had driven 72 (seven and two tenths) miles

For i and j, replace each blank with the correct vocabulary word from this lesson.

i. Full of _____, Quan gave generously to help the victims of the fire.

j. The _____ teenager was determined to help in any way possible.

More Practice See "More Practice Lesson 50" in Student Workbook.

Choose the correct word to complete sentences 1–6.

1. (*Paternal, Plausible, Tolerable*) means "bearable or
(49) moderately good."

2. *Implausible* means "not (pretty, readable, believable)."
(48)

3. *Momentary* means "lasting a (long, short) time."
(47)

4. (*Prudent, Literate, Illiterate*) means "unable to read or
(46) write."

5. The Greek word *metamorphosis* means "(fire, talk,
(26) transformation)."

6. The word *family's* is a (plural, possessive) noun.
(13)

7. Add suffixes to the following words:
(33, 34) (a) pat + ed   (b) cry + ed

8. Write the indirect object in the following sentence:
(46)
Eva threw Aaron an eraser.

9. For a and b, write the word that is spelled correctly.
(35) (a) receiver, reciever   (b) nieghborly, neighborly

10. Write each coordinating conjunction from the following
(48) sentence:

Rufus doesn't understand English or Spanish, so I shall
speak to him in Russian.

11. Rewrite the following letter, using correct capitalization:
(41, 43) dear ms. hoo,

  the noise from your room disturbs my students.
          respectfully,
          mr. annoyd

12. Write whether the following word group is a phrase or a
(36) clause: as dogs bark and yip

13. In the following sentence, write the entire verb phrase,
(12) circling each helping verb:

Buddy must warn the others!

14. Rewrite the following sentence, using correct capitalization:

is rufus attending professor speek's french class with uncle noah?

15. Write the linking verb in the following sentence:

The new puppy grew tired of whining.

16. Write whether the following word group is a complete sentence, a sentence fragment, or a run-on sentence:

Juliet Gordon Lowe, founder of the Girl Scouts.

17. From the following sentence, write each prepositional phrase, circling the object of each preposition:

After lunch, Perlina looks at the clock, rests her head on her desk, and sleeps for thirty minutes.

18. Use a dictionary: (a) The word *limpid* is what part of speech? (b) Write its pronunciation. (c) Write its etymology.

19. Rewrite the following words, circling each silent letter:

(a) castle　　　(b) scent　　　(c) should

20. Rewrite the following sentence, adding periods as needed:

An ambulance rushed Mr Jack B Nimble to the Joan C Giddy Hospital at seven pm

21. Write the word from this list that is *not* a linking verb: look, feel, taste, swell, sound, seem, appear, grow, become, remain, stay.

22. Write each proper or limiting adjective from the following sentence:

One Labrador retriever chases a spider around Perlina's desk.

23. For the following sentence, write the correct form of the verb:

A cow (past of *swat*) flies with her tail.

24. For the verb *swat*, write the (a) present participle, (b) past
(19) tense, and (c) past participle.

25. Replace each blank with a descriptive adjective to add
(39) more detail to the word "teacher" in the sentence below.
There are many possible answers.

Ms. Hoo is a(n) _____, _____ teacher.

26. Rewrite the following lines of poetry, adding capital
(26,) letters as needed:

little miss muffet
sat on a tuffet...

27. For a–c, write the plural of each noun.
(17, 22)
(a) man of God   (b) goose   (c) match

28. Diagram the <u>simple subject</u> and <u>simple predicate</u> of each
(36) clause in the following sentence:

Mr. Annoyd calls the principal, for he demands silence
when he teaches science.

Diagram each word of sentences 29–30.

29. Can Jasmin and her friends find Rufus?
(45, 49)

30. My benevolent aunt sent me a check for twenty dollars.
(45, 46)

The Predicate Nominative

Dictation or Journal Entry

Vocabulary:

Feline is an adjective meaning "of or relating to cats or the cat family." Lions, tigers, and leopards are *feline* animals.

Canine is an adjective meaning "of, relating to, or resembling a dog." Wolves, foxes, coyotes, and jackals are *canine* animals.

More than one name can identify people, animals, or things.

Flicka was an Arabian horse.

In the sentence above, "horse" is another name for "Flicka."

Renames the Subject

A **predicate nominative** is a noun that follows the verb and renames the subject person, animal, or thing. It explains or defines the subject and is identical with it. The subject and the predicate nominative are joined by a linking verb such as *am, is, are, was, were, be, being, been, become,* or *seem.* We remember that a linking verb does not show action, nor does it "help" the action verb. Its purpose is to connect the person, animal, or thing (the subject) to its new name (the predicate nominative).

Predicate nominatives are circled in the sentences below.

Tennis is my favorite sport.

"sport" renames "Tennis"

Marina is my friend.

"friend" renames "Marina"

If we reverse the subject and the predicate nominative, as in the sentences below, the meaning of the sentence is not affected.

My favorite *sport* is tennis.

My *friend* is Marina.

Identifying the Predicate Nominative

Reversing the subject and predicate nominative in this manner helps us identify predicate nominatives. If the linking verb is not a "to be" verb, we replace it with a "to be" verb to determine whether there is a predicate nominative that renames the subject.

An *island* <u>became</u> a wildlife refuge.

An *island* <u>is</u> a wildlife refuge.

↑

"to be" linking verb

Now we reverse the subject and predicate nominative, and we see that the predicate does indeed rename the subject. The meaning is the same, so we have identified a predicate nominative.

A wildlife *refuge* <u>is</u> an island.

Predicate nominatives are more difficult to identify in interrogative sentences. Turning the question into a statement will help.

Question: Is Colonel Apple the woman with red hair?

Statement: Colonel Apple is the woman with red hair.

In the statement above, we see that "woman" renames "Colonel Apple." Therefore, "woman" is a predicate nominative.

Compound Predicate Nominatives

Predicate nominatives may be compound, as in the sentences below.

Our winter *sports* <u>are</u> (skiing), (skating), and (sledding).

The best *writers* that week <u>were</u> (Grace) and (Chris).

Diagramming

In a diagram, the predicate nominative is indicated by a line that slants toward the left. Here we diagram the simple subject, linking verb, and predicate nominatives of some of the sentences above.

Flicka was an Arabian horse.

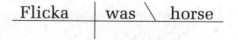

Marina is my friend.

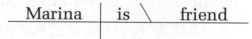

Our winter sports are skiing, skating, and sledding.

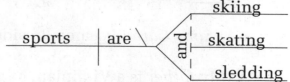

Example Diagram the simple subject, linking verb, and predicate nominatives of the following sentences. The simple subject is italicized and the linking verb is underlined to help you.

(a) Georgia's *exports* <u>are</u> cotton, peaches, peanuts, and poultry.

(b) *Savannah* <u>was</u> Georgia's first capital.

(c) *Atlanta* <u>became</u> the capital of Georgia.

(d) *Boll weevils* <u>were</u> terrible pests.

Solution (a)

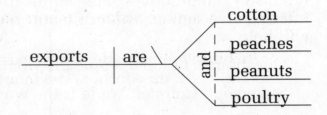

(b)

Savannah | was \ capital

(c)

Atlanta | became \ capital

(d)

Boll weevils | were \ pests

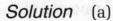 **Practice** For a and b, replace each blank with the correct vocabulary word.

a. Dogs are _____ animals.

b. Cats are _____ animals.

For c–f, diagram the <u>simple subject</u>, <u>linking verb</u>, and <u>predicate nominatives</u> in each sentence.

c. *Lake Placid* <u>became</u> a resort.

d. <u>Was</u> *Uncle Sam* a real person?

e. *Jimmy Carter* <u>became</u> President in 1976.

f. My *father* <u>is</u> a Virginian.

Review Set 51   Choose the correct word to complete sentences 1–6.

1. Benevolence causes people to be (evil, generous, greedy).
(50)

2. Extreme temperatures can be (plausible, frugal, intolerable) if you do not have proper clothing.
(49)

3. An implausible excuse is (true, unlikely, believable).
(48)

4. A momentous occasion is (short, sad, important).
(47)

5. A (tributary, mesa, delta), a triangular-shaped area of sand and silt, may form at the mouth of a river.
(13)

6. The word *benevolence* is a(n) (abstract, concrete) noun.
(11)

7. Add suffixes to the following words:
(33, 34)   (a) happy + est   (b) big + er

8. Write the indirect object in the following sentence:
(46)

Esperanza gave Isabel her porcelain doll.

9. For a and b, write the word that is spelled correctly.
(35)   (a) freind, friend   (b) weighing, wieghing

10. Write the seven common coordinating conjunctions listed in Lesson 48.
(48)

11. Rewrite the following sentence, using correct capitalization:
(41, 43)

mr. annoyd would send the bearded dragon back to central australia.

12. Write whether the following word group is a phrase or a clause: a black-collared lizard and its friends
(36)

13. In the following sentence, write the entire verb phrase, circling each helping verb:
(12)

Laborers have been picking grapes in the hot sun.

14. Rewrite the following song title, using correct capitalization:

(25)

"there's a hole in the bucket"

15. Write the predicate nominative in the following sentence:

(51)

Esperanza remains the most memorable character.

16. Write whether the following word group is a complete sentence, a sentence fragment, or a run-on sentence:

(23)

Esperanza loved her family's ranch in Mexico.

17. From the following sentence, write each prepositional phrase, circling the object of each preposition:

(44)

During the blizzard, Uray leans into the wind and walks toward home.

18. Use a dictionary: (a) The word *nuthatch* is what part of speech? (b) Write its pronunciation. (c) Write its etymology.

(27,30)

19. Rewrite the following words, circling each silent letter:

(28, 29)

(a) knowing   (b) ache   (c) bright

20. Rewrite the following sentence, adding periods as needed:

(47, 50)

Dr Payne will mail the bill to Mr Jack B Nimble, 531 Candlestick Rd

21. Write the linking verb from the following sentence:

(31)

The papayas smelled sweet and ripe.

22. Write each proper or limiting adjective from the following sentence:

(40, 42)

A Russian wolfhound joins the search for Jasmin's pets.

23. For the following sentence, write the correct form of the verb:

(9)

Jasmin (present of *cherish*) all her pets.

24. For the verb *verify*, write the (a) present participle, (b) past tense, and (c) past participle.

(19)

25. Replace each blank with a descriptive adjective to add more detail to the word "expression" in the sentence below. There are many possible answers.

Mr. Annoyd wears a(n) _____, _____ expression.

26. Rewrite the following sentence, adding capital letters as needed: mr. annoyd says, "please be quiet."

27. For a–c, write the plural of each noun.

(a) glass of milk   (b) child   (c) glassful

28. Diagram the simple subject and simple predicate of each clause in the following sentence: Since the principal has gone to lunch, his secretary will handle the complaint if she is able.

Diagram each word of sentences 29–30.

29. Ms. Hoo is Jasmin's teacher and the wife of William's cousin.

Hint:

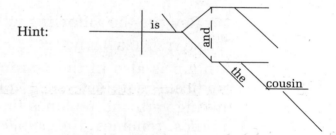

30. Our canine friends are giving Mr. Annoyd a headache.

Noun Case, Part 1: Nominative and Possessive

We can group nouns into three **cases:** *nominative, possessive,* and *objective.* The case of the noun explains how the noun is used in the sentence. In this lesson, we will learn to identify nouns that are in the nominative and possessive cases.

Nominative Case

SUBJECT OF A SENTENCE

A noun is in the **nominative case** when it is the <u>subject</u> of a sentence. In the sentence below, the noun *lizard* is in the nominative case because it is the subject of the sentence.

A *lizard* lies in the sun.

PREDICATE NOMINATIVE

A noun is also in the **nominative case** when it is used as a predicate nominative. A <u>predicate nominative</u> follows a linking verb and renames the subject. In the sentence below, *reptiles* renames the subject, lizards. *Reptiles* is in the nominative case because it is a predicate nominative.

Lizards are *reptiles.*

Possessive Case

We are familiar with nouns that show possession or ownership. These nouns are in the **possessive case**. In the sentence below, the possessive noun *Jasmin's* is in the possessive case.

Rufus is *Jasmin's* lizard.

Example

Tell whether the italicized noun in each sentence is in the nominative case or the possessive case. If it is in the nominative case, tell whether it is the subject of the sentence or a predicate nominative.

(a) A *mouse* nibbled my toe.

(b) A cricket is an *insect.*

(c) *Rufus's* cage is empty.

Solution (a) The word *mouse* is in the **nominative case.** It is the **subject of the sentence.**

(b) The word *insect* is in the **nominative case.** It is a **predicate nominative;** it follows the linking verb *is* and renames the subject.

(c) *Rufus's* is in the **possessive case.** It shows possession; it tells "whose cage."

✓**Practice** For sentences a–e, tell whether the italicized noun is in the nominative case or the possessive case. If it is in the nominative case, tell whether it is the subject of the sentence or a predicate nominative.

a. The long green *lizard* ate two crickets.

b. Mr. Stoneman is the *principal.*

c. The *principal's* eyes popped open.

d. Have the *dogs* located the reptiles?

e. Green is my favorite *color.*

For f and g, replace each blank with the correct vocabulary word from this lesson.

f. Horses are _____ creatures.

g. Cows are _____ creatures.

Review Set Choose the correct word to complete sentences 1–6.
52

1. A cat is a (feline, canine) animal.
(51)

2. (*Benevolent, Malicious, Imprudent*) means "desiring to do
(50) good; kind."

3. *Tolerable* means "(unbearable, terrible, bearable)."
(49)

4. *Plausible* and *implausible* are (synonyms, antonyms,
(48) homophones).

5. A (tributary, peninsula, isthmus) is a stream that flows
(13) into a larger stream or river.

6. The word *herd* is a (compound, collective) noun.
(11)

7. Add suffixes to the following words:
(33, 34) (a) merry + ly   (b) admit + ed

8. Write the indirect object in the following sentence:
(46)

Miguel hands Esperanza a rosebush.

9. For a and b, write the word that is spelled correctly.
(35) (a) relief, releif   (b) wieghty, weighty

10. Write each coordinating conjunction from the following
(48) sentence:

I called to Rufus in Russian and French, yet he did not respond.

11. Rewrite the following letter, using correct capitalization:
(41, 43) dear mr. annoyd,

       please believe me. i am trying to keep my class quiet.
                         seriously,
                         ms. hoo

12. Write whether the following word group is a phrase or a
(36) clause: as the lizard blinks

13. In the following sentence, write the entire verb phrase,
(12) circling each helping verb:

Esperanza might have given up on life.

14. Rewrite the following sentence, using correct
(38) capitalization:

does aunt rosa believe that officer ambush has an invisible car?

15. Write the predicate nominative in the following sentence:
(51)

The rosebush was a gift.

16. Write whether the following word group is a complete
(23) sentence, a sentence fragment, or a run-on sentence:

An elaborate home with many servants.

17. From the following sentence, write each prepositional phrase, circling the object of each preposition:
(44)

Esperanza is full of love for the land.

18. Use a dictionary: (a) The word *mangy* is what part of
(27,30) speech? (b) Write its pronunciation. (c) Write its etymology.

19. Rewrite the following words, circling each silent letter:
(28, 29)
    (a) column   (b) match   (c) who

20. Rewrite the following sentence, adding periods as needed:
(47, 50)

Ms Hatti will begin teaching on Sept 9

21. Write whether the following sentence is declarative,
(2) interrogative, imperative, or exclamatory:

Did you see the lush green forests of West Virginia?

22. Write each adjective from the following sentence:
(40, 42)
A helpful student counted the clear, glass marbles.

23. For the following sentence, write the correct form of the
(10) verb:

Spotty (past of *stir*) the paint.

24. For the verb *stir*, write the (a) present participle, (b) past
(19) tense, and (c) past participle.

25. Write whether the circled word in the sentence below is
(52) in the nominative case or the possessive case:

Cattle are bovine (creatures)

26. Rewrite the following outline, adding periods and capital
(26, 47) letters as needed:

    i bovine animals
      a oxen
      b antelope
      c cows

27. For a–c, write the plural of each noun.
(17, 22)

(a) science teacher   (b) ox   (c) thief

28. Diagram the simple subject and simple predicate of each
(36) clause in the following sentence: When he returns, Mr.
Stoneman will visit Ms. Hoo unless she has gone home.

Diagram each word of sentences 29–30.

29. My dad is a skillful carpenter and my best friend.
49, 51)

Hint: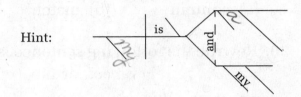

30. Rufus and his buddy showed the dog their sharp teeth.
(46, 49)

LESSON 53

Noun Case, Part 2: Objective

Dictation or Journal Entry

Vocabulary:

Olfactory is an adjective meaning "of or relating to the sense of smell." The nose is our *olfactory* organ.

Auditory is an adjective meaning "of or relating to the sense of hearing." Ears are our *auditory* organs.

We have learned to identify nouns that are in the nominative and possessive cases. In this lesson, we will see examples of nouns that are in the objective case.

Objective Case A noun is in the **objective case** when it is used as a *direct object*, an *indirect object*, or the *object of a preposition*. Let's review these "objects."

Direct Object A noun or pronoun is called a **direct object** when it is the direct receiver of the action of the verb. Direct objects are circled in the sentences below.

Rigo made (lunch).
(Rigo made *what*?)

I picked (cotton).

Who will prepare (dinner)?

Indirect Object An **indirect object** is the noun or pronoun that tells "to whom" or "for whom" the action was done. In the following examples, the indirect objects are circled.

Did you bring (Fido) a snack?
(Did you bring a snack for *Fido*?)

The runner passed (Tim) the baton.
(The runner passed the baton to *Tim*.)

Please send (Kristina) a postcard.
(Please send a postcard to *Kristina*.)

Object of a Preposition A noun or pronoun that follows a preposition is called the **object of a preposition**. Objects of the prepositions are circled in the examples below.

at the (museum)   over the (top)

around the (lake)   besides (him)

near (her)   after the (show)

Example 1 For sentences, a–c, tell whether each circled noun is a direct object, an indirect object, or the object of a preposition.

(a) Esther fried (Marissa) an egg.

(b) I sweep the (sidewalk) on Mondays.

(c) Justin fell off the (chair).

Solution (a) *Marissa* is an **indirect object.** It tells "for whom" the egg was fried.

(b) *Sidewalk* is a **direct object.** It is the receiver of the action verb *sweep.*

(c) *Chair* is the **object of the preposition** *off.*

Example 2 Tell whether the circled noun is in the nominative, possessive, or objective case.

(a) Andrew and Ryan studied (pelicans).

(b) My hair is shorter than (Kay's).

(c) Vivian is an artistic (student).

(d) An alligator slides into the (water).

Solution (a) *Pelicans* is a direct object. Therefore, it is in the **objective case.**

(b) *Kay's* is a possessive noun. Therefore, it is in the **possessive case.**

(c) *Student* is a predicate nominative. Therefore, it is in the **nominative case.**

(d) *Water* is the object of a preposition. Therefore, it is in the **objective case.**

Practice For sentences a–f, write whether the circled noun is a direct object (D.O.), an indirect object (I.O.), or the object of a preposition (O.P.).

a. Fido leaped over the (wall).

b. Grant threw (Aaron) the ball.

c. Serena caught the (ball).

d. A lizard sat upon the (rock).

e. Mahalia plays the (violin).

f. I gave my (dog) a bath.

For g–j, write whether the circled noun is in the nominative, possessive, or objective case.

g. Does (Fido) need water?

h. Crows are eating the (corn).

i. Erica borrowed (Gloria's) pen.

j. Gloria loaned (Erica) a pen.

For k and l, replace each blank with the correct vocabulary word from this lesson.

k. The sense of hearing is our _____ sense.

l. The sense of smell is our _____ sense.

Review Set 53

Choose the correct word to complete sentences 1–6.

1. Rebecca is taking a college class called "Equine Care."
(52) She is studying (birds, fish, horses).

2. A dog is a (feline, canine) animal.
(51)

3. *Benevolent* means "desiring to do (evil, homework,
(50) good)."

4. (*Imprudent, Intolerable, Illiterate*) means " unbearable;
(49) unable to be endured."

5. A (tributary, strait, hemisphere) is one half of Earth.
(14)

6. The word *firefighters* is a (plural, possessive) noun.
(13)

7. Add suffixes to the following words:
(33, 34)
  (a) cry + s   (b) top + ing

8. Write the indirect object in the following sentence:
(46)
Ernesto handed the fiddler a bow.

9. For a and b, write the word that is spelled correctly.
(35) (a) feild, field　　　　　　　(b) conciet, conceit

10. Write the seven common coordinating conjunctions
(48) listed in Lesson 48.

11. Rewrite the following sentence, using correct
(41, 43) capitalization:
in the midwest, people attend rodeos for entertainment.

12. Write whether the following word group is a phrase or a
(36) clause: in the shaggy dog's left ear

13. In the following sentence, write the entire verb phrase,
(12) circling each helping verb:
By next week, Ernesto will have completed his report.

14. Rewrite the following book title, using correct
(25) capitalization: *little house on the prairie*

15. Write the predicate nominative in the following sentence:
(51)
Is Niagara Falls the most famous waterfall in the world?

16. Write whether the following word group is a complete
(23) sentence, a sentence fragment, or a run-on sentence:
The Winter Olympics was held at Lake Placid, NY, it is a
famous resort.

17. From the following sentence, write each prepositional
(44) phrase, circling the object of each preposition:
From the city of Hershey in Pennsylvania comes much of
the world's chocolate.

18. Use a dictionary: (a) The word *malice* is what part of
(27,30) speech? (b) Write its pronunciation. (c) Write its
etymology.

19. Rewrite the following words, circling each silent letter:
(28, 29)
(a) knock　　　　(b) lamb　　　　(c) guess

20. Rewrite the following sentence, adding periods as needed:
(47, 50)

Dr Jo B Ngo will see you at two pm tomorrow

21. Write the word from this list that could *not* be a linking
(31) verb: is, am, are, was, wart, be, being, been, look, feel.

22. Write each adjective from the following sentence:
(40, 42)

A glorious rainbow arches above the smooth, glacial
lake.

23. For the following sentence, write the correct form of the
(14) verb:

We (future of *paint*) the fence tomorrow.

24. For the verb *dip*, write the (a) present participle, (b) past
(19) tense, and (c) past participle.

25. Write whether the circled word in the sentence below is
(52, 53) in the nominative, possessive, or objective case:

The puppy wagged its short (tail).

26. Rewrite the following sentence, adding capital letters as
(26) needed:

mr. stoneman said, "perhaps i shall cancel school until
friday."

27. For a–c, write the plural of each noun.
(17, 22)

(a) bird of prey   (b) Friday   (c) century

28. Diagram the simple subject and simple predicate of each
(36) clause in the following sentence:

If chaos continues, Mr. Stoneman will cancel school until
Ms. Hoo captures the animals.

Diagram each word of sentences 29–30.

29. Dan's little sister might become a serious student and
(49, 51) President of the United States.

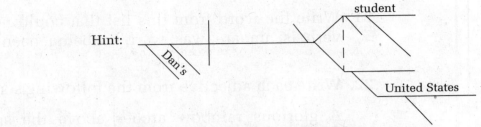

Hint:

30. Adam and Eva sent me their new address.
(46, 49)

LESSON 54

The Predicate Adjective

We have learned that a predicate nominative follows a linking verb and *renames* the subject.

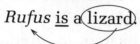

Rufus is a lizard.

"Lizard" renames Rufus.

Describes the Subject   A **predicate adjective** follows a linking verb and *describes* or gives more detail about the subject.

Rufus is shy.

"Shy" describes Rufus.

In the sentence above, the word "shy" is a predicate adjective. It describes "Rufus"— shy Rufus.

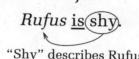

Lulu was lonely.

In the sentence above, the word "lonely" is a predicate adjective. It describes "Lulu"— lonely Lulu.

The linking verb that connects the subject to the predicate adjective may be a "to be" verb (*is, am, are, was, were, be, been*), but other linking verbs such as *become, seem, feel, appear, look, taste,* and *smell* also can link the predicate adjective to the subject.

Lulu <u>looks</u> sad.

The *lemon* <u>tastes</u> sour.

Identifying Predicate Adjectives   To help us identify the predicate adjective, we can replace a possible linking verb with a "to be" verb.

Lulu <u>is</u> sad.

↑

"to be" verb

In the sentence above, we see that "sad" describes the subject "Lulu"— sad Lulu. Therefore, "sad" is a predicate adjective.

The *lemon* <u>is</u> sour.

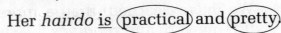

"to be" verb

In the sentence above, we see that "sour" describes the subject "lemon"— sour lemon. "Sour" is a predicate adjective.

Compound Predicate Adjectives

A predicate adjective may be compound, as in the sentence below. Predicate adjectives are circled.

Her *hairdo* <u>is</u> (practical) and (pretty)

Diagramming

We diagram a predicate adjective in the same way we diagram a predicate nominative. Here is a diagram of the simple subject, linking verb, and predicate adjectives of the sentence above:

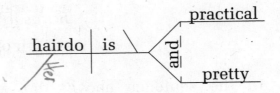

Example

Diagram the simple subject, linking verb, and predicate adjectives in sentences a–d.

(a) Squirrels <u>are</u> arboreal.

(b) That monkey <u>appears</u> tame.

(c) Some amphibians <u>look</u> scary.

(d) Wyoming <u>seems</u> high and windy.

Solution

(a)

| Squirrels | are \ arboreal |

(b)

| monkey | appears \ tame |

(c)

| amphibians | look \ scary |

(d)

✓ **Practice** For sentences a–d, diagram the simple subjects, linking verbs, and predicate adjectives.

    a. Bison <u>are</u> plentiful in Wyoming.

    b. Beets and hay <u>have been</u> profitable there.

    c. The state <u>became</u> wealthy and famous.

    d. Designers <u>were</u> creative with the flag.

For e and f, replace each blank with the correct vocabulary word from this lesson.

    e. _____ creatures live in trees.

    f. An _____ lives both on land and in water.

✓ **Review Set 54** Choose the correct word(s) to complete sentences 1–8.

    1. Grandpa could not smell the burning casserole, for he
    (53) had lost his (olfactory, auditory, tactile) sense.

    2. A cow is a (bovine, canine, equine) creature.
    (52)

    3. A (cat, bird, dog) is a feline animal.
    (51)

    4. (Illiterate, Avaricious, Benevolent) people make the
    (50) world a better place because of their kindness.

    5. (Latitude, Longitude) lines form circles running east and
    (15) west, parallel to the equator.

    6. The word *firefighters* is a(n) (abstract, concrete) noun.
    (11)

    7. Bob (tryed, tried) not to laugh.
    (33, 34)

    8. His (neighbor, nieghbor) (believes, beleives) the tall tale.
    (35)

9. Write the indirect object in the following sentence:

(46)

Conrad lent Erik money for lunch.

10. Write each coordinating conjunction in the following

(48) sentence:

British Columbia and Alberta mine coal, but the Yukon Territory mines silver.

11. Rewrite the following letter, using correct capitalization:

(41, 43) dear officer ambush,

please stop those who speed on fourth street.
respectfully,
josef habib

12. Write whether the following word group is a phrase or a

(36) clause: before Egbert saw me

13. In the following sentence, write the entire verb phrase,

(12) circling each helping verb:

You must have seen the dense forests in Washington.

14. Rewrite the following sentence, using correct

(38) capitalization:

esperanza desperately wants grandma to join her.

15. Write the predicate adjective in the following sentence:

(54)

Jasmin seems hopeful.

16. Write whether the following word group is a complete

(23) sentence, a sentence fragment, or a run-on sentence:

Kentucky's Fort Knox Gold Vault, the nation's gold depository.

17. From the following sentence, write each prepositional

(44) phrase, circling the object of each preposition:

From dawn until dusk, the family picked strawberries and put them in baskets.

18. Use a dictionary: (a) The word *maize* is what part of

(27,30) speech? (b) Write its pronunciation. (c) Write its etymology.

19. Rewrite the following words, circling each silent letter:
(28, 29)

    (a) wreath   (b) adjust   (c) calf

20. Rewrite the following outline, adding capital letters and
(47, 50) periods as needed:

    i cities in delaware
       a wilmington—capital
       b lewes—whaling colony

21. Write whether the following sentence is declarative,
(2) interrogative, imperative, or exclamatory:

    Which state is the "Garden State"?

22. Write each adjective from the following sentence:
(40, 42)

    Taste this delicious, ripe tomato from fertile New Jersey.

23. For the following sentence, write the correct form of the
(9) verb:

    Spotty (present of *pry*) open the paint can.

24. For the verb *pry*, write the (a) present participle, (b) past
(19) tense, and (c) past participle.

25. Write whether the circled word in the sentence below is
(52, 53) in the nominative, possessive, or objective case:

    The (puppy) wagged its short tail.

26. Rewrite the following lines of poetry, adding capital
(15) letters as needed:

    no one can say
    what will happen today.

27. For a–c, write the plural of each noun.
(17, 22)

    (a) lunch break   (b) calf   (c) story

28. Diagram the simple subject and simple predicate of each
(36) clause in the following sentence: If Ms. Hoo finds Rufus,
she will scold him, for he has caused trouble.

Diagram each word of sentences 29–30.

29. My cousin has been feeling joyful and optimistic.
(49, 54)

30. Adam and Eva gave us a book with beautiful illustrations.
(46, 49)

Comparison Adjectives

Adjectives are often used to compare nouns or pronouns. These **comparative adjectives** have three forms that show greater or lesser degrees of quality, quantity, or manner: **positive**, **comparative**, and **superlative**. Below are examples of the positive, comparative, and superlative forms of some adjectives.

POSITIVE	COMPARATIVE	SUPERLATIVE
small	smaller	smallest
slow	slower	slowest
hard	harder	hardest
silly	sillier	silliest
busy	busier	busiest

Positive Form The positive form describes a noun or pronoun without comparing it to any other. (Do not confuse *positive* with *good*. Here, *positive* simply means "possessing the quality." The quality itself may be good, bad, or neutral.)

Dan is *tall*.

Bananas are *tasty*.

Ms. Hoo is *busy*.

Comparative Form The comparative form compares **two** persons, places, or things.

Dan is *taller* than Tina.

Are bananas *tastier* than apples?

Ms. Hoo is *busier* than Ms. Lu.

Superlative Form The superlative form compares **three or more** persons, places, or things.

Of all the students, Dan is the *tallest*.

Are bananas the *tastiest* of all the fruits?

Ms. Hoo is the *busiest* of the four teachers.

Example 1 Choose the correct adjective for each sentence.

(a) My cat is (fat, fatter, fattest) than yours.

(b) Of the three, Krystal is the (wise, wiser, wisest).

(c) Jo is the (fast, faster, fastest) of the two runners.

(d) Of all the characters, Tim was the (funny, funnier, funniest).

Solution (a) My cat is **fatter** than yours. We use the comparative form because we are comparing two cats.

(b) Of the three, Krystal is the **wisest.** We use the superlative form because we are comparing three or more people.

(c) Jo is the **faster** of the two runners. We use the comparative form because we are comparing only two.

(d) Of all the characters, Tim was the **funniest.** We use the superlative form because we are comparing three or more characters.

Forming Comparison Adjectives How we create the comparative and superlative forms of an adjective depends on how the adjective appears in its positive form. There are three main categories to remember.

One-Syllable Adjectives We create the comparative form of most one-syllable adjectives by adding *er* to the end of the word. The superlative form is created by adding *est*.

POSITIVE	COMPARATIVE	SUPERLATIVE
red	redder	reddest
proud	prouder	proudest
large	larger	largest

Two-Syllable Adjectives Most adjectives with two or more syllables do not have comparative or superlative forms. Instead, we use the word "more" (or "less") before the adjective to form the comparative, and the word "most" (or "least") to form the superlative.

POSITIVE	COMPARATIVE	SUPERLATIVE
genteel	more genteel	most genteel
timid	less timid	least timid
reliable	more reliable	most reliable

Two-Syllable Adjectives That End in y

When a two-syllable adjective ends in *y*, we create the comparative and superlative forms by changing the *y* to *i* and adding *er* or *est*.

POSITIVE	COMPARATIVE	SUPERLATIVE
crazy	crazier	craziest
scratchy	scratchier	scratchiest
happy	happier	happiest

Exceptions

There are exceptions to these guidelines. Below are a few examples of two-syllable adjectives whose comparative and superlative forms are created by adding *er* or *est*.

POSITIVE	COMPARATIVE	SUPERLATIVE
little (size, not amount)	littler	littlest
quiet	quieter	quietest
stable	stabler	stablest
yellow	yellower	yellowest
clever	cleverer	cleverest
simple	simpler	simplest

We check the dictionary if we are unsure how to create the comparative or superlative form of a two-syllable adjective.

Spelling Reminders

Remember that when adding *er* or *est* to the positive form of an adjective, we often must alter the word's original spelling. We apply the same rules we use when adding *ed* to form a past-tense verb.

When an adjective ends <u>with</u> **two or more consonants**, *er* or *est* is simply added to the positive form of the adjective.

dark	darker	darkest
young	younger	youngest
light	lighter	lightest

When an adjective ends with a **single consonant following one vowel**, we double the final consonant before adding *er* or *est*.

sad	sadder	saddest
fit	fitter	fittest

When an adjective ends with a **single consonant following two vowels**, we do not double the final consonant.

loud	louder	loudest
cool	cooler	coolest

When a one-syllable adjective ends in **w, x, or y preceded by a vowel**, we do not double the final consonant.

new	newer	newest
gray	grayer	grayest

When a two-syllable adjective ends in **y**, we change the y to i before adding *er* or *est*.

dizzy	dizzier	dizziest
wavy	wavier	waviest

When an adjective ends with a **silent e**, we drop the e and add *er* or *est*.

brave	braver	bravest
blue	bluer	bluest

Example 2 Complete the comparison chart by adding the comparative and superlative forms of each adjective.

POSITIVE	COMPARATIVE	SUPERLATIVE
(a) long	_____	_____
(b) dull	_____	_____
(c) mighty	_____	_____
(d) beautiful	_____	_____
(e) big	_____	_____
(f) tame	_____	_____

Solution

POSITIVE	COMPARATIVE	SUPERLATIVE
(a) long	longer	longest
(b) dull	duller	dullest
(c) mighty	mightier	mightiest
(d) beautiful	more beautiful (or less beautiful)	most beautiful (or least beautiful)
(e) big	bigger	biggest
(f) tame	tamer	tamest

Practice Choose the correct adjective for each sentence, and write whether it is comparative or superlative.

    a. Your backpack is (bigger, biggest) than mine.

    b. Jenny is the (younger, youngest) of the three children.

    c. Luis is the (more, most) artistic of all the students.

    d. Are you (sleepier, sleepiest) in the morning or in the evening?

    e. Isn't this kitten the (cute, cuter, cutest) of the litter?

    f. Rose raced Clara home, but Clara was (faster, fastest).

For g and h, give the comparative and superlative of each adjective.

    g. loud   **h.** plausible

For i and j, replace each blank with the correct vocabulary word from this lesson.

    i. A person with _____ is refined and courteous.

    j. A _____ person is polite.

Review Set 55 Choose the correct word(s) to complete sentences 1–9.

    1. Frogs, toads, and salamanders are amphibians, for they
    (54) live on (toadstools, boats, land) and in water.

    2. Shandra had her hearing tested. It was called an
    (53) (olfactory, auditory, vision) test.

    3. A (dog, cat, cow) is a bovine creature.
    (52)

    4. Like dogs, foxes and coyotes have (feline, canine, bovine)
    (51) characteristics.

    5. The imaginary lines of (latitude, longitude) pass through
    (15) the North and South poles.

    6. The word *committee* is a (compound, collective) noun.
    (11)

    7. Juan is (fameous, famous) for his (funy, funny) jokes.
    (33, 34)

8. Have the (thieves, theives) (received, recieved) (there,
(5, 35) their) punishment?

9. Boomer was the (small, smaller, smallest) of the two
(55) puppies.

10. Write the seven common coordinating conjunctions
(48) listed in Lesson 48.

11. Rewrite the following sentence, using correct
(41, 43) capitalization:

many quakers settled in the northeast.

12. Write whether the following word group is a phrase or a
(36) clause: with Quan and his little sister

13. Write the indirect object in the following sentence:
(46)
Troy handed Tanner a book from the shelf.

14. Rewrite the following book title, using correct
(25) capitalization:

a new dictionary of quotations

15. Write the predicate adjective in the following sentence:
(54)
Those biscuits smell delicious.

16. Write whether the following word group is a complete
(23) sentence, a sentence fragment, or a run-on sentence:

Pennsylvania was named after William Penn.

17. From the following sentence, write each prepositional
(44) phrase, circling the object of each preposition:

Throughout the year, a group of exercisers walks daily on
the path around the park.

18. Use a dictionary: (a) The word *linguist* is what part of
(27,30) speech? (b) Write its pronunciation. (c) Write its
etymology.

19. Rewrite the following words, circling each silent letter:
(28, 29)
(a) could   (b) guide   (c) whose

20. Rewrite the following sentence, adding periods as needed:
(47, 50)

Mario M DeSurra provided these instructions: on Mon, Feb 2, go west to Arrival St to see the groundhog

21. Write the word from this list that could *not* be a linking
(31) verb: look, feel, taste, swell, sound, seem, appear.

22. Write each adjective from the following sentence:
(40, 42)

The frigid, blustery wind caused watery eyes and red noses.

23. For the following sentence, write the correct form of the
(10) verb:

The paint (past of *dry*) quickly.

24. For the verb *dry*, write the (a) present participle, (b) past
(19) tense, and (c) past participle.

25. Write whether the circled word in the sentence below is
(52, 53) in the nominative, possessive, or objective case.

Bozo is a cute (puppy).

26. Rewrite the following sentence, adding capital letters as needed:

(26)

ms. hoo said, "please take your seats."

27. For a–c, write the plural of each noun.

(17, 22) (a) flower box   (b) shovelful   (c) bunch

28. Diagram the simple subject and simple predicate of each clause in the following sentence:

(36)

Ms. Hoo smiled and her students cheered when Jasmin found Rufus in her desk.

Diagram each word of sentences 29–30.

29. That black snake looks hungry and dangerous.
(45, 49)

30. Adam and Eva baked Ms. Hoo a loaf of bread.
(45, 46)

LESSON 56

Irregular Comparison Adjectives

Some adjectives have irregular comparative and superlative forms. We must learn these if we haven't already.

POSITIVE	COMPARATIVE	SUPERLATIVE
little (amount, not size)	less	least
good, well	better	best
bad, ill	worse	worst
far	farther	farthest
many, much	more	most

Little or Few? We use *little*, *less*, and *least* with things that cannot be counted. We use *few*, *fewer*, and *fewest* with things that can be counted.

> CANNOT BE COUNTED:
> My parrot shows *less* desire for vegetables than for fruits.

> CAN BE COUNTED:
> Does the parrot eat *fewer* vegetables than fruits?

Much or Many? We use *much* with things that cannot be counted, and we use *many* for things that can be counted.

> CANNOT BE COUNTED:
> There is not *much* time to complete this assignment.

> CAN BE COUNTED:
> We still have *many* assignments to complete.

Example 1 Choose the correct adjective for each sentence.

(a) (Little, Less, Least) snow falls in the valley than in the mountains.

(b) That storm was the (baddest, worst) one in history.

(c) There are (less, fewer) holidays in June than in November.

(d) Last year, (less, fewer) smog polluted the air.

(e) (Many, Much) of the birds have flown south.

Solution   (a) **Less** snow falls in the valley than in the mountains. (The sentence is comparing snowfall in two places, so we use the comparative form of "little.")

(b) That storm was the **worst** one in history. ("Baddest" is not a word.)

(c) There are **fewer** holidays in June than in November. ("Holidays" can be counted.)

(d) Last year, **less** smog polluted the air. ("Smog" cannot be counted.)

(e) **Many** of the birds have flown south. ("Birds" can be counted.)

Avoid Double Comparisons   We do not use double comparisons. In other words, we do not use *more* with *er,* or *most* with *est.*

NO: The speed skater was *more faster* than the ice skater.
YES: The speed skater was *faster* than the ice skater.

NO: She was the *most healthiest* person at the gym.
YES: She was the *healthiest* person at the gym.

Absolute Adjectives   Some adjectives do not normally permit comparison. Adjectives that represent an ultimate condition (*square, round, maximum, equal, fatal, unique, dead,* etc.) cannot be increased by degree. (For example, a square can't be "squarer" than another square; it's either square or it's not!) When necessary, careful writers can modify these adjectives by using words like *almost, near,* and *nearly* instead of *more/less* and *most/least.*

NO: That pine tree looks *deader* now.
YES: That pine tree looks *nearly dead* now.

Example 2   Choose the correct adjective for each sentence.
(a) The pigs are (noisier, more noisier) than the horses.

(b) The lion's roar was the (fiercest, most fiercest) in the jungle.

Solution   (a) The pigs are **noisier** than the horses. ("More noisier" is a double comparison. We do not use *more* with *er*.)

(b) The lion's roar was the **fiercest** in the jungle. ("Most fiercest" is a double comparison. We do not use *most* with *est*.)

✓**Practice**   For a–f, choose the correct adjective for each sentence.

a. (Much, Many) homesteaders settled here.

b. Cattle ranchers displayed (many, much) frustration with the farmers.

c. The Donner Party experienced one of the (worse, worst) tragedies of the Gold Rush.

d. (More, Most) gold was found in California than in Kansas.

e. (Few, Little) corn comes from Maine.

f. This movie was (more scary, more scarier) than the other.

For g and h, replace each blank with the correct vocabulary word from this lesson.

g. _____ people avoid hard work; they are lazy.

h. _____ people work hard.

More Practice   Choose the correct adjective for each sentence.

1. (Little, Less) rain falls in the desert than in the jungle.

2. Omar plays chess (gooder, better) than Amir.

3. That flood was the (worse, worst) ever.

4. I feel (better, weller) today than yesterday.

5. My old camera is (reliabler, more reliable) than my new one.

6. She has (more, most) benevolence than I have.

7. Who is the (more benevolent, most benevolent) of the three?

8. Were you the (wiser, wisest) of the two?

Choose the correct word(s) to complete sentences 1–10.

1. A genteel person is (malicious, imprudent, polite).
(55)

2. Arboreal animals live in (water, caves, trees).
(54)

3. *Olfactory* refers to the sense of (touch, hearing, smell).
(53)

4. A magazine article titled "Bovine Health" talks about the
(52) health of (cattle, cats, dogs).

5. A(n) (atoll, arroyo, strait) is a small river or stream, or the
(16) bed of a stream.

6. The word *Rubys* is a (plural, possessive) noun.
(13)

7. The (begining, beginning) of the story was (sader, sadder)
(33, 34) than the ending.

8. My (neice, niece) wore a (biege, beige) sweater.
(35)

9. Rita was the (tall, taller, tallest) of the three sisters.
(55)

10. Boomer's fur is (redder, more redder) than Bozo's.
(56)

11. Rewrite the following letter, using correct capitalization:
(41, 43)

dear mr. stoneman,

we have found one of the lost critters, but i do not know where the others are.

regretfully,
ms. hoo

12. Write whether the following word group is a phrase or a
(36) clause: if you blink

13. Write each coordinating conjunction in the following
(48) sentence:

Nevada nor Oregon grows much cotton, but Alabama and Texas do.

14. Rewrite the following sentence, using correct
⁽³⁸⁾ capitalization:

professor u. r. thair teaches history and spanish.

15. Write the predicate nominative in the following sentence:
⁽⁵¹⁾
Tuesday's lunch will be spaghetti.

16. Write whether the following word group is a complete
⁽²³⁾ sentence, a sentence fragment, or a run-on sentence:

Nebraska and Montana grow wheat North Dakota does
too.

17. From the following sentence, write each prepositional
⁽⁴⁴⁾ phrase, circling the object of each preposition:

Traveling across the United States, one sees fields of
wheat and herds of cattle.

18. Use a dictionary: (a) The word *lynx* is what part of
^(27,30) speech? (b) Write its pronunciation. (c) Write its
etymology.

19. Rewrite the following words, circling each silent letter:
^(28, 29)
(a) whole   (b) sketch   (c) hour

20. Rewrite the following sentence, adding periods as needed:
^(47, 50)

Ms Hoo wrote, "All assignments are due Fri, Apr 21"

21. Write whether the following sentence is declarative,
⁽²⁾ interrogative, exclamatory, or imperative:

That ear of corn is gigantic!

22. Write each adjective from the following sentence:
^(40, 42)
The white, fluffy cotton comes from small bushes planted
in long rows.

23. For the following sentence, write the correct form of the
⁽⁹⁾ verb:

Spotty (present of *polish*) the car.

24. For the verb *hop*, write the (a) present participle, (b) past
⁽¹⁹⁾ tense, and (c) past participle.

25. Write whether the circled word in the sentence below is
(52, 53) in the nominative, possessive, or objective case.

Bozo chases his(tail).

26. Rewrite the following outline, adding periods and capital
(26, 47) letters as needed:

    i common pets
      a dogs
      b cats
      c birds

27. For a–c, write the plural of each noun.
(17, 22)
   (a) dog dish   (b) handful   (c) sheep

28. Diagram the simple subject and simple predicate of each
(36) clause in the following sentence: Dogs are sniffing,
students are searching, and Rufus is resting.

Diagram each word of sentences 29–30.

29. Ms. Hoo's thirty students appear calmer and braver.
(49, 54)

30. Did Adam and Eva bake Ms. Hoo a loaf of wheat bread?
(45, 46)

The Comma, Part 1: Dates, Addresses, and Series

Dictation or Journal Entry

Vocabulary:

Providence usually means "God's care, control, or guidance"; sometimes it simply means "foresight" or "preparation for the future." Many early settlers depended upon *providence* for their survival on the wild frontier.

Providential means "happening by divine intervention; fortunate." A *providential* rain put out the brushfire.

Commas are the most frequently-used form of punctuation. We use commas to separate elements within sentences. Using commas correctly helps us clarify the meaning of a phrase or a sentence.

Parts of a Date We use commas to separate the **parts of a date.** When we write a complete date, we always place a comma between the day and the year.

September 9, 1850

If a complete date appears in the middle of a sentence, we place a comma after the year.

On September 9, 1850, California became a U.S. state.

If the day of the week appears as part of the date, we place a comma after the day.

Remember Tuesday, September 11, 2001.

Note: When just the month and the year appear in a sentence, no comma is required.

The historian noted July 1776 as a providential time.

Example 1 Insert commas wherever they are needed in the parts of the date in this sentence:

> Elle's birth occurred on Friday October 2 2004 at eleven o'clock in the evening.

Solution We place a comma after the day of the week (Friday). We also place a comma after the date (October 2). Lastly, because the date appears in the middle of a sentence, we place a comma after the year.

> Elle's birth occurred on Friday, October 2, 2004, at eleven o'clock in the evening.

Parts of an Address   We use commas to separate the **parts of an address** and the names of geographical places or political divisions.

The parts of a street address are separated by commas according to the following pattern:

house number and street, city, state and zip code

102 Fox Lane, Loveland, Colorado 80537

1215 Stewart Street, Wall, NJ 07719

Note: We use the state abbreviation when addressing a letter or package.

We also use commas to separate the names of geographical places or political divisions.

Kern County, California   Oaxaca, Mexico

Cambridge, England, UK   Banff, Alberta, Canada

If the city and state or country appear in the middle of the sentence, a comma is required after the state or country.

I lived in Rome, Italy, last winter.

Example 2   Insert commas wherever they are needed in these sentences.

(a) Forest rangers retrieved a bear from a swimming pool at 456 Grizzly Lane Gurrsville Oregon.

(b) The marathon began in Madison Wisconsin at eight a.m.

Solution   (a) We separate the parts of the address with commas. One comma goes after the house number and street, and another goes between the city and the state.

Forest rangers retrieved a bear from a swimming pool at 456 Grizzly Lane, Gurrsville, Oregon.

(b) We place a comma between the city and the state. We place another comma after the state because it is in the middle of a sentence.

The marathon began in Madison, Wisconsin, at eight a.m.

Words in a Series   We use commas to separate **three or more words or phrases in a series**.

Fluffy, Pepper, and Tiger are common names for cats.

The street fair offers live music, homegrown produce, homemade breads, and a variety of crafts.

Example 3 Insert commas as needed in this sentence:

Commas periods quotation marks and semicolons help make the meaning of a sentence clearer.

Solution We separate the items in the series with commas.

Commas, periods, quotation marks, and semicolons help make the meaning of a sentence clearer.

✓**Practice** For a and b, replace each blank with the correct vocabulary word from this lesson.

a. A _____ visit from my friend helped to cheer me when I was sad.

b. The avalanche survivor believes that _____ saved her life.

Rewrite sentences c–e, inserting commas where necessary to separate parts of a date.

c. Lily ran fast and broke the school record in the mile on Wednesday December 7 2005.

d. I think October 2005 was our worst hurricane season.

e. Christmas fell on Sunday December 25 in the year 2005.

Rewrite sentences f–h, inserting commas to separate parts of an address.

f. The post office has moved to 612 W. Duarte Road Arcadia California 91007.

g. Boise Idaho was Mr. Spud's birthplace.

h. Are you talking about Salem Massachusetts or Salem Oregon?

Rewrite sentences i–j, inserting commas to separate words in a series.

i. The eight parts of speech include nouns pronouns verbs adverbs adjectives prepositions conjunctions and interjections.

j. Lucy saw two gray squirrels a blue jay and three robins in the park.

More Practice See "More Practice Lesson 57" in Student Workbook.

Review Set 57 Choose the correct word(s) to complete sentences 1–10.

1. (*Industrious, Indolent, Imprudent*) means "hardworking."
(56)

2. Most people like a person who has (malice, gentility, avarice).
(55)

3. A(n) (caldera, fissure, amphibian) lives both on land and in water.
(54)

4. *Auditory* refers to the sense of (touch, seeing, hearing).
(53)

5. The Tropic of Cancer and the Tropic of (Ulysses, Capricorn, Hermes) mark the northernmost and southernmost borders of the tropics, or Torrid Zone.
(17)

6. The word *providence* is a(n) (abstract, concrete) noun.
(11)

7. Max (flys, flies) the (bigest, biggest) kite I've ever seen.
(33, 34)

8. I (beleive, believe) the (cieling, ceiling) needs another coat of paint.
(35)

9. Sergio is the (tall, taller, tallest) of the two boys.
(55)

10. She made (fewer, less) mistakes than I.
(56)

11. Rewrite the following sentence, using correct capitalization:
(41, 43)

> dear katy,
> shall we play chinese checkers after school?
> your friend,
> marta

12. Write whether the following word group is a phrase or a clause: in a steamship on the Mississippi River
(36)

13. Write the indirect object in the following sentence:
(46)

Doda gave Chris words of wisdom.

14. Rewrite the following song title, using correct (25) capitalization:

"bicycle built for two"

15. Write the predicate adjective in the following sentence:
(54)
The sunsets have been glorious.

16. Write whether the following word group is a complete (23) sentence, a sentence fragment, or a run-on sentence:

Cotton remains an important crop to many people in Mississippi.

17. From the following sentence, write each prepositional (44) phrase, circling the object of each preposition:

Inside a coal mine, a cart of coal sits on a track.

18. Use a dictionary: (a) The word *cuboid* is what part of (27,30) speech? (b) Write its pronunciation. (c) Write its etymology.

19. Rewrite the following words, circling each silent letter:
(28, 29)
(a) talk   (b) light   (c) gnat

20. Rewrite the following sentence, adding periods as needed:
(47, 50)

Dr Ngo's office has moved to 54 W Main Street.

21. Write the word from this list that could *not* be a linking (31) verb: appear, grow, become, remain, play.

22. Write each adjective from the following sentence:
(40, 42)
A huge brown bull charged at the red cape.

23. Rewrite the following sentence, adding commas as (57) needed:

Lana was born on Sunday November 4 1973 in Detroit Michigan.

24. For the verb *slam*, write the (a) present participle, (b) past (19) tense, and (c) past participle.

25. Write whether the circled word in the sentence below is
(52, 53) in the nominative, possessive, or objective case.

Boomer bit (Bozo's) tail.

26. Rewrite the following sentence, adding capital letters as
(26) needed:

nora asked, "may i help you?"

27. For a–c, write the plural of each noun.
(17, 22)
(a) dog leash   (b) baby   (c) wolf

28. Diagram the simple subject and simple predicate of each
(36) clause in the following sentence: Ms. Hoo thinks that
Jasmin should take Rufus home because he has caused
too much trouble in her classroom.

Diagram each word of sentences 29–30.

29. Jasmin's shy lizard seems sorry and regretful.
(49, 54)

30. Did Adam and Eva offer Mr. Stoneman two slices of rye
(45, 46) bread?

Appositives

Vocabulary:
The Latin word *super* means "over, above, and beyond."

Supersonic means "moving at a speed greater than the speed of sound." A *supersonic* aircraft typically flies at a speed greater than 750 miles per hour.

Superfluous means "more than is needed or desired." My *superfluous* baggage held all sorts of woolen sweaters that I would not need in the hot Mojave desert.

Appositives A word or group of words that immediately follows a noun to identify or give more information about the noun is called an **appositive.** In the sentences below, the appositives are italicized.

> Charleston, *the capital of West Virginia,* lies on the Kanawha River.
>
> My friends *Raj and Sue* blow glass ornaments.
>
> Sergio Cruz, *my grandfather,* plays the trumpet.
>
> The game *chess* requires concentration and skill.

Example 1 Identify the appositives from each sentence.
(a) The Delta Queen, a riverboat, tours the Mississippi River.

(b) A monument in Alabama reminds us of the dreaded insect boll weevil.

Solution (a) The appositive **riverboat** gives more information about the noun "Delta Queen."

(b) The appositive **boll weevil** identifies the noun "insect."

Improving Our Writing Using appositives skillfully can improve our writing. With an appositive, we can combine two choppy sentences to make one good one.

TWO CHOPPY SENTENCES:

Esperanza is a rich girl in Mexico. Esperanza loves porcelain dolls and pretty dresses.

ONE GOOD SENTENCE:

Esperanza, *a rich girl in Mexico,* loves porcelain dolls and pretty dresses.

Example 2 Combine each pair of choppy sentences to make one longer sentence by using an appositive.

(a) Miguel loves Esperanza. Esperanza is the daughter of his boss.

(b) Esperanza and Mama travel to Mexicali. Mexicali is a city near the border of California.

Solution (a) **Miguel loves Esperanza, the daughter of his boss.**

(b) **Esperanza and Mama travel to Mexicali, a city near the border of California.**

Diagramming an Appositive We diagram an appositive by placing it in parentheses beside the noun it identifies or describes.

Esperanza's friend Isabel is a student.

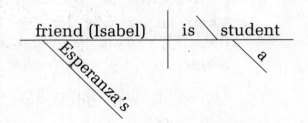

If the appositive contains adjectives, we place them on slanted lines directly beneath the appositive.

The woman in the blue dress is Rosalba, a farm worker.

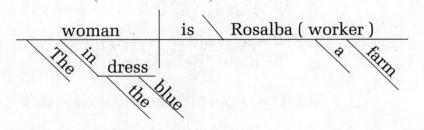

Practice For a–c, replace each blank with the correct vocabulary word from this lesson.

a. _____ advice is not needed or desired.

b. We heard a loud noise as the _____ aircraft broke the sound barrier.

c. The Latin word _____ means "over, above, and beyond."

For d and e, write the appositive from each sentence.

d. Robert flew to Atlanta, the capital of Georgia.

e. The spice cinnamon makes muffins tasty.

f. Diagram the sentence below.

Ben Chu, an artist, draws cartoons.

For g and h, combine each pair of sentences into one sentence by using an appositive.

g. Ms. Hoo is my teacher. Ms. Hoo wants me to succeed.

h. Mr. Stoneman encourages students to try hard. Mr. Stoneman is principal of Giggly School.

Review Set 58

Choose the correct word to complete sentences 1–10.

1. When Jasper was lost in the forest, he hoped that
(57) (liability, dogma, providence) would bring him safely home.

2. A(n) (indolent, industrious, benevolent) person avoids
(56) hard work.

3. (*Imprudent, Malicious, Genteel*) means " polite and
(55) well-behaved."

4. An arboreal plant is like a (vegetable, flower, tree).
(54)

5. The (Arctic, Torrid) Zone is the warm, tropical region
(18) between the Tropic of Cancer and the Tropic of Capricorn.

6. The word *worksheet* is a (compound, collective) noun.
(11)

7. Max (trys, tries) to brush Bozo's (mated, matted) fur.
(33, 34)

8. I (received, recieved) a wedding invitation from my
(35) (neighbor, nieghbor).

9. Of the two captains, Sergio is the (wise, wiser, wisest).
(55)

(56) **10.** Elle has (less, fewer) freckles than I.

11. Rewrite the following letter, using correct capitalization:
(41, 43)

dear ms. hoo,

        pets are not allowed at mudvalley middle school.

                regards,

                mr. stoneman

12. Write whether the following word group is a phrase or a
(36) clause: for I understand

13. Write the seven coordinating conjunctions listed in
(48) Lesson 48.

14. Rewrite the following sentence, using correct
(38) capitalization:

did you, auntie, call dr. rizkalla?

15. Write the predicate nominative in the following sentence:
(51)

Ms. Hoo has been a teacher for twenty years.

16. Write whether the following word group is a complete
(23) sentence, a sentence fragment, or a run-on sentence:

Slater Mill, one of the first textile mills in North America.

17. From the following sentence, write each prepositional
(44) phrase, circling the object of each preposition:

Despite our fatigue, we paddled against the strong current
toward the distant shore.

18. Use a dictionary: (a) The word *cryptic* is what part of
(27,30) speech? (b) Write its pronunciation. (c) Write its
etymology.

19. Write the appositive in the following sentence:
(58)

Boston, the site of the first World Series, remains a
popular tourist spot.

20. Rewrite the following sentence, adding periods as needed:
(47, 50)

The bridge on First Ave will be closed Dec and Jan

21. Write whether the following sentence is declarative, interrogative, imperative, or exclamatory:

(2)

This map shows the physical features of Florida.

22. Write each adjective from the following sentence:

(40, 42)

Two swimmers discovered gooey tar on the bottoms of their feet.

23. Rewrite the following sentence, adding commas as needed:

(57)

Nancy raises cattle sheep chickens and horses.

24. For the verb *reply*, write the (a) present participle, (b) past tense, and (c) past participle.

(19)

25. Write whether the circled word in the sentence below is in the nominative, possessive, or objective case.

(52, 53)

Bozo likes wheat toast with (cinnamon)

26. Rewrite the following lines of poetry, adding capital letters as needed:

(15)

smile at your troubles
and pop them like bubbles.

27. For a–c, write the plural of each noun.

(17, 22)

(a) watch dog   (b) earful   (c) candy

28. Diagram the simple subject and simple predicate of each clause in the following sentence: Jasmin says that the dogs caused the trouble and that Rufus was innocent.

(36)

Diagram each word of sentences 29–30.

29. Mr. Stoneman, the principal, looks stern and irritable.

(54, 58)

30. Jasmin gave Rufus two handfuls of large crickets.

(45, 46)

The Comma, Part 2: Direct Address and Academic Degrees

Dictation or Journal Entry

Vocabulary:

The Latin word *lumen* means "light."

Luminous means "shining, giving light." A *luminous* moon brightened the trail on our midnight hike.

Illuminate means "to give light to; light up." I hope the moon will *illuminate* the dark path tonight.

In this lesson, we will discuss more uses for commas.

Nouns of Direct Address

A **noun of direct address** names the person who is being spoken to (the person who is receiving the information in the sentence). The noun can be the person's name or a "name" you are using for him or her. Nouns of direct address can appear anywhere in a sentence. We offset them with commas.

Mikaela, stand by the heater to get warm.

Why, Gordon, did you say that?

Watch out for the bees, Norma!

There may be more than one noun of direct address in a sentence. Also, like any noun, a noun of direct address can be modified by adjectives. We offset the entire noun phrase with commas, as in the sentences below.

Here are your awards, Claude and Irmgard.

Be careful, my dear Tina, or you'll wake the baby.

Example 1 Insert commas to offset the noun of direct address in the sentence below.

Dirk where were you born?

Solution We insert a comma after "Dirk" because he is being spoken to. Dirk is a noun of direct address.

Dirk, where were you born?

Example 2 Insert commas to offset the noun of direct address in the sentence below.

Go outside muddy dog where you are happiest.

Solution We offset the entire noun phrase "muddy dog" because the dog is being spoken to and "muddy" modifies "dog."

Go outside, muddy dog, where you are happiest.

Academic Degrees When an **academic degree** or similar title follows a person's name, it is usually abbreviated. Here are some abbreviations you're likely to see:

M.D. (Doctor of Medicine)

D.D.S. (Doctor of Dental Surgery)

D.V.M. (Doctor of Veterinary Medicine)

Ph.D. (Doctor of Philosophy)

Ed.D. (Doctor of Education)

D.D. (Doctor of Divinity)

R.N. (Registered Nurse)

L.P.N. (Licensed Practical Nurse)

M.B.A. (Master of Business Administration)

We use commas to offset academic degrees or other titles that follow a person's name.

Camilla Vera, C.P.A., works long hours.

Doc's professional name is R. Ferrar, Ed.D.

Example 3 Insert commas to offset the academic degree in this sentence.

June Hetzel Ph.D. chairs the department.

Solution Since "Ph.D." is an academic degree, it is offset with commas.

June Hetzel, Ph.D., chairs the department.

Practice Rewrite sentences a and b, using commas to offset nouns of direct address.

a. Baukien we learned a new song yesterday.

b. Please remember my dear friends that I shall return soon.

Rewrite sentences d and e, using commas to offset academic degrees or other titles.

c. Carrie Prince R.N. cares for newborn babies.

d. My cat's health is very important to Carla Wheat D.V.M.

For f–h, replace each blank with the correct vocabulary word from this lesson.

    e. The Latin word _____ means "light."

    f. Without electricity, we can use candles to _____ our home at night.

    g. _____ flames gave the room a warm glow.

More Practice   See "More Practice Lesson 59" in Student Workbook.

Review Set 59   Choose the correct word to complete sentences 1–10.

    1. The Latin word (*loqui, placare, super*) means "over, above, and beyond."
(58)

    2. A providential event is a (disastrous, unfortunate, fortunate) event.
(57)

    3. *Industrious* means "(lazy, crazy, hardworking)."
(56)

    4. *Genteel* means "(rude, polite, silly)."
(55)

    5. The (savanna, tundra, atoll) is a warm, tropical, treeless, grassy plain where you might see elephants and giraffes.
(19)

    6. The word *Jennys* is a (plural, possessive) noun.
(13)

    7. I believe the (winer, winner) of the race became (fameous, famous).
(33, 34)

    8. Did the (cheif, chief) (recieve, receive) my message?
(35)

    9. Abby is the (friendlier, friendliest) of the three kittens.
(55)

    10. Abby has caught (less, fewer) mice than Easton.
(56)

    11. Rewrite the following sentence, using correct capitalization:
(41, 43)

         on a humid afternoon in the south, my cousins gather at the northeast corner of the park to play checkers.

    12. Write whether the following word group is a phrase or a clause: after the final scene in the play
(36)

13. Write the indirect object in the following sentence:
(46)

Doda told Chris the story of Laughing Lois.

14. Rewrite the following poem title, using correct
(25) capitalization:

"when icicles hang by the wall"

15. Write the predicate adjective in the following sentence:
(54)

I feel energetic today!

16. Write whether the following word group is a complete
(23) sentence, a sentence fragment, or a run-on sentence:

Maps can show the physical features they can also show
population and climate.

17. From the following sentence, write each prepositional
(44) phrase, circling the object of each preposition:

For this assignment, we shall post outlines of the states
on the walls around the room.

18. Rewrite the following words, circling each silent letter.
(28, 29)

(a) wrinkle (b) calm

19. Use an appositive to combine the following two
(58) sentences into one sentence.

Nevada is the "silver state."

Nevada borders five other states.

20. Rewrite the following sentence, adding periods as needed:
(47, 50)

On Thurs at nine am, I shall attend a lecture on the life of
Dr Martin L King

21. Write the word from this list that could *not* be a linking
(31) verb: is, am, are, was, were, be, fleeing, been, look, feel, taste.

22. Write each adjective from the following sentence:
(40, 42)

He offered a generous solution to the ugly controversy.

23. Rewrite the following sentence, adding commas as
(57, 59) needed:

Ms. Hoo have you seen my lunch my backpack or my history book?

24. For the verb *smile*, write the (a) present participle, (b)
(19) past tense, and (c) past participle.

25. Write whether the circled word in the sentence below is
(52, 53) in the nominative, possessive, or objective case.

Bozo likes wheat (toast) with cinnamon.

26. Rewrite the following sentence, adding capital letters as
(26) needed:

mr. stoneman replied, "no, jasmin, i have not fired your teacher."

27. For a–c, write the plural of each noun.
(17, 22)
(a) topic sentence   (b) rosebush   (c) Jenny

28. Diagram the simple subject and simple predicate of each
(36) clause in the following sentence: Jasmin is weeping, for Mr. Stoneman says that Rufus must go.

Diagram each word of sentences 29–30.

29. Ms. Hoo, Jasmin's teacher, is an artist and a poet.
(51, 58)

30. Ms. Hoo wrote Jasmin a poem about crickets.
(45, 46)

The Comma, Part 3: Appositives

Dictation or Journal Entry

Vocabulary:

Opportune means "suitable, appropriate, or well-timed." Your phone call was *opportune*, for I was wishing to speak with you.

Inopportune means "occurring at a bad time; inconvenient." I received an *inopportune* phone call as I was leaving in a hurry.

In this lesson, we will discuss another use for commas.

Appositives

An **appositive** is a word or group of words that immediately follows a noun to identify or give more information about the noun. In the sentence below, "Mr. Trusty" is an appositive. Notice how commas offset it from the rest of the sentence.

> Our new librarian, Mr. Trusty, dusted each shelf.

In the sentence below, "Anne Frank" is also an appositive. But it is not offset by a comma. Why?

> The author Anne Frank wrote a diary during the Holocaust.

Essential and Nonessential Appositives

Whether or not an appositive is offset with commas depends on how essential it is to the meaning of the sentence.

Let's look at the first sentence, above. If we remove the appositive, the sentence still makes sense:

> Our new librarian dusted each shelf.

The phrase "our new librarian" has already identified the person the sentence is about. The appositive "Mr. Trusty" is informative but **nonessential** to the meaning of the sentence. **Nonessential appositives are offset with commas.**

Now let's remove the appositive from the second sentence:

> The author wrote a diary during the Holocaust.

The author? Which author? This sentence no longer makes sense. The appositive "Anne Frank" is **essential** to the meaning of the sentence. **Essential appositives are not offset by commas.**

Example 1   Insert commas where necessary in the sentence below.

> Pam Muñoz Ryan author of *Esperanza Rising* wrote about her grandmother.

Solution   If we remove the appositive, "author of *Esperanza Rising*," the meaning of the sentence is still clear. (Pam Muñoz Ryan wrote about her grandmother.) Therefore, it is a nonessential appositive, and we offset it with commas.

> **Pam Muñoz Ryan, author of *Esperanza Rising*, wrote about her grandmother.**

Example 2   Insert commas where necessary in the sentence below.

> My friend Manny pitched three innings.

Solution   If we remove the appositive, "Manny," the reader is left to wonder *which* friend, and the meaning of the sentence is lost. Therefore, it is an essential appositive, and we do not offset it with commas.

> **My friend Manny pitched three innings.**

Practice   For sentences a and b, write the appositive and write whether it is essential or nonessential.

√ **a.** Sixth grader Chris played first base.

√ **b.** Katie, the girl with black silky hair, caught the fly ball.

Rewrite sentences c–f, using commas where necessary to offset each nonessential appositive. If no commas are necessary, do not rewrite the sentence.

c. Hans Christian Andersen author of "The Princess and the Pea" wrote many entertaining stories for children.

d. The great Austrian composer Wolfgang Amadeus Mozart wrote music for many different instruments.

e. Dr. May the town's only physician is busy during flu season.

f. My friend Melody has red hair.

For g and h, replace each blank with the correct vocabulary word from this lesson.

g. Unfortunately, we encountered an _____ detour on our way to the concert, so we were late.

h. I found an _____ sale on the peaches I needed to make jam.

More Practice See "More Practice Lesson 60" in Student Workbook.

Review Set 60 Choose the correct word to complete sentences 1–10.

1. The Latin word (*super, placare, lumen*) means "light."
(59)

2. *Supersonic* means "moving at a speed (greater, less, much less) than the speed of sound."
(58)

3. (Meridian, Elocution, Providence) is God's care, control, or guidance; or foresight.
(57)

4. (*Industrious, Indolent, Prudent*) means "lazy."
(56)

5. A (plateau, fissure, chasm) is a flat land area at a high elevation.
(21)

6. The word *time* is a(n) (abstract, concrete) noun.
(11)

7. Rufus (crys, cries) the (bigest, biggest) tears I've ever seen.
(33, 34)

8. My (friend, freind) drives a (frieght, freight) train.
(35)

9. Of the two libraries, this one is the (quieter, quietest).
(55)

10. There are not (much, many) mice in my house.
(56)

11. Rewrite the following letter, using correct capitalization:
(41, 43)
    dear cousin anabel,

    please meet me at chop sticks palace on tuesday.
                                        love,
                                        marta

12. Write whether the following word group is a phrase or a clause: if you remember
(36)

13. Write each coordinating conjunction that you find in the
(48) following sentence:

I must do the work now or later, so I might as well do it
now.

14. Rewrite the following sentence, using correct
(38) capitalization:

why, dr. mejares, must i study a foreign language?

15. Write the predicate nominative in the following sentence:
(51) Chris has been a violinist in the orchestra for two years.

16. Write whether the following word group is a complete
(23) sentence, a sentence fragment, or a run-on sentence:

Dentists can use computers to analyze teeth.

17. From the following sentence, write each prepositional
(44) phrase, circling the object of each preposition:

She sprinted out the door and down the street to the post
office.

18. Use a dictionary: (a) The word *hedge* is what part of
(27,30) speech? (b) Write its pronunciation. (c) Write its
etymology.

19. Rewrite the following sentence, using commas to offset
(60) the nonessential appositive:

My father Mr. Curtis can repair your broken computer.

20. Rewrite the following sentence, adding periods as needed:
(47, 50)
Were Mr and Mrs Hahn married on Mt Wilson?

21. Write whether the following sentence is declarative,
(2) interrogative, imperative, or exclamatory:

Please sit down on the floor.

22. Write each adjective from the following sentence:
(40, 42)
The mature, gentle dentist in the white coat filled my two
cavities.

23. Rewrite the following sentence, adding commas as (57, 59) needed:

I spoke with Ann Wong R.N. on Monday January 2 2006.

24. For the verb *pity*, write the (a) present participle, (b) past (19) tense, and (c) past participle.

25. Write whether the circled word in the sentence below is (52, 53) in the nominative, possessive, or objective case.

Bozo is my favorite (dog)

26. Rewrite the following outline, adding periods and capital (26, 47) letters as needed:

i crops in iowa
    a corn
    b oats
    c soybeans

27. For a–c, write the plural of each noun.
(17, 22)
    (a) journal entry   (b) can of corn   (c) truckful

28. Diagram the simple subject and simple predicate of each (36) clause in the following sentence: If Rufus leaves, the other critters will miss him, for he is their friend.

Diagram each word of sentences 29–30.

29. The titmouse, a small bird, is acrobatic and musical.
(51, 58)

30. The tiny titmouse whistles us a song about spring.
(45, 46)

Overused Adjectives •
Unnecessary Articles

Dictation or Journal Entry

Vocabulary:

Intuition is an instinctive feeling or knowledge about something that has happened or is going to happen. Mom's *intuition* told her that the train would be late.

Intuitive means "instinctive; known without the benefit of reason." Franco is an *intuitive* coach; he knows how his team will play in each game.

Overused Adjectives

Many people make the mistake of using the same adjectives over and over again. In this lesson we will learn to choose more vivid adjectives. Some of the adjectives that people use too often are as follows:

great	bad	wonderful
nice	terrible	fine
good	awful	okay

While there is nothing wrong with the adjectives above, we should try to use more specific or interesting ones if we can. We can always consult the dictionary or thesaurus for more choices.

WEAK: It was a *great* story.

BETTER: It was a *thrilling* (or *moving, stimulating, breathtaking, exciting, hilarious, hair-raising*) story.

WEAK: My uncle is *nice.*

BETTER: My uncle is *kind* (or *gracious, generous, warmhearted, loving, jovial, friendly*).

WEAK: Geraldine feels *fine* today.

BETTER: Geraldine feels *healthy* (or *energetic, elated, upbeat, fantastic, cheerful, happy*) today.

Example 1

Rewrite each sentence, replacing each overused adjective with a more vivid one.

(a) We had a *good* trip.

(b) The damage was *bad.*

(c) This soup tastes *terrible.*

(d) My day was *wonderful.*

Solution Our answers will vary. Here are some possibilities:

(a) We had a (**pleasant, delightful, enjoyable**) trip.

(b) The damage was (**disastrous, frightful, dreadful**).

(c) This soup tastes (**gross, disgusting, wretched, horrid**).

(d) My day was (**magnificent, refreshing, incredible**).

Unnecessary Articles We have learned that the articles *a, an*, and *the* are adjectives. Sometimes they are used unnecessarily. Avoid these errors:

We do not use *the* before "both."

NO: I called *the both* of them.
YES: I called *both* of them.

NO: Please help *the both* of them with their math.
YES: Please help *both* of them with their math.

We do not use *a* or *an* after the phrases "kind of," "sort of," or "type of."

NO: I like that *kind of a* person.
YES: I like that *kind of* person.

NO: She is not that *type of a* teacher.
YES: She is not that *type of* teacher.

Example 2 Rewrite each sentence correctly.

(a) Palmer wrote the both of those poems.

(b) What kind of a snake is that?

Solution (a) **Palmer wrote both of those poems.** (We remove the word *the*. It is not used before "both.")

(b) **What kind of snake is that?** (We remove the word *a*. We do not use it after "kind of.")

✓ **Practice** Rewrite sentences a–d, replacing each overused adjective with a more interesting or specific one.

a. We had *awful* weather.

b. She gave a *good* speech.

c. Louise wore a *nice* dress.

d. This milk smells *bad*.

Rewrite sentences e and f correctly.

e. That sort of a bug frightens me.

f. The babies were tired, so we put the both of them to bed.

For g and h, replace each blank with the correct vocabulary word from this lesson.

g. _____ is a noun meaning "a type of knowledge."

h. _____ is an adjective meaning "instinctive."

✓ **Review Set 61**

Choose the correct word to complete sentences 1–10.

1. (*Opportune*, *Inopportune*, *Arboreal*) means "suitable, or
(60) well-timed."

2. The Latin word *lumen* means "(dark, light, cow)."
(59)

3. (*Prudent*, *Plausible*, *Supersonic*) means "moving at a
(58) speed greater than the speed of sound."

4. Providence is God's (wrath, judgment, care) or guidance.
(57)

5. (Its, It's) is the possessive form of *it*.
(6)

6. The word *jury* is a (compound, collective) noun.
(11)

7. Let us speak (gentlely, gently) to Rufus, for he is (sader,
(33, 34) sadder) than ever.

8. Those politicians will not forfeit (thier, their) strong
(35) (beleifs, beliefs).

9. Of the three classrooms, Mr. Hush's is the (quieter,
(55) quietest).

10. Margaret has (less, fewer) mice than Debby.
(56)

11. Rewrite the following sentence, using correct
(41, 43) capitalization:

do citrus trees grow in the west?

12. Write whether the following word group is a phrase or a
(36) clause: in the path of a buffalo stampede

13. Write the indirect object in the following sentence:
(46)

The docent gave Rosella a tour of the historic hotel.

14. Rewrite the following title, using correct capitalization:
(25)

the heart of a chief

15. Write the predicate adjectives in the following sentence:
(54)

The Heart of a Chief is delightful and educational.

16. Which sentence is written correctly? Choose A or B:
(61)

A. I like the both of those songs.

B. I like both of those songs.

17. From the following sentence, write each prepositional
(44) phrase, circling the object of each preposition:

Down the hill and across the meadow galloped the horse.

18. Rewrite the following words, circling each silent letter:
(28, 29)

(a) scissors   (b) pneumonia   (c) through

19. Use an appositive to combine the following two
(58) sentences into one sentence.

Mr. Cabrera is my next-door neighbor.

Mr. Cabrera owns a Mexican restaurant in Los Angeles.

20. Rewrite the following sentence, adding periods as needed:
(47, 50)

Dr Y I Knap rests each day at two pm

21. Write the word from this list that could *not* be a linking
(31) verb: is, am, are, was, were, be, being, been, cook, feel, taste.

22. Write each adjective from the following sentence:
(40, 42)

Ambitious inventors in tiny Massachusetts created the versatile volleyball and popular basketball.

23. Rewrite the following sentence, adding commas as
(57, 59) needed:

Dr. Chu you have an appointment with Thomas Curtis
M.B.A. on Tuesday January 2 2007.

24. For the verb *beg*, write the (a) present participle, (b) past
(19) tense, and (c) past participle.

25. Write whether the circled word in the sentence below is
(52, 53) in the nominative, possessive, or objective case.

Bozo jumps (fences).

26. Rewrite the following sentence, adding capital letters as
(26) needed:

miss fortune asked, "have you seen my purse?"

27. For a–c, write the plural of each noun.
(17, 22)
    (a) trench   (b) human right   (c) dishful

28. Diagram the simple subject and simple predicate of each
(36) clause in the following sentence: When Rufus cries, his
nose runs, and he gets the hiccups.

Diagram each word of sentences 29–30.

29. Catalina, a small island off the coast of California, looks
(51, 58) hilly and barren.

30. Toby handed me a brochure about tours around Catalina.
(45, 46)

Pronouns and Antecedents

Dictation or Journal Entry
Vocabulary:
Intrepid means "fearless." *Intrepid* news reporters braved the raging hurricane in order to show the public the severity of the storm.

Cowardice is a lack of courage. *Cowardice* prevented me from speaking in public.

Pronouns

A **pronoun** is a word that takes the place of a noun or a noun phrase. Rather than using the same noun over and over again, we use pronouns.

Without pronouns, our language would be quite tiresome:

> Mr. Hurshee was eating Mr. Hurshee's breakfast on Mr. Hurshee's way to work. Unfortunately, Mr. Hurshee's milk dribbled down the front of Mr. Hurshee's shirt. Now Mr. Hurshee needs to ask Mr. Hurshee's sister to bring Mr. Hurshee a clean shirt ...

Pronouns (italicized) simplify the passage:

> Mr. Hurshee was eating *his* breakfast on *his* way to work. Unfortunately, *his* milk dribbled down the front of *his* shirt. Now *he* needs to ask *his* sister to bring *him* a clean shirt ...

Pronouns are the words (such as *he, she, it, we, they*) we use to refer to people, places, and things that have already been mentioned. Pronouns are italicized in the examples below.

> Andrés kicked the ball, and *he* watched *it* fly over Wally's head.

In the sentence above, the pronoun *he* replaces "Andrés," and the pronoun *it* replaces "ball."

Antecedents

The noun or noun phrase to which the pronoun refers is called the **antecedent.** The prefix *ante* means "before," and the root *ced* means "go." The antecedent usually "goes before" the pronoun. In the example above, "Andrés" and "ball" are antecedents for the pronouns *he* and *it.*

Notice the antecedents for the pronouns *her* and *it* in this sentence:

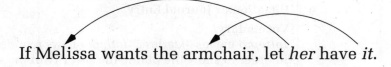

If Melissa wants the armchair, let *her* have *it*.

The antecedent of the pronoun *her* is "Melissa," and the antecedent of the pronoun *it* is "armchair."

Often we find an antecedent in an earlier sentence:

> Yesterday Gus (antecedent) made tortillas (antecedent). *He* ate *them* for lunch today.

Sometimes the antecedent comes after the pronoun:

> Although *she* dislikes watching football, Jan (antecedent) reluctantly goes to the game.

An antecedent might be another pronoun:

> *They* (antecedent) finished *their* essays.

A pronoun can also have more than one antecedent:

> After Dunlap (antecedent) and Shelby (antecedent) cut the flowers, *they* made a beautiful arrangement.

Likewise, a noun can serve as the antecedent for more than one pronoun.

> Otis (antecedent) had the flu when *he* ran *his* first race.

Example 1 Write the antecedent for each italicized pronoun in a–d. (Example: his/Tony)

(a) Todd rubs *his* chin while *he* thinks.

(b) Although *he* prefers playing, Jacob works hard.

(c) Opal bathed the dog. *She* also brushed *it*.

(d) It took them a whole week to harvest *their* big crop.

Solution (a) ***his*/Todd, *he*/Todd**

(b) ***he*/Jacob**

(c) ***she*/Opal, *it*/dog**

(d) ***their*/them**

Each pronoun needs a clear antecedent. The meaning of the sentence below is unclear because the antecedent is unclear.

The doctor said *she* eats too much sugar.

Who eats too much sugar?
What is the antecedent of *she*?

The following sentences are unclear because they each contain a pronoun that has more than one possible antecedent:

Yin and Eunice painted *her* fence.

Whose fence?
Yin's? Eunice's?

Emory left Evan with *his* horse.

Which is the antecedent of *his*?
Is it Emory, or is it Evan?

Amy picked up Beth when *she* was finished.

Does *she* refer to Amy or to Beth?

To make our meaning clear, we can use nouns instead of pronouns, we can rearrange a few words, or we can rewrite the whole sentence:

Yin and Eunice painted Yin's fence.

Emory left his horse with Evan.

When Amy was finished, she picked up Beth.

Example 2   Write the clearer sentence of each pair.
(a) She hurried to the parade.

Rosemary hurried to the parade.

(b) Ted played soccer with Ned and broke his toe.

Ted broke his toe while playing soccer with Ned.

Solution   (a) We choose the second sentence because it clearly tells *who* hurried to the parade.

Rosemary hurried to the parade.

(b) We choose the second sentence because it clearly tells *whose* toe broke.

Ted broke his toe while playing soccer with Ned.

✓ **Practice**   For a–d, give the antecedent for each italicized pronoun.
a. Opal left the pet store, but *she* returned the next day.

b. Juan wants to learn all *he* can.

c. Clem and Violet rode llamas to my house, but *they* left *them* outside.

d. Although the umbrella was old, *it* still kept Quan dry.

For e and f, write the clearer sentence of each pair.

e. While Elle and Amelia were waiting, she wrote her essay.

While Elle and Amelia were waiting, Elle wrote her essay.

f. It sputtered and coughed.

The engine sputtered and coughed.

For g and h, replace each blank with the correct vocabulary word from this lesson.

g. I saw no _____ among the brave soldiers.

h. One _____ hero risked his life to save his friend.

Review Set 62

Choose the correct word(s) to complete sentences 1–10.

1. (Elocution, Intuition, Proclamation) is an instinctive
(61) knowledge.

2. *Inopportune* means "occurring at a (bad, good, perfect)
(60) time."

3. *Luminous* means "(singing, shining, laughing)."
(59)

4. The Latin word *super* means "(above, beneath, under)."
(58)

5. A plateau is a flat land area at a (high, low) elevation.
(21)

6. The word *jury's* is a (plural, possessive) noun.
(13)

7. Rufus feels (happyest, happiest) when others are
(33, 34) (smiling, smileing).

8. Moto was (relieved, releived) when his (nieghbor,
(35) neighbor) put out the fire.

9. Mr. Hush's is the (quieter, quietest) of the two
(55) classrooms.

10. Mr. Hush's is the (quietest, most quietest) room in the
(56) school.

11. Rewrite the following letter, using correct capitalization:
(41, 43) dear mrs. roper,

    i wish to commend your intrepid assistant for capturing the run-away cheetah last wednesday.

                        gratefully,

                        mr. ortiz

12. Write the antecedent of the circled pronoun in the
(62) following sentence:

Miss Fortune bought a new purse, but she left (it) on the bus.

13. Write the coordinating conjunction that you find in the
(48) following sentence:

Opal and her daddy live in a trailer park.

14. Rewrite the following sentence, using correct
(38) capitalization:

may i keep this stray dog, daddy?

15. Write the predicate nominative in the following sentence:
(51)

Is Mr. Yu an electrician?

16. Which sentence is written correctly? Choose A or B:
(61)

    A. Ms. Hoo drives that kind of a car.

    B. Ms. Hoo drives that kind of car.

17. From the following sentence, write each prepositional
(44) phrase, circling the object of each preposition:

During the storm, Patches ran around the room and finally crawled under the sofa.

18. Use a dictionary: (a) The word *hectic* is what part of
(27, 30) speech? (b) Write its pronunciation. (c) Write its etymology.

19. Rewrite the sentence below, using commas to offset the
(60) nonessential appositive.

Rosa's youngest sister Violeta has chickenpox.

20. Rewrite the following sentence, adding periods as needed:
(47, 50)

Mr Dew now lives on S Olive St in Sacramento

21. Write whether the following sentence is declarative,
(2) interrogative, imperative, or exclamatory:

Keep your dog on a leash.

22. Write each adjective from the following sentence:
(40, 42)

A smelly, mangy, stray dog wins the affection of Opal and
her daddy.

23. Rewrite the following sentence, adding commas as
(57, 59) needed:

Mora we were on vacation in Oskaloosa Iowa.

24. For the verb *steady*, write the (a) present participle, (b)
(19) past tense, and (c) past participle.

25. Write whether the circled word in the sentence below is
(52, 53) in the nominative, possessive, or objective case.

(Bozo's) ears flap in the wind.

26. Rewrite the following lines of poetry, adding capital
(15) letters as needed:

cut thistles in May,
they'll grow in a day...

27. For a–c, write the plural of each noun.
(17, 22) (a) Gómez   (b) waltz   (c) woman

28. Diagram the simple subject and simple predicate of each
(36) clause in the following sentence:

Restless horses stomp, and hungry cows moo as Olaf
delivers their hay.

Diagram each word of sentences 29–30.

29. Today's weather in Pennsylvania appears sunny but cold.
(45, 54)

30. Punxsutawney Phil, a famous groundhog, gave us his
(46, 58) prediction concerning winter.

The Comma, Part 4: Greetings and Closings; Last Name First

Dictation or Journal Entry

Vocabulary:

Tenacious means "persistent; not giving up, as in a belief." Albert remained *tenacious* to the end of the debate, which he won.

Tenacity is persistence or strong adherence. The defense attorney argued the case with *tenacity*.

In this lesson, we will learn more uses for commas.

Greeting   We use a comma after the **greeting** of a friendly letter.

Dear Gloria,

My melancholy daddy,

Closing   We use a comma after the **closing** of a letter.

Sincerely yours,

Gratefully,

Example 1   Place commas where they are needed in the letter below.

Dear Monty

Thank you for the lovely flowers.

Love

Allison

Solution   We place commas after the greeting and closing of the letter.

Dear Monty,

Thank you for the lovely flowers.

Love,

Allison

Last Name First   When we alphabetize a list of names, we usually alphabetize by the person's last name. We place the last name first and the first name (followed by middle names, if any) last. They are separated by a comma, as shown:

Bui, Bao

Dunn, Mabel   *Allen, Hope*

Medrano, Omar P.

Stuart, M'kalah

Vong, Quan

Other than in lists, we don't often write names this way. When we do, we are usually referring to or "quoting from" a list. Quotation marks are a good way of indicating this:

The last name on the class list was "Zamarripa, Jean."

"Whitman, Walt" completed the list of famous American authors.

I am listed as "Jones, Jeffrey J." in the phone book.

Example 2   Insert a comma where it is needed in the sentence below.

"Aguilar Josie" was the first name on the class list.

Solution   We use a comma in inverted names.

"Aguilar, Josie" was the first name on the class list.

Practice   Rewrite a and b, inserting commas as needed.

a. Dear Tyrell

Thank you for the guest list. I see that the first name is "Abram Peter."

Gratefully,
Hepzy

b. The index lists "Carroll Lewis." as the author of "Father William."

For c and d, replace each blank with the correct vocabulary word from this lesson.

c. _____, a noun, is persistence.

d. _____, an adjective, means "not giving up."

Review Set 63   Choose the correct word(s) to complete sentences 1–10.

1. *Intrepid* means "(fearful, cowardly, fearless)."
(62)

2. Cedric's (elocution, intuition, optimism) warned him that
(61) it would rain on parade day.

3. *Opportune* means "(inconvenient, well-timed, lazy)."
(60)

4. (*Indolent, Dispensable, Luminous*) means "shining, or
(59) giving light."

5. To (disclose, conceal, placate) is to calm the hostility of,
(22) or appease.

6. The word *tenacity* is a(n) (abstract, concrete) noun.
(11)

7. Simon tells (funy, funny) jokes (dayly, daily).
(33, 34)

8. Can anyone (decieve, deceive) the police (chief, cheif)?
(35)

9. Of the twins, Trin has the (redder, reddest) hair.
(55)

10. Trin's hair is the (reddest, most reddest) in the whole
(56) family.

11. Rewrite the following letter, adding commas and capital
(43, 63) letters as needed:

dear mrs. roper

i appreciate your tenacity in arguing my case in court
on thursday.

gratefully

mr. palma

12. Write whether the following word group is a phrase or a
(36) clause:

with a bar of soap and a bucket of water

13. Write the indirect object in the following sentence:
(46)

Opal gives Gertrude directions.

14. Rewrite the following title, using correct capitalization:
(25)

because of winn-dixie

15. Write the predicate adjectives in the following sentence:
(54)

Winn-Dixie now looks clean and attractive.

✓**16.** Replace the overused adjective below with one that is
(61) more descriptive. There are many possible answers.

That was a _____ nice _____ story.

17. From the following sentence, write each prepositional phrase, circling the object of each preposition:
(44)

I have been wondering about you since Tuesday.

18. Use a dictionary: (a) The word *cephalic* is what part of speech? (b) Write its pronunciation. (c) Write its etymology.
(27, 30)

19. Use an appositive to combine the following two sentences into one sentence.
(58)

Pewny is my youngest cousin.

Pewny eats my broccoli for me.

20. Rewrite the following sentence, adding periods as needed:
(47, 50)

The dog's collar costs $250 (two dollars and fifty cents)

21. Write the linking verb from the following sentence:
(31)

Miss Franny is the city's librarian.

22. Write each adjective from the following sentence:
(40, 42)

She wears a shimmery green dress.

23. Rewrite the following sentence, adding commas as needed:
(57, 59)

Luis you may pick up your order on Monday Wednesday or Friday.

24. For the verb *tap*, write the (a) present participle, (b) past tense, and (c) past participle.
(19)

25. Write whether the circled word in the sentence below is in the nominative, possessive, or objective case.
(52, 53)

Bozo's (ears) flap in the wind.

26. Rewrite the following sentence, adding capital letters as needed:
(26)

inez asked, "who spilled the paint?"

27. For a–c, write the plural of each noun.
(17, 22)

(a) sea serpent   (b) sheep   (c) thief

28. Diagram the simple subject and simple predicate of each
(36) clause in the following sentence:

Lily made fewer errors on today's test than she did on the
last test because she has been studying.

Diagram each word of sentences 29–30.

29. Was Friday's dictation long and difficult?
(45, 54)

30. Jason, a rancher from Idaho, baked me a gigantic potato
(46, 58) from his garden.

There are five main categories of pronouns: personal, relative, indefinite, interrogative, and demonstrative. We will begin with personal pronouns.

Just like nouns, **personal pronouns** refer to people and things (and also places, if you think of a place as an "it"). In the following sentences, the personal pronouns are italicized.

He will help *them*.

Do *you* have *my* jacket?

They say *we* must not touch *it*.

It is the largest city in the nation.

There are three forms of personal pronouns: person, number, and case.

Person   *First person* is the speaker: *I, me, mine, we, us, ours.*

I try hard.

We shall succeed.

That error was *mine*.

Second person is the person being spoken to: *you, yours.*

Will *you* come also?

All of *you* are invited.

That invitation is *yours*.

Third person is the person being spoken about: *he, she, it, him, her, his, hers.*

He and *she* will come.

They will come also.

That dog is *hers*.

Send *it* to *him*.

Example 1 For each sentence below, write the pronoun and tell whether it is first person, second person, or third person.

(a) We studied reptiles.

(b) Pann pitches her the ball.

(c) Did you read the entire book?

Solution (a) *We* is **first person.** It indicates the speaker.

(b) *Her* is **third person,** the person being spoken about.

(c) *You* is **second person,** the person being spoken to.

Number Some personal pronouns are singular:

I, me, mine, you, yours, he, him, his, she, her, hers, it

Others are plural:

we, us, ours, you, yours, they, them, theirs

Notice that *you* and *yours* appear in both lists. These words can be either singular or plural. In fact, we cannot always tell which is meant.

Example 2 For a–d, write each personal pronoun and tell whether it is singular or plural.

(a) *They* left.   (b) That's *mine.*

(c) Flora has *hers.*   (d) *You* are welcome.

Solution (a) *They* is **plural.**   (b) *Mine* is **singular.**

(c) *Hers* is **singular.**   (d) *You* might be **singular** or **plural.** We can't tell.

Case Just like nouns, pronouns appear in **cases.** We remember that case shows how a noun or pronoun is used in a sentence.

Some pronouns are used as *subjects*:

He eats clams. *They* want some too. *I* don't. Does *she* save the shells?

Others are used as *objects*:

Elle eats *them* also. (direct object)

Bert gave *her* the last one. (indirect object)

James is waiting for *us*. (object of a preposition)

Some pronouns show *possession*:

Is this *yours?*

Claude lost *his.*

I hid *mine.*

Theirs are sour.

Example 3 Tell whether each circled pronoun shows possession or whether it is used as a subject or an object. If it is an object, tell what kind (direct object, indirect object, object of a preposition).

(a) Meg sent (her) a postcard.

(b) Yesterday, (she) mowed the lawn.

(c) Bently believes (him).

(d) This is (yours).

Solution (a) The pronoun *her* is an **indirect object.**

(b) The pronoun *she* is the **subject** of the sentence.

(c) The pronoun *him* is a **direct object.**

(d) The pronoun *yours* shows **possession.**

Practice For a and b, replace the blank with the correct vocabulary word from this lesson.

a. _____ behavior is not morally right.

b. _____ behavior is morally right.

For sentences c–e, write the personal pronoun and tell whether it is first, second, or third person.

c. Maya agrees with me.

d. He agrees with Maya.

e. Do you agree with Maya?

For f and g, write the personal pronoun and tell whether it is singular or plural.

f. Please help us.   **g.** Take me too.

For h–k, tell whether the circled personal pronoun is used as a ~~subject,~~ direct object, ~~indirect object,~~ object of a preposition, or whether it shows possession.

h. (I) wonder what will happen next.

i. Sid greets (her) with a smile.

j. Ms. Hoo hands (us) new books.

k. The pleasure is (ours).

More Practice For sentences 1–5, write each personal pronoun and write whether it is first, second, or third person. Also write whether it is singular or plural. (Example: 1. we, first person plural; you, second person singular)

1. May we help you?

2. Are they ethical?

3. Please pour him some water.

4. They folded their laundry and placed it over there.

5. Will you hear my opinion?

For sentences 6–10, write each personal pronoun and label it "subject," "object," or "possessive."

6. All the girls except her wore green.

7. We took our ducks to the lake and freed them.

8. I gave them my word.

9. They trust me.

10. She listens to us.

Review Set 64 Choose the correct word(s) to complete sentences 1–10.

1. (*Tenacious*, *Supersonic*, *Luminous*) means "persistent;
(63) not giving up."

2. (Avarice, Cowardice, Valor) is a lack of courage.
(62)

3. Intuition is an instinctive (desire, habit, knowledge).
(61)

4. An (opportune, inopportune) thunderstorm rained on our parade.
(60)

5. *To placate* means "to (disturb, anger, calm)."
(22)

6. The word *barnyard* is a (compound, collective) noun.
(13)

7. I (moped, mopped) the floor and (dryed, dried) it with a towel.
(33, 34)

8. My best (freind, friend) plays right (feild, field).
(35)

9. We don't have (much, many) apples left.
(56)

10. The pronoun *I* is (first, second, third) person (singular, plural).
(64)

11. Rewrite the following letter, adding commas and capital letters as needed:
(43, 63)

dear mr. palma

i shall represent you in the philadelphia courthouse as long as your behavior remains ethical.

sincerely

mrs. roper

12. Write the antecedent of the circled pronoun in the following sentence:
(62)

Miss Fortune bought a new purse, but (she) left it on the bus.

13. Write each coordinating conjunction that you find in the following sentence:
(48)

Yuntao or Pearlin painted this stunning watercolor.

14. Rewrite the following sentence, using correct capitalization:
(38)

my mother, dr. ting lacy, studied latin.

15. Write the predicate nominative in the following sentence:
(51)

The first day (of winter) is today.

16. Write whether the following sentence is a complete
(23) sentence, a run-on sentence, or a sentence fragment:

Without ever poking his head out of his protective shell.

17. From the following sentence, write each prepositional
(44) phrase, circling the object of each preposition:

Floyd hides in the corner opposite Harry for two hours.

18. Rewrite the word *bridge*, circling the silent letter.
(28, 29)

19. Rewrite the sentence below, using commas to offset the
(60) nonessential appositive.

Chester the biggest cat on the farm is disturbing the hens.

20. Rewrite the following sentence, adding periods as needed:
(47, 50)

Mrs Ross gave us these directions: Go north to Vista St
and turn right

21. Write whether the following sentence is declarative,
(2) interrogative, imperative, or exclamatory:

The turtle pulled his head into his shell.

22. Write whether the following word group is a phrase or a
(36) clause:

if you wash with soap

23. Rewrite the following sentence, adding commas as
(57, 59) needed:

Boise Idaho will be my destination John.

24. For the verb *supply*, write the (a) present participle, (b)
(19) past tense, and (c) past participle.

25. Write whether the circled pronoun in the sentence below
(64) is used as a subject or an object.

Bozo barks at me.

26. Rewrite the following outline, adding periods and capital
(26, 47) letters as needed:

    i new hospital staff
     a dr eric koesno
     b ms cherry clegg, rn

27. For a–c, write the plural of each noun.
(17, 22)

    (a) can opener   (b) wolf   (c) radio

28. Diagram the simple subject and simple predicate of each
(36) clause in the following sentence:

Omar made fewer errors on today's homework than he
did on yesterday's because he has been working hard.

Diagram each word of sentences 29–30.

29. Has Tyrell become a serious student or a superb artist?
(45, 51)

30. Tyrell, a serious student in my class, painted me a
(46, 58) beautiful portrait of his two collies.

Irregular Verbs, Part 2

We form the past tense of regular verbs by adding *d* or *ed* to the present tense of the verb. We form the past tense of irregular verbs in different ways. There are no rules for forming the past tense and past participles of these verbs. Fortunately, we recognize the principal parts of most irregular verbs just by hearing them. We must memorize the irregular verb parts that we do not know already.

Irregular verbs cause people trouble because it is easy to confuse the past and past participle.

She has gone (NOT went) to work.

The concert began (NOT begun) on time.

We can group many irregular verbs because they follow similar patterns. Here we list four groups of irregular verbs:

	VERB	PAST	PAST PARTICIPLE
1.	blow	blew	(has) blown
	know	knew	(has) known
	throw	threw	(has) thrown
	grow	grew	(has) grown
2.	bear	bore	(has) borne
	tear	tore	(has) torn
	wear	wore	(has) worn
	swear	swore	(has) sworn
3.	begin	began	(has) begun
	ring	rang	(has) rung
	shrink	shrank	(has) shrunk
	sing	sang	(has) sung

drink	drank	(has) drunk
4. choose	chose	(has) chosen
freeze	froze	(has) frozen
speak	spoke	(has) spoken
break	broke	(has) broken
steal	stole	(has) stolen

Remember, there are many more irregular verbs. Some of them follow the patterns above, but others don't. Always consult the dictionary if you are unsure.

Example Write the correct verb form for sentences a–d.
(a) The pond has (froze, frozen) solid already.

(b) Dawn (threw, thrown) a snowball at Pete.

(c) My beige pants (shrank, shrunk) in the dryer.

(d) Julie has (grew, grown) two inches taller this year.

Solution (a) The pond has **frozen** solid already.

(b) Dawn **threw** a snowball at Pete.

(c) My beige pants **shrank** in the dryer.

(d) Julie has **grown** two inches taller this year.

Practice For a and b, replace each blank with the correct vocabulary word from this lesson.
a. One might show _____ by singing, clapping, or cheering.

b. Roy was _____ when he heard that he had a new nephew.

For c–j, write the correct verb form for each sentence.
c. Molly (blew, blown) up red balloons for the party.

d. Mac has (wore, worn) out his shoes.

e. Nelson (sang, sung) a new song.

f. Have you (spoke, spoken) to Kelly?

g. Rosa (tore, torn) the ticket in half.

h. Geoff had (knew, known) Patrick for years.

i. A squirrel (stole, stolen) the peanut from the jay.

j. Has the bell (rang, rung) yet?

For k–x, write the past and past participle of each verb.

k. grow	**l.** bear	**m.** ring	**n.** sink
o. sing	**p.** drink	**q.** choose	**r.** break
s. wear	**t.** know	**u.** blow	**v.** begin
w. swear	**x.** speak		

Review Set 65

Choose the correct word(s) to complete sentences 1–10.

1. (*Intrepid, Ethical, Superfluous*) means "morally right."
(64)

2. A student with (liability, cowardice, tenacity) does not
(63) give up.

3. (*Intuitive, Inopportune, Intrepid*) means "fearless."
(62)

4. *Intuitive* means "(supersonic, instinctive, superfluous)."
(61)

5. We might find sediment at the (surface, top, bottom) of a
(27) lake or pond.

6. The word *armies* is a (plural, possessive) noun.
(13)

7. The (begining, beginning) of the project was (worrisome,
(33, 34) worrysome).

8. The teacher (percieves, perceives) that Wallace has
(35) (achieved, acheived) excellence.

9. Patricia is the (better, best) of the two drummers.
(56)

10. The pronoun *we* is (first, second, third) person (singular,
(64) plural).

11. Rewrite the following letter, adding commas and capital
(43, 63) letters as needed:

dear uncle sergio

you can find her information in the directory under
blackly doris.

your niece

daniela

12. Write the antecedent of the circled pronoun in the
(62) following sentence:

A boy found Miss Fortune's purse, and (he) gave it to the
bus driver.

13. Write the indirect object in the following sentence:
(46)

Moya brought Lily a piece of granite from New
Hampshire.

14. Rewrite the following title, using correct capitalization:
(25)

the sound of music

15. Write the predicate adjective in the following sentence:
(54)

The snow-covered peaks look majestic.

16. Replace the overused adjective below with one that is
(61) more descriptive. There are many possible answers.

I had a _____ ~~good~~ _____ vacation.

17. From the following sentence, write each prepositional
(44) phrase, circling the object of each preposition:

A fat green worm was inching toward the ripest tomato
on the vine.

18. Use a dictionary: (a) The word *delude* is what part of
(27, 30) speech? (b) Write its pronunciation. (c) Write its
etymology.

19. Use an appositive to combine the following two
(58) sentences into one sentence.

Marigold likes to gallop through the mud.

Marigold is a spotted mare.

20. Rewrite the following sentence, adding periods as needed:
(47, 50)

At one am Ms Overwork tore up her essay and began
again

21. Write the word from this list that could *not* be a linking
(31) verb: look, feel, taste, swell, sound, seem, appear, grow.

22. Write whether the following word group is a phrase or a
(36) clause:

for the fourth time today

23. Rewrite the following sentence, adding commas as
(57, 59) needed:

I shall see you John on Tuesday January 16 2007.

24. For the irregular verb *blow*, write the (a) present
(10, 65) participle, (b) past tense, and (c) past participle.

25. Write whether the circled pronoun in the sentence below
(64) is used as a subject or an object.

(She) is Bozo's best friend.

26. Rewrite the following lines of poetry, adding capital
(15) letters as needed:

a man of words and not of deeds
is like a garden full of weeds.

27. For a–c, write the plural of each noun.
(17, 22)
    (a) eyelash   (b) bagful   (c) soprano

28. Diagram the simple subject and simple predicate of each
(36) clause in the following sentence:

Miss Fortune lost her new purse, but Hector found it
before a thief did.

Diagram each word of sentences 29–30.

29. Hector remains an honest young man and Miss Fortune's
(45, 51) hero.

30. Hector, an honest young man, handed the bus driver Miss
(46, 58) Fortune's purse.

Nominative Pronoun Case

Dictation or Journal Entry

Vocabulary:

Contrite means "regretful for an offense; sorry." Jerome was *contrite* after mistreating his brother.

Contrition is regret for an offense. Jerome showed his *contrition* by apologizing to his brother.

Nominative Case

We remember that nouns can be grouped into three cases: nominative, objective, and possessive. We also remember that the same is true of pronouns. In this lesson we will concentrate on the **nominative case.** A pronoun used as a subject or predicate nominative is in the nominative case.

She wears sunglasses. (subject)

The girl in sunglasses is *she.* (predicate nominative)

I raked the leaves. (subject)

It was *I* who raked the leaves. (predicate nominative)

He will speak. (subject)

It is *he* who will speak. (predicate nominative)

We are the grammar experts. (subject)

The grammar experts are *we.* (predicate nominative)

Example 1

Complete this chart by replacing each blank with the correct nominative case pronoun.

NUMBER	PERSON		NOMINATIVE CASE (subject or predicate nominative)
Singular	First		_____
	Second		_____
	Third	(masc.)	_____
		(fem.)	_____
		(neuter)	_____
Plural	First		_____
	Second		_____
	Third		_____

Solution   We complete the chart as follows:

NUMBER	PERSON		NOMINATIVE CASE (subject or predicate nominative)
Singular	First		_I_
	Second		_you_
	Third	(masc.)	_he_
		(fem.)	_she_
		(neuter)	_it_
Plural	First		_we_
	Second		_you_
	Third		_they_

Subjects   These sentences use nominative case personal pronouns as subjects:

> *I* sang a solo.

> *He* joined the choir.

When we use the pronoun *I* as part of a compound subject, it is polite to refer to ourselves last:

> Erica and *I* were born in Alaska.

> Ricardo and *I* are cousins.

Example 2   Which sentence is more polite?

> Both *we* and *they* like the snow.

> Both *they* and *we* like the snow.

Solution   It is more polite to refer to ourselves (we) last.

> **Both *they* and *we* like the snow.**

Example 3   Write a sentence using a nominative case personal pronoun as a subject.

Solution   Your answer will be unique. Here are some correct examples:

> ***We* shall memorize a poem.**
> ***They* have begun the race.**
> **Ashley and *she* broke the silence.**

Predicate Nominatives These sentences use nominative case personal pronouns as predicate nominatives.

The culprit was *he* in the tall hat.

The officer in charge is *she.*

Predicate nominatives can also be compound:

The drummers are Adriana and *he.*

The vocalists will be *she* and *I.*

Example 4 Write a sentence using a nominative case pronoun as a predicate nominative.

Solution Your answer will be unique. Here are some correct examples:

It was *I* who rang the bell.

The best singer is *he.*

Your entertainers will be *they* and *I.*

Practice **a.** Study the nominative case pronoun chart from Example 1. Then try to reproduce it from memory. You may abbreviate (1st, 2nd, 3rd, sing., pl., etc.).

b. Unscramble these words to make a sentence with a personal pronoun as a subject:

writers   excellent   they   are

c. Unscramble these words to make a sentence with a personal pronoun as a predicate nominative:

writer   best   he   was   the

For d and e, replace each blank with the correct vocabulary word from this lesson.

d. _____, an adjective, means "sorry."

e. _____, a noun, is regret for an offense.

f. Write the sentence that is more polite:

I and she wore green.

She and I wore green.

g. Write each nominative case pronoun from this list: me, him, I, she, them, they, he, her, we, us.

Choose the nominative case pronoun for sentences h–k.

h. The woman in the photo is (she, her).

i. The highest jumpers were Jessica and (her, she).

j. The man in the red car was (him, he).

k. It is (I, me).

Review Set 66 Choose the correct word(s) to complete sentences 1–10.

1. (*Tenacious*, *Ethical*, *Elated*) means "having high spirits."
(65)

2. Cheating on a test is (ethical, unethical).
(64)

3. A(n) (extravagant, frugal, tenacious) person does not give
(63) up.

4. Cowardice is a lack of (fear, intuition, courage).
(62)

5. (Igneous, Metamorphic, Sedimentary) rocks form in
(27) layers from materials deposited by water, wind, or ice.

6. The word *contrition* is a(n) (abstract, concrete) noun.
(11)

7. My uncle always (prefered, preferred) (sunnyer, sunnier)
(33, 34) weather.

8. Before we leave for the airport, I shall (wiegh, weigh)
(35) each (piece, peice) of luggage.

9. We have (less, fewer) bananas than oranges.
(56)

10. The pronoun *you* is (first, second, third) person.
(64)

11. Rewrite the following letter, adding commas and capital
(43, 63) letters as needed:

dear aunt beki

    can you come to mother's birthday party on monday
may 5?

                your niece

                daniela

12. Write the antecedent of the circled pronoun in the
(62) following sentence:

A boy found Miss Fortune's purse, and he gave (it) to the
bus driver.

13. Write each coordinating conjunction that you find in the
(48) following sentence:

Fawzy and Jean hiked to Vernal and Nevada Falls, but
they were too tired to climb Half Dome.

14. Rewrite the following sentence, using correct
(38) capitalization:

leonard learned all about geology from his father, dr.
trent, but nothing about english.

15. Write the predicate nominative in the following sentence:
(51)

John Muir was the first president of the Sierra Club.

16. Write whether the following sentence is a complete
(23) sentence, a run-on sentence, or a sentence fragment:

Because of a young Scotsman named John Muir.

17. From the following sentence, write each prepositional
(44) phrase, circling the object of each preposition:

With Yosemite's Half Dome in the background, the
photograph reminds me of our long hike to the falls.

18. Rewrite the word *guide*, circling the silent letter.
(28, 29)

19. Rewrite the sentence below, using commas to offset the
(60) nonessential appositive.

My littlest brother Andrew found a worm in his apple.

20. Rewrite the following sentence, adding periods as needed:
(47, 50)
On Dec 24, 1914, Mr John Muir died at the age of
seventy-six

21. Write the nominative case pronoun to complete the
(66) following sentence:

The man in the green jacket is (he, him).

22. Write whether the following word group is a phrase or a
(36) clause:

if you make faces in the mirror

23. Rewrite the following sentence, adding commas as
(57, 59) needed:

Jacob I would like you to meet Yin Yu D.D.S.

24. For the irregular verb *bear*, write the (a) present
(10, 65) participle, (b) past tense, and (c) past participle.

25. Write whether the circled pronoun in the sentence below
(64) is used as a subject or an object.

Bozo trusts her.

26. Rewrite the following sentence, adding capital letters as
(26) needed:

hector said, "this purse belongs to the woman who
stepped off the bus at oak street."

27. For a–c, write the plural of each noun.
(17, 22)

(a) cup of tea   (b) cupful   (c) alto

28. Diagram the simple subject and simple predicate of each
(36) clause in the following sentence:

Bozo yipped when he saw Fifi at the dog show, for she is
a fluffy black poodle.

Diagram each word of sentences 29–30.

29. Will the winner of the dog show be Bozo or she?
(45, 51)

30. Fifi, the fluffy black poodle, showed me her sharp white
(46, 58) teeth.

The Comma, Part 5: Introductory and Interrupting Elements; Afterthoughts

---

Dictation or Journal Entry

Vocabulary:

Pertinent means "relevant, connected, or applicable." Information about Santa Fe is *pertinent* to a study of New Mexico, for Santa Fe is the capital of New Mexico.

Irrelevant means "not pertinent; unconnected." Information about polar bears is *irrelevant* to a study of New Mexico, for polar bears do not live there.

Comma = Pause

When we speak, we often pause between words. If we wrote down exactly what we were saying, most of those pauses would be indicated by commas. Pauses usually occur when we insert words or phrases that interrupt the natural flow of the sentence. Notice how commas are used to offset the italicized words, phrases, and clauses in the sentences below.

No, I would not like to live on Mars.

There, *I assume,* people cannot breathe.

Earth is more hospitable, *after all.*

These sentences show natural pauses that occur with introductory elements, interrupting elements, and afterthoughts. Let us look at more examples.

Introductory Elements

An **introductory element** begins a sentence. It sometimes expresses the writer's attitude about what is being said. An introductory element can also be a request or command.

Yes, I stayed up too late last night.

On the other hand, I finished reading the story.

Obviously, you didn't get enough sleep.

Please remember, the story captivated me.

Example 1

Rewrite these sentences, using commas to offset introductory phrases.

(a) Amazingly the wind blew down the fence.

(b) In my opinion it was the worst storm ever.

Solution   (a) "Amazingly" is an introductory element. We offset it with a comma.

Amazingly, the wind blew down the fence.

(b) The phrase "In my opinion" is an introductory element. We offset it with a comma.

In my opinion, it was the worst storm ever.

Interrupting Elements   An **interrupting element** appears in the middle of a sentence, interrupting the flow from subject to verb to object. An interrupting element can be removed without changing the meaning of the sentence.

Deserts, *it would seem*, are home to many reptiles.

Catch the bus, *if you can*, before noon.

Jeremy, *not Mark,* was playing the trumpet.

Example 2   Rewrite these sentences, using commas to offset interrupting phrases.

(a) How in the world you ask did we walk that far?

(b) He wanted soup not salad for lunch.

Solution   (a) We look for a word or phrase that interrupts the flow of the sentence and can be removed without changing its meaning. (It's not unusual to find that you must read the sentence two or three times in order to decide.) In this sentence, the phrase "you ask" is an interrupting element, so we offset it with commas.

How in the world, **you ask,** did we walk that far?

(b) The phrase "not salad" is an interrupting element. We offset it with commas.

He wanted soup, **not salad,** for lunch.

Afterthoughts   **Afterthoughts** are similar to introductory and interrupting elements except that they are added to the ends of sentences.

The key is under the mat, *by the way.*

I am fine, *thank you.*

Her uncle raises sheep, *if I remember correctly.*

Some afterthoughts turn the sentence into a question:

It's not too late, *is it?*

Hand me that wrench, *would you?*

We all have to help, *don't we?*

Example 3 Rewrite these sentences, using commas to offset afterthoughts.

(a) Red means "stop" of course.

(b) You don't smoke do you?

Solution (a) The phrase "of course" is an afterthought, so we offset it with a comma.

Red means "stop," **of course.**

(b) The questioning phrase "do you" is an afterthought. We offset it with a comma.

You don't smoke, **do you?**

Practice Rewrite sentences a and b, inserting commas to offset introductory elements.

a. Yes I speak English.

b. Of course not everyone does.

Rewrite sentences c and d, inserting commas to offset interrupting elements.

c. His grandfather I believe came from Denmark.

d. The camel it is said has no sense of humor.

For e and f, replace each blank with the correct vocabulary word from this lesson.

e. Your birth date is _____ to the story of your life.

f. The temperature of the Indian Ocean is probably _____ to the story of your life.

More Practice See "More Practice Lesson 67" in Student Workbook.

Review Set 67 Choose the correct word(s) to complete sentences 1–10.

1. (*Tenacious, Avaricious, Contrite*) means "regretful for an offense; sorry."
(66)

2. *Elated* means "having (low, high, depressed) spirits."
(65)

3. (*Ethical, Unethical, Avaricious*) means "morally right."
(64)

4. Isabel is (intuitive, avaricious, tenacious); she does not give up.
(63)

5. An explosion or collapse of the center of a volcano might create a(n) (savanna, atoll, caldera).
(28)

6. The word *Rufus's* is a (plural, possessive) noun.
(13)

7. Emil (frys, fries) the (flatest, flattest) pancakes I've ever seen.
(33, 34)

8. Is the senator with the (breifcase, briefcase) (conceited, concieted)?
(35)

9. Of all the illnesses, this is the (worse, worst).
(56)

10. The pronoun *she* is (first, second, third) person (singular, plural).
(64)

11. Rewrite the following letter, adding commas and capital letters as needed:
(63, 67)

dear daniela

yes i shall come to your mother's party on monday may 5.

love
aunt beki

12. Write the antecedent of the circled pronoun in the following sentence:
(62)

Miss Fortune asked the bus driver if he had seen (her) purse.

13. Write the indirect object in the following sentence:
(46)

The ranger gave us information about the Tuolumne Meadows.

14. Rewrite the following title, using correct capitalization:
(25)

the red pony

15. Write the predicate adjective in the following sentence:
(54)

John Muir was passionate about nature.

16. Which sentence is written correctly? Choose A or B:
(61)

   A. Both of you are silly.

   B. The both of you are silly.

17. From the following sentence, write each prepositional
(44) phrase, circling the object of each preposition:

With a child in a backpack, the woman climbed to the top
of Sentinel Dome.

18. Rewrite the word *two*, circling the silent letter.
(28, 29)

19. Use an appositive to combine the following two
(58) sentences into one sentence.

Sacramento is the capital of California.

Ms. Hoo flew to Sacramento.

20. Rewrite the following sentence, adding periods as needed:
(47, 50)

Dr Kraning will lecture on Aug 14

21. Write the nominative case pronoun to complete the
(66) following sentence:

It is (me, I) who should apologize.

22. Write whether the following word group is a phrase or a
(36) clause:

with pertinent information for my essay

23. Rewrite the following sentence, adding commas as
(57, 59) needed:

If you have time Mark please bake two potatoes some
rolls and a pie.

24. For the irregular verb *begin*, write the (a) present
(10, 65) participle, (b) past tense, and (c) past participle.

25. Write whether the circled pronoun in the sentence below
(64) is used as a subject or an object.

Does (she) like Bozo?

26. Rewrite the following outline, adding periods and capital
(26, 47) letters as needed:

    i national parks
      a yosemite
      b yellowstone

27. For a–c, write the plural of each noun.
(17, 22)
    (a) penny   (b) box of cereal   (c) trout

28. Diagram the simple subject and simple predicate of each
(36) clause in the following sentence:

Fifi growled at Bozo, for she thought that he was rude.

Diagram each word of sentences 29–30.

29. Will the winner of the dog show be Fifi or he?
(45, 51)

30. Bozo, the handsomest dog in the contest, might have
(46, 58) given Fifi a kiss.

The Comma, Part 6: Clarity

Dictation or Journal Entry

Vocabulary:

Meteorology is the study of atmospheric conditions, especially relating to weather. According to the *meteorology* report, hurricanes are forming off Florida's coast.

Ornithology is the study of birds. The *ornithology* book contained information about Western birds—their nesting, eating, and migrating habits.

Clarity

To *clarify* is to "make clear." When something is clear, it has *clarity*. We use commas to separate words, phrases, or clauses in order to **clarify meaning**, or to "make clear" the meaning of our sentences. Without commas, the meaning of the sentences below is unclear.

UNCLEAR: To Clark Kent was always a hero.
CLEAR: To Clark, Kent was always a hero.

UNCLEAR: Shortly after the bell rang.
CLEAR: Shortly after, the bell rang.

Example

Rewrite each sentence, using commas to clarify meaning.

(a) During the week it rained.

(b) To Daniel the coach was a friend.

Solution

(a) Without a comma, this sentence is incomplete. During the week it rained... *what?* They wore boots? We played inside? To avoid confusion, we insert a comma to clarify our intended meaning.

During the week, it rained.

(b) Is Daniel a coach? If we read the sentence carefully, we see that he is not. A comma makes this much clearer.

To Daniel, the coach was a friend.

Practice

Rewrite sentences a–c, using commas to clarify meaning.

a. To Karen Joyce meant trouble.

b. While passing the driver honked.

c. After John Thomas will speak.

For d and e, replace each blank with the correct vocabulary word from this lesson.

d. _____ is the study of birds.

e. _____ is the study of weather.

Review Set 68

Choose the correct word to complete sentences 1–10.

1. (*Unconnected, Pertinent, Contrite*) means "applicable or relevant."
   (67)

2. Contrition is (regret, forgiveness, pardon) for an offense.
   (66)

3. Elation is (high, low, evil) spirits.
   (65)

4. (*Ethical, Unethical, Tenacious*) means *"not* morally right."
   (64)

5. A (volcano's, chicken's, lagoon's) caldera looks like a huge basin.
   (28)

6. The sentence below is (declarative, interrogative, imperative, exclamatory).
   (2)

   Does Phil like cheeseburgers without cheese?

7. Gloria is (shoping, shopping) for a (beautyful, beautiful) dress.
   (33, 34)

8. Did they (recieve, receive) the (priest's, preist's) blessing?
   (35)

9. Of the two hail storms, the first one was (worse, worst).
   (56)

10. The pronoun *they* is (first, second, third) person (singular, plural).
    (64)

11. Rewrite the following letter, adding commas and capital letters as needed:
    (63, 67)

    dear aunt beki

        please bring paper plates cups and napkins to mom's party all right?

                              many thanks

                              daniela

12. Write the antecedent of the circled pronoun in the following sentence:
(62)

Miss Fortune asked the bus driver if (he) had seen her purse.

13. Write each coordinating conjunction that you find in the following sentence:
(48)

The Paiute and Ahwahnee people traded acorns or fish.

14. Rewrite the following sentence, using correct capitalization:
(38)

i'll ask mother for the spanish translation.

15. Write the predicate adjective in the following sentence:
(54)

Yosemite Valley's history seems rich.

16. Write whether the following is a complete sentence, a run-on sentence, or a sentence fragment:
(23)

Do you know what the word *Awahnee* means?

17. Rewrite the sentence below, using a comma to clarify the meaning.
(68)

To see that dog Bozo would do anything.

18. Use a dictionary: (a) The word *detour* is what part of speech? (b) Write its pronunciation. (c) Write its etymology.
(27, 30)

19. Rewrite the sentence below, using commas to offset the nonessential appositive.
(60)

Ms. Hoo a middle school teacher needs a vacation.

20. Rewrite the following sentence, adding periods as needed:
(47, 50)

At one pm, Mrs Sizzle arrived in Death Valley

21. Write the nominative case pronoun to complete the following sentence:
(66)

The artists were Ilbea and (her, she).

22. Write whether the following word group is a phrase or a
(36) clause:

if meteorologists predict more hail

23. Rewrite the following sentence, adding commas as
(57, 59) needed:

When you come Ms. Hoo please plan to stay until Friday
August 12.

24. For the irregular verb *choose*, write the (a) present
(10, 65) participle, (b) past tense, and (c) past participle.

25. Write whether the circled pronoun in the sentence below
(64) is used as a subject or an object.

Fifi has an umbrella with her name on(it.)

26. Rewrite the following lines of poetry, adding capital
(26, 47) letters as needed:

fuzzy Wuzzy was a bear,
fuzzy Wuzzy had no hair,
so fuzzy Wuzzy wasn't fuzzy,
was he?

27. For a–c, write the plural of each noun.
(17, 22)
(a) Rufus   (b) French fry   (c) leash

28. Diagram the simple subject and simple predicate of each
(36) clause in the following sentence:

Bozo yipped at Fifi, for he thought she was pretty.

Diagram each word of sentences 29–30.
29. Has Bozo proved faithful and obedient?
(45, 54)

30. My funny friend Phil ordered us cheeseburgers without
(46, 58) cheese.

Grammar and Writing 5   **355**   **Student Edition**
Lesson 68

Objective Pronoun Case

Dictation or Journal Entry
Vocabulary:
Unfeigned means "sincere." Misty shows *unfeigned* enthusiasm for Saturday's bike ride in the Rockies.

To *feign* is to pretend. After hiding his sister's harmonica, Ben *feigns* innocence.

We have learned that pronouns used as subjects and predicate nominatives are in the **nominative case**, and that pronouns that show possession are in the **possessive case**. In this lesson, we will focus on the **objective case**.

Pronouns are in the **objective case** when they are used as direct objects, indirect objects, or objects of a preposition.

Mosquitoes are biting *me*. (direct object)
Hand *me* the repellent. (indirect object)
Sue can sit with *me*. (object of a preposition)

Please take *them*. (direct object)
Did you give *them* directions? (indirect object)
I'll sit by *them*. (object of a preposition)

I think Ms. Hoo likes *us*. (direct object)
Please cook *us* dinner. (indirect object)
These maps belong to *us*. (object of a preposition)

Example 1 Complete this chart by replacing each blank with the correct objective case pronoun.

NUMBER	PERSON		OBJECTIVE CASE (direct object, indirect object, or object of a preposition)
Singular	First		_____
	Second		_____
	Third	(masc.)	_____
		(fem.)	_____
		(neuter)	_____
Plural	First		_____
	Second		_____
	Third		_____

Solution We complete the chart as follows:

NUMBER	PERSON		OBJECTIVE CASE (direct object, indirect object, or object of a preposition)
Singular	First		me
	Second		you
	Third	(masc.)	him
		(fem.)	her
		(neuter)	it
Plural	First		us
	Second		you
	Third		them

Direct Objects The following sentences use personal pronouns as direct objects. We remember to use objective case pronouns.

My dog likes *her.* (not *she*)

Ms. Hoo taught Ian and *me.* (not *I*)

Alex warned *them.* (not *they*)

Example 2 Write a sentence using a personal pronoun as a direct object.

Solution Your answer will be unique. Here are some correct examples:

Samuel remembers *him.*

Jill will call Alberto and *her.*

The cat might eat *it.*

Indirect Objects These sentences use personal pronouns as indirect objects. Note that the pronouns are in the objective case.

Mrs. Tran gave *her* a pen. (not *she*)

Karina loaned Nien and *me* a dollar. (not *I*)

Kelvin baked *us* biscuits. (not *we*)

Example 3 Write a sentence using an objective case personal pronoun as an indirect object.

Solution   Your answer will be unique. Here are some correct examples:

Nora will tell *him* the truth.

Anthony gave *them* a hint.

Jay read Julie and *her* the article.

Objects of a Preposition   The sentences below use personal pronouns as objects of a preposition. The pronouns are in the objective case.

The librarian read a story (to *them*) (not *they*)

Dr. Kim waited (for *me*) (not *I*)

The ducks flew (over *us*) (not *we*)

Example 4   Write a sentence using a personal pronoun as an object of a preposition.

Solution   Your answer will be unique. Here are some correct examples:

A duck lands near *them*.

Retha collects ideas from *us*.

My aunt stood behind *me*.

Compound Objects   Objective case pronouns can be compound. We politely mention ourselves last.

Mom hugged *her* and *me*. (compound direct object)

Joe gave *him* and *me* a gift. (compound indirect object)

Bees buzzed around *them* and *us*.
(compound object of a preposition)

Example 5   Choose the sentence that is both correct and polite.

Gwyn sliced an apple for me and him.

Gwyn sliced an apple for he and I.

Gwyn sliced an apple for him and me.

Gwyn sliced an apple for him and I.

Solution   The objective case pronouns are *him* and *me*. Also, we politely mention ourselves last.

Gwyn sliced an apple for him and me.

Practice   **a.** Study the objective case pronoun chart from Example 1. Then try to reproduce it from memory.

b. Unscramble these words to make a sentence with a personal pronoun as a direct object:

noise   the   frightened   her

c. Unscramble these words to make a sentence with a personal pronoun as an indirect object:

sang   Jesse   song   a   me

d. Unscramble these words to make a sentence with a personal pronoun as an object of a preposition:

sung   has   he   us   to

For e and f, replace each blank with the correct vocabulary word from this lesson.

e. Randy is sincere, showing _____ loyalty to his friends.

f. The children _____ illness, for they do not want to eat their broccoli.

g. Write the sentence that is more polite.

Don't forget me or him.
Don't forget him or me.

h. Write each objective case pronoun from this list:

| me | him | I | she | them |
| they | he | her | we | us |

Choose the objective case pronoun for sentences i–k.

i. The goose chased Duke and (he, him).

j. I'll give Isabel and (him, he) the recipe.

k. The python wrapped itself around Irvin and (me, I).

Review Set 69   Choose the correct word to complete sentences 1–10.

1. (*Relevant, Irrelevant, Placed*) means "not pertinent; unconnected."
(67)

2. (Geology, Ornithology, Meteorology) is the study of
(68) atmospheric conditions, especially relating to weather.

3. *Contrite* means "(tenacious, sorry, frugal)."
(66)

4. (Elation, Cowardice, Intuition) is high spirits.
(65)

5. A (caldera, magma, meteorite) is a meteor that has fallen
(29) to Earth.

6. The word *elephants* is a (plural, possessive) noun.
(13)

7. The pronoun *them* is (nominative, objective, possessive)
(66, 69) case.

8. The (thief, theif) boarded a (frieght, freight) train.
(35)

9. We have had (less, fewer) storms this year.
(56)

10. The pronoun *it* is (first, second, third) person (singular,
(64) plural).

11. Rewrite the following letter, adding commas and capital
(63, 67) letters as needed:

dear peter

    as i remember your maternal ancestors are listed
under hillborne winona.

                warmly
                uncle jakob

12. Write the antecedent of the circled pronoun in the
(62) following sentence:

Olivia, if the telephone rings, please answer (it.)

13. Write the indirect object in the following sentence:
(46)

The sunburn caused Dara extreme pain.

14. Rewrite the following title, using correct capitalization:
(25)

"the velveteen rabbit"

15. Write the predicate nominative in the following sentence:
(51)

The Grizzly Giant is a very tall tree.

16. Which of the sentences below is correct? Write *A* or *B*.
(61)

    A. I am writing that kind of story.

    B. I am writing that kind of a story.

17. Rewrite the sentence below, using a comma to clarify the
(68) meaning.

    To Elle Gabriel seems indispensable.

18. Rewrite the word *knee*, circling the silent letter.
(28, 29)

19. Use an appositive to combine the following two
(58) sentences into one sentence.

    Puerto Rico has beautiful rain forests.

    Puerto Rico is a U.S. territory.

20. Rewrite the following sentence, adding periods as needed:
(47, 50)

    Mr Lee N Chen sent us to 142 E Ash Ave

21. Write whether the circled pronoun in the sentence below
(64) is used as a subject or an object.

    Does (she) despise Bozo?

22. Write whether the following word group is a phrase or a
(36) clause:

    with unfeigned sympathy for Rufus

23. Rewrite the following sentence, adding commas as
(57, 59) needed:

    On June 26 2008 I shall be eighty-six my dear.

24. For the irregular verb *know*, write the (a) present
(10, 65) participle, (b) past tense, and (c) past participle.

25. Write the objective case pronoun to complete the
(69) following sentence:

    Fifi struts past Bozo and (I, me).

26. Rewrite the following sentence, adding capital letters as needed:

jasmin said, "we shall miss ms. hoo."

27. For a–c, write the plural of each noun.

(a) butterfly   (b) dollar bill   (c) peach

28. Diagram the simple subject and simple predicate of each clause in the following sentence:

Fifi lifts her nose and trots away, for she has no time for Bozo.

Diagram each word of sentences 29–30.

29. Will Fifi grow warmer and friendlier?

30. My thoughtful friend Phil brought Olivia and me bottles of cold water.

Personal Pronoun Case Forms

Dictation or Journal Entry

Vocabulary:

Linguistics is the study of human speech. *Linguistics* experts have created written languages for primitive tribes in faraway places.

A *linguist* is an authority in linguistics, or one who speaks several languages. The *linguist* explained the similarities and differences in the two languages.

Case Forms The following chart helps us to sort out the three personal pronoun **case forms:** (1) If a pronoun is a subject or predicate nominative, it is *nominative case*. (2) A pronoun used as a direct object, indirect object, or object of a preposition is *objective case*. (3) If a pronoun shows possession, it is *possessive case*.

NUMBER	PERSON		CASE		
			NOMINATIVE	OBJECTIVE	POSSESSIVE
Singular	First		I	me	mine
	Second		you	you	yours
	Third	(masc.)	he	him	his
		(fem.)	she	her	hers
		(neuter)	it	it	its
Plural	First		we	us	ours
	Second		you	you	yours
	Third		they	them	theirs

Example 1 Tell whether each italicized pronoun is nominative, objective, or possessive case.

(a) Mia, Rene, and *she* giggled.

(b) Arturo believes *her.*

(c) *Yours* is on the table.

Solution (a) **nominative case**

(b) **objective case**

(c) **possessive case**

The pronoun case form depends on how the pronoun is used in the sentence. We refer to the chart to decide which pronoun is correct for this sentence:

(We, Us) drummers will set the tempo.

The pronoun *we* identifies "drummers," which is the subject of the sentence. We use the nominative case pronoun *we* (NOT *us*) as a subject. Therefore, we write:

We drummers will set the tempo.

Example 2 Tell how the pronoun is used in each sentence (subject, direct object, indirect object, object of a preposition, or possession).

(a) Ms. Hoo thanked *him* for the gift.

(b) That car is *hers.*

(c) *We* promised to help.

(d) Shawn gave *her* a broom.

(e) Mia and Minh laughed with *them.*

Solution (a) *Him* is a **direct object.**

(b) *Hers* shows **possession.**

(c) *We* is the **subject.**

(d) *Her* is an **indirect object.**

(e) *Them* is an **object of a preposition.**

Example 3 Determine how the pronoun is used in each sentence. Then refer to the chart on page 363 to help you choose the correct pronoun. Rewrite each sentence correctly.

(a) The class elected Yiwen and (*he, him*).

(b) Both Henry and (*she, her*) have arrived.

(c) The invitation was sent to Donald and (*she, her*).

Solution (a) The pronoun is a **direct object,** so we choose the objective case pronoun *him.*

The class elected Yiwen and *him*.

(b) The pronoun is the **subject** of the sentence, so we choose the nominative case pronoun *she.*

Both Henry and *she* have arrived.

(c) The pronoun is an **object of the preposition** *to,* so we choose the objective case pronoun *her.*

The invitation was sent to Donald and *her*.

Practice For a–c, tell whether the pronoun is nominative, objective, or possessive case.

   a. Ann noticed *her.*

   b. *He* imitated an ape.

   c. The cell phone Sarah used was *his.*

For d–h, tell how the pronoun is used in each sentence (subject, direct object, indirect object, object of a preposition, or possession).

   d. The ball rolled beyond *me.*

   e. *I* listened carefully.

   f. A hornet stung *him.*

   g. Nancy tossed *her* the softball.

   h. That idea was *hers.*

For i and j, choose the correct pronoun.

   i. The Ortegas and (*they, them*) live in my city.

   j. Maurice stared at Beverly and (*I, me*).

For k and l, replace each blank with the correct vocabulary word from this lesson.

   k. Roberta wants to study _____ in college.

1. She wants to become a _____, or authority on human speech.

Choose the correct word(s) to complete sentences 1–10.

1. (Geology, Ornithology, Meteorology) is the study of
(68) birds.

2. (*Irrelevant, Unethical, Unfeigned*) means "sincere."
(69)

3. *Pertinent* means "applicable or (frugal, contrite, relevant)."
(67)

4. (Malice, Extravagance, Contrition) is regret for an
(66) offense.

5. A (caldera, magma, meteor) is a body from space that has
(29) entered Earth's atmosphere, where it burns brightly as it falls.

6. The word *linguist* is a(n) (abstract, concrete) noun.
(11)

7. The pronoun *we* is (nominative, objective, possessive)
(66, 69) case.

8. The stallion (troted, trotted) (steadyly, steadily) along the
(33, 34) parade route.

9. Fifi is the (prettiest, most prettiest) poodle in the show.
(56)

10. The pronoun *I* is (first, second, third) person (singular,
(64) plural).

11. Rewrite the following letter, adding commas and capital
(57, 63) letters as needed:

dear uncle jakob

    i found my maternal ancestors my paternal ancestors and my lost library card.

                with gratitude

                peter

12. Write the antecedent of the circled pronoun in the
(62) following sentence:

Juan chased the bus until (he) was out of breath.

13. Write each coordinating conjunction that you find in the
(48) following sentence:

Jeff or Jenna will sweep tomorrow, but Foster will do it the next day.

14. Rewrite the following sentence, using correct
(38) capitalization:

yes, dad, you have an appointment with dr. payne on monday.

15. From the following sentence, write each prepositional
(44) phrase, circling the object of each preposition.

The children scampered up the trail, over the bridge, and through the woods.

16. Write whether the following is a complete sentence, a
(23) run-on sentence, or a sentence fragment:

Providing transportation for logging crews.

17. Rewrite the sentence below, using a comma to clarify the
(68) meaning.

Soon after Ben fell asleep.

18. Use a dictionary: (a) The word *cyclone* is what part of
(27, 30) speech? (b) Write its pronunciation. (c) Write its etymology.

19. Rewrite the sentence below, using commas to offset the
(60) nonessential appositive.

Colorado the Centennial State is known for its many high mountain peaks.

20. Rewrite the following sentence, adding periods as needed:
(47, 50)

Col Robert Andrews has moved to St Louis, Missouri

21. Write the nominative case pronoun to complete the
(66) sentence below.

The linguist speaking Russian is (her, she).

22. Write whether the following word group is a phrase or a
(36) clause:

when Fifi snubs Bozo

23. Rewrite the following sentence, adding commas as
(57, 59) needed:

Professor Luna Ph.D. teaches English French and
poetry.

24. For the irregular verb *tear*, write the (a) present
(10, 65) participle, (b) past tense, and (c) past participle.

25. Which sentence is more polite? Write *A* or *B*.
(69) A. Fifi struts past me and him.

B. Fifi struts past him and me.

26. Rewrite the following outline, adding periods and capital
(26, 47) letters as needed:

i the old railroad
    a steam trains
    b jenny railcars

27. For a–c, write the plural of each noun.
(17, 22)
(a) solo   (b) sister-in-law   (c) child

28. Diagram the simple subject and simple predicate of each
(36) clause in the following sentence:

Bozo snorts and scratches, for he has fleas.

Diagram each word of sentences 29–30.

29. Will Fifi and Bozo become friends?
(45, 51)

30. Butch, an irritable chow, gives Fifi and Bozo a piece of
(46, 58) his mind.

Diagramming Pronouns

Dictation or Journal Entry
Vocabulary:
Ardor is passion and enthusiasm. Nellie spoke with *ardor* about who should be the next governor of her state.

Ardent means "passionate and zealous." My aunt is an *ardent* believer in UFOs.

As you may have already noticed, we diagram pronouns in the same way we diagram nouns.

boy	caught	fish

The boy caught a fish.

He	caught	it

He caught it.

Diagramming a sentence helps us determine which pronoun to use because it clearly shows *how* the pronoun is used in the sentence. We diagram the sentence below to help us choose the correct pronoun.

Sam talks to my brother and (*I, me*).

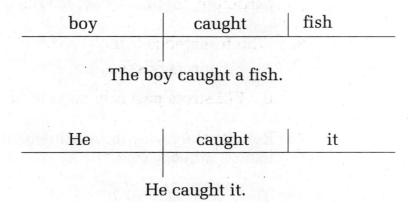

We see from the diagram that the pronoun is an object of the preposition *to*, so we choose the objective case pronoun *me*.

Sam talks to my brother and *me*.

Note: For some reason, we are more likely to use the wrong pronoun when it is part of a compound subject or object, as in the sentence above. If we remove the other half of the subject or object, the correct pronoun is usually obvious:

Sam talks to ~~my brother and~~ (*I, me*).

Our ears tell us that "talks to me" is correct. "Talks to I" does not sound right; it is incorrect.

Example   Diagram the following sentence in order to choose the correct pronoun. Then rewrite the sentence correctly.

Kevin and (*he, him*) might play soccer.

Solution   We diagram the sentence this way:

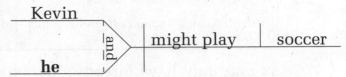

We see from our diagram that the pronoun is part of the subject of the sentence, so we choose the nominative case pronoun *he*.

Kevin and *he* might play soccer.

✓**Practice**   For a and b, replace each blank with the correct vocabulary word from this lesson.

a. The _____ politician speaks in a loud voice with many hand gestures.

b. The politician's _____ comes from strong, heartfelt feelings about the subject.

Diagram sentences c–e, choosing the correct pronoun.

c. Omar and (*him, he*) play chess.

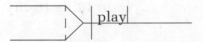

d. Nora wrote Pam and (*me, I*) a letter.

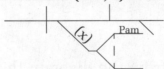

e. The captain called Ann and (*she, her*).

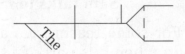

Review Set   Choose the correct word(s) to complete sentences 1–10.
71

1. (Linguistics, Ornithology, Meteorology) is the study of
(70) human speech.

(69) **2.** To (exalt, feign, humiliate) is to pretend.

3. A meteorologist studies (birds, rocks, weather).
(68)

4. Pertinent information is (relevant, irrelevant,
(67) unconnected).

5. (*Vertebrate, Valiant, Implacable*) means "having a
(30) backbone or spinal column."

6. The word *herd* is a (compound, collective) noun.
(11)

7. The pronoun *us* is (nominative, objective, possessive)
(66, 69) case.

8. Did they (acheive, achieve) (thier, their) goal?
(35)

9. We don't have (much, many) lemons on our tree.
(56)

10. The pronoun *we* is (first, second, third) person (singular,
(64) plural).

11. Rewrite the following letter, adding commas and capital
(57, 63) letters as needed:

dear quan

the deadline is monday may 10 2010.

sincerely

juan

12. Write the antecedent of the circled pronoun in the
(62) following sentence:

Juan chased the bus until it turned onto First Avenue.

13. Write the direct object in the following sentence:
(37)

Buffalo Soldiers protected the national parks.

14. Rewrite the following title, using correct capitalization:
(25)

"look for the silver lining"

15. Write the predicate nominative in the following sentence:
(51)

That large tree with yellow-green leaves and a dark trunk
is an oak.

16. Replace the overused adjective below with one that is
(61) more descriptive. There are many possible answers.

He is my _____ ⓖⓞⓞⓓ _____ friend.

17. Rewrite the sentence below, using a comma to clarify the
(68) meaning.

As you know everything needs cleaning.

18. Rewrite the word *walk*, circling the silent letter.
(29)

19. Use an appositive to combine the following two
(58) sentences into one sentence.

Kansas is the Sunflower State.

Kansas has prairies, farms, and rolling hills.

20. Rewrite the following sentence, adding periods as needed:
(47, 50)

Mr Thomas Cross, Jr, works for Barrons, Inc, in St Louis

21. Write whether the circled pronoun in the sentence below
(64) is used as a subject or an object.

Will (they) share their secret?

22. Write whether the following word group is a phrase or a
(36) clause:

without a thought about the future

23. Rewrite the following sentence, adding commas as
(57, 59) needed:

Egbert my new address is 123 Fourth Avenue
Montgomery Alabama.

24. For the irregular verb *ring*, write the (a) present
(10, 65) participle, (b) past tense, and (c) past participle.

25. Write the objective case pronoun to complete the
(69) sentence below.

Butch gave Bozo and (she, her) a fright.

26. Rewrite the following sentence, adding capital letters as needed:
(26)

olivia said, "thank you, phil."

27. For a–c, write the plural of each noun.
(17, 22)

    (a) wrench   (b) lawn mower   (c) daisy

28. Diagram the simple subject and simple predicate of each
(36) clause in the following sentence:

Butch barks and growls as Fifi and Bozo prance by.

Diagram each word of sentences 29–30.

29. Will Bozo and Butch remain enemies?
(45, 51)

30. Butch, an unfriendly dog, shows everyone the impolite
(46, 58) side of his personality.

Possessive Pronouns and Possessive Adjectives

Dictation or Journal Entry

Vocabulary:

Serene means "untroubled and peaceful." The wind ceased, leaving a *serene* landscape with still waters on the lake and quietness among the trees.

Serenity is tranquility and peace. Carlos finds *serenity* in trusting his creator.

Possessive Pronouns

We have learned that a pronoun takes the place of a noun. The possessive pronouns *mine*, *yours*, *his*, *hers*, *ours*, and *theirs* replace nouns to tell "whose."

> That's *mine*, not *yours*.

> *His* is green, and *hers* is yellow.

> *Theirs* are ready, so why aren't *ours?*

Notice that in each of the sentences above, the possessive pronoun **replaces a noun** and stands alone.

Possessive Adjectives

There is another group of words that is very similar to possessive pronouns except that they **come before a noun** rather than replace it. These words are the possessive adjectives *my, your, his, her, its, our,* and *their.*

> Please don't put *your* feet on *my* desk.

> *Her* dog is wagging *its* tail.

> Shall we move *our* tent closer to *their* cabin?

In each of the sentences above, the possessive adjective comes before a noun to tell "whose."

Many people consider these words pronouns. Others see them as adjectives because they always come before nouns to modify them. What is important is using them correctly.

POSSESSIVE ADJECTIVE (IN FRONT OF A NOUN)	POSSESSIVE PRONOUN (STANDING ALONE)
my	mine
your	yours
his	his
her	hers
its	its *(very seldom used)*
our	ours
their	theirs

Errors to Avoid Possessive pronouns do not have apostrophes. The words *yours, hers, its,* and *ours* are already possessive.

> INCORRECT: I saw Dad's car but not **your's**.
> CORRECT: I saw Dad's car but not **yours**.

> INCORRECT: The decision is **her's** to make.
> CORRECT: The decision is **hers** to make.

Also, we must not confuse contractions and possessive adjectives.

POSSESSIVE ADJECTIVE	CONTRACTION
your	you're (you are)
their	they're (they are)
its	it's (it is)

Example Choose the correct word to complete each sentence.

(a) Is (*your, you're*) dog friendly?

(b) (*Its, It's*) teeth are showing.

(c) Is the beagle (*your's, yours*) also?

(d) This dog is bigger than (*theirs, their's*).

Solution (a) Is **your** dog friendly?

(b) **Its** teeth are showing.

(c) Is the beagle **yours** also?

(d) This dog is bigger than **theirs**.

✓**Practice** Choose the correct word to complete sentences a–e.

a. The table is wobbly; (*its, it's*) legs are broken.

b. Oscar and Carmen took (*their, they're*) cat to the vet.

c. Oscar has his key, but Carmen forgot (*her's, hers*).

d. Give me (*your, you're*) opinion.

e. The brown tent is (*ours, our's*).

For f and g, replace each blank with the correct vocabulary word from this lesson.

f. High in the mountains, we enjoyed a _____ and relaxing vacation.

g. We felt _____ deep in the quiet forest.

More Practice Choose the correct word(s) to complete each sentence.

1. How do pigeons find (there, they're, their) way home?

2. (They're, There, Their) able to do it somehow.

3. That pigeon has injured (its, it's) wing.

4. Is a pigeon's eyesight better than (ours, our's)?

5. Are all these pigeons (her's, hers)?

6. Is that white dove (your's, yours)?

7. A homing pigeon could deliver (your, you're) message.

8. (It's, Its) on (its, it's) way home.

✓**Review Set 72** Choose the correct word to complete sentences 1–10.

1. A (meteorologist, ornithologist, linguist) is a language (70) expert.

2. (Intuition, Contrition, Ardor) is passion and enthusiasm. (71)

3. *Unfeigned* means "(phony, fake, sincere)." (69)

4. Ornithology is the study of (fish, reptiles, birds). (68)

5. Fish, birds, and mammals are (vertebrate, invertebrate) (30) animals.

6. The sentence below is (declarative, interrogative, (2) imperative, exclamatory).

   Can any mammals fly?

7. The pronoun *our* is (nominative, objective, possessive) (66, 69) case.

8. (Your, You're) socks are inside out.
(72)

9. That was the (better, best) of the two performances.
(56)

10. The pronoun (I, you, he, she, it, they) is second person.
(64)

11. Rewrite the following letter, adding commas and capital
(57, 63) letters as needed:

dear juan

    i cannot do my schoolwork clean my room and meet your deadline.

                     regretfully

                     quan

12. Write the antecedent of the circled pronoun in the
(62) following sentence:

Juan wishes buses would wait for (him.)

13. Write the indirect object in the following sentence:
(46)

Garen tossed the jay a peanut.

14. Rewrite the following sentence, using correct
(38) capitalization:

her classes include mathematics, latin, biology, and english.

15. Add suffixes:
(33, 34) (a) clap + ed   (b) glory + ous

16. Write whether the following is a complete sentence, a
(23) run-on sentence, or a sentence fragment:

Golden eagles soar they hold their wings in a shallow *V*-shape.

17. Rewrite the sentence below, using a comma to clarify the
(68) meaning.

Because of Clark Kent was late.

18. Use a dictionary: (a) The word *delve* is what part of
(27, 30) speech? (b) Write its pronunciation. (c) Write its etymology.

19. Rewrite the sentence below, using commas to offset the nonessential appositive.
(60)

Hawaii the Aloha State was formed by volcanic eruptions.

20. Rewrite the following sentence, adding periods as needed:
(47, 50)

Ms Hoo's note reads, "Homework due Fri, Feb 3"

21. Write the nominative case pronoun to complete the sentence below.
(66)

It was (me, I) who spilled the paint.

22. Write whether the following word group is a phrase or a clause:
(36)

if you agree

23. Rewrite the following sentence, adding commas as needed:
(57, 59)

No Egbert I did not move to Little Rock Arkansas.

24. For the irregular verb *freeze*, write the (a) present participle, (b) past tense, and (c) past participle.
(10, 65)

25. Which sentence is more polite? Write *A* or *B*.
(69)
A. Butch growled at him and me.
B. Butch growled at me and him.

26. Rewrite the following lines of poetry, adding capital letters as needed:
(15)

twinkle, twinkle, little star,
how I wonder what you are...

27. For a–c, write the plural of each noun.
(17, 22)
(a) patch   (b) dictionary   (c) basketful

28. Diagram the simple subject and simple predicate of each clause in the following sentence:
(36)

Olivia smiles and waves as Jenny and Phil jog by.

Diagram each word of sentences 29–30.

29. Will Bozo's love for Fifi remain steadfast?
(45, 54)

30. Will Fifi, the lovely poodle, give Bozo the benefit of the
(46, 58) doubt?

LESSON 73

Dependent and Independent Clauses • Subordinating Conjunctions

> **Dictation or Journal Entry**
> **Vocabulary:**
> *Sagacious* means "wise." *Sagacious* drivers obey traffic laws.
>
> *Sagacity* is wisdom. Rosita demonstrates *sagacity* by choosing her friends carefully.

Independent Clauses
There are two types of clauses. One type is the **independent clause**, also called the main clause. An independent clause expresses a complete thought.

> Max studies ornithology.

> I shall check the meteorology report.

Dependent Clauses
The other type of clause is the **dependent clause**. It cannot stand by itself and is sometimes called the subordinate clause. It depends upon additional information to complete a thought.

> If they feign illness

> When he found gold

Even though the dependent clauses above each contain a subject and a predicate, they do not complete a thought. However, if we remove the introductory words "if" and "when," they become independent clauses and can stand alone:

> They feign illness.

> He found gold.

Example 1
For a–d, tell whether the clauses are dependent or independent.

(a) as soon as she comes

(b) the pigeon flew home

(c) although it rained

(d) they find serenity

Solution
(a) This is a **dependent** clause. It depends on another clause in order to complete a thought.

(b) This is an **independent** clause. It can stand alone and does not require another clause in order to complete a thought.

(c) This is a **dependent** clause.

(d) This is an **independent** clause and can stand by itself.

Subordinating Conjunctions

A **subordinating conjunction** introduces a dependent clause. We can turn an independent clause into a dependent clause by adding a subordinating conjunction. In the dependent clauses below, *though* and *because* are subordinating conjunctions.

INDEPENDENT CLAUSE	DEPENDENT CLAUSE
I like Texas.	*Though* I like Texas,...
He looks silly.	*Because* he looks silly,...

Below are some common subordinating conjunctions. There are many more.

after	*because*	*so that*	*when*
although	*before*	*than*	*whenever*
as	*even though*	*that*	*where*
as if	*if*	*though*	*wherever*
as soon as	*in order that*	*unless*	*while*
as though	*since*	*until*	

Many of these words also function as prepositions. Sometimes phrases begin with prepositions such as *after*, *before*, *since* or *until*. In this case, these words are not subordinating conjunctions but prepositions. Remember that a clause has both a subject and a verb. Notice how the word *after* is used in the two sentences below.

SUBORDINATING CONJUNCTION:
Miners hurried to California *after* gold was found at Sutter's Mill. (introducing the **clause** "after gold was found at Sutter's Mill.")

PREPOSITION:
Miners hurried to California *after* gold. (part of the **phrase** "after gold.")

Example 2 Identify the subordinating conjunctions in the following sentences.

(a) Brad felt contrite because he had not told the truth.

(b) If I go, I'll need a ride.

Solution (a) **Because** is the subordinating conjunction. It introduces the dependent clause "because he had not told the truth."

(b) **If** is the subordinating conjunction. It introduces the dependent clause "If I go."

✓**Practice** For a–d, write whether the clause is dependent or independent.

    a. since I lacked courage

    b. the lake froze

    c. he wasted no time

    d. whenever he was in a hurry

For e–g, write each subordinating conjunction.

    e. Unless I have finished my homework, I will not play.

    f. I completed the job even though it was difficult.

    g. When Max won the game, he was elated.

For h and i, replace each blank with the correct vocabulary word from this lesson.

    h. Amir has _____; he is full of wisdom.

    i. _____ students do their homework.

More Practice See "More Practice Lesson 73" in Student Workbook.

✓**Review Set 73** Choose the correct word to complete sentences 1–10.

    1. (*Serene, Ardent, Pertinent*) means "untroubled and
    (72) peaceful."

    2. *Ardent* means "(lazy, passionate, greedy)."
    (71)

    3. Maria learns about human speech in her (ornithology,
    (70) geology, linguistics) class.

4. To feign is to (exalt, encumber, pretend).
(69)

5. An asset is something (useless, destructive, valuable).
(31)

6. The word *monkey's* is a (plural, possessive) noun.
(13)

7. The pronoun *he* is (nominative, objective, possessive)
(66, 69) case.

8. Is this sock (your's, yours)?
(72)

9. That was the (better, best) of the five performances.
(56)

10. The pronoun *she* is (first, second, third) person (singular,
(64) plural).

11. Rewrite the following letter, adding commas and capital
(57, 63) letters as needed:

dear cousin wassim

please come to my piano recital on monday april 2
2008 at grandmother's house.

> your cousin
> aleda

12. Write the antecedent of the circled pronoun in the
(62) following sentence:

I think Ms. Hoo left (her) socks by the lake.

13. From the following sentence, write each prepositional
(44) phrase, circling the object of each preposition.

We looked around the campground for bear-proof lockers
for our food.

14. Write the subordinating conjunction in this sentence:
(73) I shall play volleyball while you and Ms. Hoo swim.

15. Add suffixes:
(33, 34) (a) trap + ed   (b) cloudy + ness

16. Which sentence is correct? Write *A* or *B*.
(61) A. Willa is not that type of person.

B. Willa is not that type of a person.

17. Rewrite the sentence below, using a comma to clarify the meaning.
(68)

The day after I mopped the floor.

18. Rewrite the word *fight*, circling the silent letters.
(28, 29)

19. Use an appositive to combine the following two sentences into one sentence.
(58)

Moe is the smallest boy on the team.

Moe won the cross-country race last Saturday.

20. Rewrite the following sentence, adding periods as needed.
(47, 50)

Capt Rice lives on E Sunshine Blvd in St Petersburg

21. Write whether the circled pronoun in the sentence below is used as a subject or an object.
(64)

Onping spilled paint on Shelly and (me).

22. Write whether the clause below is dependent or independent.
(73)

if you agree

23. Rewrite the following sentence, adding commas as needed.
(57, 59)

Luey you may speak with Professor Grin Ph.D. tomorrow.

24. For the irregular verb *throw*, write the (a) present participle, (b) past tense, and (c) past participle.
(10, 65)

25. Write the objective case pronoun to complete the sentence below.
(69)

Carl gave Ann and (me, I) his opinion.

26. Rewrite the following sentence, adding capital letters as needed.
(26)

carl said, "you should paint the room mustard yellow."

27. For a–c, write the plural of each noun.
(17, 22)

(a) life   (b) Friday   (c) party

28. Diagram the simple subject and simple predicate of each
(36) clause in the following sentence:

Carl likes yellow, and Ann likes red, but I prefer blue.

Diagram each word of sentences 29–30.

29. Do Carl's comments about the paint seem sagacious?
(45, 54)

30. My sagacious cousin Carl gave Ann and me his opinion
(46, 58) on the color of paint for the room.

The Comma, Part 7: Descriptive Adjectives and Dependent Clauses

---

Dictation or Journal Entry

Vocabulary:

Redundant means "using more words than are necessary; wordy or repetitious." To call someone both wise and sagacious would be *redundant*, for wise and sagacious have the same meaning.

Redundancy is needless repetition. The phrase "large giant" is a *redundancy*, for people know that giants are large.

We remember that commas are used to indicate the natural pauses of speech. Let's look at more places where we use commas.

Descriptive Adjectives

We use a comma to separate two or more **descriptive adjectives.**

> They work at their *neat, orderly* desks.

> It was a *long, hot* summer.

There are some exceptions. For example, if one adjective is a color, we don't use a comma to separate it from another adjective.

> The *lively red* finch chirps a greeting.

One way to decide whether a comma is needed is to insert the word "and" between the adjectives.

> IF YOU COULD SAY: It was a *cold and foggy* night.
> YOU DO NEED A COMMA: It was a *cold, foggy* night.

> YOU WOULDN'T SAY: I saw an *old and green* tractor.
> SO YOU DON'T NEED A COMMA: I saw an *old green* tractor.

Example 1 Insert commas where they are needed in the sentences below.

(a) They climbed the steep rocky trail.

(b) She has bright sparkling brown eyes.

Solution (a) We place a comma between the two adjectives "steep" and "rocky."

> They climbed the **steep, rocky** trail.

(b) We separate the adjectives "bright" and "sparkling" with a comma, but we do not place a comma before the color adjective "brown."

She has **bright, sparkling brown** eyes.

Dependent Clauses We remember that a **dependent clause** cannot stand alone, while an independent clause, or main clause, makes sense without the dependent clause. We use a comma after a dependent clause when it comes before the main clause.

After they had dinner, they went for a walk.
(DEPENDENT CLAUSE)   (INDEPENDENT/MAIN CLAUSE)

However, we do **not** use a comma when the dependent clause follows the main clause.

They went for a walk after they had dinner.
(INDEPENDENT/MAIN CLAUSE)   (DEPENDENT CLAUSE)

Example 2 Insert commas as needed in the sentences below.

(a) Although she felt nervous she spoke bravely.

(b) I must keep working until the job is done.

Solution (a) We place a comma after the dependent clause "although she felt nervous" because it comes before the main clause.

Although she felt nervous, she spoke bravely.

(b) No comma is needed in this sentence because the dependent clause, "until the job is done," follows the main clause.

Practice Rewrite sentences a and b, inserting commas to separate descriptive adjectives.

a. We could hardly see through the deep, dense fog.

b. I took my biggest, warmest jacket to Minnesota, but all I really needed was my tan cotton sweater.

Rewrite sentences c–e, inserting a comma after each dependent clause.

c. When you go to the store, get a few peaches.

d. If they look bruised, buy some grapes instead.

e. As soon as you get home, we'll have lunch.

For f and g, replace each blank with the correct vocabulary word from this lesson.

    f. _____ happens when you use two or more words to say something that is clearly said by using only one of the words.

    g. "Baby kitten" is _____, for all kittens are babies.

More Practice
See "More Practice Lesson 74" in Student Workbook.

Review Set 74
Choose the correct word(s) to complete sentences 1–10.

1. (*Ardent, Supersonic, Sagacious*) means "wise."
(73)

2. Serenity is (greed, passion, peace).
(72)

3. One who has *ardor* has (indolence, passion, fleas).
(71)

4. A linguist is a (bird, weather, language) expert.
(70)

5. A good sense of humor is a(n) (asset, invertebrate, liability) for those who wish to form friendships.
(31)

6. The word *sagacity* is a(n) (abstract, concrete) noun.
(11)

7. The pronoun *him* is (nominative, objective, possessive) case.
(66, 69)

8. Is this sock (her's, hers)?
(72)

9. Lulu has (less, fewer) sheep than goats.
(56)

10. The pronoun *it* is (first, second, third) person (singular, plural).
(64)

11. Rewrite the following letter, adding commas and capital letters as needed:
(57, 63)

    dear cousin aleda

        on monday april 2 i shall be in montpelier vermont.

            regretfully

            wassim

12. Write the antecedent of the circled pronoun in the
(62) following sentence:

Ms. Hoo lost her sock, but I found (it.)

13. Write each coordinating conjunction in the following
(48) sentence:

Rudy and Lucy started a cheese business in Wisconsin,
but they left it to build a railroad.

14. Write the subordinating conjunction in this sentence:
(73)
After you see Glacier Point, go to Globe Rock.

15. Add suffixes:
(33, 34) (a) tap + ing   (b) penny + less

16. Write whether the following is a complete sentence, a
(23) sentence fragment, or a run-on sentence.

Globe Rock balances perfectly atop its pedestal.

17. Rewrite the sentence below, using a comma to clarify the
(68) meaning.

To Omar Nicasio appears malicious.

18. Use a dictionary: (a) The word *plummet* is what part of
(27, 30) speech? (b) Write its pronunciation. (c) Write its
etymology.

19. Rewrite the sentence below, using commas to offset the
(60) nonessential appositive.

Wyoming the Equality State has rugged mountains and
windy flatlands.

20. Rewrite the following sentence, adding periods as needed:
(47, 50)
He works at the Wumpit Toy Co, 12 N Main St,
Alhambra, CA

21. Write the nominative case pronoun to complete the
(66) sentence below.

The drummers were Luey and (her, she).

22. Write whether the clause below is dependent or independent.
(73)

they might shoot baskets

23. Rewrite the following sentence, adding commas as needed:
(74)

If you go to Alaska you might meet a huge friendly moose.

24. For the irregular verb *wear*, write the (a) present participle, (b) past tense, and (c) past participle.
(10, 65)

25. Write the objective case pronoun to complete the sentence below.
(69)

Ann paints with Carl and (she, her).

26. Rewrite the following outline, adding periods and capital letters as needed:
(26, 47)

i lakes
  a scenic views
  b water sports
  c houseboats

27. For a–c, write the plural of each noun.
(17, 22)

(a) opportunity   (b) police chief   (c) knife

28. Diagram the simple subject and simple predicate of each clause in the following sentence:
(36)

If you find the skunk before I return, I shall reward you.

Diagram each word of sentences 29–30.

29. Does the skunk in the basement appear angry?
(45, 54)

30. My neighbor Kim sent her mom and me a funny card with a picture of a giraffe in pajamas.
(46, 58)

Compound Sentences •
Coordinating Conjunctions

Dictation or Journal Entry
Vocabulary:
Satiable means "able to be satisfied." My kitten has a *satiable* need for human contact; it purrs and falls asleep after I stroke its fur a few times.

Insatiable means "unable to be satisfied." My puppy has an *insatiable* appetite; he's always hungry.

Compound Sentences

Two or more simple sentences (independent clauses) joined by a connecting word such as *and*, *or*, or *but* form a **compound sentence.** Only sentences closely related in thought should be joined to form a compound sentence. Below, we connect two simple sentences to form a compound sentence.

TWO SIMPLE SENTENCES:
My aunt is an office manager.
She works in Detroit.

ONE COMPOUND SENTENCE:
My aunt is an office manager, and she works in Detroit.

Here we diagram the simple subjects and simple predicates of the compound sentence above:

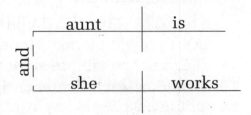

Notice that the compound sentence is made up of two independent clauses that can each stand alone and make sense. Remember that any number of independent clauses can be joined to form a compound sentence. For example, here we join four independent clauses (simple sentences) to form one compound sentence:

Jill plays the flute, and Celina beats the drums, but I just hum along, and Robert doesn't make a sound.

Coordinating Conjunctions

A **coordinating conjunction** can join two simple sentences to form a compound sentence. We have learned that the following are coordinating conjunctions:

> and but or nor for yet so

Notice how coordinating conjunctions are used in the compound sentences below.

AND INDICATES ADDITIONAL INFORMATION:
My aunt works in Detroit, *and* she likes her job.

BUT SHOWS CONTRAST:
My aunt works in Detroit, *but* she lives in Chicago.

OR SHOWS A CHOICE:
I can fly to Wisconsin, *or* I can take the bus.

Conjunctions may also connect the parts of a compound subject or predicate. Do not confuse a compound subject or a compound predicate with a compound sentence. Remember that a compound sentence has both a subject and a predicate on each side of the conjunction. A compound sentence follows this pattern:

subject <u>predicate</u>, (conjunction) *subject* <u>predicate</u>

Words <u>can hurt,</u>   (or)   *words* <u>can help</u>.
I <u>have been resting,</u>   (but)   *you* <u>have been working</u>.
Kurt <u>played</u> piano,   (and)   *Molly* <u>sang</u> a song.

Example 1

Tell whether each sentence is simple or compound. If it is compound, write the coordinating conjunction that joins the two independent clauses.

(a) *Rocio* <u>felt</u> weary, yet *he* <u>completed</u> the task.

(b) The *task* <u>was</u> difficult, but *Rocio* <u>was</u> tenacious.

(c) *Rocio* <u>scrubbed</u> and <u>mopped</u> floors all day long.

(d) The clean *floors* <u>glistened</u>, and *Rocio* <u>went</u> home.

Solution

(a) We find a subject and a predicate on each side of the conjunction: *Rocio* <u>felt</u> (conjunction), *he* <u>completed</u>. Therefore, the sentence is **compound**. The coordinating conjunction joining the two independent clauses is ***yet***.

(b) This sentence is **compound.** It consists of two independent clauses joined by the coordinating conjunction **but**.

(c) This is a **simple** sentence. It is a single, independent clause with one subject (*Rocio*) and a compound predicate (scrubbed and mopped).

(d) This is a **compound** sentence. Two independent clauses are joined by the coordinating conjunction **and**.

Diagramming To diagram the simple subjects and simple predicates of a compound sentence, we follow these steps:

1. Diagram each simple sentence, one below the other.

2. Join the two sentences with a dotted line on the left side.

3. Write the coordinating conjunction on the dotted line.

Below, we diagram the simple subjects and simple predicates of this compound sentence:

Fido is eating, so Spot is growling.

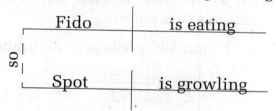

Example 2 Diagram the simple subjects and simple predicates of this compound sentence:

The mouse looked at Grandma, and she screamed.

Solution We diagram the simple subject and simple predicate of each simple sentence and place them one below the other. Then we join them with a dotted line on which we write the coordinating conjunction "and."

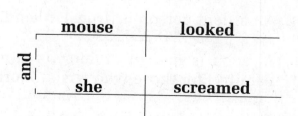

Practice For a–e, write whether each sentence is simple or compound. If it is compound, write the coordinating conjunctions that join the two or more independent clauses.

a. The *movement* of mice from the country to the city <u>made</u> Grandma nervous.

b. The *squirrel* <u>ventured</u> onto the road, but *Karen* <u>chased</u> it into the bushes.

c. *James* <u>caught</u> the sidewinder, and *Quan* <u>has measured</u> it, so *they* <u>will release</u> it now.

d. *Monica* <u>teases</u> her grandmother with all sorts of stories about mice and snakes and scary spiders.

e. *They* <u>went</u> inside, for *mosquitoes* <u>were biting</u>.

f. Diagram the simple subjects and simple predicates of this compound sentence:

You should use repellent, or bugs will bite you.

For g and h, replace each blank with the correct vocabulary word from this lesson.

g. Moto's desire to play computer games seems _____; he never wants to stop.

h. Clotilda has a _____ appetite; it is easily satisfied.

Review Set 75 Choose the correct word to complete sentences 1–10.

1. (*Pertinent, Serene, Redundant*) means "wordy."
(74)

2. (*Serenity, Sagacity, Avarice*) is wisdom.
(73)

3. *Serene* means "(troubled, angry, peaceful)."
(72)

4. An ardent person is (frugal, placid, passionate).
(71)

5. A good sense of humor is a(n) (asset, invertebrate, liability) for those who wish to form friendships.
(31)

6. The word *cluster* is a (compound, collective) noun.
(11)

7. The pronoun *his* is (nominative, objective, possessive) (66, 69) case.

8. Are these socks (theirs, their's)?
(72)

9. Of the two runners, Luey is (faster, fastest).
(56)

10. The pronoun *them* is (first, second, third) person (64) (singular, plural).

11. Rewrite the following letter, adding commas and capital (57, 63) letters as needed:

dear mrs. cruz

my new address is 12 sun avenue frankfort kentucky.

sincerely

mrs. otto

12. Write whether the sentence below is simple or (75) compound.

Ms. Hoo lost her sock, but I found it.

13. Write the predicate nominative in the following sentence:
(51)
Old Faithful is a grand geyser!

14. Write the subordinating conjunction in this sentence:
(73)
Frogs croak as Fred snores.

15. Write the word that is spelled correctly:
(35) (a) sliegh, sleigh   (b) view, veiw

16. Replace the overused adjective below with one that is (61) more descriptive. There are many possible answers.

He is a _____ ⟨nice⟩ _____ teacher.

17. Rewrite the sentence below, using a comma to clarify the (68) meaning.

With Dan Smith can accomplish much.

18. Rewrite the word *bough*, circling the silent letters.
(28, 29)

19. Use an appositive to combine the following two
(58) sentences into one sentence.

Tyrell is a tennis champion.

Tyrell is learning to play chess.

20. Rewrite the following sentence, adding periods as needed:
(47, 50)

Dr Norris's note reads, "Every 45 to 90 min, Old Faithful
erupts"

21. Write whether the circled pronoun in the sentence below
(64) is used as a subject or an object.

The dentist will see (her) tomorrow.
(36)

22. Write whether the word group below is a phrase or a
clause.

with an insatiable appetite
(74)

23. Rewrite the following sentence, adding commas as
needed:

When I swept the basement I found a sneaky stinky
skunk.
(10, 65)

24. For the irregular verb *shrink*, write the (a) present
participle, (b) past tense, and (c) past participle.
(69)

25. Which sentence is more polite? Write *A* or *B*.

A. Herb laughed with me and Ivy.

B. Herb laughed with Ivy and me.
(26)

26. Rewrite the following sentence, adding capital letters as
needed:

ivy said, "the goat is nibbling my ponytail!"
(17, 22)

27. For a–c, write the plural of each noun.

(a) liberty   (b) wish   (c) flower pot

28. Diagram the simple subject and simple predicate of each
(75) clause in the following compound sentence:

You found the skunk, so you deserve a reward.

Diagram each word of sentences 29–30.

29. Does the cavity in my tooth look deep?
(45, 54)

30. Dr. Drill, the dentist, showed Bob and Rob the X-rays of
(46, 58) their teeth.

LESSON 76

The Comma, Part 8: Compound Sentences and Direct Quotations

> **Dictation or Journal Entry**
>
> **Vocabulary:**
> *Quaint* means "attractive in an old-fashioned way, or pleasingly unusual."
> *Quaint*, narrow streets run through the old town.
>
> *Quaintness* is old-fashioned charm. We enjoyed the *quaintness* of our great grandmother's house with its antique furniture and appliances.

Compound Sentences
We remember that two sentences or independent clauses joined by a coordinating conjunction (*and, but, or, for,* etc.) is called a compound sentence. We place a comma between the first independent clause and the coordinating conjunction in a compound sentence.

> The beetle fought hard, but the bird was winning.
>
> Michael made soup, and we had it for lunch.

The following coordinating conjunctions signal the need for a comma in a compound sentence.

                    and   but   or   nor   for   yet   so

Example 1
Identify the coordinating conjunction in each compound sentence.

(a) He has not bathed, nor has he combed his hair.

(b) They can swim in the lake, or they can hike on the trail.

(c) Ivan is ill, so he cannot come with us.

Solution
(a) **nor**   (b) **or**   (c) **so**

Example 2
Insert a comma before the coordinating conjunction to separate the two independent clauses in the sentences below.

(a) They didn't camp in the desert, for it was too hot.

(b) Juan pitched the tent, and Andrew built a fire.

Solution
We place a comma between the first independent clause and the coordinating conjunction.

(a) **They didn't camp in the desert, for it was too hot.**

(b) **Juan pitched the tent, and Andrew built a fire.**

Direct Quotations We use a comma or commas to offset the exact words of a speaker, a **direct quotation**, from the rest of the sentence.

> Julia asked, "Do you know the answer?"
>
> "I think," said Mia, "that zero times six equals zero."
>
> "That is correct," said Ms. Hoo.

Notice that the comma stays next to the word it follows. If a comma follows a direct quote, the comma goes inside the quotation marks.

> YES: "Anyone can make soup," said Tom.
> NO: "Anyone can make soup", said Tom.

Example 3 Rewrite sentences a and b, inserting commas as needed to offset direct quotations from the rest of the sentence.

(a) Nora cried "Did you see that eagle? It was beautiful!"

(b) "There's a nest in that tree" explained Paul.

Solution (a) We place a comma just before Nora's words.

Nora cried, "Did you see that eagle? It was beautiful!"

(b) We place a comma after Paul's words. The comma goes inside the quotation marks.

"There's a nest in that tree," explained Paul.

Practice **a.** List the seven coordinating conjunctions.

For b–d, identify the coordinating conjunction in each sentence.

b. Ann ran fast, for she felt energetic.

c. I wrote many words, yet they were redundant.

d. Ann had already eaten, but she was still hungry.

Rewrite these compound sentences, inserting commas before the coordinating conjunctions.

e. The lake was dry and the land was parched.

f. Deer came for water but there wasn't any.

Rewrite sentences g and h, inserting commas to offset direct quotations.

g. Mary said "I've always wanted to fly."

h. "I like to see the big picture" she added.

For i and j, replace each blank with the correct vocabulary word from this lesson.

i. Jordan smiled at the _____ of the old farmhouse kitchen with its wood-burning stove and small icebox.

j. Jordan thinks the big wall phone with the crank is _____.

More Practice See "More Practice Lesson 76" in Student Workbook.

✓Review Set 76 Choose the correct word to complete sentences 1–10.

1. (*Redundant, Abundant, Satiable*) means "able to be
(75) satisfied."

2. Redundancy is needless (repetition, aggravation,
(74) irritation).

3. *Sagacious* means "(fearless, passionate, wise)."
(73)

4. *Serenity* and *tranquility* are (synonyms, antonyms).
(72)

5. A (vertebrate, meteor, panacea) is a remedy for all
(32) diseases or evils.

6. The sentence below is (declarative, interrogative,
(2) imperative, exclamatory).

The Arabian horse was magnificent!

7. The pronoun *she* is (nominative, objective, possessive)
(66, 69) case.

8. These seats are (our's, ours).
(72)

9. I have made (much, many) mistakes.
(56)

10. The pronoun *us* is (first, second, third) person (singular,
(64) plural).

11. Rewrite the following title, adding capital letters as needed:
(25)

"oh, the places you'll go"

12. Write the antecedent of the circled pronoun in the following sentence:
(62)

Mrs. Otto opened the door but forgot to close(it)

13. Write the direct object in the following sentence:
(37)

Denny will check the temperature of the water.

14. Write the subordinating conjunction in this sentence:
(73)

The frogs will stop croaking when Fred stops snoring.

15. Add suffixes:
(33, 34)

(a) funny + er   (b) grin + ing

16. Write whether the following is a complete sentence, a sentence fragment, or a run-on sentence.
(23)

Some hot springs form quiet pools others are flowing.

17. Rewrite the sentence below, using a comma to clarify the meaning.
(68)

Next doors opened everywhere.

18. From the following sentence, write each prepositional phrase, circling the object of each preposition.
(44)

Fumaroles in Earth's crust release steam through cracks and fissures.

19. Rewrite the following sentence, using commas to offset the nonessential appositive.
(60)

The mammoth a prehistoric elephant used to be plentiful in Nebraska.

20. Rewrite the following sentence, adding periods as needed:
(47, 50)

Mr and Mrs Celoni took a nine am flight to Memphis

21. Write the nominative case pronoun to complete the
(66) sentence below.

My helpers will be Mia and (him, he).

22. Write whether the clause below is dependent or
(73) independent.

as the crow flies

23. Rewrite the following sentence, adding commas and
(26, 76) capital letters as needed:

mia said "i read the lesson but i did not understand it."

24. For the irregular verb *speak*, write the (a) present
(19, 65) participle, (b) past tense, and (c) past participle.

25. Write the objective case pronoun to complete the
(69) sentence below.

Herb laughed with Ivy and (I, me).

26. Write the seven common coordinating conjunctions
(76) listed in this lesson.

27. For a–c, write the plural of each noun.
(17, 22)
(a) eyetooth   (b) toothbrush   (c) team captain

28. Diagram the simple subject and simple predicate of each
(75) clause in the following compound sentence:

Egbert is writing his essay, but Ivy is playing computer
games.

Diagram each word of sentences 29–30.
29. Does Nora's old home in the country seem quaint?
(45, 54)

30. My friend Nora will give you and me a tour of her quaint
(46, 58) house in the country.

Relative Pronouns

Dictation or Journal Entry

Vocabulary:
To a*meliorate* is to improve, or make a bad condition better. We can a*meliorate* a power shortage by turning off our lights, computers, and TVs when we are not using them.

Amelioration is improvement. The *amelioration* of the world's problems depends on our doing something about them.

Relative Pronouns

Relative pronouns play the part of subject or object in clauses:

> Mr. and Mrs. Campos, *who* adopt tortoises, enjoy their pets. (subject)

> I thought the water, *which* I had been drinking, was polluted. (object)

Relative pronouns often refer to nouns that have preceded them, making the sentence more compact.

> WORDY:
> Mrs. Wong cares for two patients, and the patients came from New Zealand.

> COMPACT:
> Mrs. Wong cares for two patients, *who* came from New Zealand.

Simple

The following are simple relative pronouns:

> *who, whom, whose, what, which, that* ←

WHO REFERS TO PEOPLE (AND SOMETIMES ANIMALS):

> The girl *who* lives next door smiled at me.

> I have a cat *who* can climb a block wall.

WHICH REFERS TO ANIMALS OR THINGS:

> The bird, *which* had already eaten, still clung to the feeder.

> She frowns at the car, *which* hasn't been washed in weeks.

THAT REFERS TO PEOPLE, ANIMALS, OR THINGS:

> He is the kind of person *that* everyone loves.

> The cow *that* escaped belongs to my uncle.

> The noise *that* I heard last night was a possum.

Example 1 Choose the correct relative pronoun for each sentence.

     (a) The woman (*who, which*) lives on the corner has a goat.

     (b) The tree, (*who, which*) had been leaning for years, finally fell down.

     (c) There is the artist (*which, that*) I told you about.

Solution   (a) We choose **who** because it refers to "woman," a person. We do not use *which* for people.

     (b) We choose **which** because it refers to "tree," a thing. We do not use *who* for things.

     (c) We choose **that** because it refers to "artist," a person. We do not use *which* for people.

Errors to Avoid The relative pronoun *who* can cause problems, because it changes form depending on the part it plays in the clause:

SUBJECT	OBJECT	POSSESSIVE
who	*whom*	*whose*

In the sentences below, we diagram the dependent clause to show how the pronoun is used.

SUBJECT:
Mrs. Cruz, *who* is my friend, will call today.

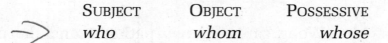

OBJECT:
Mrs. Cruz, *whom* you met, will call today.

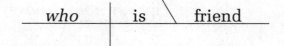

POSSESSIVE:
Mrs. Cruz, *whose* friendship I value, will call today.

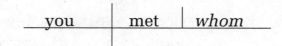
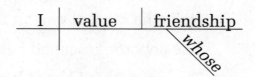

Example 2 Diagram the dependent clause to help you determine whether the pronoun is a subject or an object in the clause. Then choose the correct pronoun form.

(a) That dentist, (*who, whom*) I admire, has moved to Spain.

(b) Dr. Wu, (*who, whom*) lives in Denver, travels frequently.

(c) Mr. Green, (*who, whom*) writes music, has two daughters.

(d) Only Tony, (*who, whom*) I recognized, arrived on time.

Solution (a) That dentist, **whom** I admire, has moved to Spain. (object)

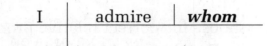

(b) Dr. Wu, **who** lives in Denver, travels frequently. (subject)

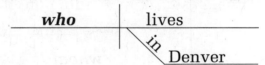

(c) Mr. Green, **who** writes music, has two daughters. (subject)

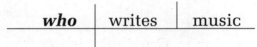

(d) Only Tony, **whom** I recognized, arrived on time. (object)

I	recognized	**whom**

Compound The following are compound relative pronouns:

> *whoever, whomever, whosoever*
> *whatever, whatsoever, whichever*

He may choose *whichever* color he wants.

Whatever you do, be there on time.

Notice that we carefully choose *whoever* or *whomever* depending on the part the compound relative pronoun plays in the clause.

You may invite *whomever* you want. (object)

Whoever is hungry may come for snacks. (subject)

Example 3 Choose the correct compound relative pronoun for this sentence:

(*Whoever, Whomever*) wants a seat should arrive early.

Solution **Whoever** wants a seat should arrive early. The pronoun is the subject, so the proper form is *who(ever)*.

Practice Choose the correct relative pronoun for sentences a–e.

a. People (*who, which*) own animals need to care for them.

b. The person (*who, whom*) took the key must return it.

Think: ? | took | key

c. I shall gladly ask (*whoever, whomever*) you want.

Think: I | shall ask | ?

d. The man (*that, which*) owns the python visits often.

e. Mr. Dolan, (*who, whom*) I have known for years, asked me to babysit his puppies.

Think: I | have known | ?

f. Diagram the dependent clause in the sentence below to show how the pronoun is used.

Emma, *who* is my best friend, helps me with math.

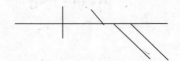

For g and h, replace each blank with the correct vocabulary word from this lesson.

    g. We can often _____ poor health by eating more nutritious foods.

    h. We can donate food and clothing for the _____ of poverty.

More Practice

Choose the correct relative pronoun for each sentence.

1. I shall thank all (who, whom) helped.

Think: ? | helped

2. Liz, (who, whom) raked the yard, worked without pay.

Think: ? | raked | yard

3. The helpers, (who, whom) I shall thank, gave me new hope.

Think: I | shall thank | ?

4. Some of the helpers, (who, whom) you know, worked until dark.

Think: you | know | ?

5. Max, (who, whom) you requested, fed the animals.

Think: you | requested | ?

6. Those (who, whom) harvested the crops were weary by nightfall.

Think: ? | harvested | crops

Review Set 77

Choose the correct word(s) to complete sentences 1–11.

1. *Quaint* means "attractive in a(n) (modern, glamorous, old-fashioned) way."
(76)

2. An insatiable appetite cannot be (understood, measured, satisfied).
(75)

3. *Redundant* means "(wise, peaceful, wordy)."
(74)

4. Sagacity is (urbanization, foolishness, wisdom).
(73)

5. *Pan American* means "including or relating to (some,
(32) small, all) countries of North, Central, and South
America."

6. The word *boss's* is a (plural, possessive) noun.
(13)

7. The pronoun *they* is (nominative, objective, possessive)
(66, 69) case.

8. (You're, Your) seats are over there.
(72)

9. You have made (less, fewer) mistakes than I.
(56)

10. The pronoun *our* is (first, second, third) person (singular,
(64) plural).

11. Dr. Kim, (who, whom) I admire, collects insects.
(77)

Think: | I | admire | ? |

12. Write whether the sentence below is simple or
(75) compound.

Anabel must call, write, or email her Uncle Rigo.

13. Write the predicate adjective in the following sentence:
(54)

Yosemite Falls is magnificent!

14. Write the subordinating conjunction in this sentence:
(73)

Uncle Rigo is scratching because he has chicken pox.

15. For a and b, write the word that is spelled correctly.
(35)

(a) pieces, peices   (b) ieght, eight

16. Which sentence is written correctly? Write *A* or *B*.
(61)

A. We need the both of you to help.

B. We need both of you to help.

17. Rewrite the sentence below, using a comma to clarify the meaning.
(68)

Without Mia Curtis is defenseless.

18. Rewrite the word *taught*, circling the silent letters.
(28, 29)

19. Use an appositive to combine the following two sentences into one sentence.
(58)

Jerusalem crickets are scary-looking bugs.

Jerusalem crickets are not poisonous.

20. Rewrite the following sentence, adding periods as needed:
(47, 50)

Mrs Lowe's baby, James L Ditter, Jr, weighs 27 lbs, 3 oz

21. Write whether the circled pronoun in the sentence below is used as a subject or an object.
(64)

Mia and (he) will be our helpers.

22. Write whether the word group below is a phrase or a clause.
(36)

the most detestable bug in the world

23. Rewrite the following sentence, adding commas and capital letters as needed:
(74)

as i stepped outside i nearly squashed the biggest ugliest bug on the planet

24. For the irregular verb *grow*, write the (a) present participle, (b) past tense, and (c) past participle.
(19, 65)

25. Which sentence is more polite? Write *A* or *B*.
(69)

A. The potato bug frightened him and me.

B. The potato bug frightened me and him.

26. Rewrite the following compound sentence, adding a comma before the coordinating conjunction.
(76)

Ivy is playing games for she has finished her essay.

27. Rewrite the following letter, adding commas and capital letters as needed.

(57, 63)

dear anabel

please call write or email me soon.

love
uncle rigo

28. Diagram the simple subject and simple predicate of each clause in the following compound sentence:

(75)

Ivy is playing games, for she has finished her essay.

Diagram each word of sentences 29–30.

✓ **29.** Is Anabel's uncle lonely and ill?

(45, 54)

30. Anabel, an excellent vocalist, could sing her uncle a song about her vacation in Maine.

(46, 58)

Pronoun Usage

Dictation or Journal Entry

Vocabulary:

Saline means "salty." Gargling with a warm *saline* solution might ameliorate your sore throat.

Salinity is saltiness. The *salinity* of the ocean helps swimmers to float.

In this lesson, we will discuss areas where pronoun usage can be troublesome.

Written vs. Spoken Language

Traditionally, pronouns that follow a form of "to be" must be in the nominative case, as in the examples below.

It is *I*.

Was it *they* who called?

I thought it was *she*.

When we write, we should follow this rule. When we are speaking, however, we tend to be less formal. Our ear tells us that in casual conversation, "It is I" sounds stiff. Instead, we are more likely to say:

It is *me*.

Was it *them* who called?

I thought it was *her*.

This relaxed pronoun usage is acceptable in casual conversation, but would be unacceptable in formal speech or any form of writing.

Now we will discuss two more areas that often cause trouble in pronoun usage.

Appositions

We remember than an appositive renames a person or thing. An **apposition** is a pronoun used to rename a noun for emphasis.

Only one student, *you*, can enter the state contest.

Ms. Hoo named the winners of the poetry contest, *you* and *me*.

The apposition must be in the same case form as the noun it renames. Consider the examples below.

SUBJECT:
We (NOT *us*) Texans are not used to cold weather.

OBJECT:
They like *us* (NOT *we*) young people.

SUBJECT:
Both players, Ina and *she* (NOT *her*), might score.

Example 1   Choose the correct apposition for this sentence:

Our class sent two helpers, Caleb and (*him, he*).

Solution   The apposition "Caleb and him" renames "helpers," which is a direct object, so we use the objective case pronoun:

Our class sent two helpers, Caleb and **him.**

Comparisons   In comparison sentences, words are sometimes omitted. This usually occurs following the words *than* or *as*.

He draws better than *I*. ("do" is omitted)

I can climb as high as *she*. ("can" is omitted)

Notice that the pronouns in the sentences above are in the nominative case because they are used as the subjects of clauses whose verbs are understood (not stated).

The pronoun used in a comparison is important because it can change the meaning of the sentence.

John loves Iowa as much as *she*. ("does" is omitted)
[MEANING: John loves Iowa as much as she does.]

John loves Iowa as much as *her*. ("he loves" is omitted)
[MEANING: John loves Iowa as much as he loves her.]

Example 2   Choose the correct pronoun for the following sentences.
(a) We write better than (*they, them*).

(b) I'm not as tall as (*she, her*).

Solution   (a) We write better than **they.** ("do" is omitted)

(b) I'm not as tall as **she.** ("is" is omitted)

✓ **Practice** Choose the correct pronoun for sentences a–e.

    a. (We, Us) boys will sing louder.

        Think: ____?____ | ____will sing____

    b. It is okay with (we, us) girls if you paint the fence.

        Think: \with\ ____?____

    c. The sudden noise startled (we, us) boys.

        Think: ___noise___ | ___startled___ | ___?___

    d. He is better at sign language than (I, me). ["am" omitted]

    e. They travel as fast as (*we, us*). ["do" omitted]

For f and g, replace each blank with the correct vocabulary word.

    f. The _____ of the sea makes it unfit to drink.

    g. Some fish cannot survive in _____ water.

More Practice Choose the correct pronoun for each sentence.

    1. Meg has more freckles than (he, him). ["does" omitted]

    2. (We, Us) students enjoy grammar.

        Think: ____?____ | ____enjoy____

    3. Ms. Hoo showed (we, us) students the diagram.

        Think: ___Ms. Hoo___ | ___showed___ | ___diagram___ \(x) ?

    4. Raul and (her, she) will rewrite the sentence.

        Think: ____?____ | ____will rewrite____

    5. I saw two new people, Lily and (her, she).

        Think: ___I___ | ___saw___ | ___?___

    6. Luey ran farther than (he, him). ["did" omitted]

7. Liz sleeps later than (she, her). ["does" omitted]

8. I sing louder than (they, them). ["do" omitted]

9. (We, Us) girls laugh together.

Think: ____?____ | ___laugh___

10. The water satisfied (we, us) hikers.

Think: ___water___ | ___satisfied___ | ___?___

✓**Review Set**
78 Choose the correct word(s) to complete sentences 1–12.

1. To (illuminate, humiliate, ameliorate) is to improve or
(77) make a bad condition better.

2. (Contrition, Elation, Quaintness) is old-fashioned charm.
(76)

3. *Insatiable* means "unable to be (destroyed, satisfied,
(75) heard)."

4. A redundant essay has more (commas, periods, words)
(74) than are necessary.

5. A(n) (dispensable, indispensable, essential) item is
(33) unimportant.

6. The word *tortoise* is a(n) (abstract, concrete) noun.
(11)

7. The pronoun *I* is (nominative, objective, possessive) case.
(66, 69)

8. This pen is (her's, hers).
(72)

9. Of the two brothers, Alex has the (curlier, curliest) hair.
(56)

10. The pronoun *their* is (first, second, third) person
(64) (singular, plural).

11. Dr. Kim, (who, whom) collects insects, will be here
(77) tomorrow.

Think: ____?____ | ___collects___ | ___insects___

12. (We, Us) students look forward to Saturdays.
(78)

Think: _____?_____|___look___

13. Write the seven common coordinating conjunctions
(48, 75) listed in lessons 48 and 75.

14. Write the subordinating conjunction in this sentence:
(73)

Some think that Alex's hair has shrunk.

15. Write the antecedent for the pronoun circled in the
(62) sentence below.

Some people think that their hair will shrink if (they) wash
it.

16. Write whether the following is a complete sentence, a
(23) sentence fragment, or a run-on sentence.

An outbreak of pinkeye among the bighorn sheep.

17. Rewrite the sentence below, using a comma to clarify the
(68) meaning.

From the sun people were burned.

18. Use a dictionary: (a) The word *despair* is what part of
(27, 30) speech? (b) Write its pronunciation. (c) Write its
etymology.

19. Rewrite the sentence below, using commas to offset the
(60) nonessential appositive.

Missouri the Show Me State lies in the center of the
continent.

20. Rewrite the following sentence, adding periods as needed:
(47, 50)

The Atlas Tile Co is located on S Third St in Rock City

21. Write the nominative case pronoun to complete the
(66) sentence below.

The most cheerful nurses were Leo and (her, she).

22. Write whether the clause below is dependent or independent.
(73)

Alex washed his hair

23. Rewrite the following sentence, adding commas and capital letters as needed:
(74)

as olaf rode a white arabian horse sven played a shiny loud trumpet.

24. For the irregular verb *swear*, write the (a) present participle, (b) past tense, and (c) past participle.
(19, 65)

25. Write the objective case pronoun to complete the sentence below.
(69)

Give the insect to Dr. Kim or (she, her).

26. Rewrite the following compound sentence, adding a comma before the coordinating conjunction.
(76)

Leo is playing games but he hasn't won any.

27. Rewrite the following title, adding commas and capital letters as needed.
(25)

a light in the attic

28. Diagram the simple subject and simple predicate of each clause in the following compound sentence:
(75)

Alex's hair has shrunk, for he washed it.

Diagram each word of sentences 29–30.

29. Whom shall we call?
(77)

30. Did Buzz the barber give Alex a short haircut?
(46, 58)

Interrogative Pronouns

Dictation or Journal Entry

Vocabulary:

To *daunt* is to discourage. The length of that novel *daunts* me, for I'll never find time to read it!

Dauntless means "not discourageable; heroic." The *dauntless* student overcame many difficulties, never gave up, and finally graduated.

When a relative pronoun introduces a question, it is called an **interrogative pronoun**. Who, whom, whose, what, which, whoever, whomever, whichever, and whatever are interrogative pronouns.

> *Who* is there?

> *What* do you want?

> *Which* shall I choose?

> *Whom* are you calling?

> *Whoever* would do that?

A sentence doesn't have to end with a question mark in order to contain an interrogative pronoun. Sometimes an interrogative pronoun introduces a question that is contained inside a declarative sentence:

> She asked *who* was there.

> Wakefield wondered *what* they wanted.

> I don't know *which* is best.

Example 1 Write each interrogative pronoun that you find in each sentence.

(a) I cannot guess what will happen next.

(b) Who ate the taco?

(c) We wonder which they'll find first.

(d) Whose smelly socks are these?

Solution (a) **what** (b) **who** (c) **which** (d) **whose**

Who* or *Whom In order to decide whether we should use *who* or *whom*, we must determine what part the interrogative pronoun plays in the sentence. If it functions as a subject or a predicate nominative, we use *who*.

Who sang the solo? (subject)

$$\underline{\text{Who} \mid \text{sang}}$$

The soloist was *who*? (predicate nominative)

$$\underline{\text{soloist} \mid \text{was} \backslash \text{who}}$$

If the interrogative pronoun is an object (direct object, indirect object, or object of a preposition), we use *whom*.

Whom did they call? (direct object)

$$\underline{\text{they} \mid \text{did call} \mid \text{Whom}}$$

Kim gave *whom* a gift? (indirect object)

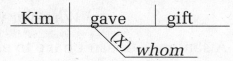

To check to see that we have used *who* or *whom* correctly, we can turn the questions above into statements, substituting *he* or *she* for *who* and *him* or *her* for *whom*.

RIGHT: They <u>did call</u> *him*.
WRONG: They <u>did call</u> *he*.

RIGHT: Kim <u>gave</u> *her* a gift.
WRONG: Kim <u>gave</u> *she* a gift.

Errors to Avoid   Do not confuse *whose* and *who's*. *Whose* is a possessive or interrogative pronoun. *Who's* is a contraction for "who is." **Possessive pronouns do not have apostrophes.**

Who's that? (Who is that?)

Whose parakeet is that?

Example 2   Choose the correct interrogative pronoun for each sentence.

(a) (Who, Whom) caught the fish?

(b) (Who, Whom) did you expect?

(c) To (who, whom) are you speaking?

(d) This one is mine, but (who's, whose) is that?

Solution (a) The pronoun is used as the subject, so we choose *who.*

Who caught the fish?

(b) The pronoun is used as an object, so we choose *whom.*

Whom did you expect?

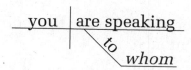

To check to see that we have used *who* or *whom* correctly, we change the question into a statement, substituting *he* or *she* for *who* and *him* or *her* for *whom.*

RIGHT: You <u>did expect</u> *him.*
WRONG: You <u>did expect</u> *he.*

(c) The pronoun is used as an object of a preposition, so we choose *whom.*

To **whom** are you speaking?

(d) *Who's* is a contraction for "who is." We choose the interrogative pronoun *whose.*

This one is mine, but **whose** is that?

Adjective or Pronoun? When *which, whose,* and *what* come before nouns, they are adjectives. When *which, whose,* and *what* stand alone, they are interrogative pronouns.

ADJECTIVE: *Which* boot goes on the right foot?
PRONOUN: *Which* goes on the right foot?

ADJECTIVE: *What* window broke?
PRONOUN: *What* broke?

ADJECTIVE: *Whose* pen is this?
PRONOUN: *Whose* is this?

Example 3 Tell whether the italicized word in each sentence is an adjective or an interrogative pronoun.

(a) I wonder *whose* cat this is.

(b) *What* is your favorite sport?

(c) *What* sport do you like best?

(d) *Which* of the two is better?

Solution (a) *Whose* comes before the noun *cat*, so it is an **adjective.**

(b) *What* stands alone, so it is an **interrogative pronoun.**

(c) *What* precedes the noun *sport*, so it is an **adjective.**

(d) *Which* stands alone. It is an **interrogative pronoun.**

Practice For a–c, write the interrogative pronoun, if any, from each sentence.

a. I could not guess what he wanted.

b. She wondered which shoes to wear.

c. Whose is that sack lunch?

For d–f, choose the correct interrogative pronoun for each sentence.

d. (Who, Whom) will you ask for help?

e. (Who's, Whose) is the little black dog?

f. (Who, Whom) wants more soup?

For g and h, write whether the italicized word is an adjective or an interrogative pronoun.

g. *What* were you thinking?

h. *Which* way shall I go?

For i and j, replace each blank with the correct vocabulary word from this lesson.

i. The ice storm might _____ some travelers.

j. The ice storm will not hinder _____ travelers.

More Practice Choose the correct word to complete each sentence.

1. (Who's, Whose) talking?

2. (Who's, Whose) phone do I hear?

3. (Who, Whom) mopped the floor?

? | mopped

4. To (who, whom) does this book belong?

To ?

5. (Who, Whom) are you calling?

you | are calling | ?

6. (Who's, Whose) the man with the long gray beard?

7. (Who's, Whose) backpack is this?

8. With (who, whom) would you like to speak?

With ?

9. (Who, Whom) will play?

? | will play

10. (Who, Whom) did you select?

you | did select | ?

✓
**Review Set
79** Choose the correct word(s) to complete sentences 1–13.

1. (*Satiable, Genteel, Saline*) means "salty."
(78)

2. Amelioration makes things (bad, better, worse).
(77)

3. Many people enjoy the quaintness of (modern, new, old)
(76) furniture.

4. *Satiable* means "able to be (counted, seen, satisfied)."
(75)

5. *Indispensable* means "(unimportant, nonessential,
(33) essential)."

6. The word *sea horse* is a (compound, collective) noun.
(13)

7. The pronoun *me* is (nominative, objective, possessive)
(66, 69) case.

8. (They're, Their) ears are green.
(72)

9. Of the three cousins, Alex has the (curlier, curliest) hair.
(56)

10. The pronoun *you* is (first, second, third) person.
(64)

11. Dr. Kim, (who, whom) the spider bit, will be more careful
(77) next time.

Think: spider | bit | ?

12. The news surprised (we, us) students.
(78)

Think: news | surprised | ?

13. (Who, Whom) did you invite?
(79)

Think: you | did invite | ?

14. Write the subordinating conjunction in this sentence:
(73)

Mieko will hike until the sun goes down.

15. Write whether the sentence below is simple or
(75) compound.

Bison are the largest mammals in Yellowstone National
Park, and they are strictly vegetarian.

16. Write the interrogative pronoun in the following
(79) sentence:

Who left their greasy fingerprints here?

17. Rewrite the sentence below, using a comma to clarify the
(68) meaning.

This Walter can do.

18. Rewrite the word *unfeigned*, circling the silent letter.
(28)

19. Use an appositive to combine the following two
(58) sentences into one sentence.

Arizona gets very little rain.

Arizona is the Grand Canyon State.

20. Rewrite the following sentence, adding periods as needed:
(47, 50)

They took water, fruit, cheese, etc, on their hike up Mt Wilson

21. Write whether the circled pronoun in the sentence below is used as a subject or an object.
(64)

That spider bit Dr. Kim and (me)!

22. From the following sentence, write each prepositional phrase, circling the object of each preposition.
(44)

All the hikers except Joe walked alongside the stream.

23. Rewrite the following sentence, adding commas and capital letters as needed:
(74)

when ms. hoo retires she will move to a quaint small town.

24. For the irregular verb *sing*, write the (a) present participle, (b) past tense, and (c) past participle.
(19, 65)

25. Which sentence is more polite? Write *A* or *B*.
(69)

A. Please give bandages to me and him.

B. Please give bandages to him and me.

26. Rewrite the following sentence, adding commas and capital letters as needed.
(26, 76)

yoli said "i was born on sunday november 4 1973 so how old am i?"

27. Rewrite the following letter, adding commas and capital letters as needed.
(57, 63)

dear uncle rigo
    if you would like i could bring you some bread cheese and grapes.

                                                        love
                                                        anabel

28. Diagram the simple subject and simple predicate of each clause in the following compound sentence:
(75)

Amy planted corn, but the ants must have harvested it.

Diagram each word of sentences 29–30.

29. The new teacher is who?
(77)

30. Badchek, the deceiver sold whom a ring with a fake
(46, 58) diamond?

Quotation Marks, Part 1

> **Dictation or Journal Entry**
>
> **Vocabulary:**
>
> A *docent* is a tour guide. On our tour of the arboretum, the *docent* explained where each tree and plant originated.
>
> A *curator* is someone who oversees, often at a museum or historical site. The museum *curator* asked us not to touch the ancient artifacts.

Direct Quotation A **direct quotation** gives a speaker's exact words. To indicate a direct quotation, we enclose the speaker's words in quotation marks.

> Ms. Hoo told me, "Don't give up."

> "You can do it," she said.

Notice that in each of the examples above, the punctuation mark following the direct quotation appears **inside** the quotation marks.

Example 1 Place quotation marks where they are needed in the sentence below.

> Tomorrow is another day, said Ms. Hoo.

Solution We place quotation marks before and after Ms. Hoo's words (including the comma that follows them).

> **"Tomorrow is another day," said Ms. Hoo.**

Direct Quotation with Explanatory Note Sometimes a direct quotation is interrupted by an **explanatory note** such as *he said, she replied, the teacher explained*, etc. We enclose in quotation marks only the speaker's exact words, not the explanatory note. Notice that both parts of the direct quotations below are enclosed in quotation marks.

> "I can't do this," moaned Jeb, "because it's too hard."

> "If you keep trying," she said, "you'll succeed."

Example 2 Place quotation marks where they are needed in the sentence below.

> Did you know, asked Ms. Hoo, that I failed geometry the first time I took it?

Solution We place quotation marks around both parts of Ms. Hoo's direct quotation, but we do not enclose the explanatory note (asked Ms. Hoo) in quotation marks.

"Did you know," asked Ms. Hoo, "that I failed geometry the first time I took it?"

Indirect Quotations An **indirect quotation** gives the main idea of what someone said, but it does not give the speaker's exact words. We do not use quotation marks with indirect quotations.

Ms. Hoo told me that I should never give up.

She explained that there is always hope for those who keep trying.

Example 3 Add quotation marks as needed in the sentence below.

Ms. Hoo said that geometry was difficult for her.

Solution **No quotations marks** are necessary, because this is not a direct quotation. It is an **indirect quotation.**

Practice For a–d, rewrite correctly each sentence that needs quotation marks. If the sentence does not need quotation marks, write "none."

   a. My classmate Jeb complains that the work is too hard.

   b. He tells me that he wants to quit school.

   c. Inch by inch, everything is a cinch, said Ms. Hoo.

   d. If you take your time, said the teacher, you'll do better work.

For e and f, replace each blank with the correct vocabulary word from this lesson.

   e. A _____ guides tourists.

   f. A _____ takes care of a museum or historical site.

More Practice See "More Practice Lesson 80" in Student Workbook.

Choose the correct word(s) to complete sentences 1–13.

1. To (ameliorate, daunt, exalt) is to discourage.
(79)

2. The *salinity* of the sea refers to its (temperature, tides, saltiness).
(78)

3. Amelioration is (destruction, improvement, cognizance).
(77)

4. (*Satiable, Ardent, Quaint*) means "attractive in an old-fashioned way."
(76)

5. (*Dispensable, Vertebrate, Indispensable*) means "absolutely necessary or essential."
(33)

6. The sentence below is (declarative, interrogative, imperative, exclamatory).
(2)

Bryce Canyon has fascinating geologic formations.

7. The pronoun *my* is (nominative, objective, possessive) case.
(66, 69)

8. (Who's, Whose) ears are green?
(79)

9. Miss BoPeep has (less, fewer) sheep than (him, he).
(56, 78) ["has" omitted]

10. The pronoun *I* is (first, second, third) person (singular, plural).
(64)

11. Miss BoPeep, (who, whom) cares for sheep, worries about wolves.
(77)

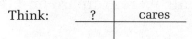

12. (We, Us) musicians need new instruments.
(78)

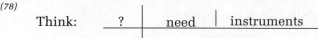

13. (Who, Whom) will play the saxophone?
(79)

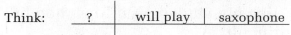

14. Write the subordinating conjunction in this sentence:
(73)

Whenever the sheep stray, Miss BoPeep worries.

15. Write the antecedent to the circled pronoun in the
(62) sentence below.

If her sheep stray, Miss BoPeep worries about (them).

16. Write the predicate adjective in the following sentence:
(54)

The old buildings in Virginia City appear quaint.

17. Rewrite the sentence below, using a comma to clarify the
(68) meaning.

For that Sven paid forty dollars.

18. Use a dictionary: (a) The word *iceberg* is what part of
(27, 30) speech? (b) Write its pronunciation. (c) Write its
etymology.

19. Rewrite the sentence below, using commas to offset the
(60) nonessential appositive.

Minnesota the Gopher State borders Lake Superior.

20. Rewrite the following sentence, adding periods as needed:
(47, 50)

The note says, "Come to the library on Sat, Feb 12"

21. Write the nominative case pronoun to complete the
(66) sentence below.

Our two docents were Amparo and (he, him).

22. Write whether the clause below is dependent or
(73) independent.

because it stings

23. Rewrite the following sentence, adding commas, capital
(76, 80) letters, and quotation marks as needed:

i like my students said ms. hoo but their animals can be
difficult.

24. For the irregular verb *break*, write the (a) present
(19, 65) participle, (b) past tense, and (c) past participle.

25. Write the objective case pronoun to complete the
(69) sentence below.

Send get-well cards to Dr. Kim and (her, she).

26. Rewrite the following outline, adding periods and capital
(26, 47) letters as needed.

    i bryce national park
      a geology
      b paleontology

27. Rewrite the following letter, adding commas and capital
(57, 63) letters as needed.

    dear anabel
      i do not like bread and cheese nor do i like grapes.
          thanks anyway
          uncle rigo

28. Diagram the simple subject and simple predicate of each
(75) clause in the following compound sentence:

A sheep has broken its leg, so Miss BoPeep must carry it.

Diagram each word of sentences 29–30.

29. Whom should Miss BoPeep notify?
(77)

30. Will Marco, the talkative, exuberant docent, give Ted and
(46, 58) me a tour of the old fort in Colorado?

Quotation Marks, Part 2

Dictation or Journal Entry

Vocabulary:
Culpable means "deserving blame." Fido is *culpable* for the disappearance of the last slice of pizza.

A *culprit* is a guilty one, or one who is accused. Fido is the *culprit*; he has pizza sauce on his whiskers.

Speaker Changes

A set of quotation marks can contain the words of only one speaker. When the speaker changes, we use a new set of quotation marks. Also, when writing dialogue (conversation), we start a new paragraph every time the speaker changes.

Notice how quotation marks are used as the speaker changes in this dialogue:

"Do you live in Tennessee?" asked Max.

"Yes, I do when I'm at home," replied the guitarist. "Where do you live?"

"My home is in Oregon," answered Max. "I have been traveling for two weeks. Do you travel much?"

"Yes," said the guitarist, "and now I am eager to go home."

Example 1

Rewrite this dialogue, inserting quotation marks as needed.

Where were you? she asked me with an angry frown.

I was at the park, I said. Were you looking for me?

Yes, I wanted you to fix my broken computer! she cried.

Solution

We know that a new paragraph means that the speaker has changed. We place quotation marks around the actual words of each speaker.

"Where were you?" she asked me with an angry frown.

"I was at the park," I said. "Were you looking for me?"

"Yes. I wanted you to fix my broken computer!" she cried.

Titles   The titles of short literary works are enclosed in quotation marks. This includes short stories, parts of books (chapters, lessons, sections, etc.), essays and sermons, one-act plays, newspaper and magazine articles, and short poems. We also enclose in quotation marks the titles of songs.

> Ogden Nash's poem "The Adventures of Isabel" makes me laugh.
>
> When I was little, Dad told me the story "William Tell."
>
> Jeb titled his essay "Life Is Hard."
>
> If you whistle "Old MacDonald" one more time, I'm going to scream.

We do not use quotation marks for larger works such as books, plays, movies, television programs, or operas. Instead, these titles are underlined or italicized (Charlotte's Web, *Mr. Popper's Penguins*). We shall discuss this more in another lesson.

Example 2   Rewrite the sentences below, inserting quotation marks where they are needed.

(a) Did they sing Happy Birthday off key?

(b) Danny wrote a poem called Ode on a Soda Can.

(c) Jeb dreads the next lesson, Dividing Decimals.

Solution   (a) We place quotation marks around "Happy Birthday" because it is a song title.

Did they sing "Happy Birthday" off key?

(b) We enclose "Ode on a Soda Can" in quotation marks because it is the name of a poem.

Danny wrote a poem called "Ode on a Soda Can."

(c) We enclose "Dividing Decimals" in quotation marks because it is the title of a lesson in a book.

Jeb dreads the next lesson, "Dividing Decimals."

Practice   For a and b, replace each blank with the correct vocabulary word from this lesson.

a. Is Fido the _____? Is he the guilty one?

b. Yes, Fido is _____. He is to blame.

Rewrite sentences c–e, inserting quotation marks as needed.

c. Have you ever read the story King Stork by Howard Pyle?

d. Can you sing the song Over the Rainbow for me?

e. The short story Gone Is Gone comes from Bohemia.

f. Rewrite this dialogue, inserting quotation marks where they are needed.

> Sit here, Molly, and tell me all about yourself. What are your hobbies?

> I like to catch butterflies and draw pictures, Molly said.

More Practice   See "More Practice Lesson 81" in Student Workbook.

Review Set 81   Choose the correct word(s) to complete sentences 1–13.

1. A (chasm, plateau, docent) is a tour guide.
(80)

2. A dauntless person is not easily (encouraged, discouraged, satisfied).
(79)

3. *Saline* means "(sweet, salty, buttery)."
(78)

4. To ameliorate is to make a bad condition (worse, terrible, better).
(77)

5. A clamor is a(n) (outcry, bird, invertebrate).
(34)

6. The word *docent's* is a (plural, possessive) noun.
(13)

7. The pronoun *their* is (nominative, objective, possessive) case.
(66, 69)

8. Are (your's, yours) green?
(72)

9. Of all the shepherds, Miss BoPeep has the (least, fewer, fewest) sheep.
(56)

10. The pronoun *we* is (first, second, third) person (singular, plural).
(64)

11. Miss BoPeep, (who, whom) you know, has lost some sheep.
(77)

Think:
you	know	?

12. They have more sheep than (us, we). ["have" omitted]
(78)

13. For (who, whom) shall we perform our music?
(79)

Think: For   ?

14. Write the subordinating conjunction in this sentence:
(73)
As soon as she finds her sheep, Miss BoPeep will relax.

15. Write whether the sentence below is simple or compound.
(75)

With great difficulty, Shirley Temple Wong moved from China to the United States of America.

16. Write the interrogative pronoun in the following sentence:
(79)

Whom shall we elect?

17. Rewrite the sentence below, using a comma to clarify the meaning.
(68)

That Alba can take with her.

18. Write the plural form of the singular noun *apology*.
(16)

19. Use an appositive to combine the following two sentences into one sentence.
(58)

Badchek is the culprit.

Badchek has fled to another country.

20. Rewrite the following sentence, adding periods as needed:
(47, 50)

Mr and Mrs Tran live at 654 S Alta Loma Dr in Austin

21. In the sentence below, is the circled pronoun used as a subject or is it used as an object?
(64)

Amparo and (he) were our docents.

22. Rewrite the sentence below, adding commas and capital
(26, 67) letters as needed.

jenny replied "no i have not seen badchek."

23. Rewrite the following sentence, adding commas, capital
(74, 80) letters, and quotation marks as needed:

if i see a suspicious malicious person said jenny i shall
call the police.

24. For the irregular verb *drink*, write the (a) present
(19, 65) participle, (b) past tense, and (c) past participle.

25. Rewrite the sentence below, adding capital letters and
(25, 81) quotation marks as needed.

let us hum the song the old gray mare.

✓ **26.** Rewrite the compound sentence below, adding a comma
(76) before the coordinating conjunction.

Fido eats my pizza yet I forgive him.

27. Rewrite the following letter, adding commas and capital
(57, 63) letters as needed.

dear officer valiant
      your mean avaricious culprit has lived in iceland
belgium and botswana.

                                  respectfully
                                  mrs. brite P.I.

28. Diagram the simple subject and simple predicate of each
(75) clause in the following compound sentence:

We must locate the culprit, or he will commit another
crime.

Diagram each word of sentences 29–30.

29. The mean, avaricious culprit is who?
(77)

30. Mrs. Brite, a clever investigator, gave the police and me a
(46, 58) thorough report on the culprit's former residences.

Demonstrative Pronouns

Pointing Pronouns   *This*, *that*, *these*, and *those* are **demonstrative pronouns.** Some people call them "pointing pronouns" because they seem to point out the person or thing being referred to, distinguishing it from others.

> *This* is an amazing world.
>
> *That* is a flying squirrel.
>
> *These* are hedgehogs.
>
> *Those* are army ants.

A demonstrative pronoun must agree in number with its antecedent (the noun that it points out).

SINGULAR:	*This* is a plateau.
PLURAL:	*These* are plateaus.
SINGULAR:	*That* is a meteorite.
PLURAL:	*Those* are meteorites.

This, These   We use *this* and *these* to point out persons or things that are nearby in space, time, or awareness.

> *This* is a calico cat.
>
> *These* are my ideas.
>
> *This* has been a busy week.

That, Those   We use *that* and *those* to point out persons or things that are farther away.

> *That* is a stray dog.
>
> *That* was a foolish idea.
>
> *Those* were the exciting games.

Errors to Avoid   We never add "here" or "there" to a demonstrative pronoun.

> NO: This *here* is my plan.
> YES: This is my plan.

NO: That *there* is the silliest young man.
YES: That is the silliest young man.

We do not use "them" in place of "these" or "those."

NO: *Them* are the ripe ones.
YES: *These* are the ripe ones.

NO: *Them* taste sour.
YES: *Those* taste sour.

Adjective or Pronoun? The demonstrative pronouns *this*, *that*, *these*, and *those* also function as demonstrative adjectives.

It is easy to tell the difference. If they stand alone, they are demonstrative pronouns. If they come before a noun, they are demonstrative adjectives.

These are too big. (pronoun)

These shoes are too big. (adjective)

He wrote *this*. (pronoun)

He wrote *this* story. (adjective)

Example Choose the correct demonstrative pronoun for each sentence, and write the noun that it points to.

(a) (This here, This) is a picture of me.

(b) Is (that, those) the reason you left?

(c) (This, These) are the shoes I like best.

(d) (Them, Those) are the ones I wore yesterday.

Solution (a) **This picture**   (b) **That reason**

(c) **These shoes**   (d) **Those ones**

✓Practice For a and b, replace each blank with the correct vocabulary word from this lesson.

    a. _____, an adjective, means "full of joy."

    b. _____, a noun, is great joy.

For c–g, choose the correct demonstrative pronoun, and write the noun it points to.

    c. (This, These) is a painting of mine.

d. (That, Those) are the colors of a sunset.

e. (This, These) is their distant relative.

f. (These, That) are my reasons for studying art.

g. (This, This here) is the key I was looking for.

Review Set 82 Choose the correct word(s) to complete sentences 1–13.

1. (*Dauntless, Saline, Culpable*) means "deserving blame."
(81)

2. A (mesa, savanna, curator) might oversee a museum or
(80) historical site.

3. *Dauntless* means "(fearful, cowardly, heroic)."
(79)

4. Salinity is (saltiness, salvation, dryness).
(78)

5. A (proclamation, meteorite, ventriloquist) is a public
(34) announcement.

6. The word *bliss* is a(n) (abstract, concrete) noun.
(11)

7. The pronoun *its* is (nominative, objective, possessive)
(66, 69) case.

8. (Who's, Whose) pencil is this?
(79)

9. Nate is the (better, best) of the two painters.
(56)

10. The pronoun *he* is (first, second, third) person (singular,
(64) plural).

11. (Who, Whom) were you expecting?
(77, 79)

> Think: ___you | were expecting | ?

12. (We, Us) musicians shall play a new song.
(78)

13. (That, Those) were comfortable shoes.
(82)

14. Write the subordinating conjunction in this sentence:
(73)
Since the water pipes froze, we have no water.

15. Add suffixes:
_(33, 34)
    (a) angry + est   (b) win + ing

16. Write whether the following is a complete sentence, a
₍₂₃₎ run-on sentence, or a sentence fragment.

Hortensia was a Zapotec from Oaxaca, Mexico.

17. Rewrite the sentence below, using a comma to clarify the
₍₆₈₎ meaning.

To Alba Dunn appears blissful.

18. Use a dictionary: (a) The word *lavish* is what part of
_(27, 30) speech? (b) Write its pronunciation. (c) Write its
etymology.

19. Rewrite the following sentence, using commas to offset
₍₆₀₎ the nonessential appositive.

Boise the capital of Idaho lies at the foot of the Rocky
Mountains.

20. Rewrite the following sentence, adding periods as needed:
_(47, 50)

Your appointment with Dr Ramos is on Mon, Jan 2

21. Write the nominative case pronoun to complete the
₍₆₄₎ sentence below.

Kurt and (he, him) have messy hair today.

22. From the following sentence, write each prepositional
₍₄₄₎ phrase, circling the object of each preposition.

An iguana scurries over the hill and around the rocks.

23. Rewrite the following sentence, adding commas, capital
_(74, 80) letters, and quotation marks as needed:

lulu said although i was born in cheyenne wyoming i
now live in salem oregon.

24. For the irregular verb *steal*, write the (a) present
_(19, 65) participle, (b) past tense, and (c) past participle.

25. Rewrite the sentence below, adding capital letters and quotation marks as needed.

(25, 81)

my aunt read me a short story called adrift on an ice pan.

26. Rewrite the compound sentence below, adding a comma before the coordinating conjunction.

(76)

Fido stole my pencil so I didn't do my homework.

27. Rewrite the following letter, adding commas and capital letters as needed.

(57, 67)

dear mrs. brite P.I.
   the culprit i believe was last seen in juneau alaska.
                      respectfully
                      officer valiant

28. Diagram the simple subject and simple predicate of each clause in the following compound sentence:

(75)

Badchek fled the country, but we shall find him, for we are detectives.

Diagram each word of sentences 29–30.

29. The mean, avaricious culprit swindled whom?

(77)

30. Officer Valiant, Mrs. Brite's assistant, sent me a message about Badchek's previous crimes.

(46, 58)

Indefinite Pronouns

Dictation or Journal Entry
Vocabulary:
To *subvert* is to destroy or corrupt. The enemy tried to *subvert* our mission.

Subversion is corruption or destruction. The enemy's *subversion* of our mission will not daunt us.

A pronoun that does not have a known antecedent is called an **indefinite pronoun.** It refers to a person or thing only generally.

Anybody can come.

Several will walk.

Something is missing.

Singular Some indefinite pronouns refer to only one person or thing. They are singular and take singular verbs:

another	anybody	anyone
anything	neither	either
everybody	everyone	everything
each	nobody	no one
nothing	other	one
somebody	someone	something
much		

Everybody <u>wants</u> success.

Each of the students <u>tries</u> hard.

Neither of us <u>is</u> going to fail.

Nothing <u>is</u> impossible.

Plural The following indefinite pronouns refer to more than one person or thing. They take plural verbs:

several	both	few
many	others	

Both <u>are</u> fine.

Few <u>were</u> quiet.

Many <u>are</u> excited.

Others <u>seem</u> nervous.

Singular or Plural The following indefinite pronouns can be singular or plural depending on their use in the sentence.

all   *any*   *more*

none   *some*   *most*

→ They are <u>plural</u> when they refer to things that <u>can be counted.</u>

Most offices <u>are</u> closed on holidays.

→ They are <u>singular</u> when they refer to something that <u>cannot be counted.</u>

Most of the pizza <u>is</u> gone.

Example 1 Write each indefinite pronoun and tell whether it is singular or plural in the sentence.

(a) *Much* has been written about college.

(b) *Each* must make his or her own decisions.

(c) *Many* of the students want more information.

(d) *All* of the snow is melting.

(e) *All* are invited to the meeting.

(f) *None* of the horses were properly shod.

Solution (a) *Much*, singular   (b) *Each*, singular

(c) *Many*, plural   (d) *All*, singular

(e) *All*, plural   (f) *None*, plural

Example 2 Choose the correct verb form (singular or plural) to match the indefinite pronoun in each sentence.

(a) *All* of you (is, are) welcome.

(b) *Many* (need, needs) surfboards.

(c) *Few* (has, have) enough patience.

(d) (Is, Are) *anything* more fun than the ocean?

Solution   (a) *All* of you **are** welcome.

(b) *Many* **need** surfboards.

(c) *Few* **have** enough patience.

(d) **Is** *anything* more fun than the ocean?

Adjective or Pronoun?   Just like demonstrative pronouns, when indefinite pronouns are placed before nouns, they function as indefinite adjectives.

Some are too ripe. (pronoun)

Some pears are too ripe. (adjective)

He gave one to *each*. (pronoun)

He gave one to *each* person. (adjective)

Agreement with Antecedents   If an indefinite pronoun is the antecedent for a personal pronoun, the personal pronoun must agree in number, person, and gender.

SINGULAR: *Everything* has *its* purpose.

(antecedent)   (personal pronoun)

PLURAL: *Both* have *their* purpose.

(antecedent)   (personal pronoun)

There is an exception. When writing, we do not use the plural *their* with the singular *everyone, everybody,* etc. When speaking, however, it has become acceptable to use *their* when *him or her* would sound awkward.

WRITTEN: *Everybody* can bring *his* or *her* own surfboard.

SPOKEN: *Everybody* can bring *their* own surfboard.

Example 3   Choose the correct personal pronoun to match the antecedent.
(a) *Something* left (their, its) footprints in the mud.

(b) *Neither* of the boys forgot (their, his) money.

(c) *Some* have paid (their, his or her) dues already.

(a) The antecedent *something* is singular, so we choose the singular personal pronoun **its**.

Something left **its** footprints in the mud.

(b) The antecedent *neither* is singular, so we choose the singular personal pronoun **his.**

Neither of the boys forgot **his** money.

(c) The antecedent *some* refers to people, who can be counted. We choose the plural personal pronoun **their.**

Some have paid **their** dues already.

✓ **Practice** For sentences a and b, write the indefinite pronoun and tell whether it is singular or plural.

  a. All of us are learning to serve the volleyball.

  b. Nobody serves the volleyball better than she.

For sentences c–e, choose the correct verb form to match the indefinite pronoun.

  c. *None* of the players (is, are) ready to play yet.

  d. *Some* of the players (is, are) ready to practice.

  e. *Each* of us (is, are) working hard.

For f–h, choose the correct personal pronoun and verb form to match the indefinite pronoun antecedent.

  f. *Something* (have, has) left (its, their) feathers here.

  g. *Many* surfers (waxes, wax) (his, her, their) surfboards every day.

  h. *None* of his poetry (sell, sells) for what (it, they) (is, are) worth.

For i and j, replace each blank with the correct vocabulary word from this lesson.

  i. Can people _____ a cruel dictatorship?

  j. Perhaps the _____ of the dictatorship will bring peace to the country.

More Practice Tell whether each indefinite pronoun is singular, plural, or either. (S = singular; P = plural; E = either)

1. both   **2.** most   **3.** anybody   **4.** neither

5. either   **6.** ones   **7.** everyone   **8.** few

9. everything   **10.** some   **11.** many   **12.** each

13. something   **14.** nothing   **15.** none   **16.** more

17. several   **18.** another   **19.** others   **20.** all

Review Set 83 Choose the correct word(s) to complete sentences 1–14.

1. (Salinity, Contrition, Bliss) is great happiness.
(82)

2. Where is the (atoll, culprit, lagoon) who stole the pizza?
(81)

3. A docent is a tour (bus, DVD, guide).
(80)

4. (*Quaint, Satiable, Dauntless*) means "heroic."
(79)

5. *Akin* means "(different, unrelated, similar)."
(35)

6. The word *committee* is a (compound, collective) noun.
(11)

7. The pronoun *they* is (nominative, objective, possessive)
(66, 69) case.

8. Is this address (their's, theirs)?
(72)

9. Nate used (less, fewer, fewest) brush strokes than I.
(56)

10. The pronoun *him* is (first, second, third) person (singular,
(64) plural).

11. The cowardly enemy (who, whom) subverted our
(77, 79) mission is hiding.

Think: ? | subverted | mission

12. A docent led (we, us) tourists around the old fort.
(78)

13. Everybody (is, are) looking for Badchek.
(83)

14. Nothing left (its, their) mark on the shiny surface.
(83)

15. Write the subordinating conjunction in this sentence:
(73)

Wherever Badchek goes, Mrs. Brite will track him.

16. Write the predicate nominative in the sentence below.
(51)

A surfboard is a long plank.

17. Rewrite the sentence below, using a comma to clarify the meaning.
(68)

Looking up Dana smiled.

18. Write the plural form of the singular noun *grandchild*.
(17, 22)

19. Use an appositive to combine the following two sentences to make one sentence.
(58)

The boll weevil ruined cotton crops in the South.

The boll weevil is an insect with a long snout.

20. Write the antecedent to the circled pronoun in the sentence below.
(62, 83)

Both had (their) umbrellas.

21. Write whether the circled pronoun in the sentence below is used as a subject or an object.
(66)

Will Officer Valiant and (she) save the day?

22. Write whether the clause below is dependent or independent.
(73)

some forgot their homework

23. Rewrite the following sentence, adding periods, commas, capital letters, and quotation marks as needed:
(76, 80)

mrs brite PI said badchek cannot escape for i have his name address and fingerprints

24. For the irregular verb *throw*, write the (a) present participle, (b) past tense, and (c) past participle.
(19, 65)

25. Write the objective case pronoun to complete the
(69) sentence below.

Badchek gave Officer Valiant and (her, she) a phony
address.

26. Rewrite the outline below, adding periods and capital
(26. 47) letters as needed.

i fun at the ocean
 a fishing
 b surfing

27. Rewrite the following letter, adding periods, commas and
(57, 67) capital letters as needed.

dear mrs brite PI
 obviously badchek does not live at 12 w palm avenue
juneau alaska that place does not exist

sincerely
officer valiant

28. Diagram the simple subject and simple predicate of each
(75) clause in the following compound sentence:

Along came the canines, but they were too late, for the
plane had left earlier.

Diagram each word of sentences 29–30.

29. Whom should the intrepid Officer Valiant arrest?
(77)

30. Badchek, a culpable coward, has written his nephew
(46, 58) seven bad checks.

Dictation or Journal Entry
Vocabulary:

Rapport is understanding and harmony in a relationship. Elle and Delbert get along well; they have good *rapport*.

Rapprochement is reestablishment of friendly relations. After an argument, Elle and Delbert sought *rapprochement*, for they wanted to be friends.

The word **italics** refers to a slightly slanted style of type that is used to indicate the titles of larger literary works or to bring special emphasis to a word or phrase in a sentence. The book title below is in italics.

The Wind in the Willows

When we handwrite material, or when the italic style of type is not available, we **underline** the word or words that would require italics in print.

<u>The Wind in the Willows</u>

Here are some of the main categories of words and phrases that should be italicized or underlined.

Longer Literary Works, Movies, CDs, etc.
We italicize or underline titles of books, magazines, newspapers, pamphlets, plays, book-length poems, television programs, movies, films, record albums, tapes, and CDs.

I used to watch TV shows like *Mister Rogers*.

Have you ever read <u>Old Yeller</u> by Fred Gipson?

Paintings and Sculptures
We italicize or underline the titles of painting, sculptures, and other works of art.

Rosa Bonheur painted *The Horse Fair* after studying horses and making many sketches.

The French artist Auguste Rodin made <u>The Thinker</u>, a statue of a man pondering some serious topic.

Ships, Planes, and Trains
We italicize or underline the names of ships, planes, and trains. (Words such as "The" and "U.S.S." are not treated as part of the vehicle's name.)

In California, we saw the *Queen Mary*, a huge ship docked in Long Beach.

They traveled by train on the <u>Coastal Express</u>.

Example 1 For sentences a–c, underline all the words that should be italicized or underlined.

(a) Charles Lindbergh's plane was called the Spirit of St. Louis.

(b) Leaves of Grass is a long poem by Walt Whitman.

(c) Blue Boy is a famous painting by Thomas Gainsborough.

Solution (a) We underline **Spirit of St. Louis** because it is the name of a plane. ("The" is not considered part of the name.)

(b) **Leaves of Grass** is a book-length poem.

(c) **Blue Boy** is a painting.

Words as Words We italicize or underline a word when the sentence calls attention to the word **as a word**.

What does the word *grandiloquent* mean?

She used *really* too often in her speech.

Squash can be a verb, but *tomato* cannot.

This is also true for numerals and lowercase letters.

Make each lowercase *b* the same height as the numeral *4*.

Foreign Words and Phrases We italicize or underline foreign words that are not used as part of everyday English language.

The French say *bonjour* in the morning.

The *beau monde* (high society) desire elegant decor.

Genus and Species Names We italicize or underline the scientific names for a genus, species, or subspecies.

Oxen, cows, and buffaloes are members of the genus *Bos*.

Bombina orientalis and *Litoria caerulea* are two species of frogs.

Example 2 For sentences a and b, underline each word that should be italicized or underlined.

(a) The verb in this sentence is are.

(b) Sans souci means "carefree" in French.

Solution (a) The sentence calls attention to the word **are**.

(b) **Sans souci** is a foreign phrase.

✓Practice For a and b, replace each blank with the correct vocabulary word from this lesson.

a. After the war, _____ occurred among the nations.

b. The teacher had good _____ with his students.

Write and underline the words that should be italicized in sentences c–g.

c. Time has been a popular magazine for decades.

d. This essay has too many little words like is.

e. The scientific name for oak tree is Quercus.

f. Spanish speakers use guapo for handsome.

g. I believe my brother sailed on the Betty Bee.

More Practice See "More Practice Lesson 84" in Student Workbook.

Review Set 84 Choose the correct word(s) to complete sentences 1–14.

1. To (conceal, encumber, subvert) is to destroy or corrupt.
(83)

2. A blissful student is (fretful, persnickety, happy).
(82)

3. *Culpable* means "deserving (praise, blame, rewards)."
(81)

4. A curator might oversee a(n) (museum, beach, ox).
(80)

5. One's relatives are one's (clamor, panacea, kin).
(35)

6. The sentence below is (declarative, interrogative, imperative, exclamatory).
(2)

The *Nina* logged at least 25,000 miles under the command of Christopher Columbus.

7. The pronoun *them* is (nominative, objective, possessive) case.
(66, 69)

8. (You're, Your) essay is interesting.
(72)

9. Of the two paragraphs, this one is the (better, best).
(56)

10. The pronoun *they* is (first, second, third) person
(64) (singular, plural).

11. The cowardly enemy, (who, whom) you know, remains
(77, 79) hidden.

Think: | you | know | ? |

12. Ben is humble, but Max is more humble than (he, him).
(78) ["is" omitted]

13. (Is, Are) everyone here?
(83)

14. (Has, Have) everyone finished (their, his or her)
(83) homework?

15. Write the subordinating conjunction in this sentence:
(73)
Ric and Mik have good rapport even though they are on opposing teams.

16. Write the interrogative pronoun in the sentence below.
(79)
What does she want?

17. Write and underline the words that should be italicized
(84) in the sentence below.

Spanish speakers greet people with buenos días.

18. Rewrite the word *palm*, circling the silent letter.
(28, 29)

19. Rewrite the following sentence, using commas to offset
(60) the nonessential appositive.

The island of Alcatraz once a federal prison lies in the middle of San Francisco Bay.

20. Write the antecedent to the circled pronoun in the
(62, 83) sentence below.

Neither had her library card.

21. Write the nominative case pronoun to complete the sentence below.
_(66)_

The most intuitive are Mrs. Brite and (him, he).

22. Write whether the word group below is a phrase or a clause.
_(36)_

with unfeigned contrition

23. Rewrite the following sentence, adding periods, commas, capital letters, and quotation marks as needed:
_(74, 80)_

officer valiant replied yes as soon as we catch badchek we shall send him to alcatraz

24. For the irregular verb _wear_, write the (a) present participle, (b) past tense, and (c) past participle.
_(19, 65)_

25. Which sentence is more polite? Write _A_ or _B_.
_(69)_
  A. Badchek has no rapport with me or his nephew.

  B. Badchek has no rapport with his nephew or me.

26. Rewrite the sentence below, adding capital letters, periods, commas, and quotation marks as needed.
_(67, 81)_

no i have not read a short story titled where the sheep went

27. Rewrite the following letter, adding periods, commas and capital letters as needed.
_(57, 67)_

dear officer valiant
    on friday february 3 2006 someone spotted badchek in columbus ohio
                    sincerely
                    mrs brite PI

28. Diagram the simple subject and simple predicate of each clause in the following compound sentence:
_(75)_

Next came the newscasters, for they wanted a good story, but Badchek had vanished.

Diagram each word of sentences 29–30.

29. Rapprochement is the reestablishment of friendly
(45, 51) relations.

30. Mrs. Brite, a dauntless investigator, shows Badchek and
(46, 58) other criminals her tenacity.

Irregular Verbs, Part 3

Dictation or Journal Entry
Vocabulary:
Pretentious means "arrogant, showy, or pompous." The *pretentious* billionaire wore flashy jewelry and looked down on common people.

Grandiloquent means "spoken pretentiously." The billionaire wearing flashy jewelry gave a *grandiloquent* account of his own accomplishments.

We have already learned that there are no rules for forming the past tense and past participle of irregular verbs. In this lesson, we will look at some additional irregular verbs.

Remember that we must memorize the principal parts of irregular verbs. To test yourself, cover the past and past participle forms, then try to write or say the past and past participle for each verb. Make a new list of the ones you miss, and work to memorize them.

VERB	PAST	PAST PARTICIPLE
beat	beat	(has) beaten
bite	bit	(has) bitten
bring	brought	(has) brought
build	built	(has) built
burst	burst	(has) burst
buy	bought	(has) bought
catch	caught	(has) caught
come	came	(has) come
cost	cost	(has) cost
dive	dove or dived	(has) dived
draw	drew	(has) drawn
drive	drove	(has) driven
eat	ate	(has) eaten
fall	fell	(has) fallen
feel	felt	(has) felt
fight	fought	(has) fought
find	found	(has) found
flee	fled	(has) fled
fly	flew	(has) flown
forget	forgot	(has) forgotten
forgive	forgave	(has) forgiven

Example 1 Write the past and past participle forms of each verb.

(a) beat   (b) bite   (c) build   (d) burst

Solution   (a) beat, **beat, (has) beaten**

(b) bite, **bit, (has) bitten**

(c) build, **built, (has) built**

(d) burst, **burst, (has) burst**

Example 2 Write the correct verb form for each sentence.

(a) Most of us (feeled, felt) sad when we said goodbye.

(b) I (fleed, fled) out the door with a lump in my throat.

(c) The last day had (come, came) too soon.

(d) It had (catched, caught) us by surprise.

Solution (a) Most of us **felt** sad when we said goodbye.

(b) I **fled** out the door with a lump in my throat.

(c) The last day had **come** too soon.

(d) It had **caught** us by surprise.

Errors to Avoid People sometimes treat a regular verb as if it were irregular. For example, the past tense of *drag* is *dragged*, not "drug." The past tense of *drown* is simply *drowned*, not "drownded." Avoid these errors by memorizing the irregular verbs and consulting a dictionary when in doubt. If the dictionary does not list the verb's principle parts, the verb is regular.

Practice For a–h, write the past and past participle form of each verb.

a. catch   **b.** come   **c.** cost   **d.** dive

e. drag   **f.** draw   **g.** drown   **h.** drive

For i–p, write the correct verb form for each sentence.

i. After I had (ate, eaten) the pie, he told me its ingredients.

j. Where did you say he (find, found) the recipe?

k. He (drived, drove) to the market.

l. The food must have (cost, costed) him twenty dollars.

m. I (forgave, forgived) him at last.

n. Marta has (catched, caught) five crayfish.

o. Thao (flied, flew) in a jet yesterday.

p. The temperature (fell, falled) as the sun went down.

For q and r, replace each blank with the correct vocabulary word from this lesson.

q. The pompous leader spoke in a _____ style, using many long words that few understood.

r. A _____ person is a show-off.

More Practice See "More Practice Lesson 85" in Student Workbook.

Review Set 85 Choose the correct word(s) to complete sentences 1–14.

1. (Subversion, Rapport, Redundancy) is understanding and
(84) harmony in a relationship.

2. (Subversion, Bliss, Salinity) is corruption or destruction.
(83)

3. *Blissful* means "full of great (fear, worry, happiness)."
(82)

4. A culprit is a(n) (innocent, guilty, blameless) one.
(81)

5. (*Dispensable, Indispensable, Akin*) means "related by
(35) blood, or of the same family."

6. The word *coaches* is a (plural, possessive) noun.
(13)

7. The pronoun *their* is (nominative, objective, possessive)
(69, 72) case.

8. My parakeet is blue; (her's, hers) is green.
(72)

9. Of the three paragraphs, this one is the (better, best).
(56)

10. The pronoun *them* is (first, second, third) person
(64) (singular, plural).

11. Do you know anyone (who, whom) gives grandiloquent
(77, 79) speeches?
Think: ____?____ | gives | speeches

12. Badchek left (we, us) detectives a clue.
(78)

13. Many have (come, came) to sketch this waterfall.
(85)

14. Several (has, have) sketched (their, his or her) friends in
(83) the foreground.

15. Write the subordinating conjunction in this sentence:
(73)
Until he arrests Badchek, Officer Valiant will not rest.

16. Write the interrogative pronoun in the sentence below.
(79)
Whose are the red mittens?

17. Write and underline the words that should be italicized
(84) in the sentence below.

Someday I shall read Rudyard Kipling's novel Kim.

18. Write the plural form of the singular noun *housefly*.
(17, 22)

19. Use an appositive to combine the following two
(58) sentences into one sentence.

The Gila monster is Arizona's biggest lizard.

The Gila monster is the only poisonous lizard in the
United States.

20. Write whether the sentence below is simple or compound.
(75)

The ship *Halve Maen* explored parts of North America,
and the *Wawona* carried lumber in Puget Sound.

21. Write whether the circled pronoun in the sentence below
(64) is used as a subject or an object.

Mrs. Brite and (he) are the most intuitive.

22. From the following sentence, write each prepositional
(44) phrase, circling the object of each preposition.

The *Wawona* was built in California's Humboldt Bay by
H.D. Bendixsen, a prominent shipbuilder.

23.
(76, 80) Rewrite the following sentence, adding periods, commas, capital letters, and quotation marks as needed:

mrs brite PI said we have not caught him but we shall before summer

24.
(19, 85) For the irregular verb *forgive*, write the (a) present participle, (b) past tense, and (c) past participle.

25.
(69) Write the objective case pronoun to complete the sentence below.

Badchek has no rapport with his nephew or (me, I).

26.
(67, 81) Rewrite the sentence below, adding capital letters, periods, commas, and quotation marks as needed.

yes i know the song i've been working on the railroad

27.
(57, 67) Rewrite the following letter, adding periods, commas, and capital letters as needed.

my dear ms hoo
> get plenty of rest exercise and fresh air
> > warm regards
> > katy diddit RN

28.
(75) Diagram the simple subject and simple predicate of each clause in the following compound sentence:

Into the room bursts Badchek, yet few recognize him, for he has grown a beard.

Diagram each word of sentences 29–30.

29.
(45, 51) Has Badchek become the caretaker of Mr. Knothead's riches?

30.
(46, 58) Did the pretentious billionaire, Mr. Knothead, assign Badchek a new task of tremendous importance?

LESSON 86

Irregular Verbs, Part 4

Dictation or Journal Entry
Vocabulary:
A *colossus* is an extremely large structure, statue, or person. Paul Bunyan was a *colossus*; he was bigger than life.

Colossal means "extremely large." Paul Bunyan had a *colossal* blue ox named Babe.

In this lesson, we will look at more irregular verbs, whose principal parts we must memorize. To test yourself, cover the past and past participle forms, then try to write or say the past and past participle for each verb. Make a new list of the ones you miss, and work to memorize them.

VERB	PAST	PAST PARTICIPLE
get	got	(has) gotten
give	gave	(has) given
go	went	(has) gone
hang (execute)	hanged	(has) hanged
hang (suspend)	hung	(has) hung
hide	hid	(has) hidden or hid
hold	held	(has) held
keep	kept	(has) kept
lay (place)	laid	(has) laid
lead	led	(has) led
lend	lent	(has) lent
lie (recline)	lay	(has) lain
lie (deceive)	lied	(has) lied
lose	lost	(has) lost
make	made	(has) made
mistake	mistook	(has) mistaken
put	put	(has) put
ride	rode	(has) ridden
rise	rose	(has) risen
run	ran	(has) run
see	saw	(has) seen
sell	sold	(has) sold

Example 1 Write the past and past participle forms of each verb.

(a) see   (b) ride   (c) go   (d) give   (e) make

Solution (a) see, **saw, (has) seen**

(b) ride, **rode, (has) ridden**

Grammar and Writing 5   458   **Student Edition**
Lesson 86

(c) go, **went, (has) gone**

(d) give, **gave, (has) given**

(e) make, **made, (has) made**

Example 2 Write the correct verb form for each sentence.
(a) The sun (rised, rose) at six a.m.

(b) Oh dear, I've (losed, lost) my homework again!

(c) Yesterday I (run, ran) three miles.

Solution (a) The sun **rose** at six a.m.

(b) Oh dear, I've **lost** my homework again!

(c) Yesterday I **ran** three miles.

Practice For a–h, write the past and past participle form of each verb.
a. hide   **b.** hold   **c.** lay   **d.** lead

e. lend   **f.** mistake   **g.** put   **h.** sell

For i–l, write the correct verb form for each sentence.
i. Willy (hided, hid) the gift under the sofa.

j. Grandpa (held, holded) the fussy baby last night.

k. I had (laid, lain) my homework on the table.

l. That sheep has (leaded, led) the others astray.

For m and n, replace each blank with the correct vocabulary word from this lesson.
m. A _____ statue overshadowed the harbor and connected two small islands.

n. The statue, a _____, stood taller than a hundred feet.

More Practice See "More Practice Lesson 86" in Student Workbook.

Choose the correct word(s) to complete sentences 1–14.

1. (*Imprudent, Bovine, Pretentious*) means "arrogant, showy,
(85) or pompous."

2. (Subversion, Rapprochement, Humiliation) leads to good
(84) rapport.

3. *Subversion* and *amelioration* are (similar, different) in
(83) meaning.

4. Bliss is great (size, strength, happiness).
(82)

5. (*Proclamation, Asset, Kin*) means "one's relatives."
(35)

6. The word *rapport* is a(n) (abstract, concrete) noun.
(11)

7. The pronoun *we* is (nominative, objective, possessive)
(66, 69) case.

8. (Who's, Whose) shoes are these?
(79)

9. Amy has (less, fewer) parakeets than finches.
(56)

10. The pronoun *we* is (first, second, third) person (singular,
(64) plural).

11. (Who, Whom) are you calling?
(77, 79)

Think:

you	are calling	?

12. Mr. Knothead is almost as silly as (me, I). ["am" omitted]
(78)

13. Some have (went, gone) to Mount Rushmore today.
(86)

14. Someone (have, has) laid (their, his or her) lunch on my
(83) desk.

15. Write the two subordinating conjunctions in the sentence
(73) below.

Mr. Knothead shrugs his shoulders as if he doesn't care
that Badchek is a thief.

16. Write the predicate adjective in the sentence below.
(54)

Do you feel optimistic?

17. Write and underline the words that should be italicized in the sentence below.
₍₈₄₎

We shall name our sailing vessel Seafoam Joy.

18. Use a dictionary: (a) The word *mime* is what part of speech? (b) Write its pronunciation. (c) Write its etymology.
_(27, 30)

19. Rewrite the following sentence, using commas to offset the nonessential appositive.
₍₆₀₎

Nashville the capital of Tennessee is famous for country music.

20. Add suffixes:
_(33, 34)

(a) messy + est   (b) thin + er

21. Write the nominative case pronoun to complete the sentence below.
₍₆₄₎

The culprits are Badchek and (they, them).

22. Write whether the following is a phrase or a clause.
₍₃₆₎

in warm, humid weather

23. Rewrite the following sentence, adding periods, commas, capital letters, and quotation marks as needed:
_(74, 80)

mrs brite PI said although a deceptive malicious witness has given me false reports i shall still find the culprit

24. For the irregular verb *drive*, write the (a) present participle, (b) past tense, and (c) past participle.
_(19, 85)

25. Write the objective case pronoun to complete the sentence below.
₍₆₉₎

A friend drove Ms. Hoo and (me, I) to the train station.

26. Rewrite the sentence below, adding capital letters, periods, commas, and quotation marks as needed.
_(67, 81)

in my opinion the short story should be titled badchek on the loose

27. Rewrite the following letter, adding periods, commas and
(57, 67) capital letters as needed.

> my dear ms hoo
>> you may see dr rivas on monday february 6
>>> warm regards
>>> katy diddit RN

28. Diagram the simple subject and simple predicate of each
(75) clause in the following compound sentence:

Jake has ridden his horse all day, so he is tired, but he
must milk the cows before bedtime.

Diagram each word of sentences 29–30.

29. Was Mr. Knothead's grandiloquent speech a joke?
(45, 51)

30. Has Mr. Knothead, the foolish billionaire, given Badchek
(46, 58) a key to the safe?

Irregular Verbs, Part 5

Dictation or Journal Entry
Vocabulary:
To *coerce* is to force. Will bandits *coerce* the bank teller to hand over the money?

Coercion is the use of force. Bandits might take the money by *coercion*.

In this lesson, we will look at one last group of irregular verbs, whose principal parts we must memorize. To test yourself, cover the past and past participle forms, then try to write or say the past and past participle for each verb. Make a new list of the ones you miss, and memorize them.

VERB	PAST	PAST PARTICIPLE
set	set	(has) set
shake	shook	(has) shaken
shine (light)	shone	(has) shone
shine (polish)	shined	(has) shined
shut	shut	(has) shut
sit	sat	(has) sat
slay	slew	(has) slain
sleep	slept	(has) slept
spring	sprang or sprung	(has) sprung
stand	stood	(has) stood
strive	strove	(has) striven
swim	swam	(has) swum
swing	swung	(has) swung
take	took	(has) taken
teach	taught	(has) taught

tell	told	(has) told
think	thought	(has) thought
wake	woke	(has) woken
weave	wove	(has) woven
wring	wrung	(has) wrung
write	wrote	(has) written

Example 1 Write the past and past participle forms of each verb.
(a) write   (b) think   (c) swim   (d) sleep   (e) stand

Solution (a) write, **wrote, (has) written**

(b) think, **thought, (has) thought**

(c) swim, **swam, (has) swum**

(d) sleep, **slept, (has) slept**

(e) stand, **stood, (has) stood**

Example 2 Write the correct verb form for each sentence.
(a) By the end of the bath, Fido had (shook, shaken) water all over the place!

(b) Salina has (wove, woven) some pretty baskets.

(c) She (swang, swung) the bat for strike two.

Solution (a) By the end of the bath, Fido had **shaken** water all over the place!

(b) Salina has **woven** some pretty baskets.

(c) She **swung** the bat for strike two.

✓**Practice** For a–h, write the past and past participle form of each verb.
a. take   **b.** set   **c.** teach   **d.** tell

e. wake   **f.** spring   **g.** strive   **h.** shut

For i–p, write the correct verb form for each sentence.

   i. Have you ever (wrote, written) a song?

   j. Mr. Sosa (sleeped, slept) well after his work was done.

   k. Have you (thought, thinked) about your future?

   l. Has Ms. Hoo ever (teached, taught) Spanish?

  m. He (telled, told) me the secret.

   n. Have you ever (woken, woke) before dawn?

   o. Mr. Otar (sitted, sat) in the shade.

   p. The door (shutted, shut) suddenly.

For q and r, replace each blank with the correct vocabulary word from this lesson.

   q. Must we _____ the dog to swallow its bad-tasting medicine?

   r. Can we accomplish this task by _____?

More Practice   See "More Practice Lesson 87" in Student Workbook.

Review Set 87   Choose the correct word(s) to complete sentences 1–14.

   1. A(n) (arroyo, tundra, colossus) is an extremely large
   ⁽⁸⁶⁾ structure, statue, or person.

   2. A grandiloquent speech is (humble, contrite,
   ⁽⁸⁵⁾ pretentious).

   3. Rapport is (discord, disharmony, understanding) in a
   ⁽⁸⁴⁾ relationship.

   4. (*Abundant, Dispensable, Avaricious*) means "greedy."
   ⁽³⁶⁾

   5. Subversion is (amelioration, benevolence, destruction).
   ⁽⁸³⁾

   6. The word *truck driver* is a (compound, collective) noun.
   ⁽¹³⁾

   7. The pronoun *us* is (nominative, objective, possessive)
   ^(66, 69) case.

8. These tools are (their's, theirs).
(72)

9. Yoli is the (better, best) of the two skaters.
(56)

10. The pronoun *I* is (first, second, third) person (singular, plural).
(64)

11. Dr. Kim, (who, whom) I called yesterday, is on vacation.
(77, 79)

Think:

I	called	?

12. I think (we, us) students should plan a field trip.
(78)

13. Yesterday afternoon, I (lied, lay) down and (sleeped, slept) for an hour.
(86, 87)

14. Each (have, has) (their, his or her) concert ticket.
(83)

15. Write the two subordinating conjunctions in the sentence below.
(73)

You may dry the dishes as I wash them if you don't mind.

16. Write whether the following is a complete sentence, a sentence fragment, or a run-on sentence.
(23)

National parks protect some of the most scenic areas in the United States.

17. Write the sentence below, adding a comma to clarify the meaning.
(68)

After the show time stood still.

18. Write the plural form of the singular noun *dropperful*.
(17, 22)

19. Use an appositive to combine the following two sentences into one sentence.
(58)

South Dakota is the Mount Rushmore state.

South Dakota has a large area of forest called the Black Hills.

20. Write the antecedent to the pronoun circled below.
(62)

Bozo likes Fifi even though (he) hardly knows her.

21.
(64)
Write whether the circled pronoun in the sentence below is used as a subject or an object.

Bozo gazes at (her) as she passes.

22.
(44)
From the following sentence, write each prepositional phrase, circling the object of each preposition.

Across the field, under the fence, and over the hill scampered the jackrabbit.

23.
(74, 80)
Rewrite the following sentence, adding periods, commas, capital letters, and quotation marks as needed:

katy diddit RN said i wrote to ms hoo but she has not written back

24.
(19, 85)
For the irregular verb *bring*, write the (a) present participle, (b) past tense, and (c) past participle.

25.
(69)
Which sentence is more polite? Write *A* or *B*.

A. A friend drove me and her to the station.

B. A friend drove her and me to the station.

26.
(67, 81)
Rewrite the sentence below, adding capital letters, periods, commas, and quotation marks as needed.

that song i believe is called over the waves

27.
(57, 67)
Rewrite the following letter, adding periods, commas, and capital letters as needed.

dear grandmother
    i have striven to do my best thank you for helping me
                 love
                 benito

28.
(75)
Diagram the simple subject and simple predicate of each clause in the following compound sentence:

Into the arena prances Fifi, and Bozo is with her, for he has become her protector.

Diagram each word of sentences 29–30.

29. Mr. Knothead's trust in Badchek is a colossal mistake.
(45, 51)

30. Ms. Hoo, the best teacher in the West, tosses Fifi and him
(46, 58) some crunchy biscuits.

The Exclamation Mark
• The Question Mark

Dictation or Journal Entry

Vocabulary:

Complacent means "content and self-satisfied." After scoring two goals, Dagny became *complacent* and did not try as hard during the rest of the soccer game.

Complacency is contentment and self-satisfaction. Because of her *complacency*, Dagny did not score any more goals in the soccer game.

Almost every sentence ends with one of three punctuation marks. The period, the exclamation mark, and the question mark are called final punctuation marks.

Exclamation Mark We use an **exclamation mark** after an exclamatory sentence (a sentence showing strong emotion).

It was a man-eating shark!

We can also use an exclamation mark after a word or phrase showing strong emotion. We call this an **interjection**.

Hooray! Well done! Oh, no!

Careful writers try to limit their use of exclamation marks. Think of it as shouting. Sometimes shouting is appropriate, but someone who shouts all the time is soon ignored. Use exclamation marks sparingly.

Question Mark We place a **question mark** at the end of an interrogative sentence (one that asks a question).

What is the collie's name?

Remember that a sentence can contain a questioning phrase without being an interrogative sentence.

I wonder what the collie's name is.

With Quotation Marks When using exclamation marks and question marks with quotation marks, we must decide whether to place the final punctuation mark *inside* or *outside* the quotation marks. We do this by determining if the final punctuation mark punctuates the whole sentence or just the part in quotation marks.

In the sentence below, only the words in quotation marks ask a question. The question mark punctuates only the direct quotation, so it goes *inside* the quotation marks.

Someone asked, "Where have you been?"

In the next sentence, the question mark punctuates the whole sentence, so it goes *outside* the quotation marks:

Have they sung "America"?

Example 1 Rewrite sentences a–d, inserting exclamation or question marks as needed.

(a) How did the Grand Canyon form

(b) What a surprise

(c) He exclaimed, "There you are"

(d) Can you sing the high notes of "The Star Spangled Banner"

Solution (a) **How did the Grand Canyon form?** (interrogative sentence)

(b) **What a surprise!** (exclamatory sentence)

(c) The exclamation mark goes inside the quotation marks because it punctuates only the direct quotation.

He exclaimed, "There you are!"

(d) The question mark goes outside the quotation marks because it punctuates the entire sentence.

Can you sing the high notes of "The Star Spangled Banner"?

✓**Practice** Rewrite sentences a–d, placing exclamation marks or question marks where they are needed.

a. Wow That sunset is spectacular

b. Do you understand Greek

c. Who painted *Blue Boy*

d. I know It's Thomas Gainsborough

For e and f, replace each blank with the correct vocabulary word from this lesson.

e. The artist's _____ kept him from doing his best work.

f. After some success, the artist became _____, no longer striving for excellence.

✓ **Review Set 88**
Choose the correct word(s) to complete sentences 1–14.

1. To (feign, ameliorate, coerce) is to force.
(87)

2. A colossal pyramid is extremely (unusual, imprudent, large).
(86)

3. *Pretentious* means "(humble, contrite, showy)."
(85)

4. Rapprochement is the (subversion, reestablishment, destruction) of friendly relations.
(84)

5. *Avaricious* means "(related, generous, greedy)."
(36)

6. The sentence below is (declarative, interrogative, imperative, exclamatory).
(2)

Hang your coat up, please.

7. The pronoun *me* is (nominative, objective, possessive) case.
(66, 69)

8. (Who, Whom) called me?
(79)

9. Yoli is the (better, best) of the two skaters.
(56)

10. The pronoun *it* is (first, second, third) person (singular, plural).
(64)

11. Dr. Kim, (who, whom) you have met, will be here soon.
(77, 79)

| Think: | you | have met | ? |

12. Can you talk as fast as (her, she)? ["can" omitted]
(78)

13. Bill has (took, taken) many photos and (hanged, hung) them on the wall.
(86, 87)

14. Both (have, has) (their, his or her) tickets.
(83)

15. Write the two subordinating conjunctions in the sentence
(73) below.

While you wash the dishes, I shall mop the floor so that
we can surprise Mom.

16. Write the predicate adjective in the sentence below.
(54)

The clouds appear luminous.

17. Write and underline the words that should be italicized
(84) in the sentence below.

Leo tried to use the word complacent in a sentence.

18. Rewrite the word *weigh*, circling the silent letters.
(28, 29)

19. Rewrite the sentence below, using commas to offset the
(60) nonessential appositive.

Dagny a complacent player seems unmotivated now.

20. Write whether the sentence below is simple or
(75) compound.

The jackrabbit leaps over small shrubs, and the hound
follows in pursuit.

21. Write the nominative case pronoun to complete the
(64) sentence below.

Bozo and (she, her) share the biscuits.

22. Write whether the following is a phrase or a clause.
(36)

with prudence and frugality

23. Rewrite the following sentence, adding capital letters and
(80, 88) punctuation marks as needed:

chloe asked have you heard from ms hoo katy

24. For the irregular verb *buy*, write the (a) present participle,
(19, 85) (b) past tense, and (c) past participle.

25. Write the objective case pronoun to complete the
(69) sentence below.

Please come with Shane and (I, me).

26. Rewrite the sentence below, adding capital letters and
(81, 88) punctuation marks as needed.

what a silly story it should be titled mr. knothead's colossal mistake

27. Rewrite the following letter, adding capital letters and
(57, 67) punctuation marks as needed.

dear benito
     have you seen my old shoes they are made out of string straw and wood

                                        love
                                        grandpa

28. Diagram the simple subject and simple predicate of each
(75) clause in the following compound sentence:

Butch has been growling, so Fifi has been cowering, yet Bozo will save her!

Diagram each word of sentences 29–30.

29. Has Mr. Knothead been imprudent?
(45, 54)

30. Bozo, a friendly dog with a mission, shows Butch and
(46, 58) them his valor.

LESSON 89

Subject-Verb Agreement, Part 1

Dictation or Journal Entry

Vocabulary:

To *languish* is to grow weak or feeble. People *languish* without proper nutrition.

Languid means "weak, lacking energy or interest." A *languid* team member dozes while the others work.

Just as a pronoun must agree with its antecedent, a verb must agree with the subject of the sentence in **person** and **number**.

Person   Verbs and personal pronouns are the only parts of speech that change their form to show person (point of view).

When we learned about the irregular verbs *be*, *have*, and *do* in Lesson 18, we used a chart similar to the one below. Here we show two regular verbs (*work* and *wish*) and one irregular verb (*be*) in the first, second, and third person. (Most regular verbs form the third person singular by adding *-s* or *-es*. The irregular verbs must be memorized.)

	SINGULAR	PLURAL
1ST PERSON	**I** work, wish, am	**we** work, wish, are
2ND PERSON	**you** work, wish, are	**you** work, wish, are
3RD PERSON	**he** works, wishes, is	**they** work, wish, are

If the subject of a sentence is in the **first person** (I, we), the verb must also be in the first person:

> *I* work hard.   *We* wish him luck.

> *I* am optimistic.   *We* are frugal.

If the subject of a sentence is in the **second person** (you), the verb must also be in the second person:

> *You* work hard.

If the subject of a sentence is in the **third person** (he, she, it, or any noun), the verb must also be in the third person:

> *He* walks two miles.   *They* walk two miles.

> *Max* wishes him luck.   *People* wish him luck.

> The *cloud* is grey.   The *clouds* are grey.

Number If the subject of a sentence is **singular**, the verb must also be singular:

I <u>work</u> hard.

He <u>wishes</u> me luck.

If the subject of a sentence is **plural**, the verb must also be plural:

We <u>work</u> hard.

They <u>wish</u> me luck.

Notice that the pronoun *you* always takes a plural verb, even when it is singular.

You <u>are</u> indispensable, Norma.

You <u>are</u> both outstanding artists.

Compound Subjects Sometimes it is difficult to determine if the subject of a sentence is singular or plural.

Compound subjects joined by *and* are considered plural and require a plural verb.

Nan and *Bert* <u>admire</u> your valor.

The *boys* and their *father* <u>restore</u> old cars.

Compound subjects joined by *or, nor, either/or,* or *neither/nor* can be singular or plural, depending on the subjects themselves.

If both subjects are singular, we use a singular verb.

Neither *Cindy* nor *Sue* <u>is</u> ready.

Either *Dan* or *Quan* <u>teaches</u> tennis.

If both subjects are plural, we use a plural verb.

Neither the *apples* nor the *cherries* <u>look</u> ripe.

My *sisters* or *brothers* <u>know</u> my nickname.

If one subject is singular and the other is plural, the verb should agree with the part of the subject it is closest to.

Neither the *cat* nor the *dogs* <u>are eating</u> today.

Either the *guitars* or the *piano* <u>sounds</u> out of tune.

Example Choose the correct verb form for each sentence.

(a) My brothers-in-law (is, are) firefighters.

(b) Either Wilbur or Mabel (has, have) the key.

(c) Neither the girls nor the boys (wants, want) homework.

(d) Eric or his sisters (sweep, sweeps) the walk daily.

Solution (a) The subject "brothers-in-law" is plural, so we use the plural verb form: My brothers-in-law **are** firefighters.

(b) When compound singular subjects are joined by *either/or*, we use the singular verb form: Either Wilbur or Mabel **has** the key.

(c) Compound plural subjects joined by *neither/nor* require the plural verb form: Neither the girls nor the boys **want** homework.

(d) When compound subjects are joined by *or,* the verb agrees with the part of the subject it is closest to: Eric or his sisters **sweep** the walk daily.

✓ Practice For a–f, choose the correct verb form for each sentence.

a. Miss Davis (was, were) contrite after the feud.

b. The Davises (was, were) were sorry they had argued.

c. Omar and he (raise, raises) chickens.

d. The hamster or the pig (make, makes) a good pet.

e. Hamsters or pigs (make, makes) good pets.

f. Neither the horses nor the cow (has, have) been fed.

For g and h, replace each blank with the correct vocabulary word from this lesson.

g. The _____ ditch digger moved slowly and did not accomplish much today.

h. Without food and water, ditch diggers will _____.

More Practice Choose the correct verb form for each sentence.

1. Neither the bass nor the drums (sound, sounds) right.

2. Either the coach or the players (is, are) stalling.

3. Salmon and trout (swim, swims) in rivers.

4. The sparrow and the finch (is, are) small birds.

5. Either a pigeon or a crow (has, have) eaten my sandwich!

6. A mouse and a rat (was, were) looking for food.

7. Either the jay or the squirrels (has, have) eaten the last peanut.

8. Neither the cats nor the dog (see, sees) the squirrel.

✓

Review Set 89 Choose the correct word(s) to complete sentences 1–15.

1. (*Pertinent, Irrelevant, Complacent*) means "content and
   (88) self-satisfied."

2. (Pessimism, Rapprochement, Coercion) is the use of
   (87) force.

3. *Colossal* means "extremely (hot, cold, large, small)."
   (86)

4. Rapprochement is the (subversion, reestablishment,
   (85) destruction) of friendly relations.

5. (*Avocado, Aviary, Avarice*) is an abstract noun meaning
   (36) "greed."

6. The word *coach's* is a (plural, possessive) noun.
   (13)

7. The pronoun *mine* is (nominative, objective, possessive)
   (66, 69) case.

8. (There, Their) cat is fluffy; (yours, your's) is sleek.
   (72)

9. Yoli has broken (less, fewer) bones than Max.
   (56)

10. The pronoun *its* is (first, second, third) person (singular,
    (64) plural).

11. Yoli, (who, whom) lives in Baltimore, jogs in the park
(77, 79) every day.

      Think: ? | lives

12. Please call (we, us) workers if you need help.
(78)

13. The knight has (keeped, kept) his promise; he has (slew,
(86, 87) slain) the dragon.

14. Neither (have, has) (their, his or her) tickets.
(83)

15. Neither Bozo nor Fifi (like, likes) Butch.
(89)

16. Write the predicate nominative in the sentence below.
(51)

Will you become a linguist someday?

17. Write and underline the words that should be italicized
(84) in the sentence below.

The artist was Monet, and the painting is called Pool of
Waterlilies.

18. Write the plural form of the singular noun *paintbrush*.
(17, 22)

19. Use an appositive to combine the following two
(60) sentences into one sentence.

Tina spends three hours a day training her dog.

Tina is Butch's owner.

20. Add suffixes:
(33, 34)

    (a) worry + some   (b) funny + er

21. Write whether the circled pronoun in the sentence below
(69) is used as a subject or an object.

Although Bozo loves biscuits, he shares (them).

22. Write whether the clause below is dependent or
(73) independent.

plants languish without sunlight

23. Rewrite the following, adding capital letters and
(80, 88) punctuation marks as needed:

leo shouted help since you are taller than i can you reach that apple

24. For the irregular verb *draw*, write the (a) present
(19, 85) participle, (b) past tense, and (c) past participle.

25. Write the objective case pronoun to complete the
(69) sentence below.

Please give Fifi and (he, him) some flea soap.

26. Rewrite the sentence below, adding capital letters and
(67, 81) punctuation marks as needed.

that song i think is called little bunny fufu

27. Rewrite the following letter, adding capital letters and
(63, 88) punctuation marks as needed.

dear tina

why is your dog so crabby have you taught him no manners

with concern
cousin juan

28. Write the two subordinating conjunctions in the sentence
(73) below.

Although it is late, we shall work until we finish.

Diagram each word of sentences 29–30.

29. Has the imprudent Mr. Knothead become a victim of
(45, 51) Badchek's criminal behavior?

30. Does Butch, a crabby dog without manners, give Fifi and
(46, 58) him a rude snarl?

LESSON 90

Subject-Verb Agreement, Part 2

> **Dictation or Journal Entry**
>
> **Vocabulary:**
> *Innocuous* means "harmless and innocent." His comment was *innocuous;* it did not hurt my feelings.
>
> *Noxious* means "harmful and injurious." Breathing *noxious* fumes made her cough.

Problems with subject-verb agreement occur when it is difficult to identify the subject of the sentence. Until we do that, we cannot determine whether it is singular or plural.

Words Between the Subject and Verb

Words that come between the subject and the verb must not distract us. Be aware of prepositional phrases, appositives, and other words that might be mistaken for the subject of the sentence. Diagramming the simple subject and simple predicate helps us to determine which verb form to use.

The letter (to my cousins) (was, were) lost in the mail.

letter	was (not were)

Every one (of you) (knows, know) your times tables.

one	knows (not know)

Adrian, who lives in the mountains, (is, are) here.

Adrian	is (not are)

Example 1 Diagram the simple subject and simple predicate in order to show the correct verb form for each sentence.

(a) A box of pencils (was, were) on her desk.

(b) The arrival of my grandparents (give, gives) me joy.

(c) The cobra, like many snakes, (is, are) dangerous.

(d) The noise of the parrots (disturb, disturbs) me.

Solution   (a) A box of pencils **was** on her desk.

$$\underline{\text{box} \mid \text{was}}$$

(b) The arrival of my grandparents **gives** me joy.

$$\underline{\text{arrival} \mid \text{gives}}$$

(c) The cobra, like many snakes, **is** dangerous.

$$\underline{\text{cobra} \mid \text{is}}$$

(d) The noise of the parrots **disturbs** me.

$$\underline{\text{noise} \mid \text{disturbs}}$$

Reversed Subject-Verb Order

If the subject follows the verb, we can better identify the subject by diagramming:

Around the corner (is, are) my aunt's house.

$$\underline{\text{house} \mid \text{is}}$$

There on the porch (was, were) the empty paint buckets.

$$\underline{\text{buckets} \mid \text{were}}$$

Here (comes, come) the Morgan horses.

$$\underline{\text{horses} \mid \text{come}}$$

There (is, are) many fleas on that dog.

$$\underline{\text{fleas} \mid \text{are}}$$

There (was, were) some slow, plodding horses in the parade.

$$\underline{\text{horses} \mid \text{were}}$$

Example 2   Diagram the simple subject and simple predicate in order to show the correct verb form for each sentence.

  (a) There (is, are) tall, skinny palm trees near the hotel.

  (b) In the shadows (sit, sits) an orange-and-white calico cat.

  (c) There (was, were) different colors of granite in the area.

  (d) First in the relay races (was, were) our school!

Solution   (a) There **are** tall, skinny palm trees near the hotel.

  (b) In the shadows **sits** an orange-and-white calico cat.

cat	sits

  (c) There **were** different colors of granite in the area.

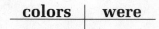

  (d) First in the relay races **was** our school!

school	was

✓ **Practice**   Diagram the simple subject and simple predicate in order to determine the correct verb form for sentences a–e.

  a. In the scrapbook (was, were) pictures of my mother.

  b. On the road to the small town (was, were) two gas stations.

  c. Here (is, are) the more practical kinds of fabric.

  d. There (goes, go) the leader of the rabble-rousers.

  e. Down the road (come, comes) trucks full of cement.

For f and g, replace each blank with the correct vocabulary word from this lesson.

  f. Unfortunately, _____ gases in the chemistry lab made some people sick.

  g. This chemical is _____; it will not harm you.

More Practice Choose the correct verb form for each sentence.

  1. A bowl of cherries (sit, sits) on the table.

  2. That sack of onions (weigh, weighs) ten pounds.

  3. A busload of students (is, are) coming.

  4. There (go, goes) the canoes!

  5. There (is, are) many kinds of snakes.

  6. The sound of many trumpets (break, breaks) the silence.

  7. The aroma of muffins in the oven (make, makes) me hungry.

  8. That man with the bushy eyebrows (look, looks) stern.

Review Set 90 Choose the correct word(s) to complete sentences 1–15.

  1. To (ameliorate, tolerate, languish) is to grow weak or
  (89) feeble.

  2. Complacency is self-satisfaction and (subversion,
  (88) rapprochement, contentment).

  3. Coercion is the use of (soap, water, force).
  (87)

  4. A colossus is an extremely (small, thin, large) structure,
  (86) statue, or person.

  5. An encumbrance is a hindrance or (meridian, delta,
  (37) burden).

  6. A basket of muffins (sell, sells) for ten dollars.
  (90)

  7. The word *meteorite* is a(n) (abstract, concrete) noun.
  (11)

8. (Who's, Whose) are those tools?
(79)

9. Of all the skaters, Yoli has broken the (least, less, fewer,
(56) fewest) bones.

10. The pronoun *our* is (first, second, third) person (singular,
(64) plural).

11. Pac and Theo, (who, whom) you mentioned, drove to St.
(77, 79) Paul.

Think:

you	mentioned	?

12. The ducks are loud, but the goose is louder than (them,
(78) they). ["are" omitted]

13. The sun has (rose, risen), and Jasper has (woke, woken).
(86, 87)

14. Everything (has, have) (their, its) place.
(83)

15. Neither Bozo nor his friends (like, likes) Butch.
(89)

16. Write whether the following is a complete sentence, a
(23) sentence fragment, or a run-on sentence:

Pretending not to notice the bathing bird.

17. Rewrite the sentence below, using a comma to clarify the
(68) meaning.

With this Olga can repair the chair.

18. Use a dictionary: (a) The word *dicast* is what part of
(27, 30) speech? (b) Write its pronunciation. (c) Write its
etymology.

19. Rewrite the following sentence, using commas to offset
(58) the nonessential appositive.

Frankfort the capital of Kentucky lies along the Kentucky
River.

20. Write the antecedent to the circled pronoun in the
(62) sentence below.

Bozo likes the biscuits, but he shares them.

Grammar and Writing 5

484

21. Write the nominative case pronoun to complete the
(64) sentence below.

Badchek's worst foes are Officer Valiant and (her, she).

22. From the following sentence, write each prepositional
(44) phrase, circling the object of each preposition.

During the night, a hard-working ant inches toward my
muffins.

23. Rewrite the following, adding capital letters and
(80, 88) punctuation marks as needed:

lucy cries watch out a branch has broken and it might fall
on you

24. For the irregular verb *beat*, write the (a) present
(19, 85) participle, (b) past tense, and (c) past participle.

25. Write the objective case pronoun to complete the
(69) sentence below.

Let's walk Bozo and (she, her) around the block.

26. Rewrite the sentence below, adding capital letters and
(67, 81) punctuation marks as needed.

as i remember ms hoo wrote an article titled my students'
lovable pets

27. Rewrite the following letter, adding capital letters and
(57, 67) punctuation marks as needed.

dear juan
    i have only had butch for two months three days one
hour and five minutes please be patient with me
                  your cousin
                  tina

28. Write the two subordinating conjunctions in the sentence
(73) below.

Though the soil is rocky and hard, Max is planting tulip
bulbs wherever he can.

Diagram each word of sentences 29–30.

29. Butch's snarls are scary but innocuous.
(45, 54)

30. Tina, an industrious trainer, will be giving Butch several
(46, 58) lessons on courtesy in public places.

LESSON 91

Subject-Verb Agreement, Part 3

> **Dictation or Journal Entry**
> **Vocabulary:**
> To *obfuscate* is to confuse or make unclear. The newspaper article actually *obfuscated* the situation surrounding the murder case.
>
> *Obfuscation* is confusion or muddling. The suspect's *obfuscation* of the facts prevented anyone from knowing the truth.

Indefinite Pronouns We remember that some indefinite pronouns are singular, some are plural, and some can be either. If an indefinite pronoun is the subject of a sentence, the verb must agree with it in number. (See Lesson 83 for the complete list of indefinite pronouns.)

SINGULAR	*Everybody* is welcome.
PLURAL	*Few* are poisonous.
SINGULAR	*Some* was gone.
PLURAL	*Some* were asleep.

Prepositional Phrases Sometimes people are confused when a prepositional phrase comes between the subject and predicate. Diagramming the simple subject and simple predicate helps us to see which verb is correct.

Neither of his friends (lives, live) nearby.

Neither	lives

Each of you (has, have) talents.

Each	has

Many on the team (was, were) complacent.

Many	were

Several on the shelf (look, looks) ancient.

Several	look

Example 1 Choose the correct verb form for each sentence.

(a) Somebody (were, was) here.

(b) Few (have, has) such courage.

(c) Nobody in these classes (know, knows) my nickname.

Solution (a) The indefinite pronoun *somebody* is singular. It takes a singular verb: Somebody **was** here.

(b) The indefinite pronoun *few* takes a plural verb: Few **have** such courage.

(c) The indefinite pronoun *nobody* takes a singular verb: Nobody in these classes **knows** my nickname.

Contractions Contractions can cause us to use the wrong verb. We expand them, if necessary, to be sure the subject and verb agree.

The *pelican* isn't (<u>is</u> not) on the pier.

The *pelicans* aren't (<u>are</u> not) on the pier.

The *boy* wasn't (<u>was</u> not) culpable.

The *boys* weren't (<u>were</u> not) culpable.

She doesn't (<u>does</u> not) feign ignorance.

They don't (<u>do</u> not) feign ignorance.

Errors to Avoid The contraction *there's* ("there is" or "there has") can only be used with singular subjects.

There's (there <u>is</u>) only one *shoe* here.

There's (there <u>has</u>) been a *mistake*.

NO: There's two *pelicans* on the pier.

YES: There <u>are</u> two *pelicans* on the pier.

 Also, we do not use the contraction *ain't.* It is not a word.

She isn't (NOT ain't) here.

I haven't (NOT ain't) seen her.

Example 2 Choose the correct contraction for each sentence.

(a) (There's, There are) Robert's brothers.

(b) Ismael (don't, doesn't) need any help.

(c) My socks (hasn't, haven't) any holes yet.

(d) The information (ain't, isn't) pertinent.

Solution (a) The subject, *brothers,* is a plural noun, so we use a plural verb: There **are** Robert's brothers.

(b) *Ismael* is a singular subject: Ismael **doesn't** need any help.

(c) *Socks* is a plural subject, so we use a plural verb: My socks **haven't** any holes yet.

(d) *Ain't* is not a word, so we choose *isn't*: The information **isn't** pertinent.

✓ **Practice** For a–e, choose the correct verb form or contraction for each sentence.

    a. The librarian exclaimed, "You (ain't, aren't) going to believe this!"

    b. Someone with flowers (is, are) at the door.

    c. The dogs and their owner (wasn't, weren't) trespassing.

    d. (There's, There are) only two slices left.

    e. Each of the students (have, has) something to do.

For f and g, replace each blank with the correct vocabulary word from this lesson.

    f. Because of her _____ in telling the story, I do not know what really happened.

    g. Please do not _____. Just tell me what happened.

More Practice Choose the correct verb form for each sentence.

    1. Everybody (is, are) trying to find Badchek.

    2. Either (is, are) all right with me.

    3. Each (need, needs) help.

    4. Neither (want, wants) to admit it.

    5. One of her teachers (is, are) tutoring her.

    6. Anybody in the upper grades (know, knows) Ms. Hoo.

7. Nobody in all the classes (has, have) swum faster than she.

8. Anyone with pets (understand, understands) Tina's frustration.

9. (There's, There are) two blue herons!

10. (There's, There are) another blue heron!

11. Mom (ain't, isn't) home yet.

12. John (don't, doesn't) have lunch money.

13. Meg and Liz (don't, doesn't) have any either.

14. We (ain't, aren't) finished reading.

15. They (isn't, aren't) finished either.

✓**Review Set 91** Choose the correct word(s) to complete sentences 1–16.

1. (*Colossal, Pretentious, Innocuous*) means "harmless and
(90) innocent."

2. (*Ardent, Intrepid, Languid*) means "weak, lacking energy
(89) or interest."

3. *Complacent* means "(tenacious, unethical, content) and
(88) self-satisfied."

4. To coerce is to (pretend, improve, force).
(87)

5. A heavy suitcase or a large debt might be a(n) (plateau,
(37) savanna, encumbrance).

6. There (was, were) eighteen in our group.
(90)

7. The word *army* is a (compound, collective) noun.
(11)

8. Is this (you're, your) hammer?
(72)

9. Bozo is the (friendlier, friendliest) of the two dogs.
(56)

10. The pronoun *your* is (first, second, third) person.
(64)

11. (Who, Whom) is it?
(77, 79)

Think: it | is \\ ?

12. Josef is packing (we, us) helpers a lunch.
(78)

13. Yesterday Ali (lead, led) the race, for she (swam, swum)
(86, 87) faster than anyone else.

14. Many on the team (has, have) (their, his or her) socks
(83, 91) inside out.

15. My brother or my sister (know, knows) my middle name.
(89)

16. (There's, There are) holes in my old backpack.
(91)

17. Write and underline the words that should be italicized in
(84) the sentence below.

Only one train, the Skeedaddle, will take you to Frazzle
Park.

18. Rewrite the word *freight*, circling the silent letters.
(28, 29)

19. Use an appositive to combine the following two
(60) sentences into one sentence.

Mount Whitney has more climbers than any other peak in
the Sierra Nevada.

Mount Whitney is California's tallest mountain.

20. Write whether the sentence below is simple or
(75) compound.

Not every pioneer survived the dangerous journey across
the Sierra Nevadas.

21. Write whether the circled pronoun in the sentence below
(64) is used as a subject or an object.

Will Officer Valiant and (she) catch Badchek?

22. Write whether the clause below is dependent or
(73) independent.

as they obfuscate the facts

23. Rewrite the following, adding capital letters and
(80, 88) punctuation marks as needed:

harold yells don't go before you leave i must warn you
about the dangers

24. For the irregular verb *fall*, write the (a) present participle,
(19, 85) (b) past tense, and (c) past participle.

25. Which sentence is more polite? Write *A* or *B*.
(69)
A. Harold gave them and me some advice.

B. Harold gave me and them some advice.

26. Rewrite the outline below, adding capital letters and
(26, 47) punctuation marks as needed.

i aesop's fables
a the tortoise and the hare
b the lion and the mouse
c the cat and the bell

27. Rewrite the following letter, adding capital letters and
(57, 67) punctuation marks as needed.

dear tina
please come to our family reunion in jefferson city
missouri on tuesday january 2 2007
your cousin
juan

28. Write the two subordinating conjunctions in the sentence
(73) below.

As soon as the bell rings, I shall leave unless Ms. Hoo
needs my help.

Diagram each word of sentences 29–30.

29. Will Ms. Hoo's retirement be restful and serene?
(45, 54)

30. Is your friend Josef packing us a lunch of fruit, nuts, and
(46, 58) bread with butter?

LESSON 92

Subject-Verb Agreement, Part 4

Dictation or Journal Entry

Vocabulary:

Concise means "brief and to the point." The sentence was *concise*, leaving out all unnecessary words.

Conciseness is shortness of speech or writing. *Conciseness* is the opposite of wordiness.

In this lesson, we shall look at nouns that can cause difficulty with subject-verb agreement.

Collective Nouns We remember that a collective noun refers to a group or unit (a collection of people, places, animals, or things). Most of the time, these nouns take singular verbs.

If the group or unit is "acting" as one, we use a singular verb.

The *class* <u>elects</u> a treasurer.

The *team* <u>is</u> tenacious.

A *bunch* of bananas <u>sits</u> in the bowl.

However, if members of the group are "acting" individually, we use a plural verb.

The *majority* <u>finish</u> the race.

What *fraction* of the runners <u>quit</u>?

A *bunch* of people <u>wait</u> in line.

Special Nouns Some nouns refer to a single "thing" but are still considered plural. When used as the subject of a sentence, nouns such as *pants, slacks, trousers, scissors, pliers, shears,* and *eyeglasses* require plural verbs.

These *scissors* <u>are</u> sharp.

His *slacks* <u>were</u> too long.

However, watch for sentences like the one below. The word *pair* is the subject. *Pair* is singular and takes a singular verb.

This *pair* of scissors <u>is</u> sharp.

Other nouns, especially ones that end in -s, appear to be plural but are considered singular. Nouns such as *measles*, *mumps*, *news*, and *lens* require singular verbs.

The *news* <u>is</u> good!

Measles <u>is</u> less common now.

Some nouns have the same form whether they are singular or plural. *Corps*, *series*, *means*, *species*, and *gross*, as well as many animal names (*sheep*, *trout*, *bison*, *salmon*, etc.), are some examples. Use the meaning of the sentence to decide which verb form to use.

SINGULAR: This *series* of novels <u>is</u> captivating.

PLURAL: Two new *series* <u>are</u> coming.

SINGULAR: That *sheep* <u>looks</u> lost.

PLURAL: Several *sheep* <u>have</u> wandered away.

Finally, nouns that end in -ics, such as *mathematics*, *economics*, *ethics*, *athletics*, *acoustics*, and *politics,* can also be either singular or plural, depending on their meaning in the sentence. If we are referring to a body of knowledge, the noun is singular. If we are referring to a series of actions, the noun is plural:

Body of knowledge: *Mathematics* <u>is</u> my favorite subject.

Series of actions: Her *mathematics* <u>are</u> accurate.

Example   Choose the correct verb form for each sentence.
(a) Economics (is, are) an interesting field of study.

(b) The committee (decide, decides) how to raise money.

(c) Some species (is, are) nearly extinct.

(d) Mumps (was, were) miserable and painful.

Solution   (a) "Economics" is singular, for it is a body of knowledge. Economics **is** an interesting field of study.

(b) "Committee" is a collective noun, and its members are acting as one. The committee **decides** how to raise money.

(c) The adjective "some" tells us that "species" is plural. Some species **are** nearly extinct.

(d) "Mumps" is singular. Mumps **was** miserable and painful.

✓Practice Choose the correct verb form for sentences a–d.

a. An army of ants (cover, covers) my sandwich.

b. A popular dog species (is, are) the golden retriever.

c. The hotel staff (has, have) chosen new uniforms.

d. The evening news (was, were) on at seven o'clock.

For e and f, replace each blank with the correct vocabulary word from this lesson.

e. A _____ sentence does not contain unnecessary words.

f. The document's _____ make it quick and easy to read.

✓Review Set 92 Choose the correct word to complete sentences 1–16.

1. To (coerce, ameliorate, obfuscate) is to confuse or make
(91) unclear.

2. *Noxious* and *innocuous* are (synonyms, antonyms,
(90) homophones).

3. To languish is to grow (strong, courageous, weak).
(89)

4. Complacency is contentment and self-(destruction,
(88) defence, satisfaction).

5. Arrogant, boastful people (humiliate, exalt, humble)
(38) themselves.

6. Here (comes, come) my friends.
(90)

7. The sentence below is (declarative, interrogative,
(2) imperative, exclamatory).

There's a pack of wolves!

8. To (who, whom) were you speaking?
(79)

9. Some people don't use (much, many) adjectives.
(56, 83)

10. The pronoun *your* is (nominative, objective, possessive)
(66, 69) case.

11. The winner of the race was (who, whom)?
(77, 79)

Think:

winner	was \ ?

12. Mrs. Brite is more tenacious than (me, I). ["am" omitted]
(78)

13. I have (sat, sitted) in the saddle and have (rode, ridden)
(86, 87) all day long.

14. No one in the group (has, have) (their, his or her) sun
(83, 91) glasses.

15. The girls and their mother (hike, hikes) every weekend.
(89)

16. The whole batch of muffins (has, have) burned in the
(92) oven!

17. Write and underline the words that should be italicized in
(84) the sentence below.

Pytilia melba is a species of finch, a small bird from Africa.

18. Write the plural form of the singular noun *finch*.
(17, 22)

19. Rewrite the sentence below, using commas to offset the
(58) nonessential appositive.

The melba finch an aggressive bird eats seeds and insects.

20. Add suffixes.
(33, 34)

(a) penny + less   (b) true + ly

21. Write the nominative case pronoun to complete the
(64) sentence below.

I heard that Max and (him, he) tied for second.

22. Write whether the following is a phrase or a clause.
(36)

for the sun shone

23. Rewrite the following, adding capital letters and
(80, 88) punctuation marks as needed:

may i please have more broccoli asked mateo

24. For the irregular verb *find*, write the (a) present
(19, 85) participle, (b) past tense, and (c) past participle.

25. Write the objective case pronoun to complete the
(69) sentence below.

Dad served Mateo and (I, me) more broccoli.

26. Rewrite the sentence below, adding capital letters and
(26, 47) punctuation marks as needed.

dad said i'm sorry luz the broccoli is all gone

27. Rewrite the following letter, adding capital letters and
(57, 67) punctuation marks as needed.

dear juan

may i bring butch he is my friend companion and
guard dog

your cousin
tina

28. Write the two subordinating conjunctions in the sentence
(73) below.

After the bell rang, I stayed in the classroom because Ms.
Hoo needed help.

Diagram each word of sentences 29–30.

29. Ms. Hoo's faithful helpers are Onping and I.
(45, 51)

30. My father, an expert in the field of nutrition, served
(46, 58) Mateo and me two big spoonfuls of broccoli.

Negatives • Double Negatives

Negatives   Negatives are modifiers, usually adverbs, that mean "no" or "not." We will learn more about adverbs later. In this lesson, we will learn to recognize negatives and to use them correctly. Negatives are italicized in the sentences below.

He *never* saw her.

She had *nowhere* to go.

We had *scarcely* enough water.

They do *not* hear you.

Here is a list of common negatives:

no	*not*	*never*
hardly	*scarcely*	*barely*
nowhere	*none*	*no one*
nothing	*nobody*	

Because the word *not* is a negative, the contraction *n't* is also a negative:

Some people do*n't* like broccoli.

Kelly is*n't* pretentious.

We have*n't* many pets.

Example 1   Write each negative that you find in these sentences.

(a) I could barely see the road ahead.

(b) No one believed that Moe had nothing to hide.

(c) She did not invite anybody, so nobody came.

(d) Hardly anyone knew it was her birthday.

Solution   (a) **barely**   (b) **No one, nothing**

           (c) **not, nobody**   (d) **Hardly**

Double   We use only one negative to express a negative idea. In the
Negatives English language, two negatives in the same clause "cancel
             each other out" and the idea becomes positive again.
             Therefore, it is incorrect to use two negatives with one verb.
             We call this a **double negative,** and we avoid it.

> NO: Liz *never* needs *no* help.
> YES: Liz *never* needs help.
> YES: Liz needs *no* help.
>
> NO: Bob has*n't no* comb.
> YES: Bob has*n't* a comb.
> YES: Bob has *no* comb.
>
> NO: *Scarcely none* are left.
> YES: *Scarcely any* are left.
> YES: Almost *none* are left.

Example 2   Choose the correct word to complete each sentence.
           (a) We (could, couldn't) hardly hear the speaker.

           (b) Minh doesn't want (no, any) pie.

           (c) Your brother isn't (nothing, anything) like mine.

           (d) Scarcely (nobody, anybody) could hear the speaker.

Solution   (a) "Couldn't" and "hardly" are both negatives, so we choose
               "could." We **could** hardly hear the speaker.

           (b) "Doesn't" and "no" are both negatives. (To *not* want *no*
               pie is to want some pie!) Minh doesn't want **any** pie.

           (c) "Isn't" and "nothing" are both negatives. Your brother
               isn't **anything** like mine.

           (d) "Scarcely" and "nobody" are both negatives. Scarcely
               anybody could hear the speaker.

Correcting Double Negatives To correct a double negative, we can replace one of the negatives with a positive word. Look at the positive forms of the negatives below.

NEGATIVE		POSITIVE
hardly	→	almost
no	→	any, a
nobody	→	anybody
nowhere	→	anywhere
never	→	ever
neither	→	either
none	→	any
no one	→	anyone
nothing	→	anything

Kate didn't do ~~nothing~~. (anything)

She is not ~~no~~ cheater. (a)

I don't want dessert ~~neither~~. (either)

Example 3 Rewrite this sentence, correcting the double negative:

Neither of them saw nobody.

Solution We replace the second negative, *nobody*, with a positive form—*anybody*:

Neither of them saw *anybody*.

Remember that a sentence can contain more than one negative, as long as they are not in the same clause. The sentence below is not an example of a double negative because each negative is in a different clause.

I *didn't* go to the store, so I have *no* milk.

Rare Exceptions On rare occasions, a double negative can be used for effect. Consider the following sentences:

The game was so easy, I *couldn't not* win!

Kim *barely, barely* made it on time.

In sentences such as these, the double negative is deliberate. Most double negatives, however, are unintended and incorrect. They are often heard in speech, but that is no excuse for using them.

Practice Choose the correct word to complete sentences a–e.

a. They (had, hadn't) scarcely any more time.

b. We (could, couldn't) see no smoke.

c. I have never done (anything, nothing) more fun!

d. That hasn't (ever, never) happened to me before.

e. They're not (ever, never) going to find us.

For f and g, replace each blank with the correct vocabulary word from this lesson.

f. The teacher said our essays should be a _____ of five hundred words and not more than a thousand.

g. For _____ test scores, we must study hard.

More Practice Choose the correct word to complete these sentences.

1. I haven't eaten (no, any) snails, and I don't expect to eat (none, any) soon.

2. Ben didn't want (no, any) snails either.

3. Mia doesn't want (nobody, anybody) to see her new haircut.

4. The barber doesn't (neither, either).

5. They haven't shown (no one, anyone).

6. Mia hasn't gone (nowhere, anywhere).

7. Ben didn't eat (none, any) of those snails.

8. He hasn't (never, ever) met Ms. Hoo.

9. Luz has hardly (no, any) money left.

10. Ben didn't eat (nothing, anything).

Choose the correct word(s) to complete sentences 1–16.

1. (*Colossal, Irrelevant, Concise*) means " brief and to the point."
(92)

2. Obfuscation makes things (clear, happy, unclear).
(91)

3. *Innocuous* means "(harmful, harmless, colossal)."
(90)

4. A languid person lacks (energy, money, patience).
(89)

5. The words *encumbrance* and *burden* are (homophones, synonyms, antonyms.)
(37)

6. There (go, goes) the geese!
(90)

7. The word *goose's* is a (plural, possessive) noun.
(13)

8. I (can, can't) hardly see through the fog.
(93)

9. Joy built the (bigger, biggest) of the two sand castles.
(56)

10. The pronoun *me* is (first, second, third) person (singular, plural).
(64)

11. (Who, Whom) borrowed (her's, hers)?
(72, 79)

Think: _____?_____ | ___borrowed___

12. Please listen to (we, us) experts.
(78)

Think: to ?

13. Max has (maked, made) the beds, and I have (shook, shaken) the dust out of the rugs.
(86, 87)

14. One of the girls (haven't, hasn't) any of (their, her) books today.
(83, 91)

15. The girls or their mother (plant, plants) bulbs each fall.
(89)

16. (There's, There are) mice in that closet!
(92)

17. Rewrite the sentence below, adding a comma to clarify
(68) the meaning.

For sewing machines are helpful.

18. Write the plural form of the singular noun *queen of*
(17, 22) *Spain.*

19. Use an appositive to combine the two sentences below
(60) into one sentence.

Olympia is the capital of Washington.

The people of Olympia are called "Olympians."

20. Write whether the following sentence is simple or
(75) compound.

Moe will prepare the meal, and Manny will wash the
dishes.

21. Write whether the circled pronoun in the sentence below
(64) is used as a subject or an object.

I heard that Max and (he) tied for second.

22. From the following sentence, write each prepositional
(44) phrase, circling the object of each preposition.

Aboard ship, they traveled along the coastline, amid a
pod of whales.

23. Rewrite the following, adding capital letters and
(80, 88) punctuation marks as needed:

that broccoli tastes delicious exclaims mateo

24. For the irregular verb *build*, write the (a) present
(19, 85) participle, (b) past tense, and (c) past participle.

25. Write the objective case pronoun to complete the
(69) sentence below.

I voted for Dr. Kim and (she, her).

26. Rewrite the sentence below, adding capital letters and
(26, 47) punctuation marks as needed.

luz said please cook more broccoli dad

27. Rewrite the following letter, adding capital letters and
(57, 67) punctuation marks as needed.

dear tina
　　　there is a dog hotel at 43 state street jefferson city
missouri

　　　　　　　　　　your cousin
　　　　　　　　　　juan

28. Write the two subordinating conjunctions in the sentence
(73) below.

Whenever Butch goes to school with Tina, he hides
where no teachers can see him.

Diagram each word of sentences 29–30.

29. Optimum conditions are the best or most favorable.
(45, 54)

30. Will the dog hotel in Jefferson City offer Butch optimum
(46, 58) conditions of comfort and convenience?

The Hyphen: Compound Nouns and Numbers

The **hyphen** is a punctuation mark used to connect elements of compound words and to express numbers.

Compound Nouns

We have learned that some compound nouns are hyphenated. There are no absolute rules for spelling a compound noun as one word, as two words, or hyphenated. However, certain categories of compound nouns are often hyphenated.

- Compound nouns that end in prepositional phrases:

right-of-way	brother-in-law	stick-in-the-mud
artist-at-large	man-about-town	attorney-at-law

- Compound nouns containing the prefix *ex-* or *self-* or the suffix *-elect*:

ex-manager	self-discipline	mayor-elect

- Compound nouns that are units of measurement:

board-foot	man-hour	light-year

- Compound nouns that end with the prepositions *in*, *on*, or *between*:

drive-in	stand-in	trade-in
add-on	goings-on	go-between

Nouns Without Nouns?

The English language is so flexible that we can create nouns from almost any part of speech. Look at the last category (compound nouns that end with prepositions) and notice that some of them don't contain an actual noun. Following are more examples of compound nouns formed from other parts of speech. We join the elements (words) with hyphens.

go-getter	show-off	has-been
get-together	look-alike	have-nots
sit-up	know-how	talking-to

The dictionary lists many of these words. But no dictionary can show every single combination of words that might make up a compound noun. If you have the need for a unique combination, use any similar words you can find in the dictionary to decide how to punctuate your compound noun.

Example 1 Write the words that should be hyphenated in sentences a–c. Be prepared to use the dictionary.

(a) We must always have self control.

(b) My chili was runner up in the contest.

(c) He is arrogant; he's a know it all.

Solution These compound words need hyphens:

(a) **Self-control** contains the prefix *self-* and so should be hyphenated.

(b) The dictionary tells us that **runner-up** is hyphenated.

c) **Know-it-all** is being used as a noun but doesn't actually contain a noun. It should be hyphenated. (The dictionary lists *know-it-all* as an informal noun or adjective.)

Numbers Hyphens are often used to join elements in the expression of numbers and inclusive sets or sequences.

Numbers as Words We use a hyphen in compound numbers from twenty-one to ninety-nine:

forty-five   one hundred fifty-two copies

fifty-first day   two twenty-fifths ($\frac{2}{25}$)

A Range of Numbers A hyphen is used to indicate a range of numbers or an inclusive set or sequence.

pages 11-22   the years 1980-1990

60-70 percent   the week of May 10-17

Because the hyphen takes the place of words in pairs such as *from/through*, *from/to*, or *between/and*, we do not use one of the words and a hyphen.

INCORRECT: between 1986-1991

CORRECT: between 1986 and 1991

Example 2 Write the numbers that should be hyphenated in sentences a–c.

(a) Ms. Hoo is forty eight.

(b) He was born on the twenty sixth of February.

(c) The story appears on pages 80 88.

Solution (a) **Forty-eight** is hyphenated because it is a number between 21 and 99.

(b) **Twenty-sixth** is hyphenated because it is a number between 21 and 99.

(c) The numerals **80-88** are hyphenated because they represent a sequence.

✓Practice For a and b, replace each blank with the correct vocabulary word from this lesson.

a. If Godfry continues to argue and fight, his friends might _____ him, for they don't like conflict.

b. Does Godfry fear _____ from the group?

For c–f, write each expression that should be hyphenated. Use the dictionary, if necessary.

c. Do you have the know how to repair a flat tire?

d. I read the write up in the newspaper.

e. You have twenty five minutes to complete the test.

f. She will attend summer camp August 13 20 at Cedar Cove.

More Practice For 1–8, use words to write each number.

1. 25   2. 47   3. 76   4. 98

5. 21st   6. 32nd   7. 45th   8. 83rd

Write each expression that should be hyphenated in sentences 9–12. Use a dictionary, if necessary.

9. Practice will give you self confidence.

10. Hauling those boxes was a real work out!

11. My energetic sister in law is a go getter.

12. I must not eat all the ice cream; I must use self restraint.

√**Review Set 94** Choose the correct word(s) to complete sentences 1–16.

1. (*Optimum, Minimum, Noxious*) means "best or most
(93) favorable."

2. Conciseness is (wordiness, silliness, shortness) of speech
(92) of writing.

3. To obfuscate is to (ameliorate, confuse, coerce).
(91)

4. *Noxious* means "(harmless, innocuous, harmful)."
(90)

5. To (exalt, humiliate, praise) is to lower the pride or
(38) dignity of; to shame or embarrass.

6. A can of peaches (sit, sits) on the shelf.
(90)

7. The word *ostracism* is a(n) (concrete, abstract) noun.
(11)

8. We don't have (no, any) rice.
(93)

9. Joy built the (bigger, biggest) of the four sand castles.
(56)

10. The pronoun *me* is (nominative, objective, possessive)
(66, 69) case.

11. (Their's, Theirs) is here, but (your's, yours) is missing.
(72, 79)

12. Dr. Kim has collected more potato bugs than (me, I).
(78) ["have" omitted]

13. Dan has (wove, woven) blankets and (selled, sold) them
(86, 87) for cash.

14. Two in the group (haven't, hasn't) read (their, his or her)
(83, 91) books.

15. Either the birds or the collie (wake, wakes) first.
(89)

16. Measles (was, were) common when Grandma was a child.
(92)

17. Write and underline the words that should be italicized
(84) in the sentence below.

The word patch can be either a noun or a verb.

18. Use a dictionary: (a) The word *deluxe* is what part of
(27, 30) speech? (b) Write its pronunciation. (c) Write its
etymology.

19. Rewrite the sentence below, adding hyphens as needed.
(94)

Forty two people attended the get together.

20. Write the antecedent of the circled pronoun in the
(62) sentence below.

The ostrich hid (its) head in the sand.

21. Write the nominative case pronoun to complete the
(64) sentence below.

My distant cousins are Max and (them, they).

22. Write whether the following is a phrase or a clause.
(36)

to be ostracized

23. Rewrite the following, adding capital letters and
(80, 88) punctuation marks as needed:

if butch howls will you quiet him asked tina

24. For the irregular verb *catch*, write the (a) present
(19, 85) participle, (b) past tense, and (c) past participle.

25. Which sentence is more polite? Write *A* or *B*.
(69)
A. Did you vote for Dr. Kim and me?

B. Did you vote for me and Dr. Kim?

26. Rewrite the sentence below, adding capital letters and
(81) punctuation marks as needed.

i shall title my essay the smooth enjoyable voyage

27. Rewrite the following letter, adding capital letters and
(57, 67) punctuation marks as needed.

> my dear cousin
> > butch will stay with me for he requires a soft bed
> healthful food and lots of attention
> > > > love
> > > > tina

28. Write the two subordinating conjunctions in the sentence
(73) below.

> Butch gets more attention than he wants when he goes to
> school.

Diagram each word of sentences 29–30.

29. The ostracism of classmates can be cruel and unkind.
(45, 54)

30. Butch's owner, Tina, handed me a long, leather leash and
(46, 58) a bowl for Butch's food.

LESSON 95

Adverbs That Tell "How"

> **Dictation or Journal Entry**
> **Vocabulary:**
> *Paltry* means "having little or no value; insignificant." Nicholas only received a *paltry* salary for all his hard work.
>
> *Paltriness* is insignificance. The *paltriness* of Nicholas's salary offends him.

Adverbs are descriptive words that modify or add information to verbs, adjectives, and other adverbs. They answer the questions "how," "when," "where," "why," and "how much" (or "to what extent"). The italicized adverbs below modify the verb *whispers*.

HOW:	Eric whispers *quietly*.
WHEN:	He whispers *now*.
WHERE:	He whispers *there*.
WHY:	He whispers *because*.
HOW MUCH:	He whispers *more*.

"How" An adverb that tells "how" usually modifies a verb or verb phrase and often ends in the suffix *-ly*. For example, let's think about how Lucy skates:

Lucy skates *happily*.

Lucy might also skate *gracefully, smoothly, cautiously, clumsily, recklessly,* or *slowly*. These adverbs all answer the question "how."

Example 1 Write the adverbs that tell "how" from this sentence:

The ice broke loudly and suddenly.

Solution The adverbs **loudly** and **suddenly** tell "how" the ice broke.

Suffix *-ly* Below are the adjective and adverb forms of some nouns. Notice that the adverb is formed by adding *-ly* to the adjective.

NOUN	ADJECTIVE	ADVERB
bliss	*blissful*	*blissfully*
nature	*natural*	*naturally*
help	*helpful*	*helpfully*
danger	*dangerous*	*dangerously*
sense	*sensible*	*sensibly*

Of course, not every word that ends in *-ly* is an adverb. *Lovely, friendly, orderly,* and *lonely* are all adjectives.

Adjective or Adverb? Some words, such as *hard, fast, right, early,* and *long,* have the same form whether they are used as adjectives or adverbs. However, we can always tell how the word is being used because an adjective <u>modifies a noun or pronoun</u>, and an <u>adverb modifies a verb, adjective, or other adverb.</u>

ADJECTIVE:	The test was *hard.* (modifies the noun "test")
ADVERB:	Jim worked *hard.* (modifies the verb "worked")
ADJECTIVE:	It was a *fast* race. (modifies the noun "race")
ADVERB:	Rita ran *fast.* (modifies the verb "ran")
ADJECTIVE:	I ate an *early* lunch.
ADVERB:	I ate lunch *early.*

We must learn to see the difference between an adverb and a predicate adjective. Look at the following sentence:

> The dog looks friendly.

It might seem that *friendly* tells "how" the dog looks. But we remember that we can identify a predicate adjective by replacing a possible linking verb (looks) with a "to be" verb:

> The dog *was* friendly. (friendly dog)

The word *friendly* describes the dog, not the act of looking. It is an adjective. Compare this to a sentence containing an action verb:

> A tiger moves silently.

If we replace an action verb with a "to be" verb, the sentence no longer makes sense:

> A tiger *is* silently? (silently tiger?)

Silently does not describe the tiger. It describes the act of moving. It is an adverb.

Example 2 Tell whether the italicized word in each sentence is an adjective or adverb. Also, tell which word it modifies.

(a) Amber paddled *hard* against the current.

(b) The long, *hard* trip was worth it.

(c) Two wild monkeys grew *friendly.*

Solution (a) The word *hard* is an **adverb. It modifies the verb "paddled."** *Hard* tells "how" Amber paddled.

(b) The word *hard* is an **adjective. It modifies the noun "trip."** *Hard* tells "what kind" of trip.

(c) The word *friendly* is an **adjective. It modifies the noun "monkeys."** *Friendly* tells "what kind" of monkeys.

✓**Practice** For sentences a–c, write each adverb that tells "how," and write the word or phrase it modifies.

a. A prince sits proudly on the throne.

b. Fast, powerful vehicles burn fuel rapidly.

c. Mario repaired the computer quickly and easily.

For d–g, write whether the italicized word is an adjective or an adverb, and write the word or phrase it modifies.

d. His lecture seemed *long*.

e. Did he speak *long*?

f. Max made a *right* turn.

g. Max turned *right*.

For h and i, replace each blank with the correct vocabulary word from this lesson.

h. The _____ of her argument caused her to lose the debate.

i. _____ arguments will not win a debate.

✓**Review Set**
95

Choose the correct word(s) to complete sentences 1–16.

1. To (ostracize, obfuscate, ameliorate) is to cut off or
(94) exclude from a group.

2. The minimum is the (least, most, biggest) possible.
(93)

3. A (colossal, concise, cumbersome) sentence leaves out
(92) unnecessary words.

4. Obfuscation is (avarice, confusion, clarity).
(91)

5. The words *exalt* and *humiliate* are (homophones,
(38) synonyms, antonyms).

6. Dan, one of the triplets, (is, are) flying a kite.
(90)

7. The word *football* is a (compound, collective) noun.
(13)

8. She doesn't keep (no, any) secrets.
(93)

9. Mac counted (less, fewer) sheep than goats.
(56)

10. The pronoun *we* is (first, second, third) person (singular,
(64) plural).

11. (Who, Whom) shall I send?
(79)

Think:

I	shall send	?

12. Please give (us, we) students more time.
(78)

13. Jo (mistook, mistaken) me for someone else; she (thinked,
(86, 87) thought) I was a movie star.

14. Some in the group (haven't, hasn't) read (their, his or her)
(83, 91) books.

15. Either the collie or the birds (wake, wakes) first.
(89)

16. Mumps (was, were) common when Grandma was a child.
(92)

17. Write and underline the words that should be italicized
(84) in the sentence below.

Michelangelo sculpted a marble statue called David.

18. Write the plural form of the singular noun *can opener*.
(17, 22)

19. Rewrite the sentence below, adding hyphens as needed.
(94)

For exercise, we did seventy five sit ups.

20. Write whether the sentence below is simple or
(75) compound.

Melody is swimming in the pool, but Daisy is taking a
nap.

21.
₍₆₉₎ Write the objective case pronoun to complete the sentence below.

I called my cousin Luz and (he, him).

22.
₍₇₃₎ Write whether the clause below is dependent or independent.

she received a paltry sum

23.
_(80, 88) Rewrite the following, adding capital letters and punctuation marks as needed:

juan said i rented a large room for the party but only a few people are coming

24.
_(19, 85) For the irregular verb *eat*, write the (a) present participle, (b) past tense, and (c) past participle.

25.
₍₉₅₎ From the sentence below, write each adverb and the word or phrase it modifies.

Most of the students in this class write skillfully.

26.
₍₈₁₎ Rewrite the sentence below, adding capital letters and punctuation marks as needed.

the scariest chapter was titled lost in the jungle

27.
_(57, 67) Rewrite the following sentence, adding capital letters and punctuation marks as needed.

the colors of the rainbow as i recall are red orange yellow green blue indigo and violet

28.
₍₇₃₎ Write the two subordinating conjunctions in the sentence below.

It looks as though Butch will stay with me since dogs are not welcome at the party.

Diagram each word of sentences 29–30.

29. Dr. Kim's contribution to the discussion of exotic
(45, 54) perfumes was minimal and paltry.

30. Dr. Kim, an entomologist, shows us his enthusiasm for
(46, 58) beetles and moths.

Using the Adverb *Well*

Dictation or Journal Entry

Vocabulary:

Perjury is lying under oath. In the courtroom the witness committed *perjury*; she lied under oath.

To *perjure* is to make oneself guilty of lying under oath. Can you prove that the witness *perjured* herself?

Good The words *good* and *well* are difficult parts of speech. *Good* is a descriptive adjective or a predicate adjective. It modifies a noun or pronoun, as in these sentences:

Dad is a *good* cook.
(descriptive adjective modifying "cook")

He makes *good* spaghetti.
(descriptive adjective modifying "spaghetti")

The spaghetti tastes *good*.
(predicate adjective describing "spaghetti")

Well The word *well* is usually an adverb. It modifies an action verb and explains "how" someone does something.

That tenor sings *well*.

Rene plays basketball *well*.

How *well* do you write?

We do not use the word *good* as an adverb.

NO: Oscar dances *good*.
YES: Oscar dances *well*.

NO: This tool works *good*.
YES: This tool works *well*.

Example 1 Replace each blank with *well* or *good*.

(a) Elle slept _____.

(b) Did you have a _____ vacation?

(c) James paints _____.

(d) He is a _____ painter.

Solution (a) Elle slept **well**. *Well* is an adverb that modifies the verb *slept*. It tells "how" Elle slept.

(b) Did you have a **good** vacation? *Good* is an adjective that modifies the noun *vacation*.

(c) James paints **well.** *Well* is an adverb that modifies the verb *paints*. It tells "how" James paints.

(d) He is a **good** painter. *Good* is an adjective that modifies the noun *painter*.

Feeling Well? The word *well* is used as an adjective when referring to the state of one's health. You feel *good* about passing a test, for example, but when you wish to state that you are in good health, it is preferable to say that you are *well*.

> She feels *well* today.
>
> Is she *well*, or is she sick?

Example 2 Choose either *well* or *good* to complete each sentence.
  (a) I don't think she feels (good, well).

  (b) Frank felt (well, good) about helping his brother.

Solution (a) I don't think she feels **well.** We use *well* when referring to one's health.

  (b) Frank felt **good** about helping his brother. We do not use *well* because we are not referring to the state of Frank's health.

✓ **Practice** Choose the correct descriptive word for sentences a–e.
  a. The girls worked (good, well) together on the costumes.

  b. Dan did a (good, well) job in the chorus.

  c. He can carry a tune fairly (good, well).

  d. Kurt is a (good, well) pianist.

  e. He directs the chorus (good, well).

For f and g, replace each blank with the correct vocabulary word from this lesson.
  f. I shall not _____ myself by telling a lie in court.

  g. _____ is a crime.

More Practice Choose the correct descriptive word for each sentence.

1. Corn grows (good, <u>well</u>) in Iowa.

2. How (good, well) did you sleep last night?

3. Miguel cooks (good, well).

4. He is a (good, well) cook.

5. His waffles taste (good, well).

6. Freddy feels (good, well) about his grades.

7. Todd and Suzi paint (well, good).

8. They've made some (good, well) paintings.

9. April sings (good, well).

10. Onping is a (good, well) singer too.

Review Set 96 Choose the correct word(s) to complete sentences 1–16.

1. (*Paltry, Essential, Akin*) means "having little or no value;
(95) insignificant."

2. If you exclude a person from the group, you (ameliorate,
(94) obfuscate, ostracize) him or her.

3. *Optimum* means "(worst, best, least)."
(93)

4. *Conciseness* and *wordiness* are (synonyms, antonyms,
(92) homophones).

5. A dogma is a formally stated belief that is viewed as
(39) (questionable, true, false).

6. There (is, are) two empty seats.
(90)

7. Ms. Hoo explains things (good, well).
(96)

8. She (has, hasn't) scarcely enough time.
(93)

9. Of all the hikers, I had the (tireder, tiredest) legs.
(56)

10. The pronoun *we* is (nominative, objective, possessive)
(64) case.

11. This booth is (our's, ours); (their's, theirs) is over there.
(72)

12. Uray is as polite as (him, he). ["is" omitted]
(78)

13. Yesterday Gloria (lended, lent) me a book, so I (writed,
(86, 87) wrote) her a thank-you note.

14. Neither of the boys (have, has) made (their, his) lunch.
(83, 91)

15. The sisters or their brother (feed, feeds) the goldfish.
(89)

16. The basketball team (board, boards) the bus.
(92)

17. Write and underline the words that should be italicized
(84) in the sentence below.

I borrowed the fantasy book Alice in Wonderland.

18. Write the plural form of the singular noun *lilac bush*.
(17, 22)

19. Rewrite the sentence below, adding hyphens as needed.
(94)

Thirty three show offs were trying to get attention.

20. Write the antecedent of the circled pronoun in the
(62) sentence below.

Venita polished her bicycle and rode (it) to the park.

21. Write whether the circled pronoun in the sentence below
(64) is used as a subject or an object.

She winked at her baby brother and blew (him) a kiss.

22. Write whether the following is a phrase or a clause.
(36)

because hounds have an excellent sense of smell

23. Rewrite the following, adding capital letters and
(80) punctuation marks as needed:

my aunt asked if i would like any lemons oranges or
avocados from her trees

24. For the irregular verb *bite*, write the (a) present participle,
(19, 85) (b) past tense, and (c) past participle.

25. From the sentence below, write each adverb and the
(95) word or phrase it modifies.

Perlina slept blissfully through the math class.

26. Rewrite the sentence below, adding capital letters and
(81) punctuation marks as needed.

jason wrote a poem and titled it if i were an ant

27. Rewrite the following sentence, adding capital letters and
(57, 67) punctuation marks as needed.

please remember i have moved to 960 fox lane frazzle
park oregon

28. Write the three subordinating conjunctions in the
(73) sentence below.

Before I leave, I must call Officer Valiant so that he will
know where I am going.

Diagram each word of sentences 29–30.

29. Badchek's outrageous testimony in court must have been
(45, 54) perjury.

30. Dr. Axle, a herpetologist, provided Lily and me valuable
(46, 58) information about reptiles and amphibians.

LESSON 97

The Hyphen: Compound Adjectives

> **Dictation or Journal Entry**
>
> **Vocabulary:**
>
> To *plagiarize* is to take someone else's work or ideas and call them your own. We must not *plagiarize* when we write our reports.
>
> *Plagiarism* is idea theft; it is using someone else's work or ideas as if they were your own. *Plagiarism* is against the law.

We have seen how hyphens are used in compound nouns and with numbers. In this lesson we will learn more uses for hyphens.

Compound Adjectives Just as we combine words to form compound nouns, we can combine words to form **compound adjectives**. A compound adjective is a group of words that works *as a unit* to modify a noun in order to express a single thought. It is not a list of adjectives, each modifying a noun in its own way.

> COMPOUND ADJECTIVE: *hand-woven* basket
>
> TWO ADJECTIVES: *pretty yellow* basket
>
> COMPOUND ADJECTIVE: *soundproof* room
>
> TWO ADJECTIVES: *neat, clean* room
>
> COMPOUND ADJECTIVE: *blue and white* shirt
>
> THREE ADJECTIVES: *floppy brown straw* hat

As shown above, compound adjectives can be spelled as one word, left as separate words, or hyphenated. How they appear is sometimes a matter of rule but is often a matter of custom or style. The following guidelines will help you form many compound adjectives confidently.

Clarity Our goal is to make our meaning as clear as possible to the reader. When we use hyphens to join two or more words, it helps the reader understand that the words are to be read as a single unit. This prevents confusion. Consider this sentence:

> The tailor made jackets for boys are stunning.

The reader, seeing a subject (tailor), a verb (made), and a direct object (jackets), is likely to misread the sentence. So we hyphenate the compound adjective for greater clarity:

> The tailor-made jackets for boys are stunning.

Borrowed Phrases and Clauses
One of the ways we modify nouns is by borrowing descriptive phrases and clauses and using them as compound adjectives. Hyphens help join words that work as a unit to modify a noun.

Prepositional Phrases
When we use a prepositional phrase to modify a noun, it is functioning as a compound adjective. If it comes *before* the noun, it should be hyphenated.

> We need an *up-to-date* report.
> (The report must be *up to date.*)

> We had an *after-dinner* snack.
> (We had a snack after dinner.)

Words out of Order
When we borrow a descriptive phrase or clause and place it before a noun, we often eliminate or rearrange some of the words. To help them express a single thought, words that are out of their normal order can be held together by hyphens.

> He wore *grass-stained* pants.
> (His pants were *stained with grass.*)

> Please feed that *hungry-looking* cat.
> (The cat *looks hungry.*)

An Exception
We *do not* use a hyphen in a compound adjective that begins with an adverb ending in *-ly*.

> a *nicely swept* porch, a *securely fastened* gate

> the *newly hired* worker, my *painfully swollen* foot

Number + Unit of Measure
We use a hyphen when joining a number to a unit of measure to form a compound adjective.

> *48-foot* cable, *ten-mile* run, *thirty-year* loan

We *do not* use a hyphen when the number alone modifies the noun:

> 48 feet, ten miles, thirty years

Fractions
We use a hyphen in a fraction that functions as an adjective.

> Terry was elected by a *two-thirds* majority.

> The tank was *three-fourths* full.

If the numerator or the denominator of a fraction is already hyphenated, *do not* use another hyphen:

> A *five twenty-fifths* increase equals a *one-fifth* increase.

We *do not* use a hyphen if the fraction functions as a noun.

Two thirds of the birds were pigeons.

Example 1 Write the words that should be hyphenated in sentences a–e.

(a) Did you hear that high pitched noise?

(b) We have had above average temperatures.

(c) Let's look at the mail order catalog.

(d) Sam drew a four foot line in the dirt.

(e) Four fifths of the boys had bare feet.

Solution (a) We hyphenate **high-pitched** because the words work as unit to modify the noun *noise* with a single thought.

(b) We hyphenate **above-average** because it is a prepositional phrase that comes before and modifies the noun *temperatures*.

(c) We hyphenate **mail-order** to help it retain its meaning (a catalog for ordering things through the mail).

(d) We hyphenate **four-foot** because it is a compound adjective formed by a number and a unit of measure.

(e) **None.** We do not hyphenate the fraction four fifths because it functions as a noun.

Dictionary Clues Remember, dictionaries cannot contain all the compound words we can create. If you are faced with an unfamiliar compound, you can search the dictionary for similar compounds and use them as clues.

Other Uses for Hyphens We use hyphens to avoid confusion or awkward spelling, and to join unusual elements.

With Prefixes and Suffixes If you add a prefix or suffix to a word, and the resulting word is misleading or awkward, use a hyphen for clarity.

Will you *re-cover* (not *recover*) the chair with new fabric?

It had a hard, *shell-like* (not *shelllike*) surface.

Also, use a hyphen to join a prefix to any proper noun.

pro-American, mid-July, post-World War II

Hyphens are used to combine unusual elements into single expressions.

When a letter (or group of letters) modifies a word in a compound noun or adjective, a hyphen is often used.

A-frame, L-shaped, PG-rated, U-turn, T-shirt

We can also use a hyphen to join numbers in expressions such as the following:

The score at halftime was *27-43*.

You have a *fifty-fifty* chance of winning.

Example 2 Write the words, if any, that should be hyphenated in sentences a–d. Be prepared to use the dictionary.

(a) Ted must research the house for his wallet.

(b) Are they really anti American?

(c) You must make a U turn here.

(d) They agreed to split the cost sixty forty.

Solution (a) We hyphenate **re-search** to avoid misleading the reader.

(b) We hyphenate **anti-American** because we are joining a prefix and a proper noun.

(c) We consult the dictionary and find that **U-turn** is a hyphenated term.

(d) We use a hyphen to form the expression **sixty-forty**.

Practice Write the words, if any, that should be hyphenated in sentences a–e.

a. They built an A frame cabin.

b. We could see a rapidly approaching storm.

c. Let's recover the chair with green velvet.

d. He drank an eight ounce glass of water.

e. Mud coated shoes sat on the porch.

For f and g, replace each blank with the correct vocabulary word from this lesson.

f. _____ is idea theft.

g. To steal someone else's work or ideas is to _____.

✓ **Review Set 97**

Choose the correct word(s) to complete sentences 1–16.

1. (Cognizance, Avarice, Perjury) is lying under oath.
(96)

2. (Benevolence, Perjury, Paltriness) is insignificance.
(95)

3. To ostracize is to (include, invite, exclude).
(94)

4. The minimum wage is the (most, highest, lowest) wage allowed.
(93)

5. (*Placid, Invertebrate, Dogmatic*) means "stating beliefs in an authoritative and often arrogant manner."
(39)

6. A book of stamps (cost, costs) how much?
(90)

7. Sleep (good, well) tonight.
(96)

8. We don't have (no, any) homework.
(93)

9. I've read (less, fewer) pages than he.
(56)

10. The pronoun *our* is (first, second, third) person (singular, plural).
(64)

11. (Who's, Whose) clicking their pencil?
(79)

12. Joe showed (we, us) herpetologists a poison dart frog.
(78)

13. Len has (gave, given) me six tennis lessons. He has (teached, taught) me many skills.
(86, 87)

14. Someone with many pets (have, has) several chores in (their, his or her) daily routine.
(83, 91)

15. Neither the goldfish nor the hamster (sing, sings) like my canary.
(89)

16. Your scissors (is, are) dull.
(92)

17. Write and underline the words that should be italicized in the sentence below.
(84)

With pen and ink, Rembrandt drew A Thatched Cottage by a Tree.

18. Use a dictionary: (a) The word *entrap* is what part of speech? (b) Write its pronunciation. (c) Write its etymology.
(27, 30)

19. Rewrite the sentence below, adding hyphens as needed.
(94, 97)

I spent forty five minutes scrubbing my paint stained shirt.

20. Write whether the sentence below is simple or compound.
(75)

Avocado growers water frequently and spray for pests.

21. Write the nominative case pronoun to complete the sentence below.
(66)

My favorite musicians are you and (her, she).

22. Write whether the clause below is dependent or independent.
(73)

astronomers can study stars and planets more closely with a telescope

23. Rewrite the following, adding capital letters and punctuation marks as needed:
(80, 88)

meg asks would you like any lemons oranges or avocados

24. For the irregular verb *feel*, write the (a) present participle, (b) past tense, and (c) past participle.
(19, 85)

25. From the sentence below, write each adverb and the word or phrase it modifies.
(95)

Nan writes her essays concisely.

26. Rewrite the sentence below, adding capital letters and punctuation marks as needed.
(81)

an interesting article was titled the return of the lynx

27. Rewrite the following sentence, adding capital letters and
(57, 67) punctuation marks as needed.

herbert my oldest brother graduated on june 16 2006

28. Write the two subordinating conjunctions in the sentence
(73) below.

Even though I reminded her, Perlina forgot that we would
have a math test on Friday.

Diagram each word of sentences 29–30.

29. Mother's elementary school was a four-mile hike from
(45, 54) her home.

30. Arachnologist Mari Hunt showed Dan and them her large
(46, 58) collection of spiders and scorpions.

Adverbs That Tell "Where"

We have learned to identify adverbs that tell "how." In this lesson, we will learn to identify adverbs that tell "where." Again, let's think about how Lucy skates:

Lucy skates happily.

"Where" Now, let's think about **where** Lucy skates:

Lucy skates everywhere.

She might also skate *away, nearby, home, outside, inside, here, there,* or *anywhere.*

Here are some common adverbs that tell "where:"

near	*anywhere*	*up*	*in*
far	*everywhere*	*here*	*out*
down	*nowhere*	*there*	*home*
above	*somewhere*	*away*	*inside*
under	*around*	*ahead*	*outside*

We remember that words like *in, out*, and *down* can also be prepositions. But in order to function as a preposition, a word must have an object. When a word like *in, out,* or *down* does not have an object, it is an adverb.

PREPOSITION: He went *out* the door. (object "door")

ADVERB: He went *out.* (no object)

Example 1 For sentences a–d, write each adverb that tells "where," and give the verb or verb phrase that it modifies.

(a) Fido ran ahead.

(b) I shall stop there.

(c) We looked everywhere for the lost treasure.

(d) Everyone looked upward during the national anthem.

Solution   (a) The word *ahead* tells "where" Fido ran.

(b) The word *there* modifies the verb *stop.* It tells "where" I shall stop.

(c) The word *everywhere* modifies the verb *looked.* It tells "where" we looked.

(d) The word *upward* modifies the verb phrase *looked.* It tells "where" everyone looked.

Diagramming Adverbs   We diagram adverbs just as we do adjectives. We write the adverb on a slanted line under the word it modifies. Here we diagram this sentence:

Lucy skates *nearby.*

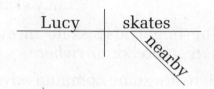

Example 2   Diagram this sentence: Abe walks home.

Solution   The adverb *home* tells "where" Abe walks, so we diagram the sentence like this:

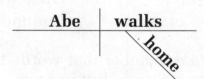

✓**Practice**   For sentences a–d, write each adverb that tells "where," and give the verb or verb phrase that it modifies.

a. Rufus can nap anywhere.

b. The cows have come home.

c. Fifi might have gone out.

d. Butch wanders around.

Diagram sentences e and f.

e. Beki and Ed wait outside.

f. He locked his key inside.

For g and h, replace each blank with the correct vocabulary word from this lesson.

g. Unfortunately I have a _____ of weeds in my garden.

h. Weeds are _____ among the tomato plants.

Choose the correct word(s) to complete sentences 1–16.

1. To (plagiarize, ostracize, languish) is to take someone
(97) else's work or ideas and call them your own.

2. To perjure is to (speak, testify, lie) under oath.
(96)

3. *Paltry* means "(significant, insignificant, benevolent)."
(95)

4. Ostracism is the act of (including, rapprochement,
(94) excluding).

5. (Concrete, Abstract) nouns name tangible things.
(11, 40)

6. Hilda, the gymnast with long curls, (wear, wears) strong
(90) perfume.

7. I had a (good, well) sleep.
(96)

8. We (have, haven't) hardly (any, no) money left.
(93)

9. Nester is the (more, most) benevolent of the two.
(56)

10. The pronoun *our* is (nominative, objective, possessive)
(66, 69) case.

11. Are these (they're, there, their) seats?
(72)

12. Oscar swam farther than (them, they).
(78)

13. Beki (losed, lost) her key, so she (standed, stood) outside,
(86, 87) wondering what to do.

14. (There's, There are) several deer in the yard.
(83, 91)

15. Neither the goldfish nor the hamsters (sing, sings) like my
(89) canary.

16. My slacks (is, are) too long.
<small>(92)</small>

17. Write and underline the words that should be italicized in the sentence below.
<small>(84)</small>

Greg sometimes writes were when he means "where."

18. Write the plural form of the singular noun *car part*.
<small>(17, 22)</small>

19. Rewrite the sentence below, adding hyphens as needed.
<small>(94, 97)</small>

James hammered twenty four nails into two by four lumber.

20. Add suffixes.
<small>(33, 34)</small>

(a) jog + ing   (b) try + ed

21. Write whether the circled pronoun in the sentence below is used as a subject or an object.
<small>(64)</small>

Of course, you and (she) are the best drummers.

22. Write whether the following is a phrase or a clause.
<small>(36)</small>

underneath the table with the checkered cloth

23. Rewrite the following, adding capital letters and punctuation marks as needed:
<small>(80, 88)</small>

i patted the goat's head and it took a bite of my sleeve exclaimed rondo

24. For the irregular verb *fly*, write the (a) present participle, (b) past tense, and (c) past participle.
<small>(19, 85)</small>

25. From the sentence below, write each adverb and the word or phrase it modifies.
<small>(95, 98)</small>

Dan suddenly leaps up.

26. Rewrite the sentence below, adding capital letters and punctuation marks as needed.
<small>(81)</small>

riding home from denver colorado my sister sang old macdonald had a farm over and over again

27. Rewrite the following sentence, adding capital letters and
_(57, 67) punctuation marks as needed.

on the other hand you could paint the table red white or blue

28. Write the two subordinating conjunctions in the sentence
₍₇₃₎ below.

Because she is prudent, Perlina does her homework even though it takes a long time.

Diagram each word of sentences 29–30.

29. Does that two-liter bottle of water look empty?
_(45, 54)

30. Arachnologist Mari Hunt carefully lifted up each
_(58, 98) specimen.

Word Division

Dictation or Journal Entry

Vocabulary:

A *prologue* is an introduction to a play, speech, or other written work. The *prologue* of the story told about the main character's birth.

An *epilogue* is a section added to the end of a written work as an explanation, summary, or conclusion. The *epilogue* of the story told about the main character's death.

When writing, we use a hyphen to divide a word if we run out of room at the end of a line. It is important to know *where* (or *whether*) to divide a word.

Note: Using a computer does not free us from this responsibility. Many "automatic" word divisions are unacceptable in good writing.

Observe the following guidelines when dividing a word.

Between Syllables Words can be divided only between syllables. We check the dictionary if we are in doubt about how a word is divided. The hyphen always appears with the first half of the word.

con- ceal   na- ture   tim- ber   tun- dra

One-Letter Syllables A one-letter syllable should not be divided from the rest of the word.

uten- sil (not u- tensil)

avi- ary (not a- viary or aviar- y)

Because of this, two-syllable words such as the following are never divided:

erase   handy   amaze   idle

When a word contains a one-letter syllable, we divide the word *after* that syllable.

presi- dent (not pres- ident)

nega- tive (not neg- ative)

experi- ence (not exper- ience)

Compound Words Divide a compound word between its elements. If the word is already hyphenated, divide it *after* the hyphen.

water- proof (not wa- terproof)

window- shop (not win- dow-shop)

mass- produce (not mass-pro- duce)

Prefixes and Suffixes Divide a word after a prefix or before a suffix.

un- ethical (not unethi- cal or uneth- ical)

power- ful (not pow- erful)

Longer Words Some longer words contain more than one possible dividing place. We divide them as needed to fit the line.

per- tinent *or* perti- nent

re- dundant *or* redun- dant

Do Not Divide Some words and expressions are never divided.

One-Syllable Words One-syllable words cannot be divided, no matter how many letters they contain. Remember that even when you add -*ed*, some words are still one syllable.

pleased   feigned   breathed   straight

Short Words Words with four letters should not be divided even if they are more than one syllable.

redo   very   alto   logo

Also, we do not divide contractions or abbreviations.

Example Use hyphens to divide each of the words. Remember that not all words should be divided. Use the dictionary if necessary.

(a) paltry   (b) erupt   (c) epilogue

(d) paltriness   (e) grandchildren   (f) sliced

Solution (a) We divide between syllables: **pal- try**

(b) We do not divide a one-letter syllable from the rest of the word. **Erupt** cannot be divided.

(c) We divide a word *after* a single-letter syllable: **epi- logue**

(d) We divide a word *before* a suffix: **paltri- ness**

(e) We divide a compound word between its elements: **grand- children**

(f) We do not divide one-syllable words. **Sliced** cannot be divided.

Practice Use a hyphen to divide words a–f. Remember that not all words should be divided. Use the dictionary if necessary.

a. adapt   b. candid   c. chocolate
d. liar   e. couldn't   f. forty-seven

For g and h, replace each blank with the correct vocabulary word from this lesson.

g. A(n) _____ comes at the beginning of a book.

h. A(n) _____ comes at the end of a book.

More Practice Divide each word correctly.

1. thought   2. blissful

3. antidote   4. akin

5. conceal   6. supersonic

7. can't   8. contrite

9. lagoon   10. feign

11. abrupt   12. paltry

13. ignite   14. perjure

15. prepare   16. shouldn't

17. paddle   18. trapped

19. hemisphere   20. prologue

Review Set 99 Choose the correct word(s) to complete sentences 1–16.

1. (*Paltry, Profuse, Minimum*) means "abundant or plentiful."
(98)

2. (Plagiarism, Ostracism, Subversion) is idea theft.
(97)

3. Perjury is (testifying, speaking, lying) under oath.
(96)

4. A paltry sum has (much, great, little) value.
(95)

5. (*Tangible, Intangible, Avaricious*) means "not able to be felt with the sense of touch."
(40)

6. There (was, were) some interesting spiders in the garage.
(90)

7. Yesterday I was ill, but today I feel (good, well).
(96)

8. She (ain't, hasn't) done (no, any) homework today.
(93)

9. Nester is the (more, most) benevolent of all.
(56)

10. The pronoun *them* is (first, second, third) person (singular, plural).
(64)

11. (Who's, Whose) kitten is that?
(79)

12. I think that (we, us) painters need help.
(78)

13. Paco had (swang, swung) the bat, and Leah had (ran, run) to second base before the pitcher threw the ball.
(86, 87)

14. I don't know if (there's, there are) any venomous snakes in this area.
(83, 91)

15. The brothers and their sister (is, are) climbing Mount Whitney.
(89)

16. My glasses (was, were) broken.
(92)

17. Write and underline the words that should be italicized in the sentence below.
(84)

With oil on canvas, John Constable painted The White Horse.

18. Write the plural form of the singular noun *handful*.
(17, 22)

19. Rewrite the sentence below, adding hyphens as needed.
(94, 97)

Watching the penguin's egg hatch was a once in a lifetime experience.

20. Use a hyphen to divide each word correctly.
(99)

(a) won't   (b) epilogue

21.
(69) Write the objective case pronoun to complete the sentence below.

I asked Nien and (her, she) about Ms. Hoo.

22.
(73) Write whether the clause below is dependent or independent.

if you need my help on Saturday morning

23.
(80, 88) Rewrite the following, adding capital letters and punctuation marks as needed:

ms hoo do goats normally eat sweaters asked rondo

24.
(19, 85) For the irregular verb *cost*, write the (a) present participle, (b) past tense, and (c) past participle.

25.
(95, 98) From the sentence below, write each adverb and the word or phrase it modifies.

Nien gladly sits nearby.

26.
(81) Rewrite the sentence below, adding capital letters and punctuation marks as needed.

i read an article titled russia's giant bears

27.
(57, 67) Rewrite the following sentence, adding capital letters and punctuation marks as needed.

lee b guo RN has moved to 940 fast lane atlanta georgia

28.
(73) Write the two subordinating conjunctions in the sentence below.

When you come, we'll bake bread if there's time.

Diagram each word of sentences 29–30.

29. Does Celly, the twenty-year-old horse, look healthy?
(45, 54)

30. My cousin in Montana faithfully mails me up-to-date
(58, 98) photographs of her rabbits and chickens.

Adverbs That Tell "When"

We have learned to identify adverbs that tell "how" and "where." In this lesson, we will learn about adverbs that modify a verb to tell "when." Again, let's think about how and where Lucy skates:

HOW: Lucy skates *happily*.

WHERE: Lucy skates *everywhere*.

"When"   Now we will think about **when** Lucy skates:

Lucy skates *often*.

She might also skate *daily*, *weekly*, *monthly*, or *today*.

Here are some common adverbs that tell "when."

afterward	daily	never	then
again	early	nightly	tomorrow
always	ever	now	tonight
before	hourly	often	weekly
constantly	late	someday	yearly
currently	monthly	soon	yesterday

Adverb Position   An adverb usually appears near the verb it modifies.

Abe will *soon* leave for home.

Abe will leave *soon* for home.

But an adverb can appear almost anywhere in a sentence.

Soon Abe will leave for home.

Abe will leave for home *soon*.

Even though the adverb *soon* modifies the verb *leave* in each of the sentences above, it is not necessarily placed near the verb. Since the placement of the adverb can vary, we must learn to identify adverbs even when they are separated from the verbs they modify.

Example 1   For each sentence, write the adverb that tells "when" and the verb or verb phrase it modifies.

    (a) Tomorrow my sister might cut her own hair.

    (b) Fido sometimes eats avocados.

    (c) Why did you come to the picnic late?

Solution   (a) The adverb *tomorrow* tells "when" my sister *might cut*. *Tomorrow* modifies the verb phrase *might cut*.

    (b) The adverb *sometimes* modifies the verb *eats*.

    (c) The adverb *late* modifies the verb phrase *did come*.

Example 2   Diagram this sentence: My aunt swims daily.

Solution   We place the adverb *daily* under the verb *swims*:

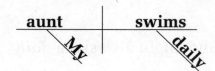

Practice   For sentences a–d, write the adverb that tells "when" and the verb or verb phrase it modifies.

    a. Tonight you and Mom and I will build a campfire.

    b. We can fish in the stream later.

    c. Have you ever seen a wombat?

    d. I read about wombats yesterday.

Diagram sentences e and f.

    e. Ms. Hoo gives grammar tests weekly.

    f. My cousin won again.

For g and h, replace each blank with the correct vocabulary word from this lesson.

    g. We show _____ when we exercise bad manners.

    h. We show _____ when we treat others with respect.

Choose the correct word(s) to complete sentences 1–16.

1. A (profusion, panacea, prologue) is an introduction to a
⁽⁹⁹⁾ play, speech, or other written work.

2. A profusion is an (adjective, asteroid, abundance).
⁽⁹⁸⁾

3. To plagiarize is to steal someone's (ideas, car, money).
⁽⁹⁷⁾

4. If you lie under oath, you (excuse, perjure, embarrass)
⁽⁹⁶⁾ yourself.

5. *Cognizant* means having "(fleas, friends, knowledge)."
⁽⁴¹⁾

6. There (was, were) some chipped paint on the door.
⁽⁹⁰⁾

7. They shoot baskets (good, well).
⁽⁹⁶⁾

8. He (has, hasn't) hardly made (no, any) errors.
⁽⁹³⁾

9. Nan caught (less, fewer) fish than I.
⁽⁵⁶⁾

10. The pronoun *them* is (nominative, objective, possessive)
^(66, 69) case.

11. (Your, You're) mail has arrived; (ours, our's) has not.
⁽⁷²⁾

12. They aren't as optimistic as (us, we).
⁽⁷⁸⁾

13. As I left, I (holded, held) the six-layer cake with one hand
^(86, 87) and (shut, shutted) the door with the other.

14. Each of those boxes (contain, contains) a surprise.
^(83, 91)

15. Neither the brothers nor their sister (have, has) reached
⁽⁸⁹⁾ the summit yet.

16. A team of experts (have, has) written a report.
⁽⁹²⁾

17. Write and underline the words that should be italicized
⁽⁸⁴⁾ in the sentence below.

Have you read The Forbidden Door?

18. Write the plural form of the singular noun *pocket knife*.
^(17, 22)

19. Rewrite the sentence below, adding hyphens as needed.
(94, 97)

Julio has completed fifty four life sized drawings.

20. Use a hyphen to divide each word correctly.
(99)

(a) equal   (b) unfeigned

21. Write the nominative case pronoun to complete the
(64) sentence below.

The two best spellers are Nien and (he, him).

22. Write whether the following is a phrase or a clause.
(36)

since some lizards run on their hind legs

23. Rewrite the following, adding capital letters and
(80, 88) punctuation marks as needed:

rondo you have a hole in your shirt exclaims ms hoo

24. For the irregular verb *fight*, write the (a) present
(19, 85) participle, (b) past tense, and (c) past participle.

25. From the sentence below, write each adverb and the
(95, 98) word or phrase it modifies.

Perlina quickly tiptoes out.

26. Rewrite the sentence below, adding capital letters and
(81) punctuation marks as needed.

carl sandburg wrote the poem buffalo dusk

27. Rewrite the following sentence, adding capital letters and
(57, 67) punctuation marks as needed.

this library book was due friday february 3 2006 i believe

28. From the sentence below, write each adverb that tells
(100) "when."

I shall never do that again!

Diagram each word of sentences 29–30.

29. Has Celly, your twenty-year-old stallion, grown tamer?
(45, 54)

30. I often send my cousin in Montana pictures of myself.
(58, 98)

Adverbs That Tell "How Much"

"How Much" or "To What Extent"

Some adverbs tell "how much" or "to what extent." These adverbs are sometimes called **intensifiers** because they add intensity (either positive or negative) to the words they modify.

Notice how the adverbs in the sentences below add intensity to the words they modify.

I felt *rather* shy.

He tries *awfully* hard.

She was *too* excited to sleep.

You are *most* welcome.

Lucy skates *quite* gracefully.

They *just* arrived.

Some adverbs that tell "how much" or "to what extent" are easy to identify because they end in -*ly*. However, many others do not. Here are some common intensifiers:

absolutely	*almost*	*altogether*
awfully	*barely*	*completely*
especially	*even*	*extremely*
fully	*hardly*	*highly*
incredibly	*just*	*least*
less	*most*	*not*
partly	*quite*	*rather*
really	*so*	*somewhat*
terribly	*thoroughly*	*too*
totally	*vastly*	*very*

An adverb that tells "how much" or "to what extent" usually modifies an adjective or another adverb. However, it occasionally modifies a verb.

MODIFYING AN ADJECTIVE

We were *so* elated!

The adverb *so* modifies the adjective *elated* and tells "how elated" we were.

MODIFYING ANOTHER ADVERB

Lucy skated *rather* carelessly.

The adverb *rather* modifies the adverb *carelessly* and tells "how carelessly" Lucy skated.

MODIFYING A VERB

Ivan *completely* agrees with you.

The adverb *completely* modifies the verb *agree* and tells "to what extent" Ivan agrees.

Example 1 For each sentence, write the adverb that tells "how much" or "to what extent" and give the word it modifies.

(a) The weather changed very quickly.

(b) Am I too late?

(c) Have they dusted the shelves thoroughly?

(d) The leader was not pretentious.

Solution (a) The adverb *very* modifies *quickly*, another adverb.

(b) The adverb *too* modifies the predicate adjective *late*.

(c) The adverb *thoroughly* modifies the verb phrase *Have dusted*.

(d) The adverb *not* modifies the adjective *pretentious*.

Diagramming Adverbs That Modify Adjectives or Other Adverbs We have learned to diagram adverbs that modify verbs. Now we will diagram adverbs that modify adjectives or other adverbs. As shown in the examples that follow, we place the adverb on a line underneath the adjective or other adverb that is being modified:

Max writes *quite* concisely.

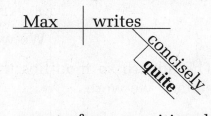

An adverb may be a part of a prepositional phrase, as in the sentence below. The adverb *rather* modifies the adjective *bumpy,* which modifies the noun *road,* which is the object of the preposition *along.*

We rode along a *rather* bumpy road.

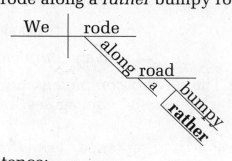

Example 2   Diagram this sentence:

Extremely dangerous snakes include cobras.

Solution   We place the adverb *extremely* underneath the adjective it modifies, *dangerous,* which describes "snakes."

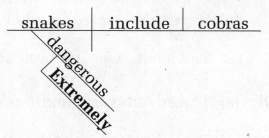

Not   Since the word *not* is an adverb, contractions like *couldn't* contain the adverb *not.* When we diagram contractions, we diagram *n't* as an adverb:

I could*n't* believe it!

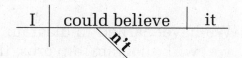

Example 3 Diagram this sentence:

Don't ostracize her.

Solution We place the adverb *not* (*n't*) under the verb phrase *Do ostracize.*

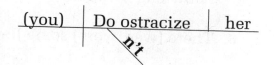

✓ **Practice** For sentences a–e, write each adverb that tells "how much" or "to what extent" and the word it modifies.

   a. That incredibly talented vocalist has a sore throat.

   b. We almost missed the train.

   c. Max was talking too fast.

   d. I couldn't understand him!

   e. He left in a terribly grumpy mood.

For f and g, replace each blank with the correct vocabulary word from this lesson.

   f. That character is an _____. I do not understand her.

   g. She is an _____ character.

Diagram sentences h and i.

   h. The two places are vastly different.

   i. He does his work very diligently.

More Practice See "More Practice Lesson 101" in Student Workbook.

✓ **Review Set 101** Choose the correct word(s) to complete sentences 1–16.

   1. (Plagiarism, Propriety, Perjury) is conformity with what
   (100) is proper and appropriate.

   2. An epilogue comes at the (beginning, middle, end) of a
   (99) written work.

3. *Profuse* means "(scarce, abundant, quaint)."
(98)

4. Plagiarism is idea (creation, theft, sale).
(97)

5. (*Avaricious, Implacable, Cognizant*) means "having knowledge; aware."
(41)

6. There (was, were) some June bugs on the door.
(90)

7. They are (good, well) players.
(96)

8. There (is, isn't) scarcely (no, any) chicken feed in the bag.
(93)

9. Among the five of us, Nan caught the (fewer, fewest) fish.
(56)

10. The pronoun *us* is (first, second, third) person (singular, plural).
(64)

11. (Who's, Whose) dog is barking?
(79)

12. A muddy field slows (we, us) soccer players.
(78)

13. I (telled, told) her where I (hided, hid) the chocolate.
(86, 87)

14. One of the cougars (pounce, pounces) on a toy rabbit.
(83, 91)

15. Either the hens or the rooster (have, has) pecked that hole in the door.
(89)

16. My camera lens (have, has) a scratch.
(92)

17. Rewrite the sentence below, adding a comma to make the meaning clear.
(68)

For Amparo Marco will do his best.

18. Write the plural form of the singular noun *chief of staff*.
(17, 22)

19. Rewrite the sentence below, adding hyphens as needed.
(94, 97)

Forty two English speaking scientists have come from Japan.

20. Use a hyphen to divide each word correctly.
(99)

(a) amaze   (b) silverware

21. Write the objective case pronoun to complete the sentence below.
(69)

Ms. Hoo gave trophies to Nien and (he, him).

22. Write whether the following clause is dependent or independent.
(73)

Daisy zooms down the street on her bicycle

23. Rewrite the following, adding capital letters and punctuation marks as needed:
(80, 88)

students asks ms hoo have you studied well

24. For the irregular verb *forget*, write the (a) present participle, (b) past tense, and (c) past participle.
(19, 85)

25. From the sentence below, write each adverb and the word or phrase it modifies.
(95, 98)

She timidly glances around.

26. Rewrite the sentence below, adding capital letters and punctuation marks as needed.
(60, 81)

the last chapter how they caught the culprit is my favorite

27. Rewrite the following sentence, adding capital letters and punctuation marks as needed.
(57, 67)

yes neil b smart phd teaches chemistry physics and russian

28. From the sentence below, write each adverb that tells "when" or "how much."
(100, 101)

The train arrived terribly late.

Diagram each word of sentences 29–30.

29. My Arabian stallion, Celly, has now become rather lazy.
(45, 54)

30. Don't you feed Celly rich green alfalfa hay very often?
(58, 98)

Dictation or Journal Entry

Vocabulary:

Candor is honesty and openness. I appreciate Juan's *candor*; he does not hide his true feelings.

Candid means "honest and straightforward; sincere." Juan gave me a *candid* response; he did not hide the truth.

Like adjectives, some adverbs can express the three degrees of comparison: positive, comparative, and superlative. Below are examples of the positive, comparative, and superlative forms of some adverbs.

POSITIVE	COMPARATIVE	SUPERLATIVE
soon	sooner	soonest
near	nearer	nearest
sweetly	more sweetly	most sweetly
early	earlier	earliest

Positive   The positive form describes an action without comparing it to anything.

Kelly came *late.*

Comparative   The comparative form compares the action of **two** people, places, or things.

Kelly came *later* than Amy.

Superlative   The superlative form compares the action of **three or more** people, places, or things.

Of the three, Kelly came *latest.*

Example 1   Choose the correct adverb form for each sentence.

(a) Of the two boys, Jay laughed (harder, hardest).

(b) Of your many jokes, that one was (funnier, funniest).

Solution   (a) Of the two boys, Jay laughed **harder.**

(b) Of your many jokes, that one was **funniest.**

Forming Comparison Adverbs

We form comparison adverbs the same way we form comparison adjectives. How we create the comparative and superlative forms of an adverb depends on how the adverb appears in its positive form. There are two main categories to remember.

One-Syllable Adverbs

We create the comparative form of most one-syllable adverbs by adding *er* to the end of the word. The superlative form is created by adding *est*.

POSITIVE	COMPARATIVE	SUPERLATIVE
late	later	latest
soon	sooner	soonest
tall	taller	tallest

Two-Syllable Adverbs

Most adverbs with two or more syllables don't have comparative or superlative forms. Instead, we put the word "more" (or "less") in front of the adverb to form the comparative, and the word "most" (or "least") to form the superlative.

POSITIVE	COMPARATIVE	SUPERLATIVE
often	more often	most often
carefully	more carefully	most carefully
happily	less happily	least happily

Since most adverbs are formed by adding the suffix *-ly* to an adjective, the rule above applies to most adverbs.

Irregular Comparison Adverbs

Some adverbs have irregular comparative and superlative forms. We must learn these if we haven't already.

POSITIVE	COMPARATIVE	SUPERLATIVE
little	less	least
good, well	better	best
badly	worse	worst
far	farther	farthest
much, some	more	most

We check the dictionary if we are unsure how to create the comparative or superlative form of any adverb.

Example 2

Complete the comparison chart by adding the comparative and superlative forms of each adverb.

POSITIVE	COMPARATIVE	SUPERLATIVE
(a) far	_____	_____
(b) well	_____	_____
(c) sadly	_____	_____
(d) quietly	_____	_____

Solution

POSITIVE	COMPARATIVE	SUPERLATIVE
(a) far	**farther**	**farthest**
(b) well	**better**	**best**
(c) sadly	**more sadly**	**most sadly**
(d) quietly	**more quietly**	**most quietly**

✓**Practice** Write the correct adverb form for sentences a–e.

a. The lions are roaring (more ferociously, most ferociously) than the tigers.

b. In our family, Lily does her chores (more quickly, most quickly).

c. I like this story (better, best) than the other one.

d. Of the four batters, Rudy hit the ball (farther, farthest).

e. I sing (worse, worst) than you, but he sings (worse, worst) of all.

For f and g, replace each blank with the correct vocabulary word from this lesson.

f. A _____ person is honest and sincere.

g. Lucy is honest and open. She demonstrates _____.

More Practice Write the correct adverb for each sentence.

1. My father cooks (weller, better) than I.

2. He is the (better, best) in our family.

3. I walk (farther, farthest) than she.

4. She practices (less, least) than he.

5. Of the four players, he practices (less, least).

6. Of the two, he drives (slower, slowest).

7. He works (longer, longest) than I.

8. She hits the ball (harder, hardest) than I.

Review Set 102
Choose the correct word(s) to complete sentences 1–16.

1. An (encumbrance, enigma, amphibian) is a riddle or
(101) mystery.

2. Impropriety is the quality of being (proper, polite,
(100) improper).

3. A prologue is a(n) (conclusion, introduction, summary)
(99) for a play, speech, or other written work.

4. In spring the garden filled with a (plagiarism, profusion,
(98) perjury) of butterflies.

5. If you are cognizant, you are (ignorant, aware, kin).
(41)

6. A bird with bright blue tail feathers (was, were) chirping
(90) nearby.

7. My friend listens (good, well).
(96)

8. There (ain't, aren't) (no, any) penguins here.
(93)

9. Among the five of us, Nan fished (longer, longest).
(102)

10. The pronoun *us* is (nominative, objective, possessive)
(64) case.

11. (Who's, Whose) there?
(79)

12. I think (we, us) champions deserve a rest.
(78)

13. Had he (got, gotten) the message before he (shined,
(86, 87) shone) his shoes?

14. Many on the team (is, are) cheering.
(83, 91)

15. Either the rooster or the hens (have, has) pecked that hole in the door.
(89)

16. Measles (was, were) more common when my grandparents were children.
(92)

17. From the sentence below, write and underline words that should be italicized.
(84)

Enigma is a noun while enigmatic is an adjective.

18. Write the plural form of the singular noun *flu virus*.
(17, 22)

19. Rewrite the sentence below, adding hyphens as needed.
(94, 97)

A color-blind painter used twenty one different colors on the kitchen walls.

20. Use a hyphen to divide each word correctly.
(99)

(a) candor   (b) erase

21. Write the nominative case pronoun to complete the sentence below.
(64)

Nien and (he, him) thanked Ms. Hoo.

22. Write whether the following is a phrase or a clause.
(36)

without a care in the world

23. Rewrite the following, adding capital letters and punctuation marks as needed:
(80, 88)

catch those thieves cries officer valiant

24. For the irregular verb *flee*, write the (a) present participle, (b) past tense, and (c) past participle.
(19, 85)

25. From the sentence below, write each adverb and the word or phrase it modifies.
(95, 98)

The officer fearlessly moves ahead.

26. Rewrite the sentence below, adding capital letters and
(60, 81) punctuation marks as needed.

omar titled his essay out of the darkness

27. Rewrite the following sentence, adding capital letters and
(57, 67) punctuation marks as needed.

our essays are due i believe on monday february 26

28. From the sentence below, write each adverb that tells
(100, 101) "when" or "how much."

Celly has now become somewhat lazy.

Diagram each word of sentences 29–30.

29. Later the wind on the lake might not be so strong.
(45, 54)

30. Almost daily I feed my lazy horse a bucket of oats with
(58, 98) molasses.

The Semicolon

Dictation or Journal Entry
Vocabulary:
Anarchy is the absence of government and law; chaos. After the government was destroyed, the country experienced *anarchy*.

Monarchy is government by one ruler. England had a *monarchy* under King Henry VIII.

The **semicolon** (;) is used as a connector. It indicates a pause longer than a comma but shorter than a colon. In this lesson, we will learn how to use the semicolon correctly.

Related Thoughts In a compound sentence, we can use a semicolon instead of a coordinating conjunction (*and, but, or, for, nor, yet, so*) between the two independent clauses. However, these clauses must contain related thoughts.

> YES: The potatoes are rotten; they smell like old shoes. (related thoughts)

> NO: The potatoes are rotten; my dad bought red apples. (not related thoughts)

Example 1 Use a semicolon instead of the coordinating conjunction in this sentence:

> He came with a question, but he left with the answer.

Solution We replace the comma and conjunction with a semicolon:

> He came with a question; he left with the answer.

Conjunctive Adverbs An adverb used as a conjunction is called a **conjunctive adverb**. Words such as *also, besides, still, however, therefore, consequently, otherwise, moreover, furthermore,* and *nevertheless* are examples of conjunctive adverbs. We place a semicolon before a conjunctive adverb.

> YES: Lisa usually curls her pigtails; *however*, today she braided them.
>   ↑

Using a comma where a semicolon is needed creates a run-on sentence:

> NO: Lisa usually curls her pigtails, *however*, today she braided them.
>   ↑

Example 2 Place a semicolon where it is needed in this sentence:

> Her feet have blisters, still, she must keep walking.

We place a semicolon before the conjunctive adverb *still*:

> Her feet have blisters; still, she must keep walking.

With Other Commas If an independent clause contains commas, we can use a semicolon to show where one independent clause ends and another one begins.

> UNCLEAR: Celina enjoys art, hiking, and tennis, and reading, softball, and music are April's favorite activities.

> CLEAR: Celina enjoys art, hiking, and tennis; and reading, softball, and music are April's favorite activities.

Semicolons can also be used to separate phrases or dependent clauses that contain commas.

> The company has offices in Sacramento, California; Salem, Oregon; and Olympia, Washington.

> She promised to feed the dogs, cats, and bird; do her homework and take out the trash; and be nicer to her sister, brother, and parents.

Example 3 Place semicolons where they are needed in sentences a and b.

(a) We drove through Boston, Massachusetts, Providence, Rhode Island, and Hartford, Connecticut.

(b) He plays the guitar, the banjo, and the mandolin, and she plays the drums, the saxophone, and the trumpet.

Solution (a) We separate each "city, state" pair of words with a semicolon for clarity:

> We drove through Boston, Massachusetts; Providence, Rhode Island; and Hartford, Connecticut.

(b) Because the independent clauses in this sentence already contain commas, we separate the two clauses with a semicolon:

> He plays the guitar, the banjo, and the mandolin; and she plays the drums, the saxophone, and the trumpet.

Practice Rewrite sentences a–c, replacing commas with semicolons where they are needed.

a. We looked at homophone pairs such as *blue, blew, hear, here,* and *no, know.*

b. We plant in the spring, we harvest in the fall.

c. I left my math book at home, moreover, I forgot my homework.

For d and e, replace each blank with the correct vocabulary word from this lesson.

d. One ruler governs a _____.

e. The absence of government is _____.

More Practice See "More Practice Lesson 103" in Student Workbook.

✓Review Set 103

Choose the correct word(s) to complete sentences 1–16.

1. (Perjury, Paltriness, Candor) is honesty and openness.
(102)

2. (*Automatic, Enigmatic, Autocratic*) means "mysterious or puzzling."
(101)

3. Propriety is (conformity, nonconformity, disagreement) with what is proper and appropriate.
(100)

4. The author wrote a(n) (prologue, epilogue, culprit) as a conclusion at the end of the essay.
(99)

5. (*Frugal, Dogmatic, Extravagant*) means "wasteful."
(42)

6. Here (come, comes) Wally and Peter!
(90)

7. My friend is a (well, good) listener.
(96)

8. Rufus (has, hasn't) hardly (no, any) fleas.
(93)

9. Of the two, Nan fished (longer, longest).
(102)

10. The pronoun *we* is (nominative, objective, possessive) case.
(64)

11. (You're, Your) seats are here; (our's, ours) are over there.
(72)

12. Liang swims faster than (me, I).
(78)

13. Rumors had (sprang, sprung) up that the villain had been
(86, 87) (hanged, hung).

14. Each of the players (is, are) cheering.
(83, 91)

15. Bob or the neighbors (recycle, recycles) aluminum cans.
(89)

16. The flock of sheep (have, has) moved to greener pastures.
(92)

17. From the sentence below, write and underline words that
(84) should be italicized.

The sailing vessel Good Hope sank off the coast of
England.

18. Rewrite the sentence below, replacing commas with
(103) semicolons where they are needed.

I remembered all the states and their capitals except for
Madison, Wisconsin, Pierre, South Dakota, and Topeka,
Kansas.

19. Rewrite the sentence below, adding hyphens as needed.
(94, 97)
Their one time offer was less desirable than a hand me
down toothbrush.

20. Use a hyphen to divide each word correctly.
(99)
(a) disclose   (b) through

21. Write the objective case pronoun to complete the
(69) sentence below.

Tyrone gave Marcela and (me, I) an enigmatic grin.

22. Write whether the following clause is dependent or
(73) independent.

after I catch a fish or two

23. Rewrite the following, adding capital letters and
(80, 88) punctuation marks as needed:

have you caught badchek asked ms hoo

24. For the irregular verb *burst*, write the (a) present
(19, 85) participle, (b) past tense, and (c) past participle.

25. From the sentence below, write each adverb and the
(95, 98) word or phrase it modifies.

Dandelions grow profusely here.

26. Rewrite the sentence below, adding capital letters and
(60, 81) punctuation marks as needed.

howard r garis a newspaperman wrote the short story
uncle wiggily and a big rat

27. Rewrite the following sentence, adding capital letters and
(57, 67) punctuation marks as needed.

the culprits it seems are badchek whipper and shadow

28. From the sentence below, write each adverb that tells
(100, 101) "when" or "how much."

Sometimes I am too frugal.

Diagram each word of sentences 29–30.

29. Today the breeze on the lake isn't very strong.
(45, 54)

30. Weekly, Howard R. Garis would write six bedtime stories
(58, 98) about Uncle Wiggily, a rabbit hero.

Sure or Surely? The word *sure* is an adjective and not an adverb. *Sure* should not take the place of the adverbs *surely, certainly,* or *really.*

NO: Joe *sure* helped.

YES: Joe *surely* helped. (modifies verb "helped")

NO: He's *sure* smart.

YES: He's *really* smart. (modifies predicate adjective "smart")

NO: You are *sure* welcome.

YES: You are *certainly* welcome. (modifies predicate adjective "welcome")

We remember that *sure* is an adjective, and we use it only as an adjective or predicate adjective, as in the sentences below.

I am *sure* of the answer. (predicate adjective)

That's a *sure* method. (adjective modifying the noun "method")

He was *sure* it would rain. (predicate adjective)

Example 1 Replace each blank with *sure* or *surely.*

(a) I (sure, surely) hope you can come.

(b) Are you (sure, surely) of your answer?

Solution (a) I **surely** hope you can come. (*Surely* is an adverb. It modifies the verb "hope.")

(b) Are you **sure** of your answer? (*Sure* is a predicate adjective. It describes the pronoun "you.")

Real or Really? Like *sure,* the word *real* is an adjective and should not take the place of the adverb *really. Real* modifies a noun or pronoun, while *really* modifies a verb, adjective, or adverb.

NO: I'm *real* happy.

YES: I'm *really* happy. (modifies predicate adjective "happy")

NO: That's a *real* big whale.

YES: That's a *really* big whale. (modifies adjective "big")

NO: Rob writes *real* well.

YES: Rob writes *really* well. (modifies adverb "well")

We remember that *real* is an adjective, and we use it only as an adjective or predicate adjective, as in the sentences below.

That stuffed toy looks like a *real* skunk. (adjective modifying the noun "skunk")

Are those diamonds *real* or fake? (predicate adjective)

Example 2 Replace each blank with *real* or *really*.

(a) Lola flew her kite (real, really) high.

(b) That toy spider looks (real, really).

Solution (a) Lola flew her kite **really** high. (*Really* is an adverb. It modifies another adverb, "high.")

(b) That toy spider looks **real**. (*Real* is a predicate adjective. It describes the noun "spider.")

Bad or Badly? The word *bad* is an adjective. It describes a noun or pronoun, and often follows linking verbs like *feel, look, seem, taste, smell*, and *is*. The word *badly* is an adverb that tells "how." We do not use *bad* as an adverb.

NO: I did *bad* on my essay.

YES: I did *badly* on my essay. (adverb that tells "how")

NO: Kate skates *bad*.

YES: Kate skates *badly*. (adverb that tells "how")

NO: That team played *bad*.

YES: That team played *badly*. (adverb that tells "how")

We remember that *bad* is an adjective, and we use it only as an adjective or predicate adjective, as in these sentences:

Victor feels *bad* today. (predicate adjective)

Rotten potatoes smell *bad*. (predicate adjective)

I earned a *bad* grade. (adjective modifying the noun "grade")

Example 3 Replace each blank with *bad* or *badly*.

(a) Last night I sang (bad, badly).

(b) Spoiled milk tastes (bad, badly).

Solution (a) Last night I sang **badly**. (*Badly* is an adverb that tells "how" I sang.)

(b) Spoiled milk tastes **bad**. (*Bad* is a predicate adjective. It describes the noun "milk.")

✓**Practice** For a and b, replace each blank with the correct vocabulary word from this lesson.

a. The _____ queen did not offer money to help the poor.

b. Her _____ was evident as she kept all her riches for herself.

Choose the correct word to complete sentences c–g.

c. Minh was (sure, surely) happy to see us.

d. They laughed (real, really) hard at the jokes.

e. It was (real, really) funny.

f. Does your skinned knee hurt (bad, badly)?

g. Yesterday, I played soccer very (bad, badly).

More Practice Choose the correct word to complete each sentence.

1. Butch (sure, surely) behaves well now.

2. He (sure, certainly) tries hard.

3. I'm (sure, really) tired.

4. Butch is (real, really) hungry.

5. He eats (real, really) well.

6. Dina skinned her knee (bad, badly).

7. It was a (bad, badly) wound.

8. Her knee hurts (bad, badly).

Choose the correct word(s) to complete sentences 1–16.

1. (Monarchy, Anarchy, Avarice) is the absence of
(103) government and law; chaos.

2. A candid remark is (phony, honest, untruthful).
(102)

3. An enigma is a (profusion, dogma, mystery).
(101)

4. Plagiarism is a(n) (impropriety, propriety, amphibian).
(100)

5. *Frugal* and *extravagant* are (synonyms, antonyms,
(42) homophones).

6. The party with my relatives (was, were) (real, really) fun.
(90, 104)

7. Tinker (sure, certainly) sings (good, well).
(96, 104)

8. There (ain't, isn't) (nobody, anybody) in the closet.
(93)

9. Of the two brothers, Joe smiles (more, most).
(102)

10. The pronoun *we* is (first, second, third) person (singular,
(64) plural).

11. (Who, Whom) have you called?
(79)

Think: you | have called | ?

12. (We, Us) swimmers saw sharks!
(78)

13. I (wringed, wrung) out the wet towel and (hanged, hung)
(86, 87) it up to dry.

14. Everyone wearing earmuffs (hear, hears) only muffled
(83, 91) noises.

15. The neighbors or Bob (recycle, recycles) aluminum cans.
(89)

16. This pair of shoes (is, are) comfortable.
(92)

17. From the sentence below, write and underline words that
(84) should be italicized.

We must catch the next train, Frazzle Express.

18. Rewrite the sentence below, replacing a comma with a semicolon where it is needed.
(103)

He remembers her face, however, her name escapes him.

19. Rewrite the sentence below, adding hyphens as needed.
(94, 97)

Mother has a curly, wash and wear hairdo.

20. Use a hyphen to divide each word correctly.
(99)

(a) tundra   (b) strait

21. Write the nominative case pronoun to complete the sentence below.
(64)

The best actors were Tinker and (her, she).

22. Write whether the following is a phrase or a clause.
(36)

where we live

23. Rewrite the following, adding capital letters and punctuation marks as needed:
(80, 88)

there's smoke shouts michael

24. For the irregular verb *dive*, write the (a) present participle, (b) past tense, and (c) past participle.
(19, 85)

25. From the sentence below, write each adverb and the word or phrase it modifies.
(95, 98)

Mom intuitively knew I was there.

26. Rewrite the sentence below, adding capital letters and punctuation marks as needed.
(60, 81)

conrad a camp counselor played the guitar and sang kookaburra

27. Rewrite the following sentence, adding capital letters and punctuation marks as needed.
(74)

as we sat around the campfire conrad told us a long scary story

28. From the sentence below, write each adverb that tells "when" or "how much."
(100, 101)

Afterward we were terribly frightened.

Diagram each word of sentences 29–30.

29. Then some of us became sleepless and rather homesick.
(45, 54)

30. Conrad, our camp counselor, certainly didn't tell us a
(58, 98) bedtime story about Uncle Wiggily.

LESSON 105

The Colon

The **colon** (:) signals to the reader that more information is to come. In this lesson we will learn to use the colon correctly.

Between Independent Clauses

We have learned that a semicolon can join two independent clauses that contain related thoughts. A colon can join two independent clauses when the first clause introduces the second or the second clause illustrates the first.

> On the camping trip, I learned an important lesson: it is wise to take along some insect repellent.

> Our tent was a mess: a jelly sandwich was smashed in the doorway, and the floor was covered with sand and dirty clothes.

Example 1 Insert colons where they are needed in these sentences.

(a) There is one sure way to pass the test do the homework.

(b) The artist was impressive he could paint with his toes.

Solution (a) The first independent clause introduces the second, so we place a colon between them:

> There is one sure way to pass the test: do the homework.

(b) The second independent clause illustrates the first. We place a colon between them:

> The artist was impressive: he could paint with his toes.

Introducing a List

We use a colon to introduce a list.

> I made a grocery list: bananas, milk, bread, and eggs.

> She certainly hopes to visit other states: Louisiana, Mississippi, Alabama, and Georgia.

> Fido knows three commands: sit, stay, and come.

We do not use a colon if the sentence is grammatically correct without it.

NO: You will need: boots, mittens, and sunglasses.

YES: You will need these things: boots, mittens, and sunglasses.

The Following,   We use a colon with the words *the following* or *as follows*
As Follows   when they introduce a list. Sometimes the list will begin on a separate line.

Gather *the following* ingredients: flour, sugar, butter, and eggs.

The ingredients are *as follows*:
  2 eggs
  1/4 cup milk
  1 teaspoon sugar

Example 2   Insert colons where they are needed in these sentences.

(a) For the hike you will need the following a compass, a water bottle, and sturdy boots.

(b) In Grandpa's tool shed are shovels, hoes, and rakes.

Solution   (a) We use a colon after the words *the following* when they introduce a list:

For the hike you will need the following: a compass, a water bottle, and sturdy boots.

(b) We do not use a colon if the sentence is grammatically correct without it. **No colon is needed in this sentence.**

Salutation of   We use a colon after a salutation in a business letter.
a Business
Letter
Madam:

Dear Mr. Tran:

Time   When we write the time of day with digits, we use a colon to separate the hours and minutes.

Class begins at 9:15 a.m.

Example 3   Insert colons where they are needed in these sentences.

(a) The show will start at 730 p.m.

(b) Dear Sir
  Please send me information...

Solution (a) We place a colon between the hours and minutes when we write the time of day. We write **7:30** p.m.

(b) We use a colon after the salutation in a business letter, so we write **Dear Sir:**

Quotations We can use a colon to introduce a quotation.

Grandma's memoirs began like this:

The youngest of six children, I was born on a small farm near Des Moines, Iowa...

Uncle Bill's letter went on: "It snowed again last night...

Example 4 Insert colons where they are needed in these sentences.

(a) Nien's speech began "Thank you for having me."

(b) Please tell me who said these words "One today is worth two tomorrows."

Solution (a) We can use a colon to introduce a quotation, so we write:

Nien's speech began: "Thank you for having me."

(b) Please tell me who said these words: "One today is worth two tomorrows."

Practice Rewrite a–d, inserting colons where they are needed

a. I shall set the alarm for 600 a.m.

b. I am taking the following classes English, math, history, science, and P.E.

c. Dear Madam

Please send me your special recipe for pea soup...

d. Abraham Lincoln spoke these words "Most folks are about as happy as they make up their minds to be."

For e and f, replace each blank with the correct vocabulary word from this lesson.

e. To destroy something sacred is to _____ it.

f. To make something sacred is to _____ it.

Choose the correct word(s) to complete sentences 1–16.

1. (Anarchy, Monarchy, Parsimony) is stinginess; extreme frugality.
(104)

2. Monarchy is government by one (congress, group, ruler).
(103)

3. Candor is (perjury, dishonesty, honesty).
(102)

4. *Enigmatic* means "(profuse, paltry, mysterious)."
(101)

5. *Extravagant* and *wasteful* are (synonyms, antonyms, homophones).
(42)

6. The rash on my toes (itch, itches) (bad, badly).
(90, 104)

7. You (sure, surely) did (good, well) on the test.
(96, 104)

8. There (ain't, isn't) (nothing, anything) in the box.
(93)

9. Of all the brothers, Joe smiles (more, most).
(102)

10. The pronoun *our* is (nominative, objective, possessive) case.
(64)

11. (Who, Whom) called you?
(79)

12. Did the shark see (we, us) swimmers?
(78)

13. We (buyed, bought) Ms. Hoo a plant.
(85)

14. Some wearing earmuffs (hear, hears) only muffled noises.
(83, 91)

15. A cat and a mouse (race, races) down the hallway.
(89)

16. The batch of cookies (is, are) baking.
(92)

17. From the sentence below, write and underline words that should be italicized.
(84)

Claude Monet, a French artist, painted The Japanese Bridge.

18. Rewrite the sentence below, replacing a comma with a semicolon where it is needed.
(103)

Rain fell, it beat on our tents.

19. Rewrite the sentence below, adding hyphens as needed.
(94, 97)

All twenty three campers wore water repellent ponchos.

20. Use a hyphen to divide each word correctly.
(99)

(a) contrite   (b) daunt

21. Write the objective case pronoun to complete the
(69) sentence below.

Conrad reads to Erik and (me, I).

22. Rewrite the following business letter, inserting colons
(105) where they are needed.

Dear Teachers

By 200 p.m., I must have the following your roll
sheets, your grades, and your seating charts.

Respectfully,
Mr. Stoneman

23. Rewrite the following, adding capital letters and
(80, 88) punctuation marks as needed:

dr kim asks is there a fire

24. Rewrite the sentence below, adding capital letters and
(57, 67) punctuation marks as needed.

yes she was born on monday may 10 1948

25. From the sentence below, write each adverb and the
(95, 98) word or phrase it modifies.

Tom generously passes fresh fruit around.

26. Rewrite the sentence below, adding capital letters and
(60, 81) punctuation marks as needed.

erik a young camper prefers stories such as uncle wiggily
and the watermelon

27. Rewrite the following sentence, adding capital letters and
(74) punctuation marks as needed.

if conrad tells another dark mysterious story we shall
turn on big bright flashlights

28. From the sentence below, write each adverb that tells ^(100, 101) "when" or "how much."

Conrad might tell another dreadfully dark story later.

Diagram each word of sentences 29–30.

29. With flashlights, we shall feel intrepid and really valiant ^(45, 54) tonight.

30. Erik, the youngest camper, surely will not loan Conrad ^(58, 98) his flashlight again.

The Prepositional Phrase as an Adverb • Diagramming

Dictation or Journal Entry

Vocabulary:

Guile is deceit or slyness. She uses *guile* to avoid punishment for her crime.

To *beguile* is to mislead or deceive. She *beguiles* her unsuspecting neighbors.

Adverb Phrases

We have learned that a prepositional phrase can function as an adjective by modifying a noun or a pronoun. A prepositional phrase can also function as an adverb. A prepositional phrase that modifies a verb, an adjective, or another adverb is called an **adverb phrase**. It answers the question "how," "when," "where," "why," or "to what extent." The italicized adverb phrases below modify the verb "skates."

HOW
Lucy skates *like a professional.*

WHEN
Lucy skates *before dinner.*

WHERE
Lucy skates *on Main Street.*

WHY
Lucy skates *for fun and exercise.*

TO WHAT EXTENT
Lucy skates *throughout the day.*

Most adverb phrases modify verbs. However, an adverb phrase can also modify an adjective or another adverb, as in the examples below.

Lucy is ready *for lunch.* (modifies predicate adjective "ready")

Lucy skates far *from home.* (modifies adverb "far")

Example 1 Write the adverb phrase, and tell which word it modifies.

(a) This path leads to the mountaintop.

(b) Exercise is good for one's health.

(c) Must we wait here in this line?

Solution (a) The adverb phrase *to the mountaintop* modifies the verb *leads.* It tells "where."

(b) The adverb phrase *for one's health* modifies the predicate adjective *good*.

(c) The adverb phrase *in this line* modifies the adverb *here*.

Diagramming   We diagram a prepositional phrase under the verb, adjective, or adverb it modifies. For example:

Lucy skates around the park.

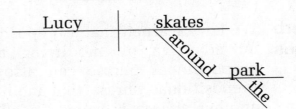

In the sentence above, the adverb phrase *around the park* modifies the verb *skates*. It tells where Lucy skates.

Example 2   Diagram the three sentences from Example 1.

Solution   (a) This path leads to the mountaintop.

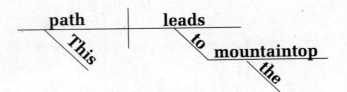

(b) Exercise is good for one's health.

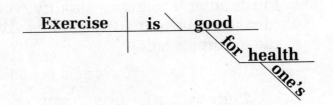

(c) Must we wait here in this line?

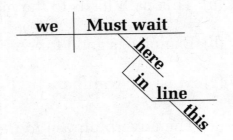

✓Practice For a–e, write each adverb phrase and tell which word it modifies.

    a. Rewards come from hard work.

    b. Nan lives in the city.

    c. Max is weary of prepositions.

    d. I am ready for another lesson.

    e. Are you wise concerning grammar?

Diagram sentences f and g.
    f. Leave a key with Mom.

    g. I am sorry about the accident.

For h and i, replace each blank with the correct vocabulary word from this lesson.
    h. Villains _____ the princess, making her think they are good people.

    i. Villains use _____ to make the princess believe they will help her.

More Practice Diagram sentences 1–5.
    1. He dove into the pond.

    2. Are you sure about your answer?

    3. Is Erik afraid of the dark?

    4. Put it under your pillow.

    5. Are you hungry for lunch?

✓Review Set 106 Choose the correct word(s) to complete sentences 1–16.
    1. To (conceal, encumber, consecrate) is to set apart as
(105) sacred or holy.

    2. *Parsimonious* means "(enigmatic, profuse, stingy)."
(104)

    3. Anarchy is the absence of (pain, hunger, government).
(103)

4. *Candid* means "(honest, dishonest, pretentious)."
(102)

5. Your paternal relatives are those on your (mother's, father's, cousin's) side of the family.
(43)

6. The fleabites on my ankle (sure, really) (itch, itches).
(90, 104)

7. I (sure, certainly) did (bad, badly) on the test.
(104)

8. We don't have (nothing, anything) to fear.
(93)

9. Of the two men, Sid travels (farther, farthest).
(102)

10. The pronoun *our* is (first, second, third) person (singular, plural).
(64)

11. (Who's, Whose) calling?
(79)

12. Sharks swim faster than (we, us).
(78)

13. I (saw, seen) him last night.
(86)

14. Anyone with strong muscles (exercise, exercises) daily.
(83, 91)

15. Either the actors or the director (sweep, sweeps) the stage.
(89)

16. Mathematics (is, are) my favorite subject.
(92)

17. From the sentence below, write and underline words that should be italicized.
(84)

Dad reads only one newspaper, the Tribune.

18. Rewrite the sentence below, replacing a comma with a semicolon where it is needed.
(103)

We saw the White House, however, we did not see the President.

19. Rewrite the sentence below, adding hyphens as needed.
(94, 97)

I pushed the fast forward button during the three hour movie.

20. Use a hyphen to divide each word correctly.
(99)

(a) beguile   (b) smashed

21. Write the nominative case pronoun to complete the
(64) sentence below.

The worst are Badchek and (she, her).

22. Rewrite the following business letter, inserting colons
(105) where they are needed.

Dear Council Members

    From greatest to least, the problems are these
traffic, graffiti, and pollution.

                    Sincerely,
                    Ms. Hoo

23. Rewrite the following, adding capital letters and
(80, 88) punctuation marks as needed:

conrad exclaims happy friday erik

24. Rewrite the sentence below, adding capital letters and
(57, 67) punctuation marks as needed.

obviously ms hoo dislikes traffic graffiti and pollution

25. From the sentence below, write each adverb and the
(95, 98) word or phrase it modifies.

We carefully searched everywhere.

26. Rewrite the sentence below, adding capital letters and
(60, 81) punctuation marks as needed.

luz a guitarist ended with the song make new friends

27. Rewrite the following sentence, adding capital letters and
(74) punctuation marks as needed.

while conrad sleeps erik plans a clever harmless prank

28. From the sentence below, write each adverb that tells
(100, 101) "when" or "how much."

Tomorrow Conrad will have very salty pancakes.

Diagram each word of sentences 29–30.

29. Wouldn't pancakes taste bad with extra salt in them?
(54, 106)

30. Will Conrad tell his friend Erik another really scary
(58, 104) story?

Preposition or Adverb?
• Preposition Usage

Preposition or Adverb? Most prepositions can also be used as adverbs. We remember that an adverb stands alone, but a preposition always has an object.

ADVERB: Lucy skates *around.*

PREPOSITION: Lucy skates *around the *corner.*

ADVERB: Lucy skates *past.*

PREPOSITION: Lucy skates *past *me.*

ADVERB: Lucy skates *along.*

PREPOSITION: Lucy skates *along the *sidewalk.*

Diagramming can help us determine whether a word is being used as an adverb or a preposition. Look at the word "around" in these two sentences:

ADVERB: We tossed *around* a ball.

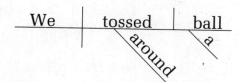

We can see that "ball" is a direct object telling what we tossed. It is not an object of a preposition.

PREPOSITION: Then we jogged *around* the field.

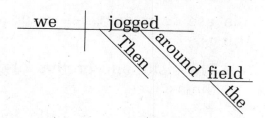

In this sentence, "field" is the object of the preposition "around."

Example 1 Tell whether the italicized word in each sentence is an adverb or a preposition.

(a) Max went *outside.*

(b) Ms. Hoo was *inside* the room.

(c) A hawk flies *above* the meadow.

(d) Rabbits hop *about.*

Solution (a) *Outside* is an **adverb** that tells where Max "went."

(b) *Inside* is a **preposition.** Its object is "room."

(c) *Above* is a **preposition.** Its object is "meadow."

(d) *About* is an **adverb** that tells where rabbits "hop."

Preposition Usage Certain pairs of prepositions are frequently misused. In this lesson, we will learn to use these prepositions correctly:

in and *into*

between and *among*

beside and *besides*

In or Into? The preposition *in* refers to position but not movement.

I am *in* the car.

She is *in* the room.

The preposition *into* refers to moving from the outside to the inside.

I climb *into* the car.

She goes *into* the room.

Between or Among? We use *between* when referring to two people, places, or things.

The sister and brother divided the peanuts *between* themselves.

There is not much difference *between* you and me.

We use *among* when referring to three or more people, places, or things.

> She is one *among* many who want the job.

> He is *among* the greatest authors of all time.

Beside or Besides? The preposition *beside* means "at the side of."

> The man stood *beside* his wife.

> She parks her car *beside* the apartment.

Besides means "in addition to" or "as well as."

> *Besides* the corn, the squash is ripe.

> Who *besides* me wants watermelon?

Example 2 Choose the correct preposition for each sentence.
(a) Please enter (in, into) the booth.

(b) She wants her dog to walk (beside, besides) her.

(c) He was (among, between) the five smallest players on the team.

Solution (a) Please enter **into** the booth.

(b) She wants her dog to walk **beside** her.

(c) He was **among** the five smallest players on the team.

Practice For sentences a–d, tell whether the italicized word is an adverb or a preposition.
a. A dove flew *by*.

b. A bandit stepped *aboard* the train.

c. Mia hurried *across* the street.

d. Please come *along*.

For e–g, choose the correct preposition.
e. She tossed the wrapper (in, into) the trash can.

f. (Among, Between) two trees, I hung a hammock.

g. Would anyone (beside, besides) Juan like to come?

For h and i, replace each blank with the correct vocabulary word from this lesson.

h. The mayor's speech was hard to follow because of his many _____.

i. If you depart from the main topic, you _____.

Review Set 107

Choose the correct word to complete sentences 1–16.

1. (Guile, Monarchy, Rapport) is deceit or slyness.
(106)

2. To (consecrate, desecrate, obfuscate) is to destroy
(105) something sacred.

3. Parsimony is (generosity, stinginess, anarchy).
(104)

4. (Anarchy, Monarchy, Propriety) is government by one
(103) ruler.

5. Your maternal relatives are those on your (father's,
(43) friend's, mother's) side of the family.

6. There (go, goes) some (real, really) fast runners!
(90, 104)

7. They (sure, surely) run (good, well).
(96, 104)

8. Carlos doesn't want (no, any) eggplant.
(93)

9. Of all the men, Sid travels (farther, farthest).
(102)

10. Badchek and his two friends sneak (in, into) the forest
(107) and divide the money (between, among) themselves.

11. (Your's, Yours) is red, but (theirs, their's) is orange.
(72)

12. Dolphins watch (we, us) swimmers.
(78)

13. Have you (saw, seen) him before?
(86)

14. Some in the class (has, have) homework to do.
(83, 91)

15. Either the director or the actors (sweep, sweeps) the
(89) stage.

16. This pair of shoes (fit, fits) perfectly.
(92)

17. From the sentence below, write and underline words that
(84) should be italicized.

In Spanish, we say adios when we leave.

18. Rewrite the sentence below, replacing commas with
(103) semicolons where they are needed.

The bus will stop in Phoenix, Arizona, Santa Fe, New Mexico, and Oklahoma City, Oklahoma.

19. Rewrite the sentence below, adding hyphens as needed.
(94, 97)

Twenty eight singers performed a one of a kind concert.

20. Use a hyphen to divide each word correctly.
(99)

(a) ardent   (b) elate

21. Write the objective case pronoun to complete the
(69) sentence below.

Will Officer Valiant arrest Badchek and (she, her)?

22. Rewrite the following business letter, inserting colons
(105) where they are needed.

Dear Counselors

Please close the cabins as follows sweep floors, take out trash, and lock doors.

Sincerely,
Mr. Vela

23. Rewrite the following, adding capital letters and
(80, 88) punctuation marks as needed:

have badchek and she fled to another country asked ms hoo

24. Rewrite the sentence below, adding capital letters and
(57, 67) punctuation marks as needed.

they have fled i believe to ottawa canada

25. From the sentence below, write whether the circled word is an adverb or a preposition.
(107)

I wrote (down) the answer.

26. Rewrite the sentence below, adding capital letters and punctuation marks as needed.
(60, 81)

i especially liked the last chapter a warm wind

27. Rewrite the following sentence, adding capital letters and punctuation marks as needed.
(74)

as the moon casts shadows erik imagines big hungry beasts outside the tent

28. From the sentence below, write each adverb that tells "when" or "how much."
(100, 101)

Later the campers will thoroughly clean their dirty tent.

Diagram each word of sentences 29–30.

29. Pancakes shouldn't taste so terribly salty.
(45, 54)

30. Will Conrad soon forgive Erik, the young camper, for that prank?
(100, 106)

LESSON 108

The Apostrophe: Possessives

Dictation or Journal Entry
Vocabulary:
Futile means "hopeless or without effect." I made a *futile* attempt to patch my leaky roof during a rainstorm.

Futility is hopelessness or ineffectiveness. Water continued to drip from the ceiling, proving the *futility* of my efforts to patch the leak.

We use the apostrophe to show possession.

Singular Possessive Nouns

To give a singular noun ownership, we add an apostrophe and an *s* (*'s*). The noun then becomes a **singular possessive noun**, as in the examples below.

SINGULAR NOUN	SINGULAR POSSESSIVE NOUN
drummer	drummer's rhythm
donkey	donkey's hooves
Cass	Cass's haircut
tree	tree's trunk
box	box's lid
Mr. Jones	Mr. Jones's smile

In a compound noun, possession is formed by adding *'s* to the last word.

brother-in-law	brother-in-law's idea
grandchild	grandchild's dream

Shared or Separate Possession

When more than one noun shares possession of something, we add *'s* to the last noun.

> Ann, Yoli, and Sara's volleyball game

When the nouns each possess something separately, we add *'s* to each noun.

> John's and Tom's signatures

Example 1 Use *'s* to make each singular noun possessive.

(a) Danny

(b) James

(c) sister-in-law

(d) fox

(e) Lisa and Daniel (daughter)

Solution   (a) **Danny's**   (b) **James's**

           (c) **sister-in-law's**   (d) **fox's**

           (e) **Lisa and Daniel's** daughter

Plural Possessive Nouns

To give a regular plural noun ownership, we add only an apostrophe. The noun then becomes a **plural possessive noun**, as in the examples below.

PLURAL NOUN	PLURAL POSSESSIVE NOUN
roller skates	roller skates' wheels
heroes	heroes' names
the Joneses	the Joneses' home

In a compound noun, possession is formed by adding *'s* to the last word.

editors in chief's opinions

brothers-in-law's hobbies

Irregular Plurals

To give an irregular plural noun ownership, add *'s*.

children	children's toys
women	women's clothing
mice	mice's nest
oxen	oxen's yoke

Many people make errors when forming plural possessive nouns. To avoid this, form the plural noun first. Then apply the guidelines above to make it possessive.

Example 2   Use the apostrophe to form a plural possessive noun from each plural noun.

           (a) cattle   (b) geese

           (c) butterflies   (d) nurses

           (e) mothers-in-law

Solution   (a) **cattle's**   (b) **geese's**

           (c) **butterflies'**   (d) **nurses'**

           (e) **mothers-in-law's**

Practice For a and b, replace each blank with the correct vocabulary word from this lesson.

    a. Do you understand the _____ of shoveling snow during a snowstorm?

    b. It is _____ to rake leaves on a windy day.

For c–h, write each word that requires an apostrophe to show possession.

    c. The two sisters-in-laws names are similar.

    d. Max, Joe, and Robs job is to paint the mural.

    e. All three kittens paws were muddy.

    f. I asked for my two friends opinions.

    g. Owning a horse was every childs dream.

    h. Is the buss tire flat?

More Practice For 1–8, make each singular noun possessive.

    1. isthmus   **2.** tributary   **3.** delta   **4.** estuary

    5. meteor   **6.** kin   **7.** story   **8.** culprit

For 9–16, make each plural noun possessive.

    9. deer   **10.** days   **11.** miners   **12.** fish

    13. girls   **14.** sheep   **15.** stories   **16.** men

Review Set 108 Choose the correct word(s) to complete sentences 1–16.

    1. To (digest, digress, beguile) is to depart from the main
    (107) subject in speaking or writing.

    2. To beguile is to (help, lead, mislead).
    (106)

    3. To consecrate is to set apart as (trash, sacred, paltry).
    (105)

    4. A parsimonious person is extremely cautious with (fire,
    (104) snakes, money).

    5. A (father, mother, brother) usually has maternal instincts.
    (43)

6. Every one of you (write, writes) (real, really) clever
(90, 104) stories.

7. You (sure, surely) write (good, well).
(96, 104)

8. There (was, wasn't) nothing in the refrigerator; it was
(93) empty.

9. Of the two classrooms, Ms. Hoo's is the (cleaner,
(102) cleanest).

10. I stood (beside, besides) the piano.
(107)

11. (Whose, Who's) game piece is yellow?
(72)

12. (We, Us) swimmers were watching dolphins.
(78)

13. I (saw, seen) him yesterday.
(86)

14. Many in the class (has, have) homework to do.
(83, 91)

15. The actors and the director (sweep, sweeps) the stage.
(89)

16. This pair of pants (fit, fits) perfectly.
(92)

17. From the sentence below, write and underline words that
(84) should be italicized.

Luey sailed on a large vessel, Wavery Bliss.

18. Rewrite the sentence below, replacing a comma with a
(103) semicolon where it is needed.

I remember Phoenix, however, I must have slept through
our stop in Santa Fe.

19. Rewrite the sentence below, adding hyphens as needed.
(94, 97)

From the third story window, she could see moss covered
rocks.

20. Use a hyphen to divide each word correctly.
(99)

(a) futile   (b) brushed

21.
(69) Write the nominative case pronoun to complete the sentence below.

Will Badchek and (she, her) go to jail?

22.
(105) Rewrite the following business letter, inserting colons where they are needed.

Dear Mr. Vela

    My cabin needs the following paint, light bulbs, carpet.

                  Sincerely,
                  Conrad Dudd

23.
(80, 88) Rewrite the following, adding capital letters and punctuation marks as needed:

conrad shouts look at that tarantula

24.
(108) For a–c, write the possessive form of each noun.

(a) boss   (b) Chris   (c) horses

25.
(107) From the sentence below, write whether the circled word is an adverb or a preposition.

We hiked (down) the mountain.

26.
(81) Rewrite the sentence below, adding capital letters and punctuation marks as needed.

erik will title his essay a long week at camp woisme

27.
(74) Rewrite the following sentence, adding capital letters and punctuation marks as needed.

when erik grows up he might become a kind thoughtful camp counselor

28.
(100, 101) From the sentence below, write each adverb that tells "when" or "how much."

Then Conrad almost lost his temper.

Diagram each word of sentences 29–30.

29. Couldn't Erik become a really responsible counselor
(45, 54) someday?

30. During the spring, we tourists viewed the magnificent
(100, 106) beauty of the Grand Canyon from different locations in
Arizona.

LESSON 109

The Apostrophe: Contractions; Omitting Digits and Letters

Dictation or Journal Entry
Vocabulary:
To *dissent* is to differ in opinion; to disagree. Those who *dissent* will vote "no" on that proposition.
Dissension is difference of opinion; disagreement. Congress was full of *dissension* over the budget.

Contractions When we combine two words and shorten one of them, we form a **contraction.** We insert an apostrophe to take the place of the letter or letters taken out.

Sometimes a verb is shortened, as in the examples below.

I have	⟶	I've
we are	⟶	we're
he will	⟶	he'll
she would	⟶	she'd
it is	⟶	it's

Other times we combine the verb and the word *not*. We shorten the word *not*, and insert an apostrophe where the letter *o* is missing.

do not	⟶	don't
is not	⟶	isn't
are not	⟶	aren't
were not	⟶	weren't
could not	⟶	couldn't

Note: the contraction *won't* (will not) is spelled irregularly.

Example 1 Use an apostrophe to write the contractions of a–d.

(a) you are   (b) they are

(c) would not   (d) did not

Solution (a) **you're**   (b) **they're**

(c) **wouldn't**   (d) **didn't**

Omitting Digits We use an apostrophe when the first two digits are omitted from the year.

$$2007 \longrightarrow \text{'07}$$

$$1996 \longrightarrow \text{'96}$$

$$1920 \longrightarrow \text{'20}$$

Omitting Letters We use an apostrophe to show that we have taken letters out of a word. In informal writing, we can leave out letters to indicate the way we imagine the words being spoken.

good morning $\longrightarrow$ good mornin'

best of luck $\longrightarrow$ best o' luck

until then $\longrightarrow$ 'til then

let them go $\longrightarrow$ let 'em go

Example 2 Rewrite sentences a–c, inserting apostrophes where they are needed.

(a) Isaac was born in 06.

(b) Clyde hollered, "Good mornin, Mervyn!"

Solution (a) **Isaac was born in '06.**

(b) **Clyde hollered, "Good mornin', Mervyn!"**

Practice For sentences a–d, write each word that needs an apostrophe.

a. I havent seen Jasmin since Tuesday.

b. He sang, "Ive been workin on the railroad..."

c. They bought the property in 48 and sold it in 02.

Make contractions of d and e.

d. should not   **e.** they would

For f and g, replace each blank with the correct vocabulary word from this lesson.

f. Some people _____ from the government's policy.

g. There is _____ among the committee members.

Review Set 109

Choose the correct word(s) to complete sentences 1–16.

1. (*Candid, Futile, Profuse*) means "hopeless or without effect."
(108)

2. A (monarchy, minimum, digression) is a departure from the main topic.
(107)

3. Guile is (honesty, deceit, candor).
(106)

4. To desecrate is to (honor, destroy, respect) something sacred.
(105)

5. (*Prudent, Imprudent, Cognizant*) means "unwise."
(44)

6. Every one of you (write, writes) (real, really) clever stories.
(90, 104)

7. That old car runs (real, really) (bad, badly).
(96, 104)

8. There (is, isn't) nobody home.
(93)

9. Of all the classrooms, Ms. Hoo's is the (cleaner, cleanest).
(102)

10. No one (beside, besides) Kim wants to swim.
(107)

11. (Who, Whom) wants to play basketball?
(79)

12. Jenny swims better than (me, I).
(78)

13. Kim (saw, seen) Jenny at the beach.
(86)

14. Someone in the family (has, have) more work to do.
(83, 91)

15. (Your, You're) right!
(109)

16. This pair of scissors (cut, cuts) (good, well).
(92, 96)

17. From the sentence below, write and underline words that should be italicized.
(84)

Have you read the book Charlotte's Web?

18. Rewrite the sentence below, replacing a comma with a
(103) semicolon where it is needed.

I am tired, nevertheless, I shall clean my room.

19. Rewrite the sentence below, adding hyphens as needed.
(94, 97) You can buy a five pound melon for ninety nine cents.

20. Use a hyphen to divide each word correctly.
(99) (a) guile   (b) beguile

21. Make contractions of a and b.
(109) (a) would not   (b) they are

22. Rewrite the following business letter, inserting colons
(105) where they are needed.

Dear Sir or Madam

    Why does my morning newspaper never arrive until
200 p.m. or later?

                                Your customer,
                                Ms. Hoo

23. Rewrite the following, adding capital letters and
(80, 88) punctuation marks as needed:

erik asked have you seen my flashlight

24. For a–c, write the possessive form of each noun.
(108) (a) artists   (b) Melody   (c) lady

25. From the sentence below, write whether the circled word
(107) is an adverb or a preposition.

She sang (throughout) the night.

26. Rewrite the sentence below, adding capital letters and
(60, 81) punctuation marks as needed.

melody my niece sang oklahoma.

27. Rewrite the following sentence, adding capital letters and
(74) punctuation marks as needed.

if she sings it again her sleepy irritable friends might
complain

28. From the sentence below, write each adverb that tells
(100, 101) "when" or "how much."

Tonight the speakers have been terribly redundant.

Diagram each word of sentences 29–30.

29. Shouldn't the youth's camp remain completely quiet
(45, 54) throughout the night?

30. In the morning, Melody the singer can give us a fine
(100, 106) concert with tunes from Broadway.

Dictation or Journal Entry

Vocabulary:
Apathy is lack of interest or concern. *Apathy* among the people resulted in few going to the polls to vote.

Apathetic means "showing little interest or concern." *Apathetic* citizens failed to go to the polls to vote.

We have learned how to join two simple sentences, or independent clauses, with a coordinating conjunction to form a compound sentence.

Jen plays the cello well, **and** she plays it every day.

independent clause   coordinating conjunction   independent clause

In a compound sentence, each of the independent clauses can stand alone. They are equal grammatical parts.

Jen plays the cello well. = She plays it every day.

Subordinate Clauses

Not all sentences are composed of equal parts. Sometimes a dependent clause is connected to an independent clause. We remember that we can turn an independent clause into a dependent clause, or **subordinate clause**, by adding a subordinating conjunction such as *after*, *although*, *because*, *even though*, *if*, *since*, or *unless*.

Jen plays the cello well ***because*** *she plays it every day*.

independent clause   subordinating conjunction   dependent clause

The subordinate clause "because she plays it every day" cannot stand alone; it is dependent on the main clause, "Jen plays the cello well."

Complex Sentence

A **complex sentence** contains one independent clause and one or more dependent, or subordinate, clauses. In the sentences below, we have underlined the independent (main) clause and italicized the subordinating conjunction that introduces the dependent clause.

She washes the dishes *after* her guests leave.

When it rains, the creek floods.

Compound-Complex Sentence

A **compound-complex sentence** contains two or more independent clauses and one or more dependent clauses. In the compound-complex sentence below, we have underlined the two independent clauses and italicized the subordinating conjunction that introduces the dependent clause.

If I skate far, <u>my toes get blisters</u>, and <u>my legs ache</u>.

<u>We can swim</u>, or <u>we can hike</u>, *since* the storm has passed.

Example

For a–d, tell whether each sentence is simple, compound, complex, or compound-complex.

(a) With his favorite book, Max retreats to a quiet place every morning.

(b) While I was waiting, time went slowly.

(c) She clicks her pen, and he taps his foot as minutes pass.

(d) I received the message, but I didn't understand it.

Solution

(a) This is a **simple** sentence. It is one independent clause.

(b) This sentence is **complex.** It has one independent clause ("time went slowly") and one dependent clause ("While I was waiting").

(c) This is a **compound-complex** sentence. It has two independent clauses ("She clicks her pen" and "he taps his foot") and one dependent clause ("as minutes pass").

(d) This is a **compound** sentence—two independent clauses joined by the coordinating conjunction "but."

Practice

For a–d, tell whether each sentence is simple, compound, complex, or compound-complex.

a. Noisy green parrots flap and squawk above.

b. Before guests come, I vacuum the floors, and Joe bakes bread.

c. This path becomes muddy and slushy as the snow melts.

d. We hurried, for we were late.

For e and f, replace each blank with the correct vocabulary word from this lesson.

e. The _____ citizen did not even know who was running for President.

f. Because of _____, some students did not study for the test.

More Practice Tell whether the sentence is simple, compound, complex, or compound-complex.

1. Ms. Hoo corrected me because I wrote *theirself.*

2. They were apathetic, so they didn't vote.

3. Do you ever dream about prepositions or nouns?

4. When the game ended, trumpets blared and people cheered.

Review Set 110 Choose the correct word(s) to complete sentences 1–16.

1. To (consecrate, meliorate, dissent) is to differ in opinion; (109) to disagree.

2. Futility is (success, hopelessness, effectiveness). (108)

3. To digress is to depart from the main (subject, character, (107) street) while speaking or writing.

4. To (languish, ostracize, beguile) is to mislead or deceive. (106)

5. *Prudent* means "(unwise, foolish, wise)." (44)

6. All of the money (go, goes) to (real, really) worthy causes. (90, 104)

7. This old car (sure, surely) runs (well, good). (96, 104)

8. There wasn't (nobody, anybody) home. (93)

9. Chloe was the (more, most) apathetic of the two. (102)

10. She stepped (in, into) the water. (107)

11. (Who's, Whose) winning the game? (79, 109)

12. Is Jenny as old as (him, he)?
(78)

13. Has Ms. Hoo (saw, seen) Badchek?
(86)

14. Everyone with dirty socks (has, have) more work to do.
(83, 91)

15. (Their, There, They're) here!
(109)

16. That bag of potatoes (smell, smells) (bad, badly).
(92, 96)

17. From the sentence below, write and underline words that
(84) should be italicized.

Apathy is a noun while apathetic is an adjective.

18. Rewrite the sentence below, replacing a comma with a
(103) semicolon where it is needed.

My room is messy, therefore, I shall clean it.

19. Rewrite the sentence below, adding hyphens as needed.
(94, 97)

My twenty year old sister took a five day vacation in
Arizona.

20. Use a hyphen to divide each word correctly.
(99)

(a) amaze   (b) airplane

21. Make contractions of a and b.
(109)

(a) you are   (b) cannot

22. Rewrite the following business letter, inserting colons
(105) where they are needed.

Dear Sir or Madam

I wish to cancel my subscription to the newspaper.

A dissatisfied customer,
Ms. Hoo

23. Rewrite the following, adding capital letters and
(80, 88) punctuation marks as needed:

at thursday's track meet grandpa yelled run amelia

24. For a–c, write the possessive form of each noun.
(108)

    (a) actors   (b) Andy   (c) James

25. From the sentence below, write whether the circled word
(107) is an adverb or a preposition.

    Elle sat (gracefully) beside her grandmother.

26. Rewrite the sentence below, adding capital letters and
(60, 81) punctuation marks as needed.

    kurt wrote the poem if i were you

27. Write whether the sentence below is simple, compound,
(110) complex, or compound-complex.

    She will wash the car, and he will feed the pets while we
    do the yard work.

28. From the sentence below, write each adverb that tells
(100, 101) "when" or "how much."

    Soon my messy room will look vastly different.

Diagram each word of sentences 29–30.

29. By this evening, my messy room will look totally clean.
(100, 101)

30. Yesterday my cousin Ted gave me a ticket to the most
(100, 106) fabulous opera!

Active or Passive Voice

Dictation or Journal Entry
Vocabulary:
Lucid means "clear; easily understood." She gave a *lucid* explanation.

To *elucidate* is to make clear or explain. The chemist *elucidated* the procedure for the experiment.

A transitive verb can be either **active** or **passive**. When the subject acts, the verb is **active.**

I <u>saw</u> the culprit.

When the subject is acted upon, the verb is **passive.**

The *culprit* <u>was seen</u> by me.

Passive verbs contain a form of "to be." Often the sentence contains a prepositional phrase beginning with "by." The subject *receives* the action; it does not *do* the action.

PASSIVE: *Lucy* <u>was followed</u> by a stray dog.

ACTIVE: A stray *dog* <u>followed</u> Lucy.

Active Voice

Writing is more exciting and powerful in the active voice. We try to use the active voice as much as possible.

WEAK PASSIVE:
The *work* <u>had been completed</u> by Mr. Tran.

STRONG ACTIVE:
Mr. Tran <u>had completed</u> the work.

WORDY PASSIVE:
We <u>were led</u> through the old house by the guide.

CONCISE ACTIVE:
The *guide* <u>led</u> us through the old house.

INDIRECT PASSIVE:
The *supplies* <u>were delivered</u> by Max to the shop.

DIRECT ACTIVE:
Max <u>delivered</u> the supplies to the shop.

Passive Voice

We see that the passive voice can be wordy and indirect. It can confuse the reader and tends to be dull. However, the passive voice does have a purpose. We use the passive voice in order to leave something unsaid. When the doer is unimportant or unknown, or when we want to emphasize the receiver of the action, we use the passive voice.

The *class* <u>was</u> totally <u>confused</u>.

All the *crops* <u>were destroyed</u> during the drought.

The *research* <u>had been completed</u>.

Example   Tell whether the verb in each sentence is active or passive voice.

(a) A young man rode a donkey.

(b) A donkey was ridden by a young man.

(c) A vulture was sighted by the bird watcher.

(d) The bird watcher sighted a vulture.

Solution   (a) The verb is **active.** The subject (man) acts.

(b) The verb is **passive.** The subject (donkey) is acted upon.

(c) The verb is **passive.** The subject (vulture) is acted upon.

(d) The verb is **active.** The subject (bird watcher) acts.

Practice   For sentences a–d, write whether the verb is active or passive voice.

a. The hungry catfish were fed by Aunt Ida.

b. Aunt Ida fed the hungry catfish.

c. The tree was hit by lightning.

d. Lightning hit the tree.

For e and f, replace each blank with the correct vocabulary word from this lesson.

e. Please _____ the entire plan.

f. Thank you for your _____ explanation. Now I understand.

Choose the correct word(s) to complete sentences 1–16.

1. (Rapport, Subversion, Apathy) is lack of interest or
(110) concern.

2. Dissension is (agreement, peace, disagreement).
(109)

3. *Futile* means "(honest, abundant, hopeless)."
(108)

4. The speaker made a (colossus, docent, digression); she
(107) departed from the main topic.

5. A(n) (prudent, imprudent, cognizant) person lacks
(44) prudence.

6. One of the trails (lead, leads) to a (real, really) beautiful
(90, 104) waterfall.

7. Melody (sure, surely) sings (well, good).
(96, 104)

8. He didn't give (no, a) lucid response.
(93)

9. Chloe was the (more, most) apathetic of all.
(102)

10. He climbs (on, onto) a raft.
(107)

11. (Who's, Whose) socks are these?
(72, 109)

12. She is older than (I, me).
(78)

13. We (saw, seen) Badchek in Austin, Texas.
(86)

14. Some on the team (have, has) dirty socks.
(83, 91)

15. (You're, Your) welcome.
(109)

16. His tan pants (fit, fits) (good, well).
(92, 96)

17. From the sentence below, write and underline words that
(84) should be italicized.

I read about the elephants in a magazine, National
Geographic.

18. Rewrite the sentence below, replacing commas with
(103) semicolons where they are needed.

We drove through Springfield, Illinois, Indianapolis,
Indiana, and Columbus, Ohio.

19. Rewrite the sentence below, adding hyphens as needed.
(94, 97)

My sister in law borrowed a six foot ladder.

20. Use a hyphen to divide each word correctly.
(99)
(a) concise   (b) washed

21. Make contractions of a and b.
(109)
(a) they will   (b) have not

22. Rewrite the following sentence, inserting a colon where it
(105) is needed.

Please excuse the following students Amy Ngo, Rod
Vargas, and Rosa Green.

23. Rewrite the following, adding capital letters and
(80, 88) punctuation marks as needed:

are you from georgia asked mark

24. For a–c, write the possessive form of each noun.
(108)
(a) states   (b) Amy   (c) Avis

25. From the sentence below, write whether the circled word
(107) is an adverb or a preposition.

Theo is running (behind) today.

26. Rewrite the sentence below, adding capital letters and
(60, 81) punctuation marks as needed.

her second song was consider yourself

27. Write whether the sentence below is simple, compound,
(110) complex, or compound-complex.

Next, I shall travel north since I have never seen
Washington, the Evergreen State.

28. From the sentence below, write each adverb that tells
(100, 101) "when" or "how much."

Later he made a more lucid statement.

Diagram each word of sentences 29–30.

29. Can you elucidate this very difficult lesson for me after
(100, 101) school?

30. Have you finally finished the very last diagram in this
(100, 106) grammar book?

LESSON 112

Interjections

Dictation or Journal Entry

Vocabulary:

To *finalize* is to finish, complete, or make final. We must *finalize* our plans for the summer.

The *finale* is the conclusion or last part, as in a musical composition, drama, fireworks display, or concert. I was in awe during the show's spectacular *finale*.

Interjections A word or short phrase used to show strong emotion is called an **interjection.** An interjection is one of the eight parts of speech. It can express excitement, happiness, joy, rage, surprise, pain, or relief. Interjections are italicized below.

Ah! Now I remember.

Ouch! I burned my finger.

Oh dear, I have forgotten your name.

Oh, excuse me. I didn't mean to interrupt.

An interjection is not a sentence and has no relationship with the words around it. For this reason, it is usually set apart from the rest of the sentence by some sort of punctuation. Generally, an exclamation point follows an interjection, but if the emotion is not very intense, a comma follows the interjection.

INTENSE: *Wow!* Did you see that shooting star?

NOT INTENSE: *Okay*, I understand now.

Below is a list of common interjections. Notice that sounds can be interjections too.

ah	*oh dear*	*ugh*	*man*
aha	*oh my*	*uh oh*	*drat*
bam	*oh yes*	*well*	*oops*
boy	*far out*	*yippee*	*bravo*
oh no	*whee*	*good grief*	*okay*
whoops	*goodness*	*ouch*	*wow*
hey	*ow*	*yikes*	*hooray*
phew	*yuck*	*hurrah*	*pow*
boo	*oh*	*shh*	*whew*

We must not overuse interjections. They lose their effectiveness when used too frequently.

Example 1   Write each interjection that you find in a–d.

(a) Good grief! You startled me.

(b) Whew! I am relieved that it's over.

(c) Okay, you are right.

(d) Yippee! Vacation is finally here.

Solution   (a) **Good grief**   (b) **Whew**

(c) **Okay**   (d) **Yippee**

Diagramming   We diagram an interjection by placing it on a line apart from the rest of the sentence.

Bravo! You finished the book.

Bravo | You | finished | book the

Example 2   Diagram this sentence:

Ugh, this problem is hard.

Solution   We place the interjection on a line apart from the rest of the sentence.

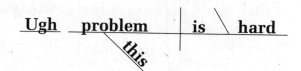

Practice   Write the interjection that you find in a–d.

a. Whoops, I made a mistake.

b. Hey, wait for me!

c. Bam! The door slammed.

d. Yuck! I stepped in the mud.

Diagram e and f.

    e. Hurrah! That is good news.

    f. Shh, people are thinking.

For g and h, replace each blank with the correct vocabulary word from this lesson.

    g. For the concert's _____, the choir sang "The Battle Hymn of the Republic."

    h. Let us _____ our schedule for publishing our own newspaper.

Review Set 112

Choose the correct word(s) to complete sentences 1–16.

    1. The finale is the (first, middle, last) part.
(112)

    2. Apathy is lack of (money, concern, food).
(110)

    3. To (finalize, elucidate, dissent) is to finish.
(112)

    4. *Lucid* means "(clear, hopeless, unclear)."
(111)

    5. To (finalize, elucidate, dissent) is to explain, or make clear.
(111)

    6. One of the twins (has, have) (real, really) curly hair.
(90, 104)

    7. Nicholas (sure, surely) draws (well, good).
(96, 104)

    8. The show didn't have (no, a) finale.
(93)

    9. Madison's speech was the (more, most) lucid of the two.
(102)

    10. She leaps (on, onto) the boat just in time.
(107)

    11. (Who's, Whose) backpack is this?
(72, 109)

    12. She is taller than (I, me).
(78)

    13. He (saw, seen) me yesterday.
(86)

    14. Some in our group (have, has) made new friends.
(83, 91)

    15. (You're, Your) essay is excellent.
(109)

16. This pair of scissors (cut, cuts) (good, well).
(92, 96)

17. Write whether the sentence below is active or passive
(111) voice.

The elephant was frightened by a mouse.

18. Rewrite the sentence below, replacing commas with
(103) semicolons where they are needed.

This bus passes through Denver, Colorado, Cheyenne,
Wyoming, and Helena, Montana.

19. Rewrite the sentence below, adding hyphens as needed.
(94, 97)

My brother in law has an eight foot python.

20. Use a hyphen to divide each word correctly.
(99)

(a) beguile   (b) guile

21. Make contractions of a and b.
(109)

(a) you are   (b) they are

22. Rewrite the following sentence, inserting a colon where it
(105) is needed.

Please call the following people James Lu, John García,
and Rachel Cohen.

23. Rewrite the following, adding capital letters and
(80, 88) punctuation marks as needed:

have you caught any fish asked daisy

24. For a–c, write the possessive form of each noun.
(108)

(a) countries   (b) Kerry   (c) Mr. Davis

25. From the sentence below, write whether the circled word
(107) is an adverb or a preposition.

Theo is running (behind) Molly.

26. Rewrite the sentence below, adding capital letters and
(60, 81) punctuation marks as needed.

for the grand finale, the band played america the
beautiful

27. Write whether the sentence below is simple, compound,
(110) complex, or compound-complex.

She is planning a trip to Cheyenne, Wyoming, for her
cousin lives there.

28. From the sentence below, write each adverb that tells
(100, 101) "when" or "how much."

Then I discovered the most pertinent information.

Diagram each word of sentences 29–30.

29. Tomorrow we shall finalize our plan for the improvement
(100, 101) of our school.

30. Ah, we have finally finished the very last diagram in this
(100, 106) grammar book.

Appendix

Dictations

At the beginning of class each Monday, students will copy their dictation to study and prepare for a test on Friday.

Week 1 Washington, D.C., our nation's capital, lies along the Potomac River, between Maryland and Virginia. Here stands the Capitol building where Congress meets to make decisions affecting our nation and the world.

Week 2 The Northeast, which includes all the coastal states from Maine south to Maryland, has become the most densely populated region of the United States. Cities such as Boston, Hartford, and New York City have grown rapidly.

Week 3 With diverse landscapes such as prairies, deep canyons, plateaus, and deserts, the sunny Southwest includes Arizona, New Mexico, Texas, and Oklahoma. The Colorado River passes through Arizona's Grand Canyon. Except in the eastern part of this region, rain is scarce.

Week 4 The Southeast has big rivers, fertile plains, and rounded mountains such as the Allegheny, Blue Ridge, and Cumberland Plateau. The Southeast is famous for its swamps, especially the Everglades, and for its mild climate with monthly rainfall that nourishes lush forests.

Week 5 The Midwest, or the American Heartland, covers the central United States from the foothills of the Rocky Mountains to Ohio and the Great Lakes. The Midwest is known for its rolling hills, fertile prairies, huge lakes, and giant rivers. In the Dakotas, we find the Badlands and the Black Hills that rise above the Great Plains.

Week 6 The West stretches from the Pacific Ocean to where the Rocky Mountains meet the Great Plains. With a variety of different climate zones, the West includes the tropical islands of Hawaii; the vast desert regions of Southern California, Nevada, and Utah; the fertile lowlands of Central California and Oregon; the forested northern coast with magnificent redwoods; and even Alaska with its ice and snow.

Week 7

The Coin
SARA TEASDALE

Into my heart's treasury
I slipped a coin
That time cannot take
Nor a thief purloin—
Oh, better than the minting
Of a gold-crowned king
Is the safe-kept memory
Of a lovely thing.

Week 8

from "A Bird Came down the Walk"
EMILY DICKINSON

A bird came down the walk:
He did not know I saw;
He bit an angle-worm in halves
And ate the fellow, raw.

And then he drank a dew
From a convenient grass,
And then hopped sidewise to the wall
To let a beetle pass.

Week 9   Before 1776, America was a group of colonies owned and ruled by England. These colonies fought for their independence in the Revolutionary War. After this war, thirteen of the colonies became the first states of the United States: Massachusetts, New Hampshire, Connecticut, Rhode Island, New York, New Jersey, Delaware, Pennsylvania,

Virginia, Maryland, North Carolina, South Carolina, and Georgia.

Week 10   July 4, 1776, is the birthday of the United States of America, for it is the day America declared its independence from England. On this day, American leaders signed the famous Declaration of Independence, which begins like this: "When, in the course of human events, it becomes necessary for one people to dissolve the political bands which have connected them with another...."

Week 11

from "Liberty"
JAMES RUSSELL LOWELL

Our fathers fought for Liberty,
They struggled long and well,
History of their deeds can tell—
But did they leave us free?

Are we free from vanity,
Free from pride, and free from self,
Free from love of power and pelf,
From everything that's beggarly?

Week 12   The Rocky Mountains are made up of sixty mountain ranges extending three thousand miles from Alaska to New Mexico. The Southern Rockies, in Utah, Colorado, and New Mexico, have the highest peaks towering more than 14,000 feet above sea level. Some of the peaks are snowcapped all year long. Here, rare and delicate snow flowers grow close to the ground.

Week 13   Tributaries that begin as far west as Montana and as far east as Pennsylvania flow into the Mississippi River, which empties into the Gulf of Mexico. From an Algonquin name meaning "great river," the Mississippi connects major cities such as Minneapolis, Minnesota; St. Paul, Minnesota;

Davenport, Iowa; St. Louis, Missouri; Memphis, Tennessee; Baton Rough, Louisiana; and New Orleans, Louisiana.

Week 14 The Great Lakes—Superior, Michigan, Huron, Erie, and Ontario—form the largest freshwater area on Earth's surface. Linking Lakes Erie and Ontario, the thirty-five-mile Niagara River sends more than fifty thousand cubic feet of water per second over Niagara Falls. The Great Lakes are so big that they are sometimes referred to as inland seas.

Week 15 The North American Plains extend across the continent from the Rocky Mountains to the Mississippi River and from Hudson Bay to the Gulf of Mexico. Covered by tall grasses, this region is the world's largest prairie. Large and small animals graze here, and weather conditions are extreme—cold and snowy in winter, and very hot during the summer. Today, much of the American prairie is planted with wheat and corn.

Week 16 The Statue of Liberty, standing in New York Harbor, is a famous American landmark. On a plaque at the base of the statue is a poem written by an American woman named Emma Lazarus. The poem ends with these words:

> Give me your tired, your poor,
> Your huddled masses yearning to breathe free,
> The wretched refuse of your teeming shore,
> Send these, the homeless, tempest-tost to me,
> I lift my lamp beside the golden door.

Week 17 Adopted June 14, 1777, the flag of the United States has symbolized the highest ideals of the nation for more than two centuries. Representing the thirteen original states, the first flag had thirteen stripes and thirteen stars. As the nation has grown, the flag's design has changed over time. A new star has been added each time another state has joined the union.

Now the flag has fifty stars representing the fifty states. People proudly fly the flag over private homes, government buildings, and ships at sea to honor this great nation.

Week 18

Star-Spangled Banner
FRANCIS SCOTT KEY

O say, can you see, by the dawn's early light,
What so proudly we hail'd at the twilight's last gleaming?
Whose broad stripes and bright stars, thro' the perilous fight,
O'er the ramparts we watch'd were so gallantly streaming?
And the rocket's red glare, the bombs bursting in air,
Gave proof thro' the night that our flag was still there.
O say, does that Star-Spangled Banner yet wave
O'er the land of the free and the home of the brave?

Week 19

In 1803, the land of the United States more than doubled with the purchase of the Louisiana Territory from the French. Thomas Jefferson hired two army officers, Meriwether Lewis and William Clark, to explore part of the purchase and to find a way across the territory to the Pacific Ocean. Lewis and Clark, along with their helpers, traveled up the Missouri River from St. Louis and spent their first winter on the Great Plains. The Shoshone people helped the expedition to cross the Rocky Mountains. They finally reached the Pacific late in November, 1805.

Week 20

Early America had few canals, for they were expensive and difficult to build. In 1825, the Erie Canal was completed, marking the beginning of the canal era in the United States. Running a distance of 363 miles, the Erie Canal connects the Hudson River to Lake Erie. This canal made it possible to easily ship manufactured goods from the East to farmers in the new Western states. The success of the Erie Canal led to the construction of many more canals before 1850.

Week 21 In the 1820s, bold and daring trappers, fur traders, and missionaries cut a path from the East to the West. The Oregon Trail, nearly two thousand miles long, began at Independence, Missouri and generally followed the Platte River to its headwaters. Then it crossed the mountains and followed the Snake River until it reached the Columbia River, which flows into the Pacific. By the 1840s, thousands of pioneers were heading West in wagon trains by way of the Oregon Trail.

Week 22 Many pioneers traveled to the western frontier in covered wagons, or prairie schooners. The most common wagons were the Conestogas, developed in Pennsylvania by descendants of German colonists. These wagons were large and heavy with beds made of hickory, maple, or oak, and covers made of waterproof canvas. Their wooden wheels had iron tires. Because of their strength, oxen, instead of mules or horses, pulled the wagons.

Week 23 In 1849, a mill worker named James Marshall found gold in a stream at John Sutter's mill near Sacramento, California. This discovery brought more than 70,000 gold seekers from all over the world to California. Not many of these "forty-niners" made a fortune. Violence, stealing, gambling, and other crimes became common in the land, for there were not enough police or courts to maintain law and order. This was one reason California voted to become a state in 1850.

Week 24 On July 1, 1862, President Abraham Lincoln signed a bill into a law called the Pacific Railroad Act, which started the building of the transcontinental railroad. The Central Pacific Railroad company began laying track from Sacramento, California, toward Omaha, Nebraska. The Union Pacific Railroad company started near Omaha and laid track toward

Sacramento. On May 10, 1869, the two lines met each other at Promontory Point, Utah.

Week 25   Henry Ford of Detroit, Michigan, built his first gasoline-powered car in 1896. In 1908, he began producing his Model T, which became very popular. Some people called these cars horseless carriages. Henry Ford developed the modern industrial assembly line for the mass production of automobiles. Automobiles changed the lives of average people more than any other invention since the wheel.

Week 26   Air travel began in the early twentieth century after Wilbur and Orville Wright made their first successful flight at Kitty Hawk, North Carolina, on December 17, 1903. The Wright brothers and others continued to experiment, adding to their scientific knowledge about aeronautics. Airplanes were used effectively in World War I, and now they are the fastest means of public transportation available.

Week 27   Born in Detroit, Michigan, the son of Swedish immigrants, Charles Lindbergh, Jr., grew up in Little Falls, Minnesota, and became a pilot. Lindbergh contributed much to aviation by charting polar routes, demonstrating high altitude flying techniques, and increasing the distance an aircraft could travel. Lindbergh's contributions made intercontinental air travel possible. He is famous for making the first solo nonstop flight across the Atlantic Ocean in 1927.

Week 28   On June 29, 1956, during Dwight D. Eisenhower's presidency, the Highway Act of 1956 became law. This began the building of the interstate highway system, 42,500 miles of highways connecting the states and tying them together. Interstate highways are marked by a number on a red, white, and blue shield. Odd-numbered highways go north and south while even-numbered highways go east and west.

Week 29   At the beginning of John F. Kennedy's presidency, the Soviet Union was winning the race for outer space. So President Kennedy set a goal for the United States to land a man on the moon and return him safely back to Earth. Although President Kennedy did not live to see this goal accomplished, an American spacecraft landed on the moon on July 20, 1969. Astronaut Neil Armstrong walked on the moon and spoke these words: "That's one small step for man, one giant leap for mankind."

Week 30

The Arrow and the Song
HENRY WADSWORTH LONGFELLOW

I shot an arrow into the air,
It fell to earth, I knew not where;
For, so swiftly it flew, the sight
Could not follow in its flight.

I breathed a song into the air,
It fell to earth, I knew not where;
For who has sight so keen and strong,
That it can follow the flight of song?

Long, long afterward, in an oak
I found the arrow, still unbroke;
And the song, from beginning to end,
I found again in the heart of a friend.

Journal Topics

A girl who wants to become a faster runner runs every day, and a boy who wants to become a better drummer plays the drums every day. In the same way, a person who wants to become a better writer should write every day.

And, just as a runner enjoys running and a drummer enjoys playing the drums, we should enjoy writing without worrying about whether or not someone is going to grade or look at our writing. We should write for the fun and satisfaction it gives us. We should write because practice will make us better writers.

A good way to practice your writing every day is to write in a journal, which can be a notebook with blank paper. When you write in a journal, you should not worry about who will read or grade your writing. This is a time for you to simply put your thoughts down on paper and perhaps try some new writing ideas.

Example   Write at least three sentences on the following topic:

Describe today's weather.

In your journal, you might write something like the following:

Leaves on trees are drooping, and so am I because today is miserably hot. I wish I were swimming or sipping lemonade instead of sitting here at my desk, doing schoolwork. I hope tomorrow is cooler.

At the beginning of class on Tuesday, Wednesday, and Thursday, you will spend five minutes writing in your journal. Each entry should be at least three sentences long. The following are suggested topics.

Topic # 1.   Write about the state, city, town, or county in which you live. Tell about what people can do or see there.

2.   Write about how you once helped someone.

3.   Write about something that you can do now that you couldn't do a few years ago.

4.   Write about something that you would like to learn to do in the future.

5. Describe the place where you are right now.

6. Describe an animal that you like.

7. If you could grow a garden, what would you plant? Why?

8. Describe a sport that you like to watch.

9. Describe an outdoor game or sport that you like to play.

10. Describe a game that you like to play indoors.

11. Describe a family member whom you admire.

12. Write about one of your friends.

13. Write about a trip you would like to take.

14. Some people enjoy the snow. Others don't. Write about how you feel about snow.

15. Write about the best teacher you have ever had.

16. What is your favorite song? Why?

17. What kinds of books do you like to read? Which is your favorite? Why?

18. What do you like to do in your free time?

19. What can you do to make the world a better place?

20. What makes you laugh? Explain.

21. Write about a time when you were thankful.

22. What special talent do you wish you had? Why?

23. What three things do you like best about yourself? Explain.

24. What can you do to help family members at home?

25. Write about the best gift you have ever received.

26. Which do you think is the best state in the United States? Why?

27. What would you like to do or be when you grow up?

28. If you could live anywhere in the universe, where would you choose to live? Why?

29. Some people are eager to travel in space; others are not. How do you feel about space travel?

30. If you had twenty dollars to spend at a produce market, what would you buy? Why?

31. How do you feel about rain?

32. What do you think about junk food?

33. How can you improve your physical fitness or your health?

34. What is your favorite school subject? Why?

35. Write about a time when you were surprised.

36. If you were to make lunch for a friend, what would you make and how would you make it?

37. Would you rather live on a mountaintop or in a valley? Why?

38. Would you rather spend a vacation at a beach or in the desert? Explain.

39. What is your favorite kind of tree? Why?

40. Write about a person whom you think is a hero.

41. What can you do to show friendship to someone?

42. How should friends treat each other?

43. Write about your favorite holiday.

44. Write about a gift that you once gave to someone.

45. Write about a gift that you would like to give to someone someday.

46. Whom do you think would make a good future President of the United States?

47. Explain how you think pumpkin pies are made.

48. How would your life be different without electricity?

49. How would your life be different without automobiles, buses, trains, and planes?

50. What is your least favorite food? Why?

51. Which school subject do you think is most important? Why?

52. Write about the hardest job you've ever had to do.

53. Are you a good cook? Explain.

54. Write about a time when you lost a tooth.

55. Write about the funniest thing that ever happened to you or to someone you know.

56. Write about sounds that you like to hear.

57. Write about sounds that you do not like to hear.

58. Some people like reptiles; others don't. How do you feel about reptiles?

59. What would you like to be famous for someday?

60. What would you do if you were invisible?

61. Write about something for which you are thankful.

62. If you were a school teacher, what subject would you like to teach? Why?

63. What can you do to make your home more cheerful?

64. Write about a generous person whom you know.

65. Describe a kind of bird that you like.

66. If you were to write a book, what would you like to write about? Why?

67. What is your favorite time of the day? Why?

68. What is your favorite season of the year? Why?

69. Do you have a favorite color? Explain.

70. What helpful advice could you give to someone younger than you?

71. Explain how to make a tasty sandwich.

72. If you could build your dream house, where would you build it and what materials would you use?

73. What is your favorite mode of transportation? Explain.

74. Some people like to eat spinach; others don't. How do you feel about eating spinach? Explain.

75. Describe yourself.

76. Write about something that happened when you were six or seven years old.

77. Write about something you learned from reading a book, newspaper, or magazine.

78. Describe how your life would be different if you were blind.

79. Write what you know about kangaroos.

80. If you owned a restaurant, what kind of food would you serve? Why?

81. Write about something you have learned from talking to someone.

82. Describe a day in the life of an eagle.

83. Describe a day in the life of a lion or tiger.

84. Explain how you think a loaf of bread is made.

85. Explain how you think clouds form and describe the kind of clouds you like best.

86. If you had wings, would you fly? How high? Where would you go?

87. Describe a typical day in the life of your father, mother, guardian, or teacher.

88. How do you feel about homework?

89. What musical instrument(s) do you like? Why?

90. What can you do to become a better student?

91. Write about something that you do well.

92. Describe a pet that belongs to you or to someone else.

93. Describe an onion.

94. Write about a friendship that you value.

95. Write what you know about bats.

96. Have you been to the doctor or dentist? Write about your experience.

97. Explain why it is important to be polite to others.

98. Write about how to plan a party.

99. Do you know someone who would make a good governor for your state? What makes you think so?

100. Are you an optimist? Are you a pessimist? Why?

Index

A, an, the (articles), 191
Abbreviations, 246
Abundant, 11
Action verb, 28
Active voice, 601
Addresses, 289
Adjective(s), defined, 186
  a, an, the, 191
  adverb, confusion with, 517
  comparison, 275
    irregular, 283
  compound adjective with
    hyphens, 522
  demonstrative, 435
  descriptive, 186
  diagramming, 191, 218, 269
  indefinite, 440
  modified by adverb, 544
  over-used, 310
  possessive, 374
  predicate adjective, 269
  prepositional phrase, 218
  proper, 202
Adverb(s), defined, 511
  adding suffixes to form, 511
  comparison, 550
  conjunctive, 556
  diagramming, 529, 539, 544, 573, 579
  distinguished from adjectives, 511
  double negatives, 498
  negatives, 498
  position of, 539
  preposition or adverb, 579
  telling how, 511
    how much, 544
    when, 539
    where, 529
  usage, 561
  using *well*, 517
Agreement, subject-verb, 474, 480, 487, 493
Akin, 167
Ameliorate, 403

Amelioration, 403
Amphibian, 269
Anarchy, 556
And (conjunction), 235, 391, 398
Antecedent, defined, 315
  agreement with pronoun, 315, 411
Antonym, 7
Apathetic, 596
Apathy, 596
Apostrophe, 585, 591
  contractions, 591
  omitted digits or letters, 591
  possessives, 585
Appositive, 295, 305
Arboreal, 269
Archipelago, 35
Ardent, 369
Ardor, 369
Arroyo, 68
Articles (*a, an, the*), 191
Asset, 144
Atoll, 68
Auditory, 263
Auxiliary verb, 49
Avarice, 171
Avaricious, 171

B

Bad or *badly*, 561
Be, 79
Beguile, 573
Benevolence, 246
Benevolent, 246
Bliss, 435
Blissful, 435
Bovine, 258
But (conjunction), 235, 391, 398

C

Caldera, 129
Candid, 550
Candor, 550
Canine, 252
Capitalization, 63, 114, 119, 181, 197, 207

Grammar and Writing 5

Student Edition
Index

abbreviations and initials, 181
areas of country, 197
family words, 181
first words of direct quotation, 119
first word of sentence, 63
first word in line of poetry, 63
greetings and closings, 197
I, 63
literary and music titles, 114
outlines, 119
proper adjectives, 202
proper nouns, 31
religions, Bible, deity, 197
seasons of the year, 207
school subjects, 181
titles of persons (family words), 181
Case, 258, 263, 327, 340, 356, 363
nominative, 258, 340
nominative pronoun, 340
objective, 263, 356
objective pronoun, 356
personal pronoun, 363
possessive, 258, 374
Certain or *certainly*, 561
Chasm, 90
Clamare, 162
Clamor, 162
Clarity, 352
Clause, 171, 380, 391, 596
dependent, 380, 386, 596
independent, 380, 391
subordinate, 380, 386, 596
Coerce, 463
Coercion, 463
Cognizance, 197
Cognizant, 197
Collective noun, 44
Colon, 567
Colossal, 458
Colossus, 458
Comma, 289, 300, 305, 322, 346, 352, 386, 398
after introductory words, 346
after dependent clauses, 386
after interjections, 606
before conjunction, 398
in appositives, 305
in compound sentence, 398
in dates, 289
in direct address, 300
in direct quotation, 398
in letter, 322
in series, 289

in titles or academic degrees, 300
reversed names, 322
separating descriptive adjectives, 386
words in a series, 289
words out of natural order, 346
Common noun, 31
Comparative form, 275, 283, 550
Comparison adjectives, 275, 283
Comparison adverbs, 550
Comparisons using pronouns, 411
Complacency, 469
Complacent, 469
Complete sentence, 19
Complex sentence, 596
Compound adjective, 522
Compound forms, hyphen in, 505, 522
Compound nouns, forming plurals, 53
Compound parts of sentence, 240
diagramming, 240
subject and verbs, 240
Compound relative pronouns, 403
Compound sentence, 391
diagramming, 391
Compound subject, with singular or plural
verb, 474
Compound word, division of, 534
Conceal, 28
Consecrate, 567
Concise, 493
Conciseness, 493
Concrete noun, 44
Conjunction(s), defined, 235, 380
coordinating, 235
in compound parts of a sentence, 235
in compound sentence, 391
subordinating, 380
list of, 380
Conjunctive adverb, 556
Contraction(s), 591
apostrophe in, 591
list of common, 591
subject-verb agreement with, 487
verb, a part of, 591
Contrite, 340
Contrition, 340
Coordinating conjunction(s), 235, 391
list of, 235, 391
Cowardice, 315
Culpable, 430
Culprit, 430
Curator, 425

D

Dates, punctuation in, 289
Daunt, 417
Dauntless, 417
Declarative sentence, 7
Delta, 53
Demonstrative adjective, 191, 435
Demonstrative pronoun, 435
Dependent clause, 380, 386
Descriptive adjective, 186, 561
Descriptive adverb, 550, 561
Desecrate, 567
Diagramming
    adjective phrases, 218
    adjectives, 191
    adverb phrases, 573
    adverbs, 529
    appositives, 295
    compound parts of a sentence, 240
    compound sentence, 391
    conjunctions, 391
    dependent clauses, 403
    direct objects, 176
    indirect objects, 224
    objects of prepositions, 218
    predicate adjectives, 295
    predicate nominatives, 252
    prepositional phrases, 218
    pronouns, 369
    verbs and subjects, 150, 240
    you understood, 7
Dictionary information, 124, 139
Digress, 579
Digression, 579
Direct address, 300
Direct object, 176
    defined, 176
    diagramming, 176
    pronoun as, 356, 411
Direct Quotation, 398
Disclose, 28
Dispensable, 155
Dissension, 591
Dissent, 591
Docent, 425
Dogma, 186
Dogmatic, 186
Dollars and cents, decimal in, 246
Double comparisons (avoiding), 283
Double negatives (avoiding), 498

E

Elated, 334

Elation, 334
Elocution, 105
Elucidate, 601
Encumber, 176
Encumbrance, 176
End punctuation, 7, 230, 246, 469
Enigma, 544
Enigmatic, 544
Epilogue, 534
Equine, 258
Essential, 3
Estuary, 35
Essential appositives, 305
Ethical, 327
Exalt, 181
Exclamation mark, 7, 469
Exclamatory sentence,
    7, 469
Extravagant, 202

F

Family words, 181
Fauna, 39
Feline, 252
Feign 356
Finale, 606
Finalize, 606
Fissure, 96
Flora, 39
Foreign words and phrases, 447
Fractions, hyphens in, 505
Fragment, sentence, 19
    defined, 19
Frugal, 202
Futile, 585
Futility, 585
Future tense, 58

G

Genteel, 275
Gentility, 275
Geo-, 31
Geography, 31
Geology, 31
Good or *well*, 517
Grandiloquent, 453
Greeting, in a letter, 197, 322
Guile, 573

H

Helping verb(s), 49
Hemisphere, 58
Homophones, 19
Humiliate, 181

Hyphen(s), 505, 522, 534
    in compound nouns, 522
    in fractions, 505
    in numbers, 505
    in word division, 534

I

Igneous rocks, 114
Ignis, 114
Ignite, 114
Illiterate, 224
Illuminate, 300
Imperative sentence, 7
Implacable, 101
Implausible, 235
Impropriety, 539
Imprudent, 212
Indefinite pronoun, 440
Independent clause, 380
Indirect object, 224
    defined, 224
    diagramming, 224
    recognizing, 224
Indirect quotation, 425
Indispensable, 155
Indolent, 283
Industrious, 283
Initials, 181
Innocuous, 480
Inopportune, 305
Insatiable, 391
Intangible, 191
Interjection, 606
Interrogative pronoun, 417
Interrogative sentence, 7, 469
Interrupting elements, 346
Intolerable, 240
Introductory elements, 346
Intuition, 310
Intuitive, 310
Intrepid, 315
Invertebrate, 139
Irregular plural noun(s), 68, 73, 101
    defined, 68
    forms, 68, 73, 101
    rules for forming, 68, 73, 101
Irregular verbs, 79, 334, 453, 458, 463
    be, have, do, 79
    defined, 79, 334
Irrelevant, 346
Isthmus, 44
Italics, 447

It's, 24
Its, 24

K

Kin, 167

L

Lagoon, 49
Lanquid, 474
Languish, 474
Last name first, 322
Latitude, 63
Liability, 144
Linguist, 363
Linguistics, 363
Linking verb(s), 144, 252, 269
Literate, 224
Longitude, 63
loqui, 105
Lucid, 601
Lumen, 300
Luminous, 300

M

Magma, 129
Malice, 218
Malicious, 218
Maternal, 207
Meridian, 58
Mesa, 90
Metamorphic rocks, 119
Metamorphosis, 119
Meteor, 134
Meteorite, 134
Meteorology, 352
Minimum, 498
Modifier(s), defined, 186, 511
    adjective as, 186, 191, 202, 218
    adverb as, 511, 517, 529, 539, 544, 550,
        561, 573
Momentary, 230
Momentous, 230
Monarchy, 556

N

Negatives, 498
    avoiding double, 498
    in contractions, 498
No and *yes*, comma after, 346
Nominative case, 258, 340
Nominative pronoun, 340, 363
Nonessential, 3
Nor (conjunction), 235

Not (adverb), 498
Noun(s), defined, 44
    abstract, 44
    adding suffixes to form, 155, 162
    as antecedents, 315
    as appositives, 295
    collective, 44
    common, 31
    compound, 53
    concrete, 44
    diagramming, 150, 176, 212, 224, 240, 252
    direct address, 300
    direct object, 176
    forming plurals of, 68, 73, 101
    indirect object, 224
    kinds of, 31, 44, 53
    modifiers, 186, 191, 202, 212
    object of preposition, 212
    possessive, 53
      as adjective, 191
    predicate nominative, 252
    proper, 31
    singular, 53
Noxious, 480

O

Obfuscate, 487
Obfuscation, 487
Object(s), 176, 212, 224, 356
    direct, 176
      diagramming, 176
    indirect, 224
      diagramming, 224
    of preposition, 212
      correct use of pronouns as, 356
      diagramming, 218
Objective case, 263, 356, 363
    pronouns in, 356, 363
Olfactory, 263
Opportune, 305
Optimism, 15
Optimum, 498
Or (conjunction), 235, 391 , 398
Ornithology, 352
Ostracism, 505
Ostracize, 505
Outline, 119, 230
    capitalization in, 119
    punctuation in, 230
Over-used adjectives, 310

P

Paltriness, 511
Paltry, 511
Panacea, 150
Pan American, 150
Parsimonious, 561
Parsimony, 561
Passive voice, 601
Past participle, 85, 334, 453, 458, 463
Past tense, 39, 85, 334, 453, 458, 463
Paternal, 207
Peninsula, 44
Period, 230, 246
    in outlines, 230
    rules for use of, 230, 246
Perjure, 517
Perjury, 517
Person, 327, 340, 363
Personal pronoun case forms, 363
    singular, 363
    list of, 363
    plural, 363
Pertinent, 346
Pessimism, 15
Phrase, 171, 212, 218, 573
    diagramming, 218, 573
Placare, 101
Placate, 101
Placid, 101
Plagiarism, 522
Plagiarize, 522
Plateau, 96
Plausible, 235
Plural(s), formation of, 53, 68, 73, 101
Possessive adjective, 374
Possessive noun, 53
    diagramming, 191
Possessive pronoun, 374
    distinguishing from contractions, 374
Predicate, 3, 11, 15, 150, 240
    compound, 240
    diagramming, 150, 240
    simple, 11
    split, 15
Predicate adjective, 269
    compound, 269
    diagramming, 269
Predicate nominative, 252
    compound, 252
    diagramming, 252
    noun as, 252
    pronoun as, 340

Preposition(s), 90, 96, 212
   list of, 90, 96
   simple, 90, 96
   object of, 212
   (understood) with indirect object, 224
Prepositional phrase, 212
   as an adjective, 218
   as an adverb, 573
   between subject and verb, 480
   diagramming, 218, 573
   indirect object, 224
Present participle, 85
Present tense, 35
Pretentious, 453
Principal parts of verbs, 85
   list of troublesome, 79, 334, 453, 458, 463
Proclamation, 162
Profuse, 529
Profusion, 529
Prologue, 534
Pronoun(s), defined, 315, 327
   antecedent of, 315
   as a subject, 340
   as an adjective, 374
   as an object, 356
   case, 363
   demonstrative, 435
   diagramming, 369
   indefinite, 440
   interrogative, 417
   nominative case, 340, 363
   number, 340, 356, 363
   objective case, 356
   person, 340, 356, 363
   personal, 327
   possessive, 374
   relative, 403
   usage, 411
Proper adjective, 202
   capitalization of, 202
Proper noun(s), 31
   abstract, 44
   capitalization of, 31
Providence, 289
Providential, 289
Prudent, 212
Punctuation
   apostrophe, 585, 591
   colon, 567
   comma, 289, 300, 305, 322, 346, 352, 386, 398
   exclamation mark, 469
   hyphen, 505, 522, 534
   italics or underline, 447
   period, 230, 246
   of appositives, 305
   of dialogue, 398
   of letters, 322, 567
   of outlines, 230
   question mark, 469
   quotation marks, 425, 430
   semicolon, 556
   underline or italics, 447

Q
Quaint, 398
Quaintness, 398
Question mark, 469
Quotation, direct, 398, 425, 430
Quotation, indirect, 430
Quotation marks, 425, 430

R
Rapport, 447
Rapprochement, 447
Real or *really*, 561
Redundancy, 386
Redundant, 386
Relative pronoun, 403
Regular verb, 39
Religions, capitalization of, 197
Renames the subject, 252
Run-on sentence, 105
   correcting, 110

S
Sagacious, 380
Sagacity, 380
Saline, 411
Salinity, 411
Salutation of letter (colon after), 567
Satiable, 391
Savanna, 85
Scarce, 11
Seasons of the year, 207
Sediment, 124
Sedimentary rocks, 124
Semicolon, 556
Sentence, defined, 3, 7
   capitalization of first word of, 63
   complex, 596
   compound, 391
   declarative, 7
   diagramming, 150, 176, 218, 224, 240, 252, 269, 295, 369, 539, 573
   exclamatory, 7
   fragment, 19, 24

imperative, 7
interrogative, 7
punctuation of, 230, 246, 289, 300, 305, 322, 346, 352, 386, 398, 425, 430, 447, 469, 556, 567
run-on, 105, 110
simple, 391
Serene, 374
Serenity, 374
Series, commas in, 289
Silent letters, 129, 134
Simple predicate, 11
Simple sentence, 391
Simple preposition, 90, 96
Simple subject, 11
Singular, 53, 327, 363
Spelling 68, 73, 101, 129, 134, 155, 162, 167
adding suffixes, 155, 162
to words ending in consonants, 162
to words ending in silent *e*, 155
to words ending in *y*, 155
plural forms, 68, 73, 101
possessives, 585
words with *ie* and *ei*, 167
words with silent letters, 129, 134
Split predicate, 15
Subject of a sentence, 11, 15, 150, 240, 340
agreement with verb, 474, 480, 487, 493
complete, 11
compound, 240
diagramming, 150, 240, 391
of imperative and interrogative sentences, 7
pronoun as, 340
simple, 11
understood, 7
Subject-verb agreement, 474, 480, 487, 493
Subordinating conjunction, 380
Subversion, 440
Subvert, 440
Suffixes, 155, 162
Superfluous, 295
Superlative degree, 275, 283, 550
Supersonic, 295
Synonym, 7

T
Tangible, 191
Tenacious, 322
Tenacity, 322
That or *which*, 403
Their, 19

There, 19
Subject-verb agreement with, 487
Timberline, 79
Titles, 114, 425, 447
Tolerable, 240
Torrid Zone, 79
Tributary, 53
Tropic of Cancer, 73
Tropic of Capricorn, 73
Troublesome verbs, 79, 334, 453, 458, 463
Tundra, 85

U
Underline or italics, 447
Unethical, 327
Unfeigned, 356

V
Val-, 110
Valiant, 110
Valor, 110
Verb(s), defined, 28, 49, 144
action, 28
active voice, 601
agreement with subject, 474, 480, 487, 493
be, 49, 79, 144
compound, 240
diagramming, 150, 240, 391
helping (auxiliary), 49
list of, 49
irregular, 79, 334, 453, 458, 463
linking, 144
passive voice, 601
principal parts of, 85
regular, 39
tense, 39
Ventriloquist, 105
Vertebrate, 139

W
Well and *good*, 517
Which or *that*, 403
Who and *whom*, 403, 417

Y
Yes and *no*, comma after, 346
You understood, 7